JUDICIAL REVIEW AND STRATEGIC BEHAVIOUR

JUDICIAL REVIEW AND STRATEGIC BEHAVIOUR

An Empirical Case Law Analysis of the Belgian Constitutional Court

Josephine De Jaegere

intersentia
Cambridge – Antwerp – Chicago

Intersentia Ltd
Sheraton House | Castle Park
Cambridge | CB3 0AX | United Kingdom
Tel.: +44 1223 370 170 | Fax: +44 1223 370 169
Email: mail@intersentia.co.uk
www.intersentia.com | www.intersentia.co.uk

Distribution for the UK and Ireland:
NBN International
Airport Business Centre, 10 Thornbury Road
Plymouth, PL6 7PP
United Kingdom
Tel.: +44 1752 202 301 | Fax: +44 1752 202 331
Email: orders@nbninternational.com

Distribution for Europe and all other countries:
Intersentia Publishing nv
Groenstraat 31
2640 Mortsel
Belgium
Tel.: +32 3 680 15 50 | Fax: +32 3 658 71 21
Email: mail@intersentia.be

Distribution for the USA and Canada:
Independent Publishers Group
Order Department
814 North Franklin Street
Chicago, IL 60610
USA
Tel.: +1 800 888 4741 (toll free) | Fax: +1 312 337 5985
Email: orders@ipgbook.com

Judicial Review and Strategic Behaviour. An Empirical Case Law Analysis of the Belgian Constitutional Court

ISBN 978-1-78068-694-3
D/2019/7849/57
NUR 820

British Library Cataloguing in Publication Data. A catalogue record for this book is available from the British Library.

FOREWORD

This is a book on the Belgian Constitutional Court and the dynamics of its judicial decision-making. It is an empirical study of the judgments rendered by this Court, revealing the strategic considerations at play, and as such is inextricably linked to the specific context of the Belgian political system.

Yet this book is so much more, and is of interest beyond Belgian borders. This is due to its contribution to more general debates in the two disciplines that it, very proficiently, combines: legal scholarship and empirical legal studies. The global value of this book – beyond the insights it offers to observers of the Belgian legal system – is therefore threefold.

First, the book contributes to the ongoing legal debate on constitutional review and the counter-majoritarian difficulty. To this end, the author views constitutional courts as deliberative institutions which provide a forum for deliberation between governments and stakeholders. In this way, it also contributes to the debate on how constitutional review is best shaped, pointing out the inherent qualities of abstract review by centralised courts from the perspective of deliberative democracy. At the same time, jurisdictions contemplating the introduction of a constitutional court can learn from this book which aspects of constitutional engineering should best be taken into account. Overall, the author is very clear in revealing how the Constitutional Court goes about making its judgments acceptable to the parties, politicians and the wider public, and how this is reflected in judicial reasoning.

Second, the book constitutes a contribution to empirical legal studies. In this discipline, much research is devoted to the factors that determine the outcome of judicial decisions. Whilst these types of studies are more commonplace in the US, this constitutes a germinal approach in Europe. In these studies, political and strategic factors have been the centre of attention, but the legal factor is often carelessly set aside. It has even been held that judicial reasoning serves as a justification *ex post* to hide what is actually going on. One reason is that legal factors are difficult to measure; another reason is that empirical scientists are often not familiar with legal reasoning and how it is intertwined with politics. In contrast to preconceptions in empirical science, political and strategic factors do not necessarily rule out the legal variable; the author, with her legal background, is well aware of that. She, very untypically, is not so much interested in the impact of the political and ideological preferences of the Court's judges. From a deliberative democracy perspective, she is much more interested in the constitutional dialogue that we witness: the participants to the dialogue and the strategic considerations in how the Court conducts the debate. Legal analysis is utilised in particular where it dissects the argumentation framework for the proportionality analysis, and then reveals through statistical evidence how this is used by the Court to address legitimacy concerns regarding constitutional review and the balance of interests. What is novel is the emphasis on how strategic considerations impact on the detail and method of legal reasoning, but not necessarily on the final outcome.

Finally, this book is truly interdisciplinary. Empirical legal studies often come down to the monodisciplinary (political or economic science) study of legal institutions, with hardly any input in the form of legal analysis. Josephine De Jaegere has succeeded in overcoming the many obstacles to conducting interdisciplinary work – not as a team, but by herself. As a qualified lawyer, she has independently trained herself in statistics and learned to perform regression analyses.

It is my hope, then, that this book will help to bridge legal and empirical scholarship on courts and contribute to a better understanding of the functioning of constitutional courts in particular. With the rise of concentrated forms of judicial review after World War II, in Europe but also beyond, comes an urgent need for this type of research.

Patricia Popelier
Professor of Law
University of Antwerp, Belgium

ACKNOWLEDGEMENTS

This book is the result of an interdisciplinary research project which I undertook at the University of Antwerp, Belgium. I would like to express my gratitude and extend my thanks to the publisher for allowing me to turn my research project into a book, and to the editor for applying the finishing touches to the manuscript.

During my studies in law, concepts such as 'empirical', 'statistics' and 'significant' were nowhere to be found. It was my supervisors, Professors Popelier (Faculty of Law) and Beyers (Faculty of Social Sciences), who introduced me to a new world: that of empirical legal analysis. For giving me this golden opportunity, I owe them my deepest gratitude. Although doing interdisciplinary research has presented me with numerous challenges, this experience has been especially enriching. I would also like to thank my supervisors for their professional guidance, as well as for their valuable and constructive critiques at every point during my research.

Further, I wish to acknowledge the vital support, both substantive and moral, of my colleagues. As an empirical *rookie*, additional assistance on methodological issues, provided by my colleagues at the Faculty of Social Sciences – in particular Sarah Arras and Iskander De Bruycker – was not only necessary, but also greatly appreciated. More generally, my colleagues at both faculties have made useful recommendations which have allowed me to improve the quality of my research.

In addition, I would like to offer my special thanks to Luc Théry and Kris De Put from the library documentation office of the Belgian Constitutional Court for providing me with the news media dataset. Without their willingness to provide me with this data, as well as regular updates, my research could not have turned out a success.

Finally, I am particularly grateful to my husband for his enthusiastic encouragement throughout my years as a research scholar. The most beautiful gift, which came almost exactly one year after my successful defence of my research project, is our little son Hector, to whom I want to dedicate this book.

CONTENTS

INTRODUCTION

A proper understanding of democratic politics needs to account for the functioning of constitutional courts. These courts play an increasingly important role in democratic policy-making. More specifically, they (usually) have the ability to nullify legislation passed by Parliament and their rulings define a framework of possible future policies. Therefore, improving our understanding of how constitutional courts write their opinions – and in particular how certain case characteristics influence different aspects (outcome, justificatory ground) of the judicial decision in that case – is a relevant research objective.

Traditionally, legal scholarship on judicial review is predominantly normative, concentrating on how courts should decide cases and to what extent they should show deference towards the legislative branch. Political scientists, on the other hand, seem more interested in what motivates judges and which factors influence their decisions. In addition, while legal scholars traditionally use qualitative methods to analyse legal texts and judicial behaviour, political scientists increasingly and predominantly answer their research questions through quantitative methods.[1] Furthermore, in contrast to the extensive body of literature on judicial behaviour in countries with a common law tradition (and especially on the US Supreme Court),[2] there is little systematic empirical knowledge relating to European constitutional courts.[3] The approach in this

1 See B Friedman, 'The Politics of Judicial Review' (2005) 84 Texas Law Review, 257, for more information on the 'separate tracks' of these academic fields.

2 Extensive overviews of this scholarship can be found in the following edited volumes: N Maveety (ed.), *The Pioneers of Judicial Behaviour* (University of Michigan Press 2003); CG Geyh (ed.), *What's Law Got To Do With It?: What Judges Do, Why They Do It, and What's at Stake* (Stanford University Press 2011), 376; and D Klein and G Mitchell (eds.), *The Psychology of Judicial Decision-Making* (Oxford University Press 2010), 337. These edited volumes include contributions by Jeffrey A Segal, Lawrence Baum, Lee Epstein, Frank Cross and Barry Friedman, among others.

3 But European scholars are currently catching up with regard to empirical research on the functioning of constitutional courts. See for example: A Dyevre, 'Unifying the Field of Comparative Judicial Politics: Towards a General Theory on Judicial Behaviour' (2010) 2 European Political Science Review, 297; M Bobek, *Comparative Reasoning in European Supreme Courts* (Oxford University Press 2013); N Garoupa et al., 'Judging Under Political Pressure: An Empirical Analysis of Constitutional Review Voting in the Spanish Constitutional Court' (2013) 29 Journal of Law, Economics and Organization, 1; J Kantorowicz and N Garoupa, 'An Empirical Analysis of Constitutional Review Voting in the Polish Constitutional Tribunal' (2015) 27 Constitutional Political Economy, 66; and V Grembi and N Garoupa, 'Judicial Review and Political Partisanship: Moving from Consensual

book is unique since it combines normative ideas on how courts should behave with an empirical analysis of the case law of the Belgian Constitutional Court (BeCC).

On the one hand, this book builds a normative framework, based on insights from deliberative theory, that sets out criteria for evaluating the performance of constitutional courts. In particular, the book discusses several 'judicial good practices' that allow the Court to enhance the deliberative component of policy-making. On the other hand, it is acknowledged that normative claims need to have a sensible idea of what may realistically shape judicial behaviour and, therefore, of what can actually be delivered. Legal theories about judicial review profit from a more empirically informed understanding of constitutional courts that builds upon and incorporates knowledge of the forces that shape their decisions.

Although the scholarship on judicial behaviour is continuously evolving, many authors have stressed that a court's functioning is influenced by its interdependent decision-making contexts. Continuing this line of research, this book argues that the consociational features of the Belgian polity may be reflected in the BeCC's case law. More specifically, the main hypothesis is that, in salient cases, the Court acts strategically – adapting certain aspects of its ruling – in order to maximise its effectiveness as a policy-maker. In other words, this book explores the relation between case salience and several aspects of the Court's decision.

The approach in this book is different from traditional research on judicial behaviour in several ways. First, scholars usually concentrate on the strategic adjustment of the final outcome – is the challenged legislation overruled or not? – and particularly on the individual judicial votes. Yet a binary categorisation of case outcomes (invalidated or not) may be too limited, considering that many courts such as the BeCC have developed diverse methods for answering a question of constitutionality. The analysis of case outcomes in this book offers a new perspective because it integrates a variety of 'in-between' modulated outcomes. Second, scholars today acknowledge that an exclusive focus on the judicial outcome may be too narrow. Instead, there is a range of judicial behaviour that

to Majoritarian Democracy' (2015) 43 International Review of Law and Economics, 1. Nonetheless, many studies on European constitutional courts are still carried out by US political scientists, for example G Vanberg, *The Politics of Constitutional Review in Germany* (Cambridge University Press 2005). In addition, there is an increasing research focus in Europe on the functioning of 'regular' courts. See for example: V Grembi and N Garoupa, 'Delays in Medical Malpractice Litigation in Civil Law Jurisdictions: Some Evidence From the Italian Court of Cassation' (2013) 8 Health Economics, Policy and Law, 423; M Westéus, 'Settlement Probability Asymmetries in the Swedish Labour Court' (2014) 38 European Journal of Law and Economics, 485; S Bielen, W Marneffe and L Vereeck, 'An Empirical Analysis of Case Disposition Time in Belgium' (2015) 11 Review of Law and Economics, 293; and P Grajzl and K Zajc, 'Litigation and the Timing of Settlement: Evidence from Commercial Disputes' (2016) 44 European Journal of Law and Economics, 287.

might reflect strategic calculations. By linking the strategical model to aspects of the ruling other than the case outcome, such as citation practices and the application of the proportionality analysis, this book offers new insights into how judges adapt their rulings in order to stimulate compliance. Third, in the current literature little attention is given to the effect of collegial judicial dynamics in the majority opinion. In Belgium, there is a balanced and collegial decision-making procedure, and the Court's rulings are presented to the public as single unanimous decisions. Therefore, this book studies how strategic considerations affect decisions at the aggregate level of the Court (both the outcome and the justificatory ground), instead of the behaviour of individual judges.

In sum, this book explores the extent to which the BeCC performs as a deliberative institution, while at the same time strategically adapting its rulings in salient cases. This central research focus can be translated into three sub-questions: (a) to what extent does the Court employ deliberative 'judicial good practices'; (b) to what extent is the Court's performance affected by strategic considerations; and (c) if the Court's rulings reflect strategic actions, does this behaviour correspond with the deliberative expectations weighing on the Court? Answering these questions will contribute to fundamental discussions about the appropriate role for judicial institutions to play in a democratic society.

In what follows, a more extensive overview is given of the structure of this book – divided into three main parts, each consisting of one or more chapters – and the subjects treated in each of these chapters.

The first part of this book explores the role of constitutional courts in democratic systems. Although many democratic countries have established some type of constitutional review, scholars still raise the counter-majoritarian objection.[4] In short, they believe that review, and possibly annulment, of legislation that was approved by (the representatives of) the people, is undemocratic. This is considered even more delicate when legislation is the result of a broad, encompassing supermajority, as is often the case in consociational democracies like Belgium. However, democracy should be defined more widely, as including both an electoral and a deliberative component. The first component, defined by the aggregation of viewpoints through and after recurring elections, is necessary but will not automatically guarantee the quality or legitimacy of policy-making. While proponents of the counter-majoritarian objection limit the definition of democracy to this electoral aspect, I believe that it is necessary to add a deliberative component defined by the concepts of inclusion, transparency, and the reasoned exchange of diverging viewpoints. Building on deliberative theory,

---

4 For its most vehement expressions, see: AM Bickel, 'Foreword: The Passive Virtues' (1961) Faculty Scholarship Series, 40; J Waldron, *Law and Disagreement* (Oxford University Press 1999); and J Waldron, 'The Core of the Case Against Judicial Review' (2006) 115 Yale Law Journal, 1346.

a multi-dimensional definition is introduced in this book to assess deliberative performance. In short, a deliberative institution should: (1) provide an inclusive forum; (2) deliberate internally; (3) produce a transparent written decision; (4) justify that decision by rational arguments; and (5) enhance constitutional dialogue. Essentially, it is argued that a strong deliberative performance can enhance the quality and legitimacy of democratic policy-making.

However, while most deliberative theorists agree on which notions and values define the 'deliberative' concept, it is unclear which institution(s) should put these into practice. On the one hand, this task could be allocated to the legislative branch. Although the virtues and malfunctions of each political system are different, the first part of this book reflects upon the democratic credentials of a (super)majoritarian decision-making process. The focus is on the Belgian polity, which is often defined as consociational. It is argued that the legislative policy-making process – maybe even more so in a consociational system – can be criticised for a lack of inclusiveness, transparency and rationality – the very elements that define the deliberative concept. On the other hand, judicial institutions seem apt to function as deliberative institutions because of the specific expectations that weigh upon them. More specifically, courts are expected to provide a decision once a case has been initiated, regardless of who the petitioner(s) is/are. Hence, they offer an inclusive forum where a variety of viewpoints can be considered. To formulate their decision, courts have to operate within the existing constitutional framework. Moreover, the reason-giving requirement is a special burden that weighs on courts. In particular, they are expected to justify their decision with legal and factual arguments.

For each key ingredient of deliberative performance, a selection of 'judicial good practices' will be highlighted and discussed. Examples include citing relevant and persuasive authorities, structuring the decision on the four-stage proportionality analysis, and communicating through constructive case outcomes. The main argument in this first part is that, when the deliberative performance of the legislative branch falls short, constitutional courts can provide an alternative route. This is not intended to demonstrate that the legislative branch cannot function as a deliberative institution, but merely to point out the potential *ex post* value of constitutional review. These good practices generate fresh considerations for the legislator to take into account when drafting new proposals. In that sense, deliberative theory helps to overcome the counter-majoritarian objections against constitutional review, because of the potential of courts to remedy malfunctions *post hoc* in the representative system.[5]

---

5 P Popelier and AA Patiño Álvarez, 'Deliberative Practices of Constitutional Courts in Consolidated and Non-Consolidated Democracies' in P Popelier, A Mazmanyan and W Vandenbruwaene (eds.), *The Role of Constitutional Courts in Multilevel Governance* (Intersentia 2013), 200.

The deliberative component should be understood as an ongoing dialogue between various institutions, centred on producing high quality outcomes.

Although it is indisputably valuable to discuss how a court *should* act in a "well-ordered constitutional democracy",[6] its authority cannot derive solely from what it ought to do. Every court, to a greater or lesser extent, is able to initiate and channel the deliberative quality of democratic policy-making. Therefore, the second part of this book explores what can be realistically expected from the BeCC.

First, like each constitutional court, the BeCC has to function within a specific institutional framework, decided upon by the legislator. This framework defines the Court's potential to act as a deliberative institution. The BeCC, and how it developed over time, is a highly interesting case study. Because constitutional review can present an obstacle for political actors in a consociational polity, the Court's competences were initially limited and served to protect consociational bargains and deal-making. The composition of the Court, with a strict parity between French-speakers and Dutch-speakers, and between 'professional' judges and former politicians, reflects these concerns. Although the strict parity has remained in place, the legislator has repeatedly extended the BeCC's competences. An evaluation of the institutional setting shows that the BeCC has developed into a fully-fledged human rights court with robust deliberative features. Nonetheless, preparatory documents show that the Court's further development was conditional on its performance as a 'reliable partner' for the legislative branch. In short, the legislator created a venue for deliberation, but at the same time built in security mechanisms to protect consociational peace.

Second, the rationale behind the Court's establishment and its further development may still weigh on the Court. More generally, judicial behaviour is believed to be constrained by the political context in which the court functions. Building on the literature on judicial behaviour, it is argued that the BeCC's case law may be (in part) shaped by strategic considerations. Under the 'strategic model', it is assumed that judges (micro level) or courts (macro level) want to maximise their effectiveness as policy-makers, but that they are also aware of their interdependent decision-making context. Importantly, contexts are always associated with expectations emanating from others who share this context.[7] Without legal incentives to guarantee compliance with its decisions, the Court is compelled to take into account the preferences of others responsible for this implementation. Moreover, the collegial constraints that follow from the double parity rule ensure that rulings always reflect the views of the different

6 CH Mendes, *Constitutional Courts and Deliberative Democracy* (Oxford University Press 2013), 5.

7 JL Gibson, 'From Simplicity to Complexity: The Development of Theory in the Study of Judicial Behavior' (1983) 5 Political Behavior, 7, 17.

sub-groups represented in the Court. The internal discussion needed to reach a collective outcome is likely to be reflected in the majority opinion. Considering these collegial and political constraints on the Court, it is no surprise that the Court (macro level) takes into account the anticipated reactions of the legislature, litigants, or other judges. More specifically, strategic behaviour may be reflected in the case outcome or, alternatively, in how the justificatory ground for the decision is formulated (e.g. through citations or the application of an argumentative framework). One of the central arguments in this book is that case salience functions as a trigger for such strategic behaviour. The strategic model assumes that the Court adapts its behaviour in line with the anticipated reactions of others, which are expected to be more pronounced in salient cases. The reason for this is that these cases have higher visibility and potentially raise major policy questions. Hence, in cases that are perceived as salient by the audience it addresses, the Court is under increased pressure to formulate the ruling – the outcome as well as the justificatory ground – in a way that stimulates acceptance and compliance. The incorporation of the logic of the strategic model can significantly enhance our understanding of the BeCC's behaviour and of the behaviour of constitutional courts in continental Europe in general.

In the third part of the book, divided into four chapters, the BeCC's case law is analysed from both a strategic and deliberative perspective. Methodologically, an interdisciplinary approach best serves the purpose of answering both the normative and empirical research questions raised. In particular, a statistical analysis of a large number of cases should be combined with in-depth legal scrutiny. For this purpose, I have built an extensive database on the case law of the BeCC, including all cases – annulment procedures as well as preliminary references – from its inception until 2015 (n=3145). A total of 55 variables were coded, which can be categorised into four sets of variables (see Annex). The first set collects information on the key features of the procedure, such the type of legislation under review or the nature (annulment/preliminary) of the procedure. The second set identifies who participated in the review procedure. A third set of variables register the content of each ruling, looking into the reference norms that were invoked and the cited authorities. The final set of variables collects information on the case outcome. In addition, I rely on a media database, provided by the Court for academic purposes.[8] This database contains information on the extent of news media attention for cases that were brought before the Court.

---

8 A special thank you to Luc Théry and Kris van Put, from the library and documentation office on the Belgian Constitutional Court, for providing me with this data (including regular updates).

In the first chapter, the concept of 'case salience' is explored. Considering that strategic behaviour is likely to be triggered by case salience, this concept needs to be translated into measurable explanatory variables. Three measures are specifically discussed: media coverage, the size of and diversity within the group of litigants, and panel size. It is considered why these measures are objective and can reasonably be expected to affect the Court's behaviour. For each salience measure, a descriptive overview is given of the collected data. Moreover, it is explored how the measures correlate with each other and with other aspects of the rulings such as the legal domain and the invoked reference norms. Although there is some level of congruence between the different types of salience, they do not overlap. Finally, an overview is given of 'highly salient' cases, of which 57 have been identified. These cases gained media coverage prior to the judicial decision, attracted a large and/or diverse group of litigants, and were decided in plenary session. Drawing on parliamentary preparatory documents and newspaper articles, it is explained why these cases can be considered controversial. In particular, many highly salient cases revolve around a political conflict (e.g. the famous *BHV* case). Others deal with issues that impact moral sensibilities, such as same-sex marriage, or attract media attention for another reason (e.g. the weapon regulation case). Considering their delicate nature, it should be expected that these are especially likely to demonstrate strategic actions by the Court.

The following three chapters are each centred on one specific aspect of the Court's case law. In particular, the case outcomes (chapter 5), citation practices (chapter 6), and the application of the proportionality analysis in fundamental rights cases (chapter 7) are scrutinised. Each of these chapters follows the same structure. First, it is discussed how the Court should shape its case law in light of the deliberative expectations that weigh on it. Special attention is paid to the reason-giving requirement and the engagement in dialogue. Next, a descriptive analysis is undertaken to reveal certain patterns in the Court's case law. Where there is a discernible evolution over time, this is illustrated by graphs. In addition, correlations are explored between each judicial practice and other case characteristics. Next, regression models lay bare which factors may influence the Court's behaviour. A number of hypotheses are tested regarding strategic actions in salient cases. After examining the presumed strategic model in a broad range of cases, the results are illustrated with isolated case examples. This allows me to contextualise the findings with concrete case material. In particular, an in-depth analysis of highly salient cases can illuminate how the BeCC manages the constraints impacting on its decisions, leading to a strategic equilibrium. Finally, throughout the analyses, references are made to other constitutional courts, indicating the relevance of the findings beyond the Belgian context.

Chapter 5 focuses on the case outcomes. From a deliberative angle, it is argued that case outcomes can be used as a vehicle to communicate with the Court's audience. Through more creative 'modulated outcomes', the Court can indicate how the legislation under review should be interpreted or altered in order for it to be applied in a constitutional manner. In this way, the Court assists ordinary courts on how to apply legislation and instructs the legislator on how to amend and draft legislation. The descriptive analysis shows that, over the years, the Court has become more willing to offer such assistance. Yet a reservation should also be noted: the Court should be more consistent in the phrasing of modulated dicta. Further, in the explanatory section, it is hypothesised that the Court may be more likely to proclaim a substantive or temporal modulation in salient cases. Proclaiming a simple invalidation in such cases entails a risk for the Court. In particular, it may lead to heavy criticism and/or non-compliance and may therefore threaten its institutional standing. Modulated outcomes do not confront the legislator in the same way. The results confirm that the Court addresses its audience in less pronounced terms when the case is particularly delicate.

Chapter 6 provides an insight into the citation practices of the BeCC. First, it is explained why citations of external authorities show that the Court has made efforts to explore all available information to answer the constitutional question. The descriptive analysis shows that the grounding of the Court's rulings has become stronger over the years. Yet, in terms of which authorities get cited, the BeCC takes a prudent approach. Often rulings are documented with only one *routine* citation to parliamentary documents. Also, the BeCC has shown an increasingly strong preference for the citation of judicial decisions, whether they be its own or those of other (inter)national courts. Citations from other sources, such as scientific studies, academic work, or advice from expert organisations, are very rare. Both the unavailability of such sources and/or the reluctance of judges to use and cite non-legal authorities are put forward as possible explanations. In the explanatory section, it is hypothesised that the Court uses more citations in salient cases in order to stimulate compliance. The findings confirm that the Court responds to external incentives and that citing authorities serves the purpose of legitimating decisions to a public audience.

The last chapter provides an in-depth analysis of how the Court uses references to the four-stage proportionality analysis to communicate with the legislator on why the constitutional challenge was accepted. From a deliberative perspective, indicating more specifically why legislation is found unconstitutional – in particular by referring to one of these stages – is important in light of the transparency requirement. Yet the descriptive analysis reveals that the Court rarely takes a structured, sequential approach with regard to the proportionality analysis. The suitability and necessity stages, which would require that the Court evaluate the empirical relation between the legislator's objective and the challenged (or alternative) measure(s), are often circumvented. Although the balancing stage also entails a difficult normative evaluation, the judges seem more comfortable with concluding that the challenged measure is disproportionate. Moreover, often the Court does not even make reference to any stage of the test. The main hypothesis in the explanatory section is that the Court, in salient cases, will be vaguer on the grounds for establishing a violation (by not referring to one of the stages of the proportionality analysis). This serves the purpose of protecting it against institutional reprisals while at the same time striking down the legislation to which the Court objects. Additional hypotheses are developed regarding the availability of information on the legislative objective and the influence of human rights case law. The regression models reveal that the vagueness of the Court's opinions is primarily due to the lack of sufficient information on the legislative objective. In that sense, legislative shortcomings prevent the Court from applying the proportionality test to its full extent. The results also suggest that the Court's reasoning patterns are influenced by the European Court of Human Rights (ECtHR), and that, in salient cases, producing a clearer opinion is considered a better strategy to stimulate compliance. In particular, more external attention on the ruling decreases the risk of open legislative defiance and protects the Court against institutional reprisals.

PART I

NORMATIVE FRAMEWORK

The Deliberative Performance of Constitutional Courts

The first part of this book builds a normative framework based on insights from deliberative theory. It is argued that, although the aggregation of viewpoints through and after recurring elections is necessary, this *electoral component* may not guarantee the quality or legitimacy of policy-making. Therefore, a *deliberative component* should be added, defined by the concepts of inclusion, transparency and the reasoned exchange of diverging viewpoints. Essentially, the deliberative component should be understood as an ongoing dialogue between various institutions, centred on producing high quality outcomes.

In order to assess deliberative performance, this book introduces a multi-dimensional definition. In particular, a deliberative institution should: (1) provide an inclusive forum; (2) deliberate internally; (3) produce a transparent written decision; (4) justify that decision by rational arguments; and (5) enhance constitutional dialogue.

The question is raised as to which institution(s) are capable of enhancing the deliberative component of democratic policy-making. As such, this chapter begins by discussing the democratic credentials of a (super)majoritarian decision-making process. The legislative process – maybe even more so in a consociational system such as the Belgian polity – can be criticised for a lack of inclusiveness, transparency and rationality, which are the very elements that define the deliberative concept. The central argument in this chapter is therefore that constitutional courts can provide an *ex post* alternative route to enhance the deliberative component of democratic policy-making. For each key ingredient of deliberative performance, a selection of 'judicial good practices' are highlighted, such as citing relevant and persuasive authorities, structuring the decision on the four-stage proportionality analysis, and communicating through constructive case outcomes. These good practices generate fresh considerations for the legislator to take into account when drafting new proposals. In that sense, deliberative theory helps to overcome the counter-majoritarian objections against constitutional review because of the potential for courts to remedy malfunctions in the representative system.

CHAPTER 1

CONSTITUTIONAL REVIEW IN DEMOCRATIC SYSTEMS

Countering the Counter-Majoritarian Objection

This first chapter explores the role of constitutional courts in democratic systems. Building on deliberative theory, a normative framework is built against which the BeCC's performance can be evaluated. This framework is defined by the key concepts of inclusiveness, rationality, transparency and dialogue. Without arguing that this framework may be applicable to any court in any period, the aim is to provide a 'middle-level' normative theory which sets out prescriptions and guidelines to be followed.[9] In particular, several judicial 'good practices' are highlighted and discussed. These will be further explored in the case law analysis in the fourth part of this book.

In sum, it is argued that a strong deliberative performance can enhance the quality and legitimacy of democratic policy-making. Because of constitutional courts' potential to remedy malfunctions in the representative system, judicial review provides a *post hoc* alternative path to enhance the deliberative component of policy-making.[10] The purpose is not to insinuate the superiority of constitutional courts in relation to the legislative branch, but to justify their place in an overall system of democratic decision-making. In that sense, deliberative theory helps to overcome the counter-majoritarian objections against constitutional review.

---

9 For more information, see CH Mendes, *Constitutional Courts and Deliberative Democracy* (Oxford University Press 2013), 5.

10 P Popelier and AA Patiño Álvarez, 'Deliberative Practices of Constitutional Courts in Consolidated and Non-Consolidated Democracies' in P Popelier, A Mazmanyan and W Vandenbruwaene (eds.), *The Role of Constitutional Courts in Multilevel Governance* (Intersentia 2013), 200.

1.1. DEMOCRATIC POLICY-MAKING: AN ELECTORAL AND A DELIBERATIVE COMPONENT

Although many democratic countries have established some type of constitutional review,[11] scholars still raise the counter-majoritarian objection.[12] Their argument derives from the idea that one of the most fundamental characteristics of a democracy is the equal opportunity for citizens, by means of elections, to participate in policy choices.[13] Even though some might disagree with the outcome of the legislative procedure, it is argued that each expressed opinion was given the greatest weight possible compatible with giving equal weight to all opinions.[14] Hence legislation is legitimate when approved by a majority of the elected representatives. According to the opponents of judicial review, courts lack the democratic legitimacy to reject or overrule this legislation. They argue that such review conflicts with the essential principles of representation and political equality.[15] In addition, as discussed at greater length in chapter 5, invalidations by a constitutional court are even more delicate when the invalidated legislation was the product of broad and encompassing supermajorities, as is often the case in consociational democracies like Belgium.

However, scholars have equally taken up the challenge to overcome this scepticism towards judicial review. Their responses to the counter-majoritarian objection are diverse and based upon different images of constitutional courts. Among other things, constitutional courts have been described as 'guardians of fundamental rights',[16] 'custodians of public deliberation',[17] and

---

11 On the global spread of constitutional review, see T Ginsburg, 'The Global Spread of Constitutional Review' in KE Whittington, RD Kelemen and GA Caldeira (eds.), *The Oxford Handbook of Law and Politics* (Oxford University Press 2010).

12 For its most vehement expressions, see: AM Bickel, 'Foreword: The Passive Virtues' (1961) Faculty Scholarship Series, 40; J Waldron, *Law and Disagreement* (Oxford University Press 1999); J Waldron, 'The Core of the Case against Judicial Review' (2006) 115 Yale Law Journal, 1346.

13 P Rosanvallon, *Le Bon Gouvernement* (Seuil 2015), 30, 197. As Rosanvallon argues, the right to vote is a constitutive element or minimal requirement of democracy.

14 J Waldron, 'The Core of the Case against Judicial Review' (2006) 115 Yale Law Journal, 1346, 1388.

15 Ibid., 1353.

16 W Sadurski, *Rights Before Courts: A Study of Constitutional Courts in Postcommunist States of Central and Eastern Europe* (Springer 2008), 107.

17 This image is attributed to, among others, Habermas and Zurn. They see the court as supervisor or 'regulatory watchdog' of the legislative process, assessing whether it was undertaken under proper deliberative circumstances. See: J Habermas, *Between Facts and Norms: Contributions to a Discourse Theory of Law and Democracy* (Polity 1996); CF Zurn, *Deliberative Democracy and the Institutions of Judicial Review* (Cambridge University Press 2007); P Popelier, 'The Court as Regulatory Watchdog: the Procedural Approach in the Case Law of the European Court of Human Rights' in P Popelier, A Mazmanyan and W Vandenbruwaene (eds.), *The Role of Constitutional Courts in Multilevel Governance* (Intersentia 2013).

'forums of principle'.[18] Each image emphasises one aspect of judicial review and, from this perspective, articulates the added value of constitutional courts in a democratic system. Essentially, these images raise expectations as to how the court *should* act in a "well-ordered constitutional democracy".[19] Recently, several authors have focused on another image: constitutional courts as deliberative institutions.[20] This multi-faceted image bundles together and supplements previous theories. It locates constitutional review within a broader conception of democratic policy-making, which includes an electoral as well as a deliberative component.[21]

The electoral component is defined by the notions of authorisation and accountability. The authority of representatives depends on the opportunity, for those citizens entitled to vote, to select the representatives who will act in their place in the policy-making process.[22] The individual or collective positions of these representatives are aggregated through a voting process, even though this might be the end-point of a deliberation phase.[23] After a certain period of time, the policy-makers are held accountable for their actions. In theory, citizens are allowed to elect an entirely different group of representatives.[24] Opponents of judicial review define democratic legitimacy by the equal opportunity to participate in the decision-making process, and argue that only elections, representation and the legislative process can guarantee the realisation of this process. Although it is necessary to aggregate viewpoints through returning elections, this will not automatically guarantee the quality or legitimacy of

18 This perception of constitutional courts is based on the idea that they are the ideal forums for constitutional reasoning, as distinct from 'ordinary politics': R Dworkin, *A Matter of Principle* (Harvard University Press 1985) and *Freedom's Law: The Moral Reading of the American Constitution* (Oxford University Press 1996).

19 CH Mendes, *Constitutional Courts and Deliberative Democracy* (Oxford University Press 2013), 5.

20 For example: J Ferejohn and P Pasquino, 'Constitutional Courts as Deliberative Institutions' in W Sadurski, *Constitutional Justice, East and West: Democratic Legitimacy and Constitutional Courts in a Comparative Perspective* (Kluwer 2002); LG Sager, *Justice in Plainclothes: A Theory of American Constitutional Practice* (Yale University Press 2006); P Popelier and AA Patiño Álvarez, 'Deliberative Practices of Constitutional Courts in Consolidated and Non-Consolidated Democracies' in P Popelier, A Mazmanyan and W Vandenbruwaene (eds.), *The Role of Constitutional Courts in Multilevel Governance* (Intersentia 2013); and CH Mendes, *Constitutional Courts and Deliberative Democracy* (Oxford University Press 2013).

21 This division is inspired by the work of LG Sager in *Justice in Plainclothes: A Theory of American Constitutional Practice* (Yale University Press 2006).

22 P Rosanvallon, *Le Bon Gouvernement* (Seuil 2015), 30, 197.

23 J Beyers, 'Policy Issues, Organisational Format and the Political Strategies of Interest Organisations' (2008) 31 West European Politics, 1188, 1196: "Although voting is key to politics, pure voting or voting that is not combined with or preceded by other interaction modes [bargaining and arguing] is somewhat rare."

24 In practice, however, the assembly of representatives remains relatively stable.

the policy-making process.[25] Even the strongest proponents of this idea have acknowledged that electoral systems can be flawed.[26]

Therefore, a second, equally important component should be added to democratic policy-making. This second element is captured by the term 'deliberative'[27] and is inspired by the theoretical literature on deliberative democracy.[28] In short, deliberative theory is defined by the concepts of inclusiveness, rationality and transparency. While the electoral component includes voting and, especially in consociational systems, bargaining, the main mode of interaction in the deliberative component is rational argument.[29] Essentially, the deliberative component aims to guarantee that the rights and interests of each member of a political community are seriously considered and taken into account. Also, those rights cannot be set aside without a proper explanation: any person is entitled to a reasoned statement as to why his or her claim was found wanting.[30] An institution that maximises its deliberative performance intensifies its democratic legitimacy.[31]

Nonetheless, it is important to stress that the electoral and deliberative components are equally important.[32] The deliberative enterprise does not aim to extinguish or supplant bargaining. The aggregation of votes remains central in democratic politics. Both components, together, are required to guarantee the democratic quality of a political system.

While most deliberative theorists agree on which notions and values define the 'deliberative' concept, it is unclear which institution(s) should put

---

25 See also P Rosanvallon, *Le Bon Gouvernement* (Seuil 2015), 21.

26 J Waldron, 'The Core of the Case against Judicial Review' (2006) 115 Yale Law Journal, 1346, 1386–8.

27 Other terms have been (and can be) used to capture the same idea. For example Rosanvallon differentiates between *"démocratie d'autorisation"*, set in place by elections, and a *"démocratie d'exercice […] qui a pour object de determiner les qualités attentues des gouvernants"*. See P Rosanvallon, *Le Bon Gouvernement* (Seuil 2015), 21.

28 The 'deliberative turn' in the theory on democracy can be located around 1990. For more information on the general concept, see: JS Dryzek, *Deliberative Democracy and Beyond* (Oxford University Press 2000); J Elster et al., *Deliberative Democracy* (Cambridge University Press 1998); A Guttman and D Thompson, 'Deliberative Democracy Beyond Process' (2002) 10 The Journal of Political Philosophy, 153; and JM Valadez, *Deliberative Democracy, Political Legitimacy and Self-Determination in Multicultural Societies* (Westview Press 2001).

29 For more information about these three modes of interaction, see: J Beyers, 'Policy Issues, Organisational Format and the Political Strategies of Interest Organisations' (2008) 31 West European Politics, 1188, 1194–1200; and J Elster et al., *Deliberative Democracy* (Cambridge University 1998), 5–12.

30 LG Sager, *Justice in Plainclothes: A Theory of American Constitutional Practice* (Yale University Press 2006), 202–3.

31 J Elster et al., *Deliberative Democracy* (Cambridge University 1998), 8; CH Mendes, *Constitutional Courts and Deliberative Democracy* (Oxford University Press 2013), 51.

32 J Elster et al., ibid., 11, 13; CH Mendes, ibid., 19, 48. See also J Knight and J Johnson, 'Aggregation and Deliberation: on the Possibility of Democatic Legitimacy' (1994) 22 Political Theory, 277, 286.

these into practice. On the one hand, this task could be allocated to the legislative branch. However, the policy-making process is often criticised for a lack of inclusiveness, transparency and rationality – the very elements that define the deliberative concept. On the other hand, judicial institutions seem appropriate candidates for deliberative performance, because of the specific expectations that weigh upon them.[33] More specifically, courts are expected to provide a decision once a case has been initiated, regardless of who the petitioner(s) is/are. To formulate this decision, they have to operate within the existing constitutional framework and their justifications must be based upon legal and factual arguments. Hence, when the legislative branch falls short, constitutional courts can provide an alternative route. Because of this potential of courts to remedy malfunctions in the representative system, deliberative theory may counter-majoritarian-based objections against constitutional review.[34]

In the next section, the electoral and deliberative components of democratic decision-making are discussed in more detail.

From an institutional and operational perspective, there are various ways to shape the electoral component. Two principal democratic representative models will be considered: a majoritarian system, where decisions are made by a simple majority of representatives, and an alternative power-sharing model, where different groups of representatives are expected to work together in the decision-making process. More attention will be paid to the latter model, also referred to as consociational or consensus democracy, because it defines the Belgian political context. Although the virtues and malfunctions of each political system are different, some general perspectives on the democratic credentials of a (super)majoritarian decision-making process will also be discussed. This is not intended to demonstrate that the legislative branch cannot function as a deliberative institution, but merely to point out the *ex post* potential value of constitutional review.

Further, building on deliberative theory, it will be explained how these courts may enhance the deliberative component of democratic policy-making. A multi-dimensional definition will be introduced to assess deliberative performance.[35]

---

33 J Ferejohn and P Pasquino, 'Constitutional Courts as Deliberative Institutions' in W Sadurski, *Constitutional Justice, East and West: Democratic Legitimacy and Constitutional Courts in a Comparative Perspective* (Kluwer 2002); and C Guarniere and P Pederzoli, *The Power of Judges: a Comparative Study of Courts and Democracy* (Oxford University Press 2003).

34 P Popelier and AA Patiño Álvarez, 'Deliberative Practices of Constitutional Courts in Consolidated and Non-Consolidated Democracies' in P Popelier, A Mazmanyan and W Vandenbruwaene (eds.), *The Role of Constitutional Courts in Multilevel Governance* (Intersentia 2013), 200.

35 This framework is inspired by the work of CH Mendes, who defined three consecutive phases of judicial deliberation: public contestation, collegial engagement and a deliberative written decision. This, in turn, builds on the work of J Ferejohn and P Pasquino in 'Constitutional Courts as Deliberative Institutions' in W Sadurski, *Constitutional Justice, East and West: Democratic Legitimacy and Constitutional Courts in a Comparative Perspective* (Kluwer 2002),

In short, a deliberative institution should: (1) provide an inclusive forum; (2) deliberate internally; (3) produce a transparent written decision; (4) justify that decision by rational arguments; and (5) enhance constitutional dialogue.

1.2. THE ELECTORAL COMPONENT

1.2.1. POWER-SHARING AS AN ALTERNATIVE TO THE MAJORITY RULE

The electoral system in a majoritarian democracy is founded on the principle of 'winner takes all': in each electoral district, parliamentary seats are allocated to the candidate or party which collects the most votes, maximising the size of the majorities.[36] Therefore, the smaller political parties rarely obtain a parliamentary seat, limiting the number of parties represented in Parliament. Most legislative decisions are taken by a simple majority, which requires the acceptance of only one or two parties. Only in exceptional situations, such as a constitutional reform, might a qualified majority be required. Although this is usually combined with or preceded by bargaining and debate, the main mode of interaction in a majoritarian system is voting. Through the voting process, all political preferences are aggregated. The decision of the majority can be imposed hierarchically and it is expected that both majority and minority acquiesce.[37]

When the viewpoints of the different political parties do not vary significantly, as is the case in a homogeneous society, such a system usually does not cause many problems. Moreover, majority and minority will usually alternate, so each political party can, by turns, influence important policy decisions.[38]

The situation, however, is different in heterogeneous societies like Belgium. These societies are characterised by segmentation into several fixed 'sub-groups', divided by religious, ethnic, socio-economic or other differences.[39] Each sub-group is represented by its own political elite with specific policy ideas,

---

who made the distinction between internal deliberation between jugdes and external dialogue with other constitutional agents. Although Mendes wanted to focus on internal deliberation, the main contribution of his book is rather to list the factors that stimulate the court's deliberative performance. See CH Mendes, *Constitutional Courts and Deliberative Democracy* (Oxford University Press 2013), 4. For criticism, see T Bustamate, 'The Ongoing Search for Legitimacy: Can a 'Pragmatic yet Principled' Deliberative Model Justify the Authority of Constitutional Courts?' (2015) 78 The Modern Law Review, 372, 375.

36 This is not necessarily an absolute majority. In some cases, it is sufficient to be the 'largest minority'.

37 J Beyers, 'Policy Issues, Organisational Format and the Political Strategies of Interest Organisations' (2008) 31 West European Politics, 1188, 1196.

38 A Lijphart, *Patterns of Democracy* (Yale University Press 1999), 31–2.

39 For the definition and characteristics of a pluralistic society, see A Lijphart, 'Consociational Theory: Problems and Prospects. A Reply' (1981) 13 Comparative Politics, 355–6.

resulting in a permanent lack of consensus. The 'winner takes all' principle would lead to a domination of the same sub-group(s), permanently excluding other minority groups from the policy process. A natural alternation between the political parties, as in majoritarian systems, does not occur. A consistent application of the majority rule would therefore lead to conflicts and destabilisation.[40]

Many political scientists have accounted for how the balancing of majorities and minorities affects the politics in pluralistic societies and have looked for an alternative to a simple majoritarian model. One of those authors is Arend Lijphart, who made it his life's work to identify counter-majoritarian solutions for heterogeneous societies. He developed several related but not interchangeable concepts:[41] 'consociationalism',[42] 'consensus democracy'[43] and the overarching concept of 'power-sharing'.[44,45] The basic underlying premise of these solutions is that they effect conflict management, by striving for a broad compromise between the sub-groups on each policy decision. To reach these compromises, permanent and detailed consultations between the sub-groups are necessary. Hence, the main mode of interaction in these systems is bargaining. As opposed to the mode of rational argument, this might not change the factual beliefs or preferences of the representatives, but it will affect their voting behaviour.[46]

Although these concepts developed by Lijphart share some general traits, some differences are to be noted. The first concept was 'consociationalism'. Consociationalist systems are typified by their pluralistic nature, which causes recurring conflicts between different sub-groups. Therefore Lijphart considered

---

40 A Lijphart, *Democracy in Plural Societies: a Comparative Exploration* (Yale University Press 1977), 25–36; and A Lijphart, *Patterns of Democracy* (Yale University Press 1999), 1–2.

41 A Lijphart, *Thinking About Democracy: Power Sharing and Majority Rule in Theory and Practice* (Routledge 2008), 8.

42 A Lijphart, 'Consociational Democracy' (1969) 21 World Politics, 207.

43 In his initial work he mentioned 'negotiation democracy' as an alternative name for this type of democracy: A Lijphart, *Democracy in Plural Societies: a Comparative Exploration* (Yale University Pres 1977), 2. However, after Armingeon developed a separate theory under this heading (see K Armingeon, 'The Effects of Negotiation Democracy: a Comparative Analysis' (2002) 41 European Journal of Political Research, 81), Lijphart distanced himself from this terminology: A Lijphart, 'The Wave of Power Sharing Democracy' in A Reynolds (ed.), *The Architecture of Democracy: Constitutional Design, Conflict Management and Democracy* (Oxford University Press 2002).

44 A Lijphart, *Power Sharing in South Africa* (Institute of International Studies, University of Berkely 1985); and A Lijphart, *Thinking About Democracy: Power Sharing and Majority Rule in Theory and Practice* (Routledge 2008).

45 For more information about the interrelation of these concepts, and criticism of Lijphart's conceptual development, see M Bogaards, 'The Uneasy Relationship Between Empirical and Normative Types in Consociational Theory' (2000) 12 Journal of Theoretical Politics, 395, 404.

46 J Beyers, 'Policy Issues, Organisational Format and the Political Strategies of Interest Organisations' (2008) 31 West European Politics, 1188, 1197.

the *good will* of the political elites and their joint efforts to reach broadly acceptable compromises to be the most essential characteristic of consociationalism.[47] In addition, he identified four essential features of consociational democracies: government by a grand coalition, proportional political representation, mutual veto-powers and segmented autonomy.[48] Lijphart paid less attention to the institutional features framing and stimulating the cooperation between sub-groups.[49] He argued, for example, that government by grand coalition could take several different institutional forms. Not only the prototypal coalition cabinet, but also other councils or committees, could serve the same function.[50] Lijphart also stated that the idea of segmented autonomy could be implemented in different ways, for example by introducing territorial federalism.[51] In short, the consociational model primarily served as a normative example for plural societies.

However, this made the concept of consociationalism difficult to measure. In reply to this criticism, Lijphart developed a binary empirical typology with ten measurable institutional variables, placing each country on a continuum, at a point between a majoritarian or – introducing a new concept – 'consensus democracy'.[52,53] While Lijphart initially relied on the *good will* of the political elites, he now acknowledged there should be arrangements that encourage or oblige communities to make public policy jointly. To overcome their differences, he argued, the structure of political power should be divided between the sub-groups, and consultations among these groups should be held along established lines.[54] Lijphart clustered the institutional variables in two separate dimensions: the executives-parties dimension and the federal-unitary dimension. As for the first dimension, the consensus model is characterised by broad

---

47 A Lijphart, 'Consociational Democracy' (1969) 21 World Politics, 207, 213; and A Lijphart, *Power Sharing in South Africa* (Institute of International Studies, University of Berkely 1985), 113.

48 A Lijphart, *Democracy in Plural Societies: a Comparative Exploration* (Yale University Press 1977).

49 A Lijphart, 'Consociational Democracy' (1969) 21 World Politics, 207, 213 and further.

50 A Lijphart, *Democracy in Plural Societies: a Comparative Exploration* (Yale University Press 1977), 25, 31.

51 Lijphart states that federal theory can be regarded as a limited and special type of consociational theory, and offers an especially attractive way of implementing the idea of segmental autonomy: A Lijphart, *Democracy in Plural Societies: a Comparative Exploration* (Yale University Pres 1977), 42–3.

52 A Lijphart, *Democracy in Plural Societies: a Comparative Exploration* (Yale University Press 1977).

53 However, it is not, as Sartori stated, merely a new name for consociationalism: G Sartori, *Comparative Constitutional Engineering: An Inquiry into Structures, Incentives and Outcomes* (New York University Press 1994), 70.

54 D Sinardet, 'From Consociational Consciousness to Majoritarian Myth: Consociational Democracy, Multi-Level Politics and the Belgian Case of Brussels-Halle-Vilvoorde' (2010) 45 Acta Politica, 346, 348–9.

multi-party coalitions, executive-legislative balance of power, a multiparty system, proportional representation and a corporatist interest group system aimed at compromise and concertation. From the federal-unitary perspective, one can recognise a consensus model when there is a federal and centralised government, bicameralism, a rigid constitution, a constitutional court responsible for judicial review and an independent central bank.[55]

Over time, other scholars have begun to take a similar institutional approach to consociationalism.[56] As a result, the current conception of consociationalism seems to cover the same institutional features as consensus democracy, in addition to the pluralistic nature of the society.

Adding to the conceptual confusion, Lijphart later introduced the alternative term 'power-sharing'.[57] This has been reused by most authors as an umbrella concept that can be defined as an "inherently accommodative set of attitudes, processes, and institutions, in which the art of governance becomes a matter of bargaining, conciliating, and compromising the aspirations and grievances of its ethnic communities".[58] From this perspective, both consociational and consensus democracies are particular types of democracies with a characteristic set of power-sharing institutions, processes and policies.[59]

In the next section, the Belgian political system is scrutinised. The analysis from a historical perspective shows that there has always been a tradition of power-sharing and compromising. Nonetheless, it equally demonstrates that there are limitations to such supermajoritarian practices.

1.2.2. THE BELGIAN POLITY: HISTORICAL OVERVIEW

Belgium is a divided society, with a tradition of cooperation between the different sub-groups in society. However, the dividing lines between these groups have evolved from being socio-religious to more language-based. When Belgium was proclaimed an independent state, the Catholics and Liberals built an alliance (the so-called *monsterverbond*) against the Dutch occupation. From previous periods of occupation, the political leaders had learned that internal disagreement made the system unstable, and therefore easily conquered.[60] Only when King Willem I from the Netherlands accepted the independence of

---

55 A Lijphart, *Patterns of Democracy* (Yale University Press 1999), 2–3.

56 M Bogaards, 'The Uneasy Relationship between Empirical and Normative Types in Consociational Theory' (2000) 12 Journal of Theoretical Politics, 395.

57 A Lijphart, *Power Sharing in South Africa* (Institute of International Studies, University of Berkely 1985).

58 MJ Esman, *An Introduction to Ethnic Conflict* (Polity Press 2004), 177–8.

59 M Bogaards, 'Democracy and Power-Sharing in Multinational States: Thematic Introduction' (2006) 8 International Journal on Multicultural Societies, 119, 122.

60 A Lijphart, 'Consociational Democracy' (1969) 21 World Politics, 207, 212–3.

Belgium in 1839 did the union between Liberals and Catholics fall apart. There was no need for structural cooperation between both parties, and Belgium evolved into a majoritarian system with two competing parties. Nevertheless, in the following decades Liberals and Catholics worked together several times in coalition governments.[61] In 1877, the Socialist party was established. Although initially this party did not obtain enough votes to be included in a (coalition) government, it soon developed into a strong third pillar.

During the first half of the twentieth century, the division into three pillars (*zuilen*) – the Catholics, Socialists and Liberals – became more pronounced. Each pillar was horizontally organised with its own political party, labour union etc. The first example of broad cooperation between the political elites of the three pillars dates back to the period after the First World War, when socio-economic and linguistic tensions began to emerge. To avoid destabilisation and the loss of legitimacy, the three political parties negotiated a compromise in 1918 with the introduction of the 'one man, one vote' principle, although this was technically incompatible with the Constitution.[62] Afterwards, cooperation came to an end, only to be re-established in 1935, when the three parties formed a coalition government that would last until after the Second World War.[63]

Although the Catholic pillar was dominant for quite some time, none of these parties (with a single exception in 1950) succeeded in obtaining an absolute majority of the votes. However, even in 1950, the Catholics could not solve the delicate 'Royal question'[64] without taking into account the opinion of the other sub-groups. When the Catholics tried to impose a decision without consulting the others, this resulted in a short civil war. Afterwards, the tradition of coalition governments – or other temporal collaborations outside the government[65] – continued. With two exceptions, in 1950 and 1954, there has not been a government consisting of only one party since the end of the Second World War.[66]

---

61 The Nothomb government from 13 April 1941 to 19 June 1845; the Van de Weyer government from 30 July 1845 to 2 March 1846; the de Decker government from 30 March 1855 to 30 October 1857. But in the first two governments mentioned there was a preponderance of Catholics.

62 'The Loppem Pact': K Deschouwer, 'From Consociation to Federation: How the Belgian Parties Won' in KR Luther and K Deschouwer (eds.), *Party Elites in Divided Societies: Political Parties in Consociational Democracy* (Routledge 1999), 75.

63 K Deschouwer, 'And the Peace Goes On? Consociational Democracy and Belgian Politics in the Twenty-First Century' (2006) 29 West European Politics, 895, 899.

64 For more information, see K Deschouwer, 'And the Peace Goes On? Consociational Democracy and Belgian Politics in the Twenty-First Century' (2006) 29 West European Politics, 895, 899.

65 An example is the School Pact of 1961. After the elections of 1958, the prime minister of the Catholic minority government reached out to the political leaders of the opposition to secretly negotiate this compromise, after years of conflict on the issue: W Dewachter, *Besluitvorming in Politiek België* (Acco 1992), 107–8; and A Lijphart, *Democracy in Plural Societies: a Comparative Exploration* (Yale University Press 1977), 33.

66 A Lijphart, 'Consociational Democracy' (1969) 21 World Politics, 207, 218.

Further, over time some of the structures designed to accommodate the separate demands of the three pillars became institutionalised.[67] For example, the regulation of employment relations is driven by formalised consultations between the labour unions and employers' organisations.[68] Because of this strong involvement of professional and special-interest organisations in the creation of public policy, Belgian consociationalism is closely linked to corporatism.[69]

During the second half of the twentieth century, socio-religious divisions diminished[70] while the Flemish movement grew stronger, cutting across this pillar structure.[71] Although its political organisation had already increased,[72] there were only a few recognised representatives on the national level to formulate Flemish interests and demands. Therefore, in his initial work, which dates back to 1969, Lijphart argued that consociationalism might not be a realisable solution to these language-based conflicts in Belgium.[73] However, Lijphart's observation was outdated before his article was published. After 1960, the aforementioned political parties started to split along language lines, and several additional (language-based) parties were established. On the one hand, the Flemish political elite aspired to eliminate any subordination at the economic, cultural, social and political level, and demanded more autonomy. On the other hand, mindful of the numerical and economic preponderance of the Flemish, the French-speaking political elite feared domination by the more conservative, more catholic Flemish elite.[74]

An important turning point in the establishment of Belgium as a super-majoritarian polity was the constitutional reform of 1970. This package deal constituted not only the first step in the devolutionary trend towards a federal

67 G Peters, 'Consociationalism, Corruption and Chocolate: Belgian Exceptionalism' (2006) 29 West European Politics, 1079, 1082.

68 These agreements are called *Collectieve Arbeidsovereenkomsten* (Collective Labour Agreements): W Dewachter, *Besluitvorming in Politiek België* (Acco 1992), 156–7.

69 Ibid., 116, 140, 144.

70 The first School Pact in 1961 is considered the end point of this period of strong pillarisation: K Deschouwer, 'From Consociation to Federation: How the Belgian Parties Won' in KR Luther and K Deschouwer (eds.), *Party Elites in Divided Societies: Political Parties in Consociational Democracy* (Routledge 1999), 90.

71 However, the socio-religious and linguistic divisions were also intertwined. While the Catholic pillar was the most important in the Flemish Region, in the Walloon Region the Socialist pillar was most prominent: T Boucké and K Vandaele, *Het Sociaal Overleg in België* (Academia Press 2003), 16.

72 The first language-based parties date from the 19th century. Although their general influence at the national level was limited, some smaller achievements at the local level were noticeable. More information can be found in E Witte, J Craeybeckx and A Meynen, *Politieke Geschiedenis van België: van 1830 tot Heden* (Standaard uitgeverij 2007), 61–4, 102–6, 157–60, 193–9, 419 and further.

73 A Lijphart, 'Consociational Democracy' (1969) 21 World Politics, 207, 221.

74 E Witte, J Craeybeckx and A Meynen, *Politieke Geschiedenis van België: van 1830 tot Heden* (Standaard uitgeverij 2007), 426–8.

state, but also introduced several power-sharing mechanisms.[75] To avoid deadlock and protect minority rights, not only the French-speaking minority in Belgium, but also other minorities (Flemings in Brussels, German-speakers in Wallonia) gained specific power-sharing rights. In addition to segmental autonomy, protection at the federal level was guaranteed, for example by parity between Dutch-speaking and French-speaking officials in the council of ministers, and a special 'alarm bell' procedure giving the French-speaking minority in Parliament certain veto powers. In short, the tradition of power-sharing between the language-groups became institutionalised. The establishment of the BeCC can also be situated within this process of institutionalisation, since it was part of the package deal implied in the second state reform of 1977.

During the last decade, criticism of the political structures of the Belgian system has become stronger. It has become increasingly difficult to establish workable governing coalitions.[76] After the elections of 2010 it took 541 days to form a government, an international record, and it took several months (139 days) to form the government in 2014. It seems more and more challenging to transcend the deeply rooted differences between Dutch-speaking and French-speaking parts. One could argue that the stabilising effect of power-sharing structures and mechanisms has declined. Nonetheless, many political elites still cling to these principles.[77]

From this historical overview, one can conclude that all three of Lijphart's concepts apply to the Belgian situation. First, the defining feature of the Belgian society is its strongly pluralistic nature. This structural division into several religious, social or language-based sub-groups is the main characteristic of a consociationalist system, but not a necessary condition to make it a consensus democracy. On the other hand, the institutionalised super-majoritarian decision-making process in Belgium seems to encompass most of the empirical characteristics of a consensus democracy. As a result, clearly the Belgian polity can also be categorised within the broad group of power-sharing democracies. Lijphart himself contributed to the confusion on the categorisation of the Belgian polity. In the context of a conference on the Belgian political system in 1980, he described Belgian democracy as the prime example of consociationalism.[78]

---

75 K Deschouwer, 'And the Peace Goes On? Consociational Democracy and Belgian Politics in the Twenty-First Century' (2006) 29 West European Politics, 895, 901–2.

76 For example: D Caluwaerts, *Confrontation and Communication: Deliberative Democracy in Divided Belgium* (Peter Lang 2012), 14, 72; and D Sinardet, 'From Consociational Consciousness to Majoritarian Myth: Consociational Democracy, Multi-Level Politics and the Belgian Case of Brussels-Halle-Vilvoorde' (2010) 45 Acta Politica, 346–7.

77 K Deschouwer, 'And the Peace Goes On? Consociational Democracy and Belgian Politics in the Twenty-First Century' (2006) 29 West European Politics, 895–911.

78 A Lijphart, *Conflict and Coexistence in Belgium: The Dynamics of a Culturally Divided Society* (Institute of International Studies, University of California 1981), 4: "Belgium can

However, his conclusion was based on a step-by-step analysis of several institutional characteristics which were the very same features he had treated in his book on consensus democracy in 1984.[79] In academic literature, Belgium has been described as a consociational, consensus, or power-sharing democracy, or as a combination of these. However, this book refers to Belgium as a consociational polity. This is on account of the broader scope of this concept, combining institutional and attitudinal features. Considering that political elites in Belgium have continuously searched for compromise, notwithstanding strong socio-religious and linguistic divisions, one can argue that its pluralistic nature remains the most distinguishing characteristic of the Belgian system.

1.2.3. THE DEMOCRATIC CREDENTIALS OF (SUPER)MAJORITARIAN DECISION-MAKING

As mentioned above, both the majoritarian and the consociational models are representative democratic systems, characterised by recurring elections. However, whereas in a majoritarian system acquiescence is expected from minority groups after the voting process, in a consociationalist system these minority groups are structurally included in the policy process. In other words, the first model emphasises the voting outcome and the latter focuses on the bargaining process (often at the executive level). In what follows, a review is conducted of some general perspectives on the democratic credentials of the (super)majoritarian decision-making process. This falls within the scope of this book because malfunctions in the policy-making process may cause the legislator to infringe upon the Constitution, which may stimulate actors to present their grievances to the constitutional court. Essentially, the virtues and flaws of each system also depend on the nature of the society in question. Here the Belgian system will be considered as an example of a consociational system.

Although we cannot underestimate the value of representation through elections, the majoritarian model has been criticised by many scholars.[80] First, the majoritarian model does not guarantee the protection of minority groups.

legitimately claim to be the most thorough example of consociational democracy, the type of democracy that is most suitable for deeply divided societies ... In fact, [it] is a more perfect example of the consociational ideal than British democracy is of the majoritarian ideal".

79 K Deschouwer, 'And the Peace Goes On? Consociational Democracy and Belgian Politics in the Twenty-First century' (2006) 29 West European Politics, 895, 899.

80 For example: JH Ely, 'Toward a Representation-Reinforcing Mode of Judicial Review' (1978) 37 Maryland Law Review, 451; JS Dryzek, 'Democratization as Deliberative Capacity Building' (2008) 42 Comparative Political Studies, 1379–80; and P Popelier and AA Patiño Álvarez, 'Deliberative Practices of Constitutional Courts in Consolidated and Non-Consolidated Democracies' in P Popelier, A Mazmanyan and W Vandenbruwaene (eds.), *The Role of Constitutional Courts in Multilevel Governance* (Intersentia 2013), 200–1.

If a majority group is treated unreasonably, it can choose to not re-elect its representatives, but the 'winner takes all' principle, as opposed to the proportional system, limits this possibility for minorities.[81] This is problematic because, notwithstanding a minimum of consensus, contemporary societies are characterised by a multiplicity of (minority) opinions.[82] The values and beliefs of the different parties will never be identical.[83] Hence political parties included in the executive coalition can effectively pursue their interests while others are – at least temporarily – excluded from the processes of political change. There is always a chance that at the next elections the 'winner takes it all' principle might run in favour of another party, resulting in an alternation of majority and minority. However, where there are multiple smaller groups, these might never obtain a majority of the votes. Also, elections do not always provide clear signals about the voters' intentions and preferences.[84] And even if all minority groups are consulted, the executive might fail to grasp their situation or interests. In addition, not all majoritarian decisions are driven by rational arguments.[85] On the contrary, public choice theories have shown that majoritarian decision procedures can be arbitrary.[86] Further, time pressure or competing priorities which appear (electorally) more pressing or salient might prevent political representatives from fully assessing the potential impact of a legislative proposal.[87] All these features weaken the democratic credentials of the outcome of a majoritarian decision-making process.[88]

According to Lijphart, the consociational model, in which minorities are structurally included in the policy process, is a better alternative in

81 JH Ely, ibid., 451, 458.

82 R Gargarella, 'Full Representation, Deliberation and Impartiality' in J Elster (ed.), *Deliberative Democracy* (Cambridge University Press 1998), 270–1; and P Rosanvallon, *Le Bon Gouvernement* (Seuil 2015), 25, 300.

83 JH Ely, 'Toward a Representation-Reinforcing Mode of Judicial Review' (1978) 37 Maryland Law Review, 459.

84 J Parkinson, *Deliberating in the Real World: Problems of Legitimacy in Deliberative Democracy* (Oxford University Press 2006), 91.

85 J Ferejohn and P Pasquino, 'The Countermajoritarian Opportunity' (2010) 13 Journal of Constitutional Law, 353, 360.

86 CF Zurn, *Deliberative Democracy and the Institutions of Judicial Review* (Cambridge University Press 2007), 65.

87 P Popelier and AA Patiño Álvarez, 'Deliberative Practices of Constitutional Courts in Consolidated and Non-Consolidated Democracies' in P Popelier, A Mazmanyan and W Vandenbruwaene (eds.), *The Role of-Constitutional Courts in Multilevel Governance* (Intersentia 2013), 201; and CR Sunstein, 'Health-Health Trade-Offs' in J Elster (ed.), *Deliberative Democracy* (Cambridge University Press 1998), 257.

88 A Mazmanyan, 'Majoritarianism, Deliberation and Accountability as Institutional Instincts of Constitutional Courts' in A Mazmanyan, P Popelier and W Vandenbruwaene (eds.), *The Role of Constitutional Courts in Mulitlevel Governance* (Intersentia 2013), 169, referring to J Ferejohn and P Pasquino, 'Constitutional Courts as Deliberative Institutions' in W Sadurski, *Constitutional Justice, East and West: Democratic Legitimacy and Constitutional Courts in a Comparative Perspective* (Kluwer 2002), 25.

heterogeneous societies.[89] He rebuts the claim that this is less democratic given the absence of a strong opposition, arguing, on the contrary, that the democratic credentials of a broad compromise are higher than those of a mere majority decision.[90] Because of this enhanced inclusiveness, some have argued that consociationalism is indeed the superior model.[91] However, although studies have shown that consociationalism can indeed effect conflict management in a pluralistic society, many authors have also raised doubts about its democratic quality.[92]

First, due to the institutionalisation of conflict management, consociationalism might not be as inclusive as is generally presumed.[93] For example, the Belgian system does not (yet) guarantee broad inclusion of all relevant (minority) interests in the policy-making process. Due to the proportional electoral system, smaller political parties – if they reach a certain threshold – are represented in Parliament. However, it should be noted that the role of this institution is rather limited in comparison with the executive branch. At the national as well as the regional levels, the majority of legislative initiatives come from (the cabinets of) government officials,[94] but not all minority groups are (permanently) represented in the government.[95] Also, instead of being attentive to individual rights, there is a strong focus on group rights.[96] Consultations among the sub-groups are held along established lines and decision-making powers are strongly delegated to the

89 Initially, he only argued that is the best option that realistically can be expected in a pluralistic society (A Lijphart (1977) 8), but his later work (e.g. A Lijphart (1985)) shows his further conviction of the merits of consociationalism, or any type of power sharing in general.

90 A Lijphart (1977) 47. Lijphart argues that "a substantial degree of oligarchy and secrecy is a common and probably unavoidable chracteristic of democratic politics everywhere".

91 B O'Leary, 'Debating Consociational Politics: Normative and Explanatory Arguments' in S Noel (ed.), *From Power Sharing to Democracy: Post-Conflict Institutions in Ethnically Divided Societies* (McGill-Queen's Press 2005). The OECD also explicitly stated that "the Belgian system draws a large part of its strength from high participation rates. Union membership is high (between 60 and 70%), and 80–90% of companies are members of an employer's federation." OECD, *Better Regulation in Europe* (OECD 2010), 21.

92 For example, Tatsuo Inoue defends the majoritarian principle and enumerates what she feels "is wrong with the Lijphart models". See T Inoue, 'Two Models of Democracy: How to Make Demos and Hercules Collaborate in Public Deliberation' in LJ Wintgens (ed.), *The Theory and Practice of Legislation: Essays in Legisprudence* (Ashgate 2005), 116 and further.

93 This is also the reason why Lijphart initially put so much emphasis on the congruent attitude of the political elite. See A Lijphart, 'Consociational Democracy' (1969) 21 World Politics, 207, 213.

94 OECD, *Better Regulation in Europe* (OECD 2010), 19: "In all governments (federal, regions, communities), ministerial cabinets [...] are often involved in law drafting (a task usually reserved for civil servants)."

95 See JS Dryzek, 'Deliberative Democracy in Divided Societies: Alternatives to Agonism and Analgesia' (2005) 33 Political Theory, 218, 222: "Elections have little meaning, as the same political parties will often govern in an oversized coalition." On Belgium specifically, see H Vuye, 'Het Parlement als Wetgevende macht, Historisch en Prospectief' in P Popelier and J Van Nieuwenhove, *Wie Maakt de Wet?* (die Keure 2006), 3–5.

96 HJ Steiner, 'Ideals and Counter-Ideals in the Struggle Over Autonomy Regimes for Minorities' (1991) Notre Dame Law Review, 1539, 1551–2.

political elite of each group. Hence, there is a close and influential connection between social groups, political parties and the government. For this reason, Belgian consociationalism is closely linked with corporatism and partitocracy.[97] The former is defined by a specific institutionalised relation between the political level and certain socio-economic organisations. By structurally integrating these organisations in the policy-making process, the political level aims to create social support for its legislative decisions. This support is important to ensure compliance with policy decisions.[98] However, access to these negotiations is limited to certain established 'representative' organisations,[99] excluding the smaller, less organised or weaker groups.[100] The latter concept, partitocracy, concerns the role of political parties in the policy-making process. In this system, parties tend to control most aspects of governing, including the allocation of positions and the appointment of many officials.[101] The relative strength of politicians during negotiations depends on the results of the elections and the proportional share of parliamentary seats. The elite nature of this policy-making process constrains the possibility for a broad range of citizens to directly and effectively participate in the policy process.[102] As a result, consociationalist systems equally fail to guarantee that all minority viewpoints are taken into account.

Second, the policy-making process in a consociational system is often criticised for its lack of transparency. Consociational bargains often reflect elite-centred negotiations at the executive level which take place behind closed doors and are dominated by political parties. This discretion is meant to create a secure environment without distractions from outside.[103] Politicians believe that acting

---

97 For Belgium, see: G Peters 'Consociationalism, Corruption and Chocolate: Belgian Exceptionalism' (2006) 29 West European Politics, 1079, 1083; and H Vuye, 'Het Parlement als Wetgevende macht, Historisch en Prospectief' in P Popelier and J Van Nieuwenhove, *Wie Maakt de Wet?* (die Keure 2006), 20.

98 T Boucké and K Vandaele, *Het Sociaal Overleg in België* (Academia Press 2003), 14, 22.

99 OECD, *Better Regulation in Europe* (OECD 2010), 17: "Belgium's current institutionalised system of consultation is based on fundamental principles of representative democracy". In practice, this means that most representative organisations are closely linked to a specific – ideologically affiliated – political party.

100 W Dewachter, *Besluitvorming in Politiek België* (Acco 1992) 141–2.

101 G Peters, 'Consociationalism, Corruption and Chocolate: Belgian Exceptionalism' (2006) 29 West European Politics, 1079, 1081.

102 M Bogaards, 'Democracy and Power-sharing in Multinational States: Thematic Introduction' (2006) 8 International Journal on Multicultural Societies, 119–120; JS Dryzek, 'Deliberative Democracy in Divided Societies: Alternatives to Agonism and Analgesia' (2005) 33 Political Theory, 218, 222; and J Parkinson, *Deliberating in the Real World: Problems of Legitimacy in Deliberative Democracy* (Oxford University Press 2006), 149. For Belgium, see W Dewachter, *Besluitvorming in Politiek België* (Acco 1992), 118, 125.

103 JS Fishkin, *When the People Speak: Deliberative Democracy and Public Consultation* (Oxford University Press 2009), 168. On the tension between political practice and transparency, see P Popelier et al., 'Transparant Consulteren in Vlaanderen: de Spanning Tussen Rationeel Wetgevingsmodel en Besluitvormingspraktijk' (2012) Tijdschrift Voor Wetgeving, 6–7.

otherwise might cause a potential threat to the delicate arrangements between the political parties.[104] Keeping the public informed would fuel discontent about the compromise and increase polarisation.[105] Afterwards, there is often no or scarce documented information available to reconstruct the negotiation process. As mentioned before, compared with the executive, the role of Parliament is limited. Therefore, preparatory parliamentary documents cannot always illuminate the justificatory ground for a policy decision. Also, the opinions of the Council of State, which – in principle – should be consulted on all draft laws, decrees and ordinances, and therefore plays an important role in *ex ante* scrutiny of draft regulations, are not widely publicised.[106] Although secrecy and elite negotiations are not unique to consociational democracies,[107] these are considered essential to achieve workable agreements. This lack of transparency not only hinders a proper political dialogue between the representatives, but also public debate in general.[108] The decision-making process does not entail direct and broad citizen participation in the policy process. Also, it makes it difficult for the politicians to be held accountable, and thus undermines the legitimacy of the system.

Third, in consociationalist systems, party elites tend to combine all sorts of political issues in large package deals in which negotiation logic – the exchange of resources through bargaining – prevails. The political parties will exchange resources to reach a large package deal that can be approved in Parliament as a whole, although they might not agree with all individual elements of the compromise.[109] Also, since these compromises are reached at the executive level and are considered very delicate, there is not much room for alterations during the parliamentary procedure. This might create a gap between what is politically opportune and accomplishable, and what would be most adequate and efficient.[110] Hence, policy outcomes strongly depend on the negotiation strategies pursued by the bargaining elites and do not necessarily reflect rational arguments that result from creative and reasoned exchanges of diverging viewpoints.[111] Although this negotiation strategy might improve acceptance

104 G Peters, 'Consociationalism, Corruption and Chocolate: Belgian Exceptionalism' (2006) 29 West European Politics, 1079, 1087.

105 M Bogaards, 'Democracy and Power-sharing in Multinational States: Thematic Introduction' (2006) 8 International Journal on Multicultural Societies, 119–120.

106 OECD, *Better Regulation in Europe* (OECD 2010), 23.

107 A Lijphart, *Power-sharing in South Africa* (Institute of International Studies, University of Berkely 1985), 111.

108 R Dahl, *On Democracy* (Yale University Press 1998), 113. Dahl calls this the dark side of representative democracy. Also see P Rosanvallon, *Le Bon Gouvernement* (Seuil 2015), 232.

109 A Lijphart, *Power-sharing in South Africa* (Institute of International Studies, University of Berkely 1985), 113: "[consociationalism] does not require that decision-makers abandon their original preferences, that they whole-heartedly support the compromises, or that they never cast a vote against a particular compromise proposal."

110 W Dewachter, *Besluitvorming in Politiek België* (Acco 1992), 121.

111 HJ Steiner, 'Ideals and Counter-Ideals in the Struggle Over Autonomy Regimes for Minorities' (1991) Notre Dame Law Review, 1539, 1551–2; JS Dryzek, 'Deliberative Democracy in

of the rule on a short-term basis, the lack of a sufficient, rational justification might cause problems in the long run. Therefore, those who are critical of consociational systems argue that package deals might be incoherent and less efficient than policy choices shaped by a single political goal or ideology.[112]

In addition, not all malfunctions discussed above can be addressed by a supermajoritarian policy process. Electoral outcomes are susceptible to various arbitrary, exogenous social, cultural or economic influences.[113] For example, many legislative proposals suffer from problems such as time pressure, competing priorities, or strategic voting.[114] In Belgium, draft legislation should normally be submitted to the Council of State for an *ex ante* evaluation. However, a large number of these drafts are submitted under the 'emergency procedure' which severely limits the capacity to carry out effective checks.[115] As in other countries, Belgian politicians also make use of 'mosaic laws'.[116] This is legislation, usually produced at the end of the year when time is running short, that combines various decisions in one bulky and fragmented law. Mosaic laws might include technical issues such as the rectification of errors or legislative lacunae, legislative reactions to judicial decisions, and even regulations with more substantial scope. When a mosaic law has a budgetary purpose, it is also nominated a 'programme law'. When using the emergency procedure for programme laws,[117] there is no time for a thorough evaluation of the proposal, nor for a substantial and critical debate.[118] Also, although these programme laws are in principle limited to budgetary issues, in practice they are (mis)used for various other reasons.[119] Usually, the quality of mosaic laws leaves much to be desired. Legal certainty can suffer when citizens have difficulties identifying and

---

Divided Societies: Alternatives to Agonism and Analgesia' (2005) 33 Political Theory, 218, 222; and M Bogaards, 'Democracy and Power-sharing in Multinational States: Thematic Introduction' (2006) 8 International Journal on Multicultural Societies, 119–120.

112 K Armingeon, 'Democracy, Consociational' in B Badie (ed.), *International Encyclopedia of Political Science* (Sage publications 2011), 557; and A Guttman and D Thompson, 'Deliberative Democracy Beyond Process' (2002) 10 The Journal of Political Philosophy, 15, 167.

113 J Knight and J Johnson, 'Aggregation and Deliberation: on the Possibility of Democatic Legitimacy' (1994) 22 Political Theory, 277, 279.

114 P Popelier and AA Patiño Álvarez, 'Deliberative Practices of Constitutional Courts in Consolidated and Non-Consolidated Democracies' in P Popelier, A Mazmanyan and W Vandenbruwaene (eds.), *The Role of Constitutional Courts in Multilevel Governance* (Intersentia 2013), 200–1.

115 OECD, *Better Regulation in Europe* (OECD 2010), 23.

116 For a comparative overview, see P Popelier, 'Mosaic Laws and Arrangement Laws: A Common Practice Respectively Not So Common Practice' (2005) European Journal of Law Reform, 47.

117 The Belgian Council of State is only given five days to judge the law. Ibid., 54.

118 Ibid., 51.

119 OECD, *Better Regulation in Europe* (OECD 2010), 22. "An agreement exists between the federal government and the parliament to limit the use of programme laws to budgetary issues. In principle, only urgent and technical issues can be included in programme laws. The federal government recognises that in practice these laws can be unhelpful to transparency and the general quality of the legislative process."

comprehending the provisions applicable to their situation. Considering that parliamentary debate on the law is often seriously curtailed, these laws may lack democratic legitimacy.[120]

From this perspective, both majoritarian and supermajoritarian decisions might not be as democratic as critics of judicial review presume. These findings are not new and have been picked up by Belgian politicians. Over the years, there have been considerable developments and achievements, at the national as well as the regional levels, driven by a growing awareness of the need to improve legislative quality.[121] For example, all governments have improved the preparatory stage, by introducing *ex ante* impact analyses to assess various policy options.[122] These procedures include, to a greater or lesser extent, and depending on the nature of the decision, scientific inquiries and consultation rounds with stakeholders. The goal is to understand the full scope of the issue, and to evaluate the necessity, efficiency, feasibility and character of different alternatives. Belgian governments have also been developing new forms of consultation, such as open online calls for comments, to reach out directly to citizens. These methods create new access possibilities alongside the traditional structures.[123]

In practice, however, these impact assessments are often circumvented through existing loopholes, such as the emergency procedure.[124] At the federal level, the procedure is also criticised because many legislative proposals fall outside the scope of its application.[125] Even when the *ex ante* analyses are carried out, short deadlines and the political culture limit their extent and efficiency. Politicians often consider the time-consuming impact assessment procedures to be redundant.[126] Once a political compromise is reached, this is implemented in a detailed legislative text by government officials within the ministerial cabinets. This does not leave much room for alterations during the

---

120 P Popelier, 'Mosaic Laws and Arrangement Laws: A Common Practice Respectively Not So Common Practice' (2005) European Journal of Law Reform, 51–53.

121 OECD, *Better Regulation in Europe* (OECD 2010), 16.

122 For more information on these *ex ante* impact assessments, see the following websites: http://www.bestuurszaken.be/reguleringsimpactanalyse (Flemish government); and http://www.vereenvoudiging.be/nl/content/impactanalyse (Federal government).

123 OECD, *Better Regulation in Europe* (OECD 2010), 21.

124 Ibid., 23; and P Van Humbeeck, 'Wetgevingsbeleid in Vlaanderen op Niveau van de Uitvoerende Macht: een Update van de Uitdagingen voor Betere Regelgeving' in P Popelier and J Van Nieuwenhove, *Wie maakt de wet?* (die Keure 2006), 108–9.

125 P T'Kindt and J Van Nieuwenhove, 'De federale voorafgaande regelgevingsimpactanalyse (RIA) – een wassen neus of een stapje vooruit?' (2014) Tijdschrift Voor Wetgeving, 168–184. The Council of State had also criticised the new system (*Parl Doc* Chamber 2012–13, no 53-2992/1, 42–9) because it did not respond to the concerns of the OECD. See OECD, *Better Regulation in Europe* (OECD 2010), 49–51, 95–136.

126 P Van Humbeeck, 'Wetgevingsbeleid in Vlaanderen op Niveau van de Uitvoerende Macht: een Update van de Uitdagingen voor Betere Regelgeving' in P Popelier and J Van Nieuwenhove, Wie maakt de wet? (die Keure 2006), 112.

parliamentary procedure.[127] Also, the impact assessments suffer from a lack of transparency. Due to scarce public information on the legislative proposal and the assessment procedure, interested actors are often too late to offer their suggestions.[128] This is even more difficult for underprivileged minorities, such as detainees and refugees. Afterwards, it is often unclear which actors were consulted and whether their grievances were taken into account.[129] Participants should at least be able to understand why their claim was found wanting. Without this feedback, the whole purpose of these consultations is defeated.[130]

In sum, not only does it seem more and more difficult to continue the cooperative tradition, some of the distinctive features of the Belgian policy-making process also appear to present barriers to effective governance.[131] Some consociational mechanisms undermine the implementation of democratic values such as inclusiveness, transparency and rational decision-making. In short, consociational bargains reflect elite-centred negotiations which take place behind closed doors. Such negotiations do not entail direct and broad citizen participation in the policy process. Also, negotiation logic might prevail over rational arguments. Notwithstanding that there has been some progress, if *ex ante* legislative evaluation is to make a real difference, important challenges need to be addressed. Examples of further improvements that could be made include the increased use of more direct forms of consultation, greater visibility in consultation processes, substantial critical debate instead of formal hearings and extensive, clear feedback. This will require further culture change and a high-level commitment.[132]

1.3. THE DELIBERATIVE COMPONENT

1.3.1. DELIBERATIVE PERFORMANCE DEFINED BY FIVE, INTERRELATED KEY ELEMENTS

As demonstrated above, democratic legitimacy should not be equated with the simple balancing of majorities and minorities. Therefore, some authors

---

127 Ibid., 116.

128 Ibid., 114.

129 W Marneffe and K Poel, 'De Federale Regelgevingsimpactanalyse: een Stand van Zaken na Zes Maanden' (2014) Tijdschrift Voor Wetgeving, 193; P Popelier et al., 'Transparant Consulteren in Vlaanderen: de Spanning tussen Rationeel Wetgevingsmodel en Besluitvormingspraktijk' (2012) Tijdschrift Voor Wetgeving, 2–12.

130 P Popelier et al., ibid., 5. According to these authors, providing feedback is one of the 'good practices' in a consultation process.

131 G Peters, 'Consociationalism, Corruption and Chocolate: Belgian Exceptionalism' (2006) 29 West European Politics, 1079, 1080.

132 OECD, *Better Regulation in Europe* (OECD 2010), 17–21.

have argued that (temporary) electoral supremacy alone cannot justify the supremacy of a political decision.[133] Democratic legitimacy equally implies that all viewpoints are seriously taken into account, with consideration for the variety of perspectives in a heterogeneous society.[134] Citizens do not only have the right to vote, but also the right to be heard and receive a proper answer.[135] Also, the outcome of a decision-making process should follow from reasoned argumentation.[136] This second element is captured by the deliberative modality and is inspired by the theoretical literature on deliberative democracy.[137]

Although there is an extensive overlap among the definitions, the term 'deliberative' covers a large range of meanings, and therefore risks creating conceptual uncertainty.[138] Nonetheless, there is a 'minimal common denominator' in the deliberative component.[139] In short, deliberative theorists posit the inclusive, transparent and reasoned weighing of interests as the means to achieve the best possible policy results.[140] Outcomes are only legitimate when all those subject to the decision in question have had the chance to participate in the decision-making process.[141] This also implies that each participant is treated with equal consideration.[142] Also, instead of relying only or predominantly on the strength of electoral success, deliberative theorists promote persuasion through better argument.[143] The main mode of interaction of the deliberative

133 A Guttman and D Thompson, 'Deliberative Democracy Beyond Process' (2002) 10 The Journal of Political Philosophy, 153–154; J Knight and J Johnson, 'Aggregation and Deliberation: on the Possibility of Democatic Legitimacy' (1994) 22 Political Theory, 277; CS Sunstein, *One Case at a Time: Judicial Minimalism on the Supreme Court* (Harvard University Press 1999), 25; and P Rosanvallon, *Le Bon Gouvernement* (Seuil 2015), 32, 213.

134 LG Sager, *Justice in Plainclothes: A Theory of American Constitutional Practice* (Yale University Press 2006), 72–6, 200–7 and 218–9; and P Rosanvallon, *Le Bon Gouvernement* (Seuil 2015), 212.

135 CH Mendes, *Constitutional Courts and Deliberative Democracy* (Oxford University Press 2013), 116.

136 J Knight and J Johnson, 'Aggregation and Deliberation: on the Possibility of Democatic Legitimacy' (1994) 22 Political Theory, 277, 284.

137 On the 'deliberative turn' in theories on democracy, see *supra*, footnote 28.

138 J Elster et al., *Deliberative Democracy* (Cambridge University Press 1998), 8; and CH Mendes, *Constitutional Courts and Deliberative Democracy* (Oxford University Press 2013), 11; and J Parkinson, *Deliberating in the Real World: Problems of Legitimacy in Deliberative Democracy* (Oxford University Press 2006), 2.

139 CH Mendes, *Constitutional Courts and Deliberative Democracy* (Oxford University Press 2013), 14, referring in footnote 2 to other publications that agree on the existence of a consolidated common denominator.

140 R Dahl, *On Democracy* (Yale University Press 1998), 85–6; and A Gutmann and D Thompson, 'Democracy and Disagreement' in R Dahl, I Shapiro and JA Cheibub, *The Democracy Sourcebook* (MIT Press 2003), 18–24.

141 J Elster et al., *Deliberative Democracy* (Cambridge University Press 1998), 8.

142 CH Mendes, *Constitutional Courts and Deliberative Democracy* (Oxford University Press 2013), 17.

143 Ibid., 16.

component is rational argument, which, in contrast with bargaining, is primarily meant to shape preferences and/or factual beliefs.[144] These arguments must be couched in terms that are accessible to everybody and could in principle be accepted by anyone.[145] After this exchange of reasons, the decision-makers should articulate the justificatory ground for their final opinion. Irrespective of whether citizens assent to the particular content of the decision, they deserve, as equals, collective feedback.[146] Although obedience is expected from those who are affected by the decision, the debating process is not closed indefinitely. On the contrary, the issue may be reopened in new rounds of debate. This continuity emphasises the long-term perspective and an openness to persuasion and prevents the ossification of the deliberation process.[147]

In what follows, the intention is not to summarise or evaluate the voluminous literature on deliberative democracy, but rather to concentrate its essential features in a framework capable of measuring deliberative performance. Building on deliberative theory, I have identified five key, interrelated elements of deliberative performance. A deliberative institution should: (1) provide an inclusive forum; (2) deliberate internally; (3) produce a transparent written decision; (4) justify that decision by rational arguments; and (5) enhance constitutional dialogue. This definition captures the fundamental notions of deliberative theory: inclusiveness, transparency, rationality and dialogue. In addition, each element can be translated into certain 'good practices'. Importantly, an institution that maximises its deliberative performance enhances its democratic legitimacy.[148]

It should be stressed that these five key elements are interlinked. Indeed, the definition implies a certain chronology. During the pre-decision phase, a deliberative institution must enable an inclusive canvassing of arguments. This gives the decision-maker(s) all necessary tools to reach a collective, reasoned conclusion. Next is the actual decision phase, which refers to the collegial

---

144 Therefore, deliberation should be *consequential*: it must somehow make a difference in determining or influencing political outcomes: JS Dryzek, 'Democratization as Deliberative Capacity Building' (2008) 42 Comparative Political Studies, 1379, 1381. Also see J Beyers 'Policy Issues, Organisational Format and the Political Strategies of Interest Organisations' (2008) 31 West European Politics, 1188, 1197.

145 JS Dryzek, 'Democratization as Deliberative Capacity Building' (2008) 42 Comparative Political Studies, 1379, 1381; A Guttman and D Thompson, 'Deliberative Democracy Beyond Process' (2002) 10 The Journal of Political Philosophy, 153, 165–6; and J Habermas, *De Nieuwe Onoverzichtelijkheid en Andere Opstellen* (Boom Meppen 1989), 90–1.

146 CH Mendes, *Constitutional Courts and Deliberative Democracy* (Oxford University Press 2013), 15, 116.

147 Ibid., 14–15.

148 J Elster et al., *Deliberative Democracy* (Cambridge University Press 1998), 8; and CH Mendes, *Constitutional Courts and Deliberative Democracy* (Oxford University Press 2013), 51.

engagement between actors involved in the deliberation process. Once a decision is adopted, it must be translated into a clear written document which includes rational arguments and which has the capacity to enhance dialogue. If not, the post-decision phase, during which the decision should be implemented, may be flawed. These consecutive phases do not form a linear time-line, but simply highlight that the five key elements are interconnected. For instance, an inclusive procedure enables the deliberative institution to engage in a comprehensive internal debate and formulate an accurate decision. Also, for a decision-making process to be truly inclusive, the deliberative institution should show that all viewpoints were seriously considered. Without transparency on the justificatory ground for the final decision, participants may feel deceived.[149] Finally, the quality of the reason-giving affects the legitimacy of the decision. Compliance with the decision can only be expected if all participants can reasonably embrace the given justification.

Although deliberative theorists seem to agree on what the deliberative component substantively includes, it is not always clear which institution should be responsible for its performance.[150] Also, as Mendes has stated, "not all institutions are designed to be deliberative and of those intended as such, not all are equally so".[151] Some deliberative theorists are sceptical about the deliberative role of courts,[152] yet many accept that they can provide an additional deliberative forum.[153] Some authors go even further and argue that, while legislators are best suited to carry out the electoral component, (constitutional) courts might be

---

149 CH Mendes, *Constitutional Courts and Deliberative Democracy* (Oxford University Press 2013), 116.

150 Most deliberative theorists have concentrated on this question. Parkinson, for example, promotes a macro conception of democracy in which a variety of institutions (but not constitutional courts) are connected together: J Parkinson, *Deliberating in the Real World: Problems of Legitimacy in Deliberative Democracy* (Oxford University Press 2006). See also JS Dryzek, 'Democratization as Deliberative Capacity Building' (2008) 42 Comparative Political Studies, 1379, 1396: "it is not always clear which sorts of institutional combinations best promote deliberative capacity in particular settings."

151 CH Mendes, *Constitutional Courts and Deliberative Democracy* (Oxford University Press 2013), 43.

152 For example: JS Dryzek, 'Legitimacy and Economy in Deliberative Democracy' (2001) 29 Political Theory, 651, 657; A Gutmann and D Thompson, 'Democracy and Disagreement' in R Dahl, I Shapiro and JA Cheibub, *The Democracy Sourcebook* (MIT Press 2003); and CF Zurn, *Deliberative Democracy and the Institutions of Judicial Review* (Cambridge University Press 2007).

153 For example: J Ferejohn and P Pasquino, 'Constitutional Courts as Deliberative Institutions' in W Sadurski, *Constitutional Justice, East and West: Democratic Legitimacy and Constitutional Courts in a Comparative Perspective* (Kluwer 2002); P Popelier and AA Patiño Álvarez, 'Deliberative Practices of Constitutional Courts in Consolidated and Non-Consolidated Democracies' in P Popelier, A Mazmanyan and W Vandenbruwaene (eds.), *The Role of Constitutional Courts in Multilevel Governance* (Intersentia 2013); and J Rawls, *Political Liberalism* (Columbia University Press 1993), 231–6.

more apt to function as deliberative institutions.[154] Both institutions are capable of reinforcing the deliberative function but courts can provide an alternative *ex post* route when the legislative branch falls short.[155] A legislative decision might be formally legitimated without necessarily meeting substantive democratic standards.[156] As accurately noted by Guarniere and Pederzoli, "The chances that individual and collective interests will use the courts depends on the judiciary's ability to answer to such claims; this, in turn has to be evaluated with respect to the ability of other institutions to respond effectively to social demands."[157]

In what follows, the five key ingredients of deliberative performance are delineated separately, with a focus on their added value in a democratic policy-making process. The main argument is that, because of the specific expectations that weigh on courts,[158] a true deliberative performance is within their reach. Courts can therefore complement and influence the democratic policy-making process in a positive way. To strengthen this argument, some of the malfunctioning aspects of the legislative decision-making process are highlighted. This is, however, not intended to demonstrate that the legislative process cannot be deliberative, but merely to point out the potential *ex post* value of constitutional review. It is important to stress that although courts may legitimately prevent majorities from compromising the rights of minorities, they may not make compromises in their name.[159] The end of each section highlights which particular judicial good practices should be expected from a deliberative constitutional court.

---

154 LG Sager, *Justice in Plainclothes: A Theory of American Constitutional Practice* (Yale University Press 2006), 74–5, 200–7.

155 See P Popelier and AA Patiño Álvarez, 'Deliberative Practices of Constitutional Courts in Consolidated and Non-Consolidated Democracies' in P Popelier, A Mazmanyan and W Vandenbruwaene (eds.), *The Role of Constitutional Courts in Multilevel Governance* (Intersentia 2013), 200; and T Bustamate, 'The Ongoing Search for Legitimacy: Can a 'Pragmatic yet Principled' Deliberative Model Justify the Authority of Constitutional Courts?' (2015) 78 The Modern Law Review, 372, 383.

156 M Van Hoecke, 'Constitutional Courts and Deliberative Democracy' in A Mazmanyan, P Popelier and W Vandenbruwaene (eds.), *The Role of Constitutional Courts in Mulitlevel Governance* (Intersentia 2013), 184.

157 C Guarniere and P Pederzoli, *The Power of Judges: a Comparative Study of Courts and Democracy* (Oxford University Press 2003), 11.

158 Ferejohn and Pasquino call them 'deliberative expectations': J Ferejohn and P Pasquino, 'Constitutional Courts as Deliberative Institutions' in W Sadurski, *Constitutional Justice, East and West: Democratic Legitimacy and Constitutional Courts in a Comparative Perspective* (Kluwer 2002), 2. Also see C Guarniere and P Pederzoli, *The Power of Judges: a Comparative Study of Courts and Democracy* (Oxford University Press 2003), 10–11, where they enumerate "specific procedural constraints."

159 T Bustamate, 'The Ongoing Search for Legitimacy: Can a 'Pragmatic yet Principled' Deliberative Model Justify the Authority of Constitutional Courts?' (2015) 78 The Modern Law Review, 372, 383.

1.3.2. CONSTITUTIONAL COURTS AS DELIBERATIVE INSTITUTIONS

1.3.2.1. Inclusiveness

A deliberative institution should first of all provide an inclusive forum where all interests, values and information are brought together and examined.[160] All those affected by a decision should be able to present their suggestions and grievances.[161] The inclusiveness of the procedure is essential for two reasons. First, an inclusive process improves the understanding of the problem at issue and amplifies information and resources.[162] The gathering of information is particularly important because no amount of hypothetical reasoning can bring out all the complexities of a policy issue.[163] In this sense, inclusiveness improves the quality of the decision.[164] In addition, an active and wide-ranging involvement can create popular support for the decision, even if not all citizens agree with the outcome.[165] As empirical research has shown, the perception that the decision-making procedure was fair is at least as important as a favourable decision for the satisfaction of the parties involved in the procedure.[166] Hence, under the condition of a transparent, qualitative justification, the perception of an inclusive procedure stimulates an effective implementation of the decision.

---

160 J Parkinson, *Deliberating in the Real World: Problems of Legitimacy in Deliberative Democracy* (Oxford University Press 2006), 150.

161 According to Dryzek, "deliberative democracy itself began [...] as a theory for which democratic legitimacy depends upon the ability of all those subject to a decision to participate in authentic deliberation": JS Dryzek, *Deliberative Democracy and Beyond* (Oxford University Press 2000), 85.

162 CH Mendes, *Constitutional Courts and Deliberative Democracy* (Oxford University Press 2013), 24.

163 A Guttman and D Thompson, 'Deliberative Democracy Beyond Process' (2002) 10 The Journal of Political Philosophy, 153, 157.

164 However, this quality is also determined by other factors. See P Popelier and et al., *Consultaties in de Wetgevingspraktijk* (Politeia 2008), 11.

165 J Knight and J Johnson, 'Aggregation and Deliberation: on the Possibility of Democatic Legitimacy' (1994) 22 Political Theory, 277; E Brems and L Lavrysen, 'Procedural Justice in Human Rights Adjudication: The European Court of Human Rights' (2013) 35 Human Rights Quarterly, 176, 178 and further; CH Mendes, *Constitutional Courts and Deliberative Democracy* (Oxford University Press 2013), 31; and P Rosanvallon, *Le Bon Gouvernement* (Seuil 2015), 213.

166 SG Grimmelikhuijsen and AJ Meijer, 'The Effects of Transparency on the Perceived Trustworthiness of a Government Organization: Evidence from an Online Experiment' (2012) Journal of Public Administration Research and Theory Advance Access, 1; E Brems and L Lavrysen, 'Procedural Justice in Human Rights Adjudication: The European Court of Human Rights' (2013) 35 Human Rights Quarterly, 176, 183–4; and MC Ponthoreau, 'l'énigme de la motivation encore et toujours l'éclairage comparatif' in F Hourquebie and MC Pontoreau (eds.), *La Motivation des Decisions des Cours Suprêmes et Cours Constitutionelles* (Bruylant 2012), 15.

In order to ensure the inclusiveness of the procedure, an institution should have an open-access policy, lowering its threshold to allow all citizens to articulate their wishes and concerns. Moreover, a deliberative institution should not remain passive, but should actively gather as many viewpoints as possible. For this purpose, the institution should consult with different individuals, interest groups, business organisations etc,[167] and should seek information from external sources like legal doctrine, case law or comparative research. In addition, inclusiveness does not only imply the opportunity to be heard, but also an obligation to listen.[168] A deliberative institution should be responsive to all arguments and counter-arguments that emerge. Each participant should receive, equal to its input, a thorough answer.[169] In conclusion, inclusiveness as a component of deliberative performance entails an open-access policy, an active engagement in the search for evidence-based decisions and an equal responsiveness to all those affected by the decision.

Thus, inclusive legislative decision-making is the first step towards high-quality, effective legislation. However, including *all* citizens in this procedure is practically impossible. Because of this problem, individuals usually authorise – through elections – a group of representatives to express their different opinions.[170] As discussed in relation to the electoral component, this process has proved to be effective but (sometimes) incomplete. Contemporary societies are characterised by a multiplicity of opinions. Viewpoints that were not strongly represented might not, possibly unconsciously, be taken into account. Equally, this might also happen deliberately, owing to time pressure or competing priorities. Consociationalist systems, which structurally include minority groups in the policy process, promoting in-depth consultations between political parties, aim to move in the direction of greater inclusiveness. However, consociationalism is also closely linked with elitism and corporatism. This implies the involvement of a fixed set of traditionally defined groups, limiting the participation potential of those who do not fit into these traditional categories.[171] Finally, some citizens, such as refugees or detainees, might not be entitled to vote, making them additionally vulnerable to violations of their rights.[172] In short, relying

---

167 J Parkinson, *Deliberating in the Real World: Problems of Legitimacy in Deliberative Democracy* (Oxford University Press 2006), 2.

168 J Knight and J Johnson, 'Aggregation and Deliberation: on the Possibility of Democatic Legitimacy' (1994) 22 Political Theory, 277, 286.

169 A process of "taking in and reflecting back": see JM Makau and DL Marty, *Dialogue and Deliberation* (Waveland Press 2013), 251. This responsiveness requirement will also be considered in section 1.3.2.4.

170 For more information on this 'scale problem', see J Parkinson, *Deliberating in the Real World: Problems of Legitimacy in Deliberative Democracy* (Oxford University Press 2006), 5–8, 26–8.

171 Ibid., 149.

172 P Popelier, 'The Belgian Constitutional Court: Guardian of Consensus Democracy or Venue for Deliberation?' in A Alen et al., *Liber Amicorum Marc Bossuyt* (Intersentia 2013), 493–4.

on electoral mechanisms to achieve the full representation of society can prove difficult.[173]

Such failures may create the need for, and reliance on, responsiveness from other institutions. In particular, constitutional courts – if this possibility is institutionally provided – can offer redress to those who were excluded from the policy process or who found their claim rejected. There are several procedural aspects regarding access to constitutional courts which may enhance the inclusiveness of the review procedure. First, individuals usually do not need (strategic) resources or wide popular support to gain access to the court, thereby offering opportunities to marginalised groups that usually have little chance of voicing their grievances in the public forum. Also, although there might be some form of docket control or certain conditions of admissibility, judges are usually expected to provide a decision once the claim has been lodged. Finally, they are obliged to hear both parties before the decision can be taken.[174]

Therefore, the review procedure provides a forum for interaction between its participants, who are all considered equals: the initiating parties who demand the annulment of the legislation at issue, the defending party who must demonstrate that the legislation is justified,[175] and the intervening parties, who can submit a memorandum to support the claim of one or the other. This allows all parties, including the government responsible for the challenged law,[176] to advance arguments in the constitutional debate that may have been overlooked or neglected in the course of the parliamentary proceedings.[177] The success of the constitutional claim does not depend on coalition-forming between political groups, but rather on the strength of the legal argument.[178] Therefore, constitutional adjudication can provide a mode of participation

---

173 R Gargarella, 'Full Representation, Deliberation and Impartiality' in J Elster (ed.), *Deliberative Democracy* (Cambridge University Press 1998) 270–1: "The system seems structurally incapable of taking into account the viewpoints of all those affected by the decision-making."

174 C Guarniere and P Pederzoli, *The Power of Judges: a Comparative Study of Courts and Democracy* (Oxford University Press 2003), 12; and A Kavanagh, *Constitutional Review under the UK Human Rights Act* (Cambridge University Press 2009), 339 and further.

175 On this 'burden of justification', see C Sunstein, *Designing Democracy* (Oxford University Press 2001), 234; and M Cohen-Eliya and I Porat, 'Proportionality and the Culture of Justification' (2011) 59 American Journal of Comparative Law, 463, 474.

176 The legislator may also introduce new or additional arguments during the review procedure, a practice that is known as *post hoc* reason-giving. See M Shapiro and A Stone Sweet, *On Law, Politics and Judicialization* (Oxford University Press 2002), 245–7.

177 P Popelier and AA Patiño Álvarez, 'Deliberative Practices of Constitutional Courts in Consolidated and Non-Consolidated Democracies' in P Popelier, A Mazmanyan and W Vandenbruwaene (eds.), *The Role of Constitutional Courts in Multilevel Governance* (Intersentia 2013), 209.

178 A Kavanagh, *Constitutional Review under the UK Human Rights Act* (Cambridge University Press 2009), 341.

which can counteract some of the ways in which normal democratic politics may disadvantage the poor and powerless in society.[179]

Additionally, courts do not only gather information from the involved parties, but can also undertake their own research. For example, judges can make use of external sources such as legal doctrine, (inter)national case law or comparative research.[180] However, it may be delicate for a court to actively undertake certain investigations (e.g. consultations, scientific inquiries) because the selection process might show prejudice. Therefore, the information available to the judges is often limited to what the directly involved participants brought before the court. Without the possibility of inviting others into the discussion, the quantity and quality of information will then depend on the salience of the specific case and the level of (public) mobilisation behind it.[181]

In conclusion, it is essential that the court's rulings follow from a critical evaluation of the available arguments, and are based on a justification that is equally responsive to all participants. Hence, an evaluation of responsiveness involves a careful review of the degree to which the court avoids making claims which are not based on evidence. This deliberative quality will be further explored in sections 1.3.2.3. and 1.3.2.4. in relation to the transparency and rationality of the justification for the judicial decision.

Judicial good practices:

- A broad interpretation of the conditions for admissibility (open access policy);
- If there is a form of docket control, transparency on the reasons for denial/acceptance;
- Research activities, including enquiries and consultations;
- Equal responsiveness to all participants, hence a proper justification (see *infra*, sections 1.3.2.3. and 1.3.2.4.).

1.3.2.2. Internal Deliberation

Next, deliberative institutions should deliberate internally so as to define and refine the assembled arguments. The participants should engage in a conversation and discuss the value of the different arguments.[182] With a shared belief in the potential existence of a 'right' answer, they will have to persuade each other and

---

179 Ibid., 343.

180 E Brems and L Lavrysen, 'Procedural Justice in Human Rights Adjudication: The European Court of Human Rights' (2013) 35 Human Rights Quarterly, 176, 188.

181 CH Mendes, *Constitutional Courts and Deliberative Democracy* (Oxford University Press 2013), 107.

182 J Parkinson, *Deliberating in the Real World: Problems of Legitimacy in Deliberative Democracy* (Oxford University Press 2006), 127, 150.

produce a collectively reasoned decision.[183] This process of persuasion assumes that the deliberators involved are willing to revise their initial opinions.[184] Although deliberation is not infallible, it is believed to produce decisions that are substantially superior to those that follow from other kinds of decision-making processes.[185]

In the legislative process, deliberation may be a prior phase to voting.[186] In this sense, voting may serve to merge reflective judgments about the common good. However, a political discussion in a consociational polity may also fall short of the ideal standard of deliberation. It is said that, while bargaining, politicians do not necessarily persuade each other with reasoned arguments. Rather, bargaining is a process of give-and-take in order to reach an agreement. Hence, the negotiation process does not aim to change the opinions of the deliberators, but to trade mutually advantageous concessions.[187] This might create a gap between what is politically opportune and accomplishable, and what would be most adequate and efficient.[188] Accordingly, policy outcomes do not necessarily reflect rational arguments that are the result of creative and reasoned exchanges of diverging viewpoints.[189] Although a negotiation strategy might improve acceptance of a rule on a short-term basis, the lack of a sufficient, rational justification might cause problems in the long run.

Constitutional courts are collegial institutions, where the judges are expected to discuss the cases internally.[190] In practice, one judge – or often the law clerk(s) working for this judge – produces an initial draft and circulates this to his or her colleagues. By doing so, the judge invites input from other judges, or their

---

183 Although there should be an ethics of consensus underlying the discussion, in the end the deliberators may reasonably disagree on the outcome: CH Mendes, *Constitutional Courts and Deliberative Democracy* (Oxford University Press 2013), 16; J Parkinson, *Deliberating in the Real World: Problems of Legitimacy in Deliberative Democracy* (Oxford University Press 2006) 150; and J Knight and J Johnson, 'Aggregation and Deliberation: on the Possibility of Democatic Legitimacy' (1994) 22 Political Theory, 277, 286.

184 CH Mendes, *Constitutional Courts and Deliberative Democracy* (Oxford University Press 2013), 16.

185 Ibid., 25.

186 J Beyers, 'Policy Issues, Organisational Format and the Political Strategies of Interest Organisations' (2008) 31 West European Politics, 1188, 1195; and CH Mendes, *Constitutional Courts and Deliberative Democracy* (Oxford University Press 2013), 27.

187 CH Mendes, *Constitutional Courts and Deliberative Democracy* (Oxford University Press 2013), 18, 27.

188 W Dewachter, *Besluitvorming in Politiek België* (Acco 1992), 121.

189 HJ Steiner, 'Ideals and Counter-Ideals in the Struggle Over Autonomy Regimes for Minorities' (1991) Notre Dame Law Review, 1539, 1551–2; JS Dryzek, 'Deliberative Democracy in Divided Societies: Alternatives to Agonism and Analgesia' (2005) 33 Political Theory, 218, 222; and M Bogaards, 'Democracy and Power-sharing in Multinational States: Thematic Introduction' (2006) 8 International Journal on Multicultural Societies, 119, 120.

190 J Ferejohn and P Pasquino, 'Constitutional Courts as Deliberative Institutions' in W Sadurski, *Constitutional Justice, East and West: Democratic Legitimacy and Constitutional Courts in a Comparative Perspective* (Kluwer 2002), 21, 24.

respective law clerks. They may answer with suggested changes to the original opinion draft. Irrespective of whether the judges are allowed to publish a separate minority opinion, in order to form a majority, the judges – or groups of judges – will need to persuade each other. When judges form this majority, they inevitably compromise their individual preferences. Yet courts are not expected to engage in bargaining, a process driven by private interests.[191] Rather, the collegial decision-making process should lead to a creative solution that was not anticipated by any one judge alone.[192]

For it to be possible to evaluate the deliberative process within the court, internal documentation or separate opinions should be available to the public. As will be discussed in the second chapter, this is not always the case. Nonetheless, the (detailed) justification included in the majority ruling may reflect the process that preceded the final decision.

Judicial good practices:

- A collegial decision-making process where judges exchange arguments and persuade each other during internal discussions.

1.3.2.3. *Transparent Justification*

When an institution has reached its final decision, this should be communicated to all those affected by what has been decided. This reason-giving requirement calls for clarity in the justificatory ground for the decision, which is essential for two reasons. First, as Shapiro argues, "a decision-maker required to give reasons will be more likely to weigh pros and cons carefully before reaching a decision than will a decision-maker able to proceed by simple fiat."[193] By meeting the requirement to give reasons, decisions become verifiable and the decision-maker can be held accountable. Therefore, it is a mechanism to avoid arbitrary decision-making.[194] Second, the quality of the reason-giving affects the degree to which decisions are perceived as legitimate. This substantive legitimacy is important, since it affects how external actors will react to the decision. On the one hand,

---

[191] Ibid., 27, 65, 130. A judicial compromise is 'principled', which means it has the common good in mind: "Negotiating personal agendas, trading votes across cases or mitigating arguments within the case, if motivated by self-interest, are plainly incompatible with adjudication."

[192] CH Mendes, *Constitutional Courts and Deliberative Democracy* (Oxford University Press 2013), 66.

[193] M Shapiro, 'The Giving Reasons Requirement' (1992) 179 The University of Chicago Legal Forum, 179–180; and P Rosanvallon, *Le Bon Gouvernement* (Seuil 2015), 229.

[194] LM Friedman et al., 'State Supreme Courts: A Century of Citation' (1981) 33 Stanford Law Review, 773, 793; and M Shapiro and A Stone Sweet, *On Law, Politics and Judicialization* (Oxford University Press 2002), 232.

citizens affected by the decision might simply be convinced by the provided reasons.[195] Acceptance might also occur despite the fact that the parties disagree with the decision. They might accept the collective outcome as the result of a reasoned exchange of diverging viewpoints.[196] Experimental research suggest that transparent reason-giving is an effective tool to ensure compliance, even for those who do not agree with the content of the decision.[197]

Therefore, an extensive but precise justification should clarify which arguments were found most persuasive.[198] The claims of those who are affected by the decision should be addressed, not by merely enumerating all individual viewpoints, but by showing that they were seriously considered.[199] A deliberative institution should show its responsiveness by being equally attentive to all claims, values and perspectives.[200] As mentioned before, failing to be responsive to all perspectives also compromises the inclusiveness of the deliberative procedure. As a corollary to this substantial requirement, the decision and its justificatory ground should also be publicly accessible for anyone interested in reading it.[201] The nature and the extent of reason-giving depends on the salience and the context of the particular decision.[202] For example, a controversial ruling might require a more detailed account of all the deliberative analyses undertaken, while a concise report can suffice when the decision is rather straightforward.

---

195 Substantive legitimacy compels acceptance by the force of its argument, while institutional legitimacy relies more on the authority of the issuer of the decision: M Bobek, *Comparative Reasoning in European Supreme Courts* (Oxford University Press 2013), 231.

196 JD Fearon, 'Deliberation as Discussion' in J Elster, *Deliberative Democracy* (Cambridge University Press 1998), 57; and M Van Hoecke, 'Constitutional Courts and Deliberative Democracy' in A Mazmanyan, P Popelier and W Vandenbruwaene (eds.), *The Role of Constitutional Courts in Mulitlevel Governance* (Intersentia 2013), 190.

197 J De Fine Licht et al., 'When Does Transparency Generate Legitimacy? Experimenting on a Context-Bound Relationship' (2014) 27 Governance: An International Journal of Policy, Administration and Institutions, 111 and further.

198 J Elster and et al., *Deliberative Democracy* (Cambridge University 1998), 9; and A Guttman and D Thompson, 'Deliberative democracy Beyond Process' (2002) 10 The Journal of Political Philosophy, 153, 156.

199 VF Comella, *Constitutional Courts and Democratic Values*, (Yale University Press 2009), 33. E Brems and L Lavrysen call this 'substantive participation', which is more than simply providing the opportunity to speak (formal participation): E Brems and L Lavrysen, 'Procedural Justice in Human Rights Adjudication: The European Court of Human Rights' (2013) 35 Human Rights Quarterly, 176, 181.

200 JM Makau and DL Marty, *Dialogue and Deliberation* (Waveland Press 2013), 245.

201 J Parkinson considers this publicity as the essence of deliberative democracy because through this publicity a deliberative institution can be held accountable: J Parkinson, *Deliberating in the Real World: Problems of Legitimacy in Deliberative Democracy* (Oxford University Press 2006), 99.

202 M Shapiro and A Stone Sweet, *On Law, Politics and Judicialization* (Oxford University Press 2002), 238; and W Lucy, 'Adjudication' in J Coleman and S Shapiro (eds.), *The Oxford Handbook of Jurisprudence and Philosophy of Law* (Oxford University Press 2002), 222–4.

In principle, legislative decisions should be discussed publicly in Parliament, resulting in an online published report.[203] These preparatory documents might be very useful for reconstructing the deliberation process, but they are often unclear and incomplete. Even if legislation is based on evidence, this might not appear in preparatory documents. Moreover, in consociational systems, much policy-making (usually big decisions and bargains) is kept deliberately opaque.[204] Not only may this affect the quality of the decision, the lack of transparency makes it difficult to evaluate the bargaining process between government officials. It is difficult to hold decision-makers accountable when there is insufficient information to evaluate their decisions.[205] As mentioned above, the clear understanding of a decision, and the sense of having been heard are important factors in stimulating acceptance.

Again, the review procedure may provide an *ex post* route to understanding why some arguments were found more persuasive than others.[206] The requirement to give reasons for their judgments is a special burden on courts.[207] Constitutional courts must clarify why they consider challenged legislation to be in accordance with the Constitution or not.[208] They are expected to carefully examine the arguments of all parties involved, and respond in a juridical and logical way.[209] In addition, judicial opinions are publicly accessible. This means that the legislator, other judges and the general public have access to the decision, as well as to the reasons underpinning it.

In constitutional adjudication, judges employ specific tools to enhance the transparency of their decisions. First, to maximise clarity on the justification

---

203 For an evaluation of the regulatory culture in Belgium, see OECD, *Better Regulation in Europe* (OECD 2010).

204 P Popelier and AA Patiño Álvarez, 'Deliberative Practices of Constitutional Courts in Consolidated and Non-Consolidated Democracies' in P Popelier, A Mazmanyan and W Vandenbruwaene (eds.), *The Role of Constitutional Courts in Multilevel Governance* (Intersentia 2013), 205.

205 See P Rosanvallon, *Le Bon Gouvernement* (Seuil 2015), 230, who calls this a "*condition essentielle*".

206 E Brems and L Lavrysen, 'Procedural Justice in Human Rights Adjudication: The European Court of Human Rights' (2013) 35 Human Rights Quarterly, 176, 186.

207 A Stone Sweet and J Mathews, 'Proportionality Balancing and Global Constitutionalism' (2008) 47 Colombia Journal of Transnational Law, 73, 78, 83; CH Mendes, *Constitutional Courts and Deliberative Democracy* (Oxford University Press 2013), 93; and T Bustamate, 'The Ongoing Search for Legitimacy: Can a 'Pragmatic yet Principled' Deliberative Model Justify the Authority of Constitutional Courts?' (2015) 78 The Modern Law Review, 372, 388: "The awareness of the 'the fact that the legitimacy of judicial review is conditional', entails a burden of justification for the decisions of the constitutional court."

208 O Fiss, *The Law as it Could Be* (New York University Press 2003), 152.

209 A Stone Sweet and J Mathews, 'Proportionality Balancing and Global Constitutionalism' (2008) 47 Colombia Journal of Transnational Law, 73, 78, 83.

for their rulings, constitutional courts may support their judgments by citing a variety of authorities.[210] Judges are expected to invoke appropriate legal authority for their decisions.[211] This provides a means for judges to relate their reasons back to other relevant sources. Ultimately, the external audience addressed by the court should be able to understand and accept the decision. The proper use of citations helps to make the decision more convincing.[212] A more detailed analysis of the role of citations in constitutional adjudication will be undertaken in chapter 6. Second, most constitutional courts have adopted a fixed argumentative framework for rights adjudication, based on the proportionality principle.[213] The last (and most important) stage of this framework, also called the 'proportionality analysis', is the 'justification test', during which the court evaluates whether the policy objective is legitimate, whether there is a causal relation between the challenged provision and this objective (rationality test), whether the least restrictive means were chosen to further that objective (necessity test), and whether the relation between the objective and the provision is proportional (proportionality test *sensu stricto*). The fixed character of the framework enhances transparency on how the decision is made. Step by step, it should be specified how information is weighted and combined to form a decision.[214] Hence, when following the justification test sequentially, the decision cannot easily be concealed behind an evasively drafted justification. The advantages and pitfalls of the use of the justification test as an argumentative framework in fundamental rights adjudication will be explored in more depth in chapter 7.

Judicial good practices:

- Consecutive application of a fixed argumentative framework;
- Citations of external authorities;
- Show responsiveness by equally addressing all perspectives.

---

210 M Bobek, *Comparative Reasoning in European Supreme Courts* (Oxford University Press 2013), 225.

211 LM Friedman et al., 'State Supreme Courts: A Century of Citation' (1981) 33 Stanford Law Review, 773, 793; and JH Merryman, 'Toward a Theory of Citations: an Empirical Study of the Citation Practice of the California Supreme Court in 1950, 1960 and 1970' (1978) 50 Southern California Law Review, 381, 418.

212 JH Merryman, ibid., 381, 418.

213 For more information on the emergence of the proportionality analysis as a global constitutional standard, see A Stone Sweet and J Mathews, 'Proportionality Balancing and Global Constitutionalism' (2008) 47 Colombia Journal of Transnational Law, 73.

214 JL Gibson, 'From Simplicity to Complexity: The Development of Theory in the Study of Judicial Behavior' (1983) 5 Political Behavior, 7, 15.

1.3.2.4. *Rational Justification*

The reason-giving requirement is about more than transparency; it comprises a requirement to give 'good' reasons.[215] This deliberative element thus explicitly relates to the substantive quality of the decision. The question then arises as to which arguments should be considered in the deliberation process. Many authors have already debated this difficult and delicate question.[216] In short, a deliberative institution should justify its decision with arguments that are relevant and correct in fact, law and logic.[217] It should take into account universal objective standards, such as the rules of evidence, methods of scientific inquiry and the values of efficiency and effectiveness.[218] It is essential that all participants in the deliberation process should be reasonably able to embrace the arguments put forward.[219] They should also have the capacity to challenge the validity of the arguments.[220] The relevance and credibility of arguments can change over time in response to new insights, interpretations or empirical evidence.[221] Ultimately, it is through the process of deliberation that the value of the circulating arguments is determined.

In principle, legislative decisions should be based on relevant social and economic considerations, as well as the best scientific information. Such calls for evidence-based legislation have become widespread, especially in recent years.[222] In general, the legislator is equipped to select the most effective measures

215 M Shapiro and A Stone Sweet, *On Law, Politics and Judicialization* (Oxford University Press 2002), 245; and CH Mendes, *Constitutional Courts and Deliberative Democracy* (Oxford University Press 2013), 25.

216 CH Mendes, ibid., 16: "this is one of the most controversial domains of deliberative theory". See also: JM Makau and DL Marty, *Dialogue and Deliberation* (Waveland Press 2013), 245–6; W Lucy, 'Adjudication' in J Coleman and S Shapiro (eds.), *The Oxford Handbook of Jurisprudence and Philosophy of Law* (Oxford University Press 2002), 228–247; and A Baker, 'Proportionality' in H Fenwick (ed.), *Judicial Review* (LexisNexis 2014), 302.

217 Brems and L Lavrysen, 'Procedural Justice in Human Rights Adjudication: The European Court of Human Rights' (2013) 35 Human Rights Quarterly, 176, 181; and M Shapiro and A Stone Sweet, *On Law, Politics and Judicialization* (Oxford University Press 2002), 244.

218 J Parkinson, *Deliberating in the Real World: Problems of Legitimacy in Deliberative Democracy* (Oxford University Press 2006), 125; and JM Makau and DL Marty, *Dialogue and Deliberation* (Waveland Press 2013), 245–6.

219 A Guttman and D Thompson, 'Deliberative Democracy Beyond Process' (2002) 10 The Journal of Political Philosophy, 153, 158. These authors argue that substantive principles are integral to the deliberative process itself.

220 JS Dryzek, *Deliberative Democracy and Beyond* (Oxford University Press 2000), 70; and J Knight and J Johnson, 'Aggregation and Deliberation: on the Possibility of Democatic Legitimacy' (1994) 22 Political Theory, 277, 285–6.

221 A Guttman and D Thompson, 'Deliberative Democracy Beyond Process' (2002) 10 The Journal of Political Philosophy, 153, 166.

222 J Verschuuren (ed.), *The Impact of Legislation* (Martinus Nijhoff 2009); and AW Seidman, RB Seidman and V Matsiborchuk, 'Legislative Deliberation and the Drafting Process: The Drafter's Role' (2015) Theory and Practice of Legislation, 341.

to achieve policy aims. This is usually determined via different methods of *ex ante* evaluation, such as consultations, impact assessments and cost-benefit analyses.[223] Yet the legislator does not always make proper factual prognoses. On the contrary, support for a statute might be influenced by various exogenous or arbitrary factors.[224] For example, public pressure may cause the legislator to take measures that may not have the desired effect simply because the public *believes* that they do have such effect.[225] Legislation may be approved without an effective assessment of its potential impact.[226] Moreover, in consociationalist systems, the bargaining process between sub-groups is mainly based upon strategies for exchanging resources and potential benefits. The result may be a compromise to which all sides can consciously assent, but not a universal agreement emerging from a creative and reasoned exchange of diverging viewpoints.[227] As mentioned before, this might improve acceptance of the rule on a short-term basis, but the lack of a sufficient, rational justification might cause problems in the long run.

Constitutional courts do not establish policies, but assess the strength of the reasons supporting a decision made by the elected branches. The question is not whether a decision is desirable or not, but whether it is compatible with the Constitution.[228] Moreover, courts are expected to justify their decisions in terms that can be universalised.[229] For that purpose, they are restricted to pre-existing legal materials and factual information.[230] When citing sources in support of

---

223 Van Gestel and De Poorter, 'Putting Evidence-Based Law Making to the Test: Judicial Review of Legislative Rationality' (2016) 4 Theory and Practice of Legislation, 155, 161.

224 Time limits and political concerns might outweigh the need for informed decision-making. See: E Bohne, 'The Politics of the *Ex Ante* Evaluation of Legislation' in J Verschuuren (ed.), *The Impact of Legislation* (Martinus Nijhoff 2009), 65; J Knight and J Johnson, 'Aggregation and Deliberation: on the Possibility of Democatic Legitimacy' (1994) 22 Political Theory, 277, 279; and JM Makau and DL Marty, *Dialogue and deliberation* (Waveland Press 2013), 245–6.

225 N Petersen, 'Proportionality and the Incommensurability Challenge – Some Lessons from the South African Constitutional Court' (2013) New York University Public Law and Legal Theory Working Papers, 16. Petersen gives the example of the death penalty, which was introduced for the mere appeasement of the public, without evidence that it has a deterring effect or contributes to reducing crime rates.

226 P Popelier and AA Patiño Álvarez, 'Deliberative Practices of Constitutional Courts in Consolidated and Non-Consolidated Democracies' in P Popelier, A Mazmanyan and W Vandenbruwaene (eds.), *The Role of Constitutional Courts in Multilevel Governance* (Intersentia 2013), 201.

227 JS Dryzek, 'Democratization as Deliberative Capacity Building' (2008) 42 Comparative Political Studies, 1379, 1388; and R Dworkin, *Freedom's Law: The Moral Reading of the American Constitution* (Oxford University Press 1996), 31.

228 O Fiss, *The Law as it Could Be* (New York University Press 2003), 152; and I Venzke, 'Judicial Authority and Styles of Reasoning: The Self-presentation Between Legalism and Deliberation' (2016) 4 Amsterdam Law School Legal Studies Research Paper, 1, 11.

229 Fiss calls this the 'neutral principle requirement': O Fiss, ibid., 163.

230 J Ferejohn and P Pasquino, 'The Countermajoritarian Opportunity' (2010) 13 Journal of Constitutional Law, 353, 366; and C Guarniere and P Pederzoli, *The Power of Judges: a Comparative Study of Courts and Democracy* (Oxford University Press 2003), 10–11.

the judicial decision, they should be applicable – or be found inapplicable – to the constitutional question.[231] Additionally, the source should be persuasive,[232] by virtue of the authority of the institution that created the document and/or because of its content.[233]

Some constitutional questions require specific expert knowledge, particularly when the legislation under review is based on normative assumptions that need empirical clarification.[234] By applying the proportionality analysis in fundamental rights adjudication, the court examines the reasonableness of the law.[235] The justification test is a factual enquiry, especially the evaluation of the challenged measure's 'suitability' and 'necessity'.[236] Because the test concerns the efficacy of the means, and the nature and acceptability of side-effects, questions about empirical causality are built into it.[237] For instance, evidence might show that the challenged measure does not advance the stated purpose, or that an equally effective measure is available that would mitigate the constitutional infringement.[238] The argumentative space implied in the proportionality test compels courts to look for evidence to substantiate their assessments.[239]

---

231 JH Merryman, 'Toward a Theory of Citations: an Empirical Study of the Citation Practice of the California Supreme Court in 1950, 1960 and 1970' (1978) 50 Southern California Law Review, 381, 420–1.

232 HP Glenn, 'Persuasive Authority' (1987) 32 McGill Law Journal, 261, 263.

233 The extent of this persuasiveness differs between legal systems: C Flanders, 'Towards a Theory of Persuasive Authority' (2009) 62 Oklamhoma Law Review, 55, 58–64; and M Bobek, *Comparative Reasoning in European Supreme Courts* (Oxford University Press 2013), 25–7.

234 N Petersen, 'Avoiding the Common-wisdom Fallacy: the Role of Social Sciences in Constitutional Adjudication' (2013) 11 International Journal of Constitutional Law, 294. For examples, see G Cumming, *Expert Evidence Definiciencies in the Judgments of the Court of the Europeion Union and the European Court of Human Rights* (Kluwer 2014), 113 and further.

235 P Popelier and AA Patiño Álvarez, 'Deliberative Practices of Constitutional Courts in Consolidated and Non-Consolidated Democracies' in P Popelier, A Mazmanyan and W Vandenbruwaene (eds.), *The Role of Constitutional Courts in Multilevel Governance* (Intersentia 2013), 215; and M Cohen-Eliya and I Porat, 'Proportionality and the Culture of Justification' (2011) 59 American Journal of Comparative Law, 463, 469–470.

236 Conversely, the 'legitimate purpose' and 'balancing' stages invoke a normative judgment: see R Sulitzeany-Kenan, M Kremnitzer and S Alon, 'Facts, Preferences and Doctrine: An Empirical Analysis of the Proportionality Judgment' (2015) 50 Law & Society Review, 348, 352.

237 P Yowell, 'Proportionality in United States Constitutional Law' in L Lazarus, C McCrudden and N Bowled (eds.), *Reasoning Rights: Comparative Judicial Engagement* (Hart Publishing 2014), 111.

238 A famous case in which the US Supreme Court cited a number of social science studies was *Brown v. Board of Education* (1954). The court used psychological evidence to establish that racial segregation of schools caused psychological harm to black students and violated the right to equal protection. Another example is *S v. Makwanyane and Another* (1995), in which the South African Constitutional Court found that there is no evidence that the death penalty is a greater deterrent of crime than imprisonment, and that the death sentence was therefore unconstitutional.

239 A Alemanno, 'The Emergence of the Evidence-based Judicial Reflex: A Response to Bar-Siman-Tov's Semiprocedural Review' (2013) The Theory and Practice of Legislation, 1, 3.

When the measure has already been in place for a while, it is easier to determine in hindsight whether the pursued goal has been reached.[240] Yet this proves more difficult when courts need to make a probability estimate of the measure's effectiveness. Challenges to legislative decisions may also put questions to the courts relating to the quality and interpretation of evidence.

There are several strategies open to judges for dealing with such empirical questions.[241] Some argue that the judicial role should be limited to the review of the adequacy of the legislative process. According to this view, constitutional courts should verify whether the major issues were addressed and that the decision is based on a proper *ex ante* evaluation (investigations, studies, impact assessments, consultations) and sufficient parliamentary debate.[242] In other words, the justification test would only require evidence that the legislation was a product of evidence-based legislative decision-making.[243] Yet a lack of transparency during the policy-making process can make it difficult to evaluate its adequacy *ex post*. In other words, the decision may be evidence-based, without this being apparent from the preparatory documents.[244] Also, although an inadequate legislative process will often result in legislation that infringes the Constitution,[245] this will not always be the case. The legislation may be substantially justified even though the process leading up to it was not executed properly.[246] Conversely, judicial deference to arguments of procedural

---

240 Van Gestel and De Poorter, 'Putting Evidence-Based Law Making to the Test: Judicial Review of Legislative Rationality' (2016) Theory and Practice of Legislation, 155, 161.

241 For an overview, see: N Petersen, 'Avoiding the Common-wisdom Fallacy: the Role of Social Sciences in Constitutional Adjudication' (2013) 11 International Journal of Constitutional Law, 294, 306–17; and I Bar-Siman-Tov, 'The Dual Meaning of Evidence-Based Judicial Review of Legislation' (2016) Theory and Practice of Legislation, 107. As Bar-Siman-Tov notes, there is currently considerable conceptual confusion on evidence-based judicial review.

242 The ECtHR has stated that national authorities must show "that they based their decisions on an acceptable assessment of the relevant facts" (*Makhmudov v. Russia* (App no 35082/04) (2008) 46 EHRR 37, para 65). See also P Popelier and C Van De Heyning, 'Procedural Rationality: Giving Teeth to the Proportionality Analysis' (2013) 9 European Constitutional Law Review, 260.

243 I Bar-Siman-Tov, 'The Dual Meaning of Evidence-Based Judicial Review of Legislation' (2016) 4 Theory and Practice of Legislation, 107, 113.

244 For a critical evaluation of *post hoc* reason-giving, see M Shapiro and A Stone Sweet, *On Law, Politics and Judicialization* (Oxford University Press 2002), 245–7.

245 See A Alemanno, 'The Emergence of the Evidence-based Judicial Reflex: A Response to Bar-Siman-Tov's Semiprocedural Review' (2013) Theory and Practice of Legislation, 1, 6, who argues that procedural shortcomings can act as "proxies for the determination of constitutionality infringements".

246 M Elliot, 'Proportionality and Deference, the Importance of a Structured Approach' (2013) 32 University of Cambridge Faculty of Law Research Papers, 1, 8. For an example, see the case of the Israeli Constitutional Court discussed in I Bar-Siman-Tov, 'The Dual Meaning of Evidence-Based Judicial Review of Legislation' (2016) Theory and Practice of Legislation, 107.

correctness is unlikely to guarantee constitutional protection to the litigants involved in the review procedure.[247]

Other scholars seek a more substantive role for the courts.[248] These point out that it is impossible to avoid scientific and technical issues when evaluating the justifiability of legislative decisions. The question of whether a policy is reasonable often depends on the data on which it is based. Therefore, it is said, courts should evaluate whether there is sufficiently convincing and robust evidence in support of the claims of the litigants – either affirming or contradicting the legislator's assumptions. For this purpose, judges can rely on the statements of policy-makers and the preparatory documents that reflect the bases for adopting the challenged measure. The initiating and intervening parties may also bring forward evidence to support their claim. Yet when no evidence is brought before the court, judges may struggle in circumstances where the proportionality assessment requires the collection of 'fresh' evidence.[249] Academic articles and scientific studies can be extremely useful as research aids, but research varies enormously in quality.[250] Also, lawyers – especially in continental Europe – are usually not trained to interpret or evaluate the accuracy or reliability of scientific evidence.[251] They may not be familiar with statistical language and may feel unqualified to draw conclusions, particularly in relation to the causal relations between different factors.[252]

Therefore, it is important to assist the judiciary on this point.[253] In particular, the (technical) input into the judicial process should be maximised and the

---

247 A pure procedural approach focuses solely on the legislative enactment process, regardless of whether the law's content raises constitutional issues. See: I Bar-Siman-Tov, ibid., 122; and Van Gestel and De Poorter, 'Putting Evidence-Based Law Making to the Test: Judicial Review of Legislative Rationality' (2016) Theory and Practice of Legislation, 155, 156–7.

248 J Monahan and L Walker, 'Judicial Use of Social Science Research' in E Mertz (ed.), *The Role of Social Science in Law*' (Ashgate 2008); A Baker, 'Proportionality' in H Fenwick (ed.), *Judicial Review* (LexisNexis 2014), 303–4; and Van Gestel and De Poorter, ibid., 155.

249 A Baker, 'Proportionality' in H Fenwick (ed.), *Judicial Review* (LexisNexis 2014), 302.

250 J Monahan and L Walker, 'Judicial Use of Social Science Research' in E Mertz (ed.), *The Role of Social Science in Law*' (Ashgate 2008), 27.

251 Most law faculties, especially in continental Europe, do not include a course on statistical methods in their curriculum. In contrast, several US law faculties have programmes and research centres that focus on empirical legal work: E Barbier de la Serre and AL Sibony, 'Expert Evidence before the EC Courts' (2008) 45 Common Market Law Review, 941–2; E Brems and L Lavrysen, 'Procedural Justice in Human Rights Adjudication: The European Court of Human Rights' (2013) 35 Human Rights Quarterly, 176, 187; and R Van Gestel and J De Poorter, 'Putting Evidence-Based Law Making to the Test: Judicial Review of Legislative Rationality' (2016) Theory and Practice of Legislation, 155, 178.

252 G Cumming, *Expert Evidence Definiciencies in the Judgments of the Court of the Europeion Union and the European Court of Human Rights* (Kluwer 2014), 79.

253 R Van Gestel and J De Poorter, 'Putting Evidence-Based Law Making to the Test: Judicial Review of Legislative Rationality' (2016) 4 Theory and Practice of Legislation, 155, 181–3.

scientific competences of judicial decision-makers should be broadened.[254] First, increasing the quantity and quality of information presented to a court increases the probability that it will reach evidence-based decisions. The defending party may introduce arguments to prove that the measure is justifiable, even when this does not follow directly from the parliamentary documents. Yet the defendants cannot occupy a uniquely privileged position in this regard. All involved parties or *amici curiae*, if they are allowed to participate (see *infra* section 2.4.),[255] should be able to bring forward information and (empirically) evaluate its significance.[256] Finally, if needed, judges should rely on existing scientific expertise or invite experts.[257] As a general guideline, courts should place confidence in expertise relative to the extent that: (a) it has undergone critical review in the scientific community; (b) it has used valid research methods; (c) it is applicable to the legal question at issue; and (d) it is supported by a larger body of research.[258] Second, although the presence of legal specialists is vital for a court to understand and solve each case within the constitutional framework, it is especially helpful when at least one of the judges (or law clerks) is trained in interpreting and evaluating empirical evidence.

When both sides in the review procedure bring forward contradictory evidence, uncertainty prevails. It must then be decided who should receive the benefit of the doubt. The court should avoid automatic and unquestioning deference to Parliament in matters of factual prognosis.[259] One possibility

254 S Jasanoff and D Nelkin, 'Science, Technology and the Limits of Judicial Competence' in WA Thomas (ed.), Science and Law: An Essential Alliance (Westview Press 1983), 16–17; and M Elliott, 'Proportionality and Deference: The Importance of a Structured Approach' in C Forsyth et al. (eds.), *Effective Judicial Review: A Cornerstone of Good Governance* (Oxford University Press 2010), 272.

255 The propensity of the US Supreme Court to cite scientific evidence is partially due to the large amount of public interest litigation and *amici curiae* involvement: D Fausten, I Nielsen and R Smyth, 'A Century of Citation Practice on the Supreme Court of Victoria' (2007) 31 Melbourne University Law Review, 733, 761.

256 M Elliott, 'Proportionality and Deference: The Importance of a Structured Approach' in C Forsyth et al. (eds.), *Effective Judicial Review: A Cornerstone of Good Governance* (Oxford University Press 2010), 274.

257 K Möller, The Global Model of Constitutional Rights (Oxford University Press 2012), 131; A Baker, 'Proportionality' in H Fenwick (ed.), *Judicial Review* (LexisNexis 2014), 303–4; and D Grimm, 'Proportionality in Canadian and German Constitutional Jurisprudence' (2007) 57 University of Toronto Law Review, 383, 388.

258 J Monahan and L Walker, 'Judicial Use of Social Science Research' in E Mertz (ed.), *The Role of Social Science in Law* (Ashgate 2008), 28. Alternatively: (a) peer review, (b) testability and falsifiability, (c) rate of error, and (d) acceptance in the scientific community. This is referred to as the 'Daubert doctrine', developed by the USSC in 509 US 579 (1993): R Van Gestel and J De Poorter, 'Putting Evidence-Based Law Making to the Test: Judicial Review of Legislative Rationality' (2016) Theory and Practice of Legislation, 155, 178.

259 I Bar-Siman-Tov, 'The Dual Meaning of Evidence-Based Judicial Review of Legislation' (2016) 4 Theory and Practice of Legislation, 107, 111–112.

is to introduce a certain scale of intensity of review: the more serious the constitutional infringement, the stronger the evidential burden on the legislator.[260] Only where the legislation emerges from a reliable process of legislative fact-finding, consultation and expert opinion should the court consider a degree of deference.[261] But until an effective standard of control is established, courts in continental Europe[262] may remain reluctant to use and cite scientific evidence.[263]

Judicial good practices:

- Citations of relevant and persuasive authorities;
- If needed, an inquiry into the empirical evidence to establish the relation between legislative means and ends.

1.3.2.5. Constitutional Dialogue

Finally, through its decisions a deliberative institution should contribute to the dialogue on how to reconcile the Constitution with the accomplishment of public policy objectives. The goal should not be to close, but rather to facilitate and enrich democratic debate. The decision, as well as the clarity of the reason-giving, should spark an interactive engagement with other actors. It should be 'consequential', meaning that it has an impact upon collective decisions or social outcome.[264] In particular, the decision can be instructive in relation to both its subject matter and the deliberative skills themselves,[265] which can be useful in new rounds of debate. In that regard, deliberation is an ongoing process aiming

---

[260] On this scale, see J Rivers, 'Proportionality, Discretion and the Second Law of Balancing' in G Pavlakos (ed.), *Law, Rights and Discourse: The Legal Philosophy of Robert Alexy* (Hart Publishing 2007), 180–3.

[261] J Rivers, 'Proportionality and Variable Intensity of Review' (2006) 65 Cambridge Law Journal, 174, 204; and M Elliott, 'Proportionality and Deference: The Importance of a Structured Approach' in C Forsyth et al. (eds.), *Effective Judicial Review: A Cornerstone of Good Governance* (Oxford University Press 2010), 272.

[262] This contrasts immensely with the citation practices of Anglo-American countries, where supreme courts regularly cite academic work and scientific evidence. See section 4.3.

[263] Petersen argues that, until then, it is best to combine these strategies. Some margin of appreciation should be left to the legislature. However, in order not to transform the margin of appreciation into marginless arbitrariness, courts have to control the limits of parliamentary discretion. The legislature only has a margin of appreciation if the social science evidence is inconclusive: N Petersen, 'Avoiding the Common-wisdom Fallacy: the Role of Social Sciences in Constitutional Adjudication' (2013) 11 International Journal of Constitutional Law, 294, 317–318.

[264] JS Dryzek, 'Democratization as Deliberative Capacity Building' (2008) 42 Comparative Political Studies, 1379, 1382.

[265] CH Mendes, *Constitutional Courts and Deliberative Democracy* (Oxford University Press 2013), 23.

at the production of high-quality decisions.[266] The dialogic dimension is the culmination of all previous elements. When the decision lacks other qualities such as responsiveness and transparency or is not well-founded, this will hamper the institution's capacity to influence individual or collective behaviour. This also counteracts the underlying premise of mutual understanding between different actors, which is essential to enable dialogue.

Within a democratic polity, constitutional dialogue may appear between several institutions. Instead of concentrating on who has the last word, the three branches of power should rather be seen as participants in a circle of debate.[267] Each participant in this interaction (the constitutional court, the legislature, other courts and the citizenry) has a distinct role to play and bears some deliberative responsibilities.[268] While constitutional review is centred on the importance of maintaining fundamental, substantive and procedural values, the legislature focuses on promoting certain social or economic goals.[269] An essential aspect of this dialogue is its ongoing character, where no branch has the last word. This does not mean that the process is never-ending, but rather that it holds the promise of reaching a decision to which *both* institutions can assent.

For the purpose of this research, this book concentrates on how constitutional courts engage in constitutional dialogue.

First, courts can incorporate legislative arguments into their rulings. During the review procedure, the government is entitled to give reasons that support the challenged legislation and to defend its view about the proper constitutional balance. In particular, the government "must disclose what it has done to formulate the policy: its investigation and research, the alternatives considered, and the reasons why the option underlying the policy was selected".[270] In that sense, the review procedure entails a 'burden of justification' on the legislative branch.[271] The legislature is considered to have considerable expertise and resources to pursue its policy objectives.[272] References to parliamentary or other preparatory documents reflect that the court not only wishes to persuade, but can also be persuaded in return.

---

266 JB Grossman and RS Wells, 'Constitutional Law and Judicial Policy Making' (John Wiley & Sons 1972), 47.

267 CH Mendes, *Constitutional Courts and Deliberative Democracy* (Oxford University Press 2013), 185.

268 E Luna, 'Constitutional Road Maps' (2000) 90 Journal of Criminal Law and Criminology, 1125, 1174.

269 LB Tremblay, 'The Legitimacy of Judicial Review: The Limits of Dialogue between Courts and Legislatures' ¾ 2005 ICON, 617, 633.

270 E Cameron, 'A South African Perspective on the Judicial Development of Socio-Economic Rights' in L Lazarus, C McCrudden and N Bowles (eds.), *Reasoning Rights: Comparative Judicial Engagement* (Hart Publishing 2014), 327.

271 C Sunstein, *Designing Democracy* (Oxford University Press 2001), 234.

272 C Bateup, 'The Dialogic Promise: Assessing the Normative Potential of Theories of Constitutional Dialogue' (2006) 71 Brooklyn Law Review, 72.

Next, constitutional courts delineate the boundaries of what is constitutionally acceptable.[273] When the court decides that there is no constitutional infringement, this provides an indirect but explicit justification for the legislative outcome. In this sense, the review procedure adds legitimacy to the challenged legislation, stimulating compliance from the litigants. Yet the review procedure can also draw attention to fundamental values that may be ignored or downplayed in the legislative process.[274] Many constitutional courts have developed methods – whether enforceable or not – for setting out incentives that stimulate a reaction from the legislator and the judiciary.[275] More specifically, courts can address their audience through creative case dicta (modulated outcomes). An in-depth study of case outcomes as vehicles for constitutional dialogue follows in chapter 5. In addition, to facilitate the follow-up of judicial recommendations, courts should make clear why the legislation was invalidated or modulated. Transparency on the justificatory ground is therefore essential. To give substantial advice to the legislator, the court can use a step-by-step analysis ('the justification test') and/or refer to external authorities.

Furthermore, the review procedure can educate the legislator on the deliberative practice itself, by exposing the faults in the legislative policy-making process. *Post hoc* reason-giving might not be sufficient to rectify the lack of inclusive dialogue and reasoned argument during the parliamentary procedure. If the constitutional court points out that the unconstitutionality of a provision is caused by a deficient deliberative performance,[276] this sends a strong signal to the legislator. It should make the legislator aware of the importance of a proper *ex ante* assessment of the legislative proposal. This can, in turn, promote a broader culture of proof, evidence and rationality in policy-making.[277] Even when

[273] Constitutional review can also have a positive effect on the quality of legislation outside the scope of a specific judgment. In particular, the threat of future constitutional censure can have an anticipatory effect on legislative outcomes: M Shapiro and A Stone Sweet, *On Law, Politics and Judicialization* (Oxford University Press 2002), 187.

[274] E Cameron, 'A South African Perspective on the Judicial Development of Socio-Economic Rights' in L Lazarus, C McCrudden and N Bowles (eds.), *Reasoning Rights: Comparative Judicial Engagement* (Hart Publishing 2014), 327.

[275] P Popelier and AA Patiño Álvarez, 'Deliberative Practices of Constitutional Courts in Consolidated and Non-Consolidated Democracies' in P Popelier, A Mazmanyan and W Vandenbruwaene (eds.), *The Role of Constitutional Courts in Multilevel Governance* (Intersentia 2013), 223; and M Shapiro and A Stone Sweet, *On Law, Politics and Judicialization* (Oxford University Press 2002), 189.

[276] For example, some representative organisations were consulted, while minority or vulnerable groups (such as detainees and refugees) were not; the scientific inquiries were implemented unsatisfactorily or the legislative decision does not logically follow from its empirical results.

[277] On this interplay between the legislator and constitutional courts, see A Alemanno, 'The Emergence of the Evidence-based Judicial Reflex: A Response to Bar-Siman-Tov's Semiprocedural Review' (2013) Theory and Practice of Legislation, 1, 13.

post hoc reasons can substantively justify the decision, the court may explicitly point out that these reasons were unavailable during the prior parliamentary procedure. This is important, since a decision-maker who is incentivised to give reasons may be less prone to arbitrary, capricious, self-interested, or otherwise unfair judgment.[278] Consequently, the case law of the court affects the quality of parliamentary debate and the policy decisions that follow from this debate.

Subsequently, the debate returns to the legislature, which considers if and how to respond to the court's decision.[279] The legislature may devise a response that accomplishes its policy objectives and is respectful of the Constitution, without simply assenting to the judicial opinion.[280,281] Finally, this legislative response may equally be challenged anew before the constitutional court. If so, it might aid the court if the legislature has incorporated the language of judicial review (e.g. 'reasonable boundaries') into parliamentary documents.[282] In this sense, both the review and the legislative procedure contribute to a continuing dialogue on how to reconcile the Constitution with the accomplishment of public policy objectives.[283]

Up to this point, this section has concentrated on the relation between the constitutional court and policy-makers. However, constitutional dialogue should ideally incorporate both society-wide and institutional perspectives.[284] First, the court's decisions may be relevant to other members of the domestic or foreign judiciary. It may help them to comprehend the outcome of the case. For domestic judges, the judgments of the BeCC provide guidelines on the interpretation and application of Belgian legislation. Foreign judges, on the other hand, may rely on the BeCC's case law for inspiration when they come across a similar constitutional question. It has been observed that constitutional courts

---

278 M Shapiro and A Stone Sweet, *On Law, Politics and Judicialization* (Oxford University Press 2002), 232.

279 A Meuwese and M Snel, 'Constitutional Dialogue: an Overview', (2013) 9 Utrecht Law Review, 129.

280 Manfredi and Kelly argue that simple compliance is not evidence of a real interactive dialogue between equals. Genuine, positive dialogue occurs when elected officials actually reflect on the implications of judicial decisions and involves some form of creative response: CP Manfredi and JB Kelly, 'Six Degrees of Dialogue: a Response to Hogg and Bushell' (1999) 37 Osgoode Hall Law Journal, 513–27.

281 C Bateup, 'Expanding the Conversation: American and Canadian Experiences of Constitutional Dialogue in Comparative Perspective' (2006) 44 New York University Public Law and Legal Theory Working Papers, 6.

282 CP Manfredi and JB Kelly, 'Six Degrees of Dialogue: a Response to Hogg and Bushell' (1999) 37 Osgoode Hall Law Journal, 515.

283 LB Tremblay, 'The Legitimacy of Judicial Review: The Limits of Dialogue between Courts and Legislatures' ¾ 2005 ICON, 617, 625.

284 C Bateup, 'The Dialogic Promise: Assessing the Normative Potential of Theories of Constitutional Dialogue' (2006) 71 Brooklyn Law Review, 76–84.

often face common issues, and that they increasingly scan foreign jurisdictions to solve these issues.[285]

Finally, the fact that the court's case law is publicly accessible for the society at large allows others, such as legal scholars or the media, to study and discuss that case law in depth.[286] It is vital to recognise the importance of involving the citizenry in ongoing debate, because it is their responsibility to select the representatives in Parliament. News reporting of a judicial decision can bring an issue to public attention and can inform public opinion. Even if the claimant loses in court, the public outcry can be such that legislators are forced to address the issue. In other words, constitutional adjudication can raise public consciousness of the merits of the case and build up political pressure in support of a potential wider campaign.[287] Therefore, the court's judgments can enrich collective deliberation. The practice of widespread debate on difficult and important constitutional questions has led scholars to the conclusion that constitutional review should be considered as a counter-majoritarian *opportunity*, not a difficulty.[288]

Judicial good practices:

- Engage with legislative arguments;
- Include signals in the case dictum and justificatory ground. These signals can relate to the substantial boundaries of what is constitutionally acceptable or to procedural faults when they have led to a constitutional infringement;
- Constitutional dialogue is the culmination of the other ingredients of deliberative performance. Hence, a lack of transparency, responsiveness, or rationality hinders the court's capacity to enhance dialogue.

1.4. CONCLUSION

In this first chapter, the focus was on the role of constitutional courts in democratic systems. It was argued that, although the aggregation of viewpoints through and after recurring elections is essential to democracy, it does not

---

285 C Moon, 'Comparative Constitutional Analysis: Should the United States Supreme Court Join the Dialogue?' (2003) 12 Washington University Journal of Law & Policy, 229, 245.

286 Van Hoecke argues that the involvement of the professional community, a public forum and the whole public sphere of society, is exactly what legitimates constitutional review: M Van Hoecke, 'Constitutional courts and Deliberative Democracy' in A Mazmanyan, P Popelier and W Vandenbruwaene (eds.), *The Role of Constitutional Courts in Mulitlevel Governance* (Intersentia 2013), 190–192.

287 A Kavanagh, *Constitutional Review under the UK Human Rights Act* (Cambridge University Press 2009), 342.

288 J Ferejohn and P Pasquino, 'The Countermajoritarian Opportunity' (2010) 13 Journal of Constitutional Law, 353, 360.

automatically guarantee the quality or legitimacy of the policy-making process. Policy-making should also include a deliberative component, consisting of five key, interrelated elements: inclusiveness, persuasion amongst colleagues, transparency, rationality and dialogue. Together, these five key elements form a deliberative practice, defined by the exchange of arguments between the decision-maker and all actors affected by their decisions. Only when the legislative branch fails to observe some of these key 'standards of excellence' is the constitutional court called upon to step into the breach.[289] From this perspective, constitutional review is not merely a "necessary evil to be tolerated for the community's self-protection against abuses of power".[290] On the contrary, when a court performs as a deliberative institution, the legal quality and legitimacy of democratic policy-making is enhanced. In this sense, deliberative theory helps to overcome the counter-majoritarian objections against constitutional review.[291]

However, not all constitutional courts fulfil these normative deliberative expectations. Every court may, to a greater or lesser extent, initiate and channel the deliberative quality of democratic policy-making. Courts must function within a certain environment, defined by institutional and political constraints. Primarily, they must have the necessary institutional tools to be able to perform as a deliberative institution. Moreover, considering that courts always need to function within a certain political context, other expectations may equally weigh upon the decision-making process. The next chapter looks into the factors that may influence judicial behaviour. To illustrate this part of the research, the Belgian Constitutional Court will be examined as a case study.

---

289 I Venzke, 'Judicial Authority and Styles of Reasoning: The Self-presentation between Legalism and Deliberation' (2016) 4 Amsterdam Law School Legal Studies Research Paper, 1, 10: "Parties typically find themselves before the court because the law has run out."

290 CH Mendes, *Constitutional Courts and Deliberative Democracy* (Oxford University Press 2013), 83.

291 P Popelier and AA Patiño Álvarez, 'Deliberative Practices of Constitutional Courts in Consolidated and Non-Consolidated Democracies' in P Popelier, A Mazmanyan and W Vandenbruwaene (eds.), *The Role of Constitutional Courts in Multilevel Governance* (Intersentia 2013), 200.

PART II

THE CONTOURS OF JUDICIAL DECISION-MAKING

The first part of this book discussed how constitutional courts may enhance the deliberative quality and legitimacy of democratic policy-making. This led to the formulation of a handful of judicial good practices, such as following a fixed argumentative framework, using relevant and persuasive citations to underpin judgments and communicating with the legislator through modulated rulings. However, deliberative performance is an intertwined and complex endeavour and may differ between courts and, importantly, between cases. Variety in a court's behaviour suggests how this court perceives its own role in democratic society. Therefore, it is enlightening to evaluate which forces play upon constitutional judging.

The second part of this book aims to build a bridge between the normative framework and the case law analysis. In particular, the factors which may influence the Belgian Constitutional Court's behaviour are explored. These contours of judicial decision-making must be recognised in order to fully comprehend the role of constitutional courts in a democratic society. These underlying contours, which form the theoretical background on which the empirical analysis is based, are set out in two chapters, titled 'The institutional framework of the Belgian Constitutional Court' (chapter 2) and 'Variation of judicial behaviour within the institutional boundaries' (chapter 3) respectively.

In chapter 2, the institutional setting of the BeCC is discussed. This framework, decided upon by the legislator, shapes the background against which the Court takes its decisions. The tools available to the Court do not only indicate the prospects of deliberation, but also affect the choices the Court (can) make(s). To provide necessary background information against which the empirical results should be understood, the establishment and further development of this institutional framework is situated within the Belgian political context. More specifically, the consociational nature of the Belgian polity is reflected in the Court's composition and its institutional tools. Special attention will be paid to the parliamentary preparatory documents, which show how the rules regarding the BeCC's decision-making process should be understood and applied.

They also show how the rationale behind the development of the Court may still raise expectations concerning its behaviour, both within the Court and from external actors.

Throughout this chapter, the extent to which the BeCC's institutional framework differs from that of other countries will be explored. The reason for the comparative exercise is to facilitate cross-country evaluations but also, at the same time, to set appropriate limits on the extent to which the findings of this study may be generalised for other constitutional courts. It also indicates the strength of the BeCC's deliberative potential in comparison to other systems. In particular, references are made to other 'Kelsenian' civil law constitutional courts in continental Europe – many of which share characteristics with the BeCC. In addition, it is also interesting to explore the setting of courts that differ considerably from the BeCC – in particular the US Supreme Court (USSC) and the South African Constitutional Court (SACC). The USSC, established long before the BeCC (1789), is usually discussed as the model example of a Supreme Court in a common law system. Moreover, taking into account that the case law of the USSC is particularly well explored by academics, this allows (especially in the empirical part of this book) for a reflection upon how different institutional environments shape judicial behaviour. The SACC – like the BeCC – functions within a heterogeneous society. Although the country's political structure does not entirely adhere to Lijphart's consociationalism, several power-sharing mechanisms have been set in place to politically involve and protect the different sub-groups in this divided society.[292] Hence, exploring the SACC's framework also enables further reflection upon the role of a constitutional court within a divided society. Also, the South African Constitution was adopted rather recently (1996) and is therefore inevitably influenced by other constitutions and charters that preceded it.[293] Therefore, as will be discussed below, the institutional framework includes many features that can be defined as deliberative.

In chapter 3, the specific case characteristics that might widen or limit the Court's room to manoeuvre within these institutional boundaries are explored. Although judicial behaviour may be fuelled by the willingness to maximise impact on the legitimacy and quality of democratic policy-making, other factors may also play a role. Many scholars, especially in the US, have tried to explain the choices justices make. This literature has produced useful insights and contributed to expanding our understanding of judicial behaviour. More specifically, a particular strand within this literature focuses on how the context

---

292 R Hopper, 'Post Apartheid South Africa: Evaluating South Africa's Institutional Design' (2008) Opticon1826, 1.

293 U Bentele, 'Mining for Gold: The Constitutional Court of South Africa's Experience with Comparative Constitutional Law' 37 (2009) Georgia Journal of International and Comparative Law, 219, 228.

wherein a Court functions influences its case law. Importantly, courts are not isolated institutions. On the contrary, as will be explained in the third chapter, prior studies have shown that courts recognise the interdependency of their behaviour in a forward-looking way. In particular, without legal mechanisms to ensure compliance with their rulings, courts must rely on other strategies to stimulate such implementation. For this purpose, they must anticipate the reactions from other relevant actors such as the legislator, litigants, 'regular' courts or the general public. Situating the Belgian Constitutional Court within its institutional and political context, it is argued that this 'strategic model' may offer an explanation for variation in the Court's case law.

CHAPTER 2

THE INSTITUTIONAL FRAMEWORK OF THE BELGIAN CONSTITUTIONAL COURT

2.1. INTRODUCTION

Institutional devices function as accelerators or brakes for the deliberative project.[294] Although a set of favourable procedural routes does not guarantee the quality of the deliberative performance, they do constitute the minimal conditions for such an aim. A relatively recent book by Mendes listed the procedural choices that legislators must make if they want to design a deliberative constitutional court.[295] Other authors have equally enumerated procedural factors furthering the deliberative potential of constitutional courts.[296] In addition, the framework may leave room to the court for self-regulation. This, in turn, may lead to a constant refinement of the procedures themselves.[297]

In this chapter, the institutional setting of the Belgian Constitutional Court – and how this developed over time – will be explored as a case study. The institutional devices of the BeCC are legally determined, in article 142 of the Constitution and the Special Law of 6 January 1989 on the Constitutional Court (from here on The Special Act). The Special Act has been updated several times. Also, many legal provisions leave room for interpretation. Therefore, the

---

294 CH Mendes, *Constitutional Courts and Deliberative Democracy* (Oxford University Press 2013), 104, 142–175. Mendes' intention was not to provide a readymade institutional design, but to enumerate all procedural, substantive and contextual 'facilitators' maximising the court's possibilities to act as a deliberator.

295 Mendes argues that its enlistment draws upon largely accepted knowledge about plausible correlations, although there is a lack of empirical evidence on each device: ibid., 148.

296 P Popelier and AA Patiño Álvarez, 'Deliberative Practices of Constitutional Courts in Consolidated and Non-Consolidated Democracies' in P Popelier, A Mazmanyan and W Vandenbruwaene (eds.), *The Role of Constitutional Courts in Multilevel Governance* (Intersentia 2013), 208–229.

297 CH Mendes, *Constitutional Courts and Deliberative Democracy* (Oxford University Press 2013), 146–147.

parliamentary preparatory documents are scrutinised in order to evaluate how the political actors meant the provisions – at the time of their inception – to be understood.

Special attention is paid to how the consociational nature of the Belgian polity has impacted upon the Court's establishment and development. Views on the compatibility between judicial review and consociationalism differ from a theoretical and practical perspective.[298] On the one hand, constitutional review is considered a useful instrument in a consociational polity. It gives minority groups additional protection against the violation of their (group) rights and gives them an additional possibility of participating in public debate. On the other hand, in practice this might not be as obvious as Lijphart argued.[299] A (partial) annulment of legislation might threaten consociational peace. Also, the transparent nature of constitutional review might conflict with the opaque nature of such policy-making. One might argue that the constraining power of judicial review could incentivise the political elite to limit the court's discretionary powers in order to protect their own political autonomy. However, a court that is conscious of its deliberative role would make maximal use of its competences and even extend them if it deems this to be appropriate. An awareness of the malfunctions in the policy-making process might even push the court towards a more activist approach. Considering this ambiguous relation between consociationalism and constitutional review, the Belgian Constitutional Court is an interesting case study.

The establishment of the Court was part of the package deal included in the second state reform of 1977, which reformed the Belgian unitary state into a federal state with regions and communities. Legislation enacted by the national and subnational assemblies was put on an equal footing, which could cause conflicts of competence between the different levels of government. Therefore, it was declared in the Community Pact of 1977 that a special court would be established as a neutral arbiter of conflicts of power between the federal and subnational levels.[300] According to this Pact, the court would be composed of both lawyers and former politicians, appointed for a period of eight years by the King,[301] on the Senate's proposal.[302] The government repeated this statement

---

298 P Popelier and W Voermans, 'Europeanization, Constitutional Review and Consensus Politics in the Low Countries' in H Vollaard, J Beyers and P Dumont (eds.), *European Integration and Consensus Politics in the Low Countries* (Routledge 2015), 94–9.

299 P Popelier, 'The Belgian Constitutional Court: Guardian of Consensus Democracy or Venue for Deliberation?' in A Alen et al., *Liber Amicorum Marc Bossuyt* (Intersentia 2013), 483.

300 The 'Community Pact' of 24 May 1977.

301 This term would be renewable: Explanatory memorandum to the draft of 23 May 1980 of the law on the institutional reform, *Parl Doc* Senate no 435/1, 11.

302 Appendix 1 to the government statement of 7 June 1977, 29.

in 1978 and explicitly added that the 'Arbitration Tribunal', already clarified by this denomination,[303] would not constitute a constitutional court. The review would therefore be limited to the constitutional and institutional provisions concerning the competences of the federal State, communities and regions.[304] Only a few years later, in 1980, the establishment of the BeCC was written into the Constitution.[305] Its composition, competences and practical functioning were further defined by the Law of 28 June 1983. The parliamentary documents preceding this law clarify what was expected from the 'Arbitration Tribunal'. In general, a role as true constitutional court (as in other European countries) was excluded because "it was not constitutionally assigned to the court to review the observation of all dispositions in the Constitution".[306] Nevertheless, the rules concerning the access to the court and the reference norms were repeatedly extended. Moreover, the BeCC interpreted these rules very broadly. Gradually, due to these legislative and judicial impulses,[307] the BeCC transformed into a venue for deliberation. The preparatory documents underlying the BeCC's establishment and reforms in 1988 and 2003 reflect the permanent quest for balance between strong, deliberative, constitutional review and the protection of consociational agreements.

In what follows, the institutional setting of the BeCC is evaluated in more detail, integrating both deliberative and consociational perspectives. Consecutively, the reference norms, the composition of the Court, access to the Court, the investigative possibilities, the sanctioning possibilities and transparency of the Court's rulings are addressed.[308]

---

303 Initially, the denomination 'Court of Conflicts' (*Hof van Conflicten*) was proposed. However, this proposition was renounced because some argued that it was rather aggressive: Report of 30 March 1983 from the commission of constitutional and institutional reform, about the draft law on the composition, competence and functioning of the constitutional court, *Parl Doc* Senate no 246/2, 57.

304 Appendix to the government statement of 28 February 1978, annex, 992.

305 Article 107*ter*, currently article 142 of the Constitution.

306 Report of 30 March 1983 from the commission of constitutional and institutional reform, about the draft law on the composition, competence and functioning of the constitutional court, *Parl Doc* Senate no 246/2, 28.

307 The link between these impulses is bi-directional: "proper devices tent to encourage deliberative attitudes; the right attitudes may lead to a constant refinement of the procedures themselves." See CH Mendes, *Constitutional Courts and Deliberative Democracy* (Oxford University Press 2013), 146.

308 Mendes argues that the classical distinctions (e.g. concentrated/diffuse systems, abstract/concrete review and weak/strong models) have a "limited, if any, bearing on deliberation". CH Mendes, *Constitutional Courts and Deliberative Democracy* (Oxford University Press 2013), 141–144.

2.2. REFERENCE NORMS

2.2.1. SHIFTING THE FOCUS: FROM FEDERALISM TO THE PROTECTION OF HUMAN RIGHTS

When the BeCC was established, its review was limited to the constitutional and institutional provisions concerning the competence allocating rules between the federal and subnational levels of government.[309] However, the first preparatory documents reveal that extensions to other constitutional provisions were already considered an option. The Minister of Institutional Reform declared that, if the 'experiment' should succeed, a further extension would not be excluded.[310] Nonetheless, this extension was postponed until 1988, and during the first period the BeCC only acted as a neutral arbiter of competences.

After long and difficult negotiations, the politicians decided in the state reform of 1988 to transfer the competences concerning educational policy to the subnational levels. Educational policy was a delicate issue, because of former conflicts on the funding of 'free' (mostly catholic) and 'official' (state) schools. These conflicts had been settled by a supermajoritarian 'School Pact', agreed upon by the three political families, in particular the Catholics, Liberals and Socialists. This Pact guaranteed the stable existence and funding of both free and official schools. While most free, religion-based schools were located in the Dutch-speaking Community, the majority of the official schools were vested in the French-speaking Community. The transfer of competences could upset the delicate balance laid down in this School Pact, because both Communities would be able, within their own territory, to make changes to the agreed funding. The Dutch-speaking Community feared that catholic schools would be disadvantaged in the French-speaking Community, and vice versa.[311]

To prevent new conflicts on educational issues, it was decided to constitutionalise the principles of educational freedom and equality, and to add these provisions to the reference norms of the BeCC. Hence, this led to the revision of article 107*ter* (now 142) of the Constitution, which regulates the competences of the BeCC. Three additional reference norms were included: articles 17, 6 and 6*bis*, provisions concerning education and the equality clause. This would ensure the legal enforcement of the guarantees inserted into the School Pacts. While this extension may have seemed innocent, it was in fact

[309] Appendix to the government statement of 28 February 1978, 992.

[310] Report of the plenary session of 16 June 1988, *Parl Doc* Senate no 30, 638.

[311] Senator Langendries (PSC): "en ce qui concerne l'enseignement, chacun sait qu'il s'agit là d'un des grands dossiers qui reviennent périodiquement dans l'histoire de notre pays et que cette matière n'est traité valablement qu'avec le consensus le plus large", report of the plenary session of 17 May 1988, *Parl Doc* Senate, no 12, 254.

quite radical. It shifted the BeCC's primary role from arbiter of competence conflicts to the protector of fundamental rights.[312]

Initially, only the provision which dealt specifically with education (article 17, now 24) was accepted as an additional reference norm. Later propositions extended the BeCC's competence to the – more general – equality clause (articles 6 and 6*bis*, now 10 and 11). This was demanded by some politicians in exchange for the transfer of educational competences to the Communities,[313] because it was considered an additional protection for the equality between the free and official schools.[314] However, the negotiators quickly realised that the equality clause was not limited to educational issues.[315] The minister of institutional reform at that time stated that this extension would protect citizens against any discrimination, including discrimination based on ideological and philosophical preferences. Therefore, the BeCC would be able to review discriminating legislation against fundamental rights in the Constitution, as well as against analogous rights in the European Convention on Human Rights (ECHR).[316] The following examples were mentioned in the preparatory parliamentary documents: a decree which grants/refuses a licence to broadcast to a radio or television station;[317] unequal treatment of men and women; and inequality during the designation procedure of public agents and fiscal discrimination.[318] The government struck out on a definite new course, adding a human rights approach to the Court's initial role as a neutral 'arbiter' of competence conflicts. Some opposition members warned government officials that they would not be able to reverse this reform by claiming that they had never intended to give the Court such extensive review competences.[319]

As for the Court's competences with regard to federalism disputes, the 1988 reform introduced another novelty. Article 30*bis* of the Special Act of 1989 stated that these competence allocations rules also include certain legally

---

312 Report of the plenary session of 14 June 1988, *Parl Doc* Senate no 22, 470.

313 Report of 8 June 1988 from the commission on constitutional and institutional reform by Lallemand and Leemans, about the reform of article 107*ter* of the Constitution, *Parl.Doc* Senate no 100-3/2, 17, 20.

314 Report of the plenary session of 14 June 1988, *Parl Doc* Senate no 24, 509. The reforms of article 17, 59*bis* and 107*ter* were considered logically and politically interconnected: see the report of the plenary session of 14 June1988, *Parl Doc* Senate no 22, 469, and no 23, 489.

315 Articles 6 and 6*bis* were considered only 'partially complementary' with article 17: see the report of the plenary session of 14 June 1988, *Parl Doc* Senate no 23, 488.

316 Report of 8 June 1988 from the commission on constitutional and institutional reform by Lallemand and Leemans, about the reform of article 107*ter* of the Constitution, *Parl Doc* Senate no 100-3/2, 2. Therefore, some commission members suggested that the regular judiciary, and not the BeCC, should be competent to judge on these fundamental freedoms.

317 Ibid., 11.

318 Report of the plenary session of 16 June 1988, *Parl. Doc* Senate no 29, 631–2.

319 Ibid., 632.

binding procedural formalities that should be executed before adopting a rule, such as consultations and common agreements.[320] This is however not a general rule, but only concerns those formalities that are mentioned in the Special Act of 8 August 1980 on institutional reform.[321] Hence, the legislature did not want to enforce other procedural requirements on the legislature, unless they imposed forms of federal cooperation.[322] However, the BeCC does protect parliamentary prerogatives of its own accord. More specifically, some constitutional clauses require that matters should be regulated by law (in contrast to executive action). In those cases, the BeCC formulates this legality principle as an individual right, and will declare legislative clauses that delegate these matters to the executive unconstitutional.[323]

The government in 1988 was reluctant to further expand the set of reference norms to other constitutional clauses, for two reasons.[324] First, it argued that this expansion would cause practical problems, as most constitutional provisions were drawn up by a constituent power that had rejected any form of judicial review.[325] Therefore, the government anticipated the insertion of new constitutional provisions which would be "less succinct, at least with regard to the fundamental rights and freedoms".[326] Secondly, it was considered a problem that the current provisions were formulated differently than those in the ECHR.[327] Because of these two reasons, the government chose a gradual, step-by-step extension of the BeCC's competences, notwithstanding that its ultimate goal was to establish a full-fledged constitutional court.[328] Therefore, the reformed article 107*ter* (now 142) stipulated that the review of the BeCC could be expanded to other constitutional articles determined by a law adopted

---

320 Article 30*bis*: "the consultation, involvement, provision of information, opinions, unanimous opinions, agreements, common agreements and proposals referred to in the Special Act".

321 MF Rigaux and B Renauld, *La Cour Constitutionelle* (Bruylant 2009), 76, 98–9.

322 P Popelier and AA Patiño Álvarez, 'Deliberative Practices of Constitutional Courts in Consolidated and Non-Consolidated Democracies' in P Popelier, A Mazmanyan and W Vandenbruwaene (eds.), *The Role of Constitutional Courts in Multilevel Governance* (Intersentia 2013), 227.

323 BeCC, 13 September 1995, case no 64/95.

324 Report of the plenary session of 16 June 1988, *Parl Doc* Senate no 30, 638.

325 Report of 8 June 1988 from the commission on constitutional and institutional reform by Lallemand and Leemans, about the reform of article 107*ter* of the Constitution, *Parl Doc* Senate no 100-3/2, 12. However, this wasn't considered a problem when the legislator, in 1946, gave the authority to the Council of State to review legislation *ex ante* against the Constitution.

326 Ibid., 12.

327 Report of 4 July 1988 from the commission on constitutional and institutional reform by Gehlen and Anciaux about the reform of article 107*ter* of the Constitution, *Parl Doc* Chamber no 457-1, 4.

328 Report of the plenary session of 14 June 1988, *Parl Doc* Senate no 22, 470, and no 24, 510.

with a 'special majority'. The latter condition was considered necessary to secure the institutional balance in later reforms.[329]

Notwithstanding the limited set of reference norms at that time, the BeCC interpreted its competences broadly. The Court used this opening to link the equality clause to other constitutional clauses.[330] As a result, it developed case law concerning fiscal, social, criminal and various other issues.[331] Therefore, when the legislator in 2003 extended the set of reference norms to all fundamental rights in the Constitution,[332] this was merely the legal validation of the existing review practice.[333] Instead of enumerating all reference norms separately, the government in 2003 chose to refer to 'Title II: The Belgians and their Rights'. The advantage of this formulation was that the BeCC's competence would expand automatically if a constitutional reform introduced new rights under this title.[334] In addition, the BeCC ingeniously extended the set of reference norms to European Law, analogous provisions in international treaties on fundamental rights and general principles of law.[335] Before the 2003 reform, the litigants had to demonstrate how the violation of these rules and principles constituted an infringement of the equality clause. Since the expansion in 2003, they can also link these rules and principles to other constitutional clauses of 'Title II'. The Court considers that, when the scope of a treaty provision is analogous to a constitutional provision, both provisions form an 'inseparable whole'.[336] The link with a national constitutional provision remains necessary.[337] Hence, although the Court still lacks the formal power to review legislation against international and European law, over time it has confirmed and even strengthened its practice of indirectly using these norms as benchmarks for constitutional review.[338]

---

329 Report of 8 June 1988 from the commission on constitutional and institutional reform by Lallemand and Leemans, about the reform of article 107*ter* of the Constitution, *Parl Doc* Senate no 100-3/2, 8.

330 The government was aware of the wider protection this review could offer. Some mentioned that every discrimination could possibly be reviewed against other rights in the Constitution or the ECHR: ibid., 2.

331 MF Rigaux and B Renauld, *La Cour Constitutionelle* (Bruylant 2009), 78.

332 Article 1 of the updated Special Act of 6 January 1989 on the Constitutional Court now refers to 'the articles of Title II, "The Belgians and their Rights", and Articles 170, 172 and 191 of the Constitution.'

333 MF Rigaux and B Renauld, *La Cour Constitutionelle* (Bruylant 2009), 67.

334 Ibid., 77–8.

335 P Popelier and K Lemmens, *The Constitution of Belgium: A Contextual Analysis* (Bloomsbury 2015), 197–8.

336 BeCC case no 136/2004, 22 July 2004, B.5.1-B.5.4.

337 BeCC case no 189/2005, 14 December 2005, B.3.5, and BeCC case no 195/2009, 3 December 2009.

338 M De Visser, *Constitutional Review in Europe: A Comparative Analysis* (Hart Publishing 2014), 203 and further.

The conclusion is that, while the protection of educational freedom and equality triggered the extension of the BeCC's competences and constituted the legislator's immediate concern, it was certainly not the only cause. The 1988 reform can be considered as the first step towards the establishment of a genuine constitutional court.[339] However, as the current Dutch-speaking President of the BeCC recently stated, the Court's role as 'guardian of federalism' is still present. Moreover, he argued that this role would regain some importance after the sixth state reform in 2011, which introduced several new complex competence allocating rules.[340]

2.2.2. EVALUATION

Usually, the set of reference norms is not discussed as a separate institutional facilitator of the deliberative ideal. This may be explained by the fact that this aspect relates more to the substance of the review procedure and not, like the other facilitators, to the decision-making procedure. However, substantial limitations may equally restrict the Court's potential to engage in a comprehensive debate.[341] In addition, when some constitutional clauses are off limits, courts must find ways to circumvent this rule, which may decrease the clarity of the justificatory ground for the ruling.

Currently, most constitutional courts have the power to review legislation against all clauses in the Constitution.[342] Although evaluating the substance of various constitutional rights provisions for different constitutional systems is beyond the scope of this book, a few provisions or constitutional principles particularly elevate the deliberative potential of constitutional courts. More specifically, in what follows the manner in which the proportionality principle, participatory requirements and international law may play a deliberation-enhancing role in constitutional adjudication is discussed. To illustrate this, the BeCC's competences are highlighted from a comparative perspective, which specifically draws upon the Constitution of South Africa (CSA) since it explicitly includes provisions relating to these deliberation-enhancing competences.

---

339 Report of 4 July 1988 from the commission on constitutional and institutional reform by Gehlen and Anciaux, about the reform of 107*ter* of the Constitution, *Parl Doc* Chamber no 457/3, 4.

340 Speech by president André Alen during the formal hearing on the occasion of his inauguration, 5 February 2013.

341 P Popelier and AA Patiño Álvarez, 'Deliberative Practices of Constitutional Courts in Consolidated and Non-Consolidated Democracies' in P Popelier, A Mazmanyan and W Vandenbruwaene (eds.), *The Role of Constitutional Courts in Multilevel Governance* (Intersentia 2013), 216.

342 Ibid., 215. For an overview of constitutional courts in the European Union, see M De Visser, *Constitutional Review in Europe: A Comparative Analysis* (Hart Publishing 2014), 229 and further.

First, the proportionality principle comes into play primarily in conflicts over fundamental rights and freedoms and the legislature's power to limit and intrude upon them. Accepting this principle as the cornerstone of human rights jurisprudence gives courts the opportunity to evaluate the reasonableness of legislation.[343] Moreover, it provides a way for the court to require the legislative branch to justify their actions on substantive grounds, which fits within the idea of a "culture of justification".[344] As explained more extensively in chapter 7, most constitutional courts have adopted a fixed argumentative framework in rights adjudication based on this principle.[345] In short, courts evaluate: (1) the legitimacy of the policy objective; (2) whether there is a causal relation between the challenged provision and this objective; (3) whether the least restrictive means were chosen to further that objective; and (4) whether the relation between the objective and the provision is proportionate.

The Constitution of South Africa, drawing upon experience in other systems, makes explicit reference to the proportionality analysis in article 36(1) regarding the limitations of rights.[346] Except for Israel, where elements of the test can also be found in section 8 of the Basic Law, nowhere else does a Constitution contain such an explicit reference.[347] The SACC has confirmed that, without a rational justifying mechanism, unequal treatment will follow.[348] Nonetheless, the constitutionalisation of the proportionality analysis does not necessarily lead to a stricter scrutiny of legislative action.[349]

The BeCC has incorporated the proportionality principle into its case law without such an explicit constitutional provision. Inspired by the case law

343 P Popelier and AA Patiño Álvarez, 'Deliberative Practices of Constitutional Courts in Consolidated and Non-Consolidated Democracies' in P Popelier, A Mazmanyan and W Vandenbruwaene (eds.), *The Role of Constitutional Courts in Multilevel Governance* (Intersentia 2013), 215.

344 M Cohen-Eliya and I Porat, 'Proportionality and the Culture of Justification' (2011) 59 American Journal of Comparative Law, 463.

345 For more information on the emergence of the proportionality analysis as a global constitutional standard, see A Stone Sweet and J Mathews, 'Proportionality Balancing and Global Constitutionalism' (2008) 47 Colombia Journal of Transnational Law, 73.

346 Article 36(1) states: "The rights in the Bill of Rights may be limited only in terms of law of general application to the extent that the limitation is reasonable and justifiable in an open and democratic society based on human dignity, equality and freedom, taking into account all relevant factors, including – (a) the nature of the right; (b) the importance of the purpose of the limitation; (c) the nature and extent of the limitation; (d) the relation between the limitation and its purpose; and (e) less restrictive means to achieve the purpose."

347 S Gardbaum, 'The Structure and Scope of Constitutional Rights' in T Ginsburg and R Dixon (eds.), *Comparative Constitutional Law* (Edward Elgar 2011), 390.

348 For a discussion of rationality, reasonableness and proportionality as standards in the case law of the SACC, see C Courtis, 'Rationality, Reasonableness and Proportionality: Testing the Use of Standards of Scrutiny in the Constitutional Review of Legislation' (2011) 4 Constitutional Court Review, 31.

349 Ibid., 45.

of the ECtHR, the BeCC applies this 'justification test' – although not always to its fullest extent – when reviewing against the equality clause (see *infra*, chapter 7). Carrying out the proportionality analysis allows courts to evaluate the deliberative quality of the legislation under review. This kind of case law may prompt the legislator to adopt the same standard of approach and act reasonably.[350] Hence, including the proportionality principle in constitutional adjudication, with or without an explicit provision in the Constitution, strongly enhances a court's deliberative potential.

The role of Parliament as a deliberative law-making body may also come under scrutiny when constitutional courts are allowed to review against constitutional participatory requirements.[351] As mentioned before, citizen engagement between elections – in addition to their representation in Parliament – may increase the quality and legitimacy of legislation. In short, by facilitating input into the legislative process, the legislator shows respect and citizens learn that their opinions are valued.[352] Also, it can change legislation for the better and is therefore the procedural mirror of the substantive work to be accomplished.[353]

The CSA explicitly proclaims that the government has a duty to adequately facilitate public involvement in the different stages of the decision-making process.[354] In addition, the SACC asserted that this right is equally protected by international and regional human rights instruments.[355] Nonetheless, according to the SACC, this is not an absolute requirement, but depends on the nature, importance and urgency of the legislation and the time and expense that public involvement may require.[356] Input should not necessarily have an impact on the outcome, but those who are interested should nonetheless be granted a reasonable opportunity to participate meaningfully.[357] Public participation

---

350 P Popelier and AA Patiño Álvarez, 'Deliberative Practices of Constitutional Courts in Consolidated and Non-Consolidated Democracies' in P Popelier, A Mazmanyan and W Vandenbruwaene (eds.), *The Role of Constitutional Courts in Multilevel Governance* (Intersentia 2013), 215.

351 KS Czapanskiy and R Manjoo, 'The Right of Public Participation in the Law-making Process and the Role of Legislature in the Promotion of this Right' 19 (2008) Duke Journal of Comparative and International Law, 1, 3.

352 Ibid., 17.

353 E Brems and L Lavrysen, 'Procedural Justice in Human Rights Adjudication: The European Court of Human Rights' (2013) 35 Human Rights Quarterly, 176, 184.

354 Sections 59, 1°, 72(1) and 188(1)(a) of the Constitution.

355 In particular articles 19 and 25 of the International Covenant on Civil and Political Rights, signed in 1966, registered and entering into force in 1976, ratified by Belgium in 1983, by the US in 1992, and by South Africa in 1998.

356 L Nyati, 'Public Participation: What has the Constitutional Court Given the Public?' (2008) 15 Law, Democracy & Development Law Journal, 102, 104.

357 SACC, *Doctors for life Int'l v. the Speaker of the Nat'l Assembly & Others 2006* (12) BCLR 1399. For a discussion of this case law, see for example: C Courtis, 'Rationality, Reasonableness and Proportionality: Testing the Use of Standards of Scrutiny in the Constitutional Review of

should supplement elections and majority rule, and is "not to conflict with or even overrule or veto them".[358]

By comparison, no such constitutional requirement can be found in the Belgian Constitution. Except for those rules that require the involvement or agreement of other federal entities,[359] the BeCC refuses to extend its competence to other procedural requirements such as the obligation to negotiate with trade unions[360] or other consultation committees,[361] or the obligation to consult the advisory opinion of the Council of State.[362] Some litigants have tried to argue that they are discriminated against vis-à-vis other citizens because they are denied the same procedural safeguards, but so far the BeCC has not accepted this argument.[363] Although shortcomings in the law-making process do not necessarily lead to legislation that is substantively unconstitutional, allowing courts to take these considerations into account would allow them to stress the importance of participation as a deliberative requirement.

Finally, adding international law and engaging with comparative jurisprudence increases the deliberative capacity of courts. This allows for reflexivity and can make judges sceptical of the arguments brought forward in the case before them.[364] In this way, more arguments are introduced into the constitutional debate, possibly transforming the constituent's initial interpretation of constitutional clauses.[365]

The CSA explicitly states that, when interpreting the Bill of Rights, courts must consider international law (and may consider foreign law).[366] In the case law of the SACC, international law has played a vital role in shaping legislation in South Africa and in protecting the rights enshrined in the CSA.[367] In some

Legislation' (2011) 4 Constitutional Court Review 31, 37; and KS Czapanskiy and R Manjoo, 'The Right of Public Participation in the Law-making Process and the Role of Legislature in the Promotion of this Right' 19 (2008) Duke Journal of Comparative and International Law, 1.

358 L Nyati, 'Public Participation: What has the Constitutional Court Given the Public?' (2008) 15 Law, Democracy & Development Law Journal, 102, 108.

359 Article 30*bis* of the Special Act on the Constitutional Court.

360 BeCC case no 107/98, 21 October 1998, B.3.1.

361 BeCC case no 136/2000, 21 December 2000, B.40.

362 BeCC case no 66/88, 30 June 1988, and BeCC case no 103/2000, 11 October 2000.

363 MF Rigaux and B Renauld, *La Cour Constitutionelle* (Bruylant 2009), 98.

364 CH Mendes, *Constitutional Courts and Deliberative Democracy* (Oxford University Press 2013), 191.

365 P Popelier and AA Patiño Álvarez, 'Deliberative Practices of Constitutional Courts in Consolidated and Non-Consolidated Democracies' in P Popelier, A Mazmanyan and W Vandenbruwaene (eds.), *The Role of Constitutional Courts in Multilevel Governance* (Intersentia 2013), 216; and CH Mendes, *Constitutional Courts and Deliberative Democracy* (Oxford University Press 2013), 190.

366 Article 39(1) of the Constitution of South Africa.

367 CD Zungu, 'The Role, Relevance and Application of International Law in South Africa' (2015) 8 International Journal of Sustainable Development, 85, 88.

countries, courts in the European Union, international and/or European law are also treated as autonomous standards for review.[368]

As mentioned above, the BeCC initially did not have the competence to review against international law (including the ECHR and EU law), but has expanded of its own accord its set of reference norms. Nonetheless, an explicit (constitutional) provision allowing the Court to take into account international and/or European legislation would encourage it to integrate these sources more strongly in its adjudication.

The conclusion is that, notwithstanding a few limitations, the BeCC interprets its set of reference norms broadly, which allows for an all-including debate and increases its impact on democratic decision-making.

2.3. COMPOSITION OF THE COURT AND INTERNAL DYNAMICS

2.3.1. THE DOUBLE PARITY RULE: ENSURING THE PROTECTION OF POLITICAL AGREEMENTS

When the BeCC was established in 1983, government officials agreed upon a double parity among the twelve judges: between professional lawyers and former politicians, and between Dutch-speaking and French-speaking judges. In principle, each case is submitted to seven judges (restricted session). Of those seven, there are at least three Dutch-speaking and three French-speaking judges. In addition, at least two judges are former politicians and at least two are legal experts.[369] When the case is relatively straightforward, the judges-rapporteurs may suggest submitting it to a 'limited procedure'.[370] If so, the case is still submitted to a panel of seven judges, but within a more limited time frame. The parties involved in the procedure are informed about this proposition and receive a short period of time (15 days) to submit a memorandum. However, either of the two presidents may submit a case to plenary session. Indeed, they are obliged to do so when at least two judges request a full session.[371]

---

368 Particularly in Italy, Hungary and Poland: M De Visser, *Constitutional Review in Europe: A Comparative Analysis* (Hart Publishing 2014), 278.

369 Article 55 of the Special Act.

370 In particular, article 72 of the Special Act determines: "If the judges-rapporteurs consider that the action for annulment is manifestly unfounded, the preliminary question evidently calls for a negative reply, or the case, owing to its very nature or the relatively straightforward nature of the issues raised therein, [this] can be settled with a judgment delivered after a preliminary procedure".

371 Article 56 of the Special Act.

Because there are no rules determining[372] or guiding[373] the decision to refer a case to the plenary session, this relies solely on the request of these judges. When the case is submitted to the BeCC in plenary session, there must be at least ten judges, with a maximum of twelve judges deciding the case. In plenary session, the double parity rule is strictly applied; in any case there are always as many Dutch-speaking as French-speaking judges.[374] All decisions, notwithstanding panel size, are adopted by a majority vote of the judges. However, as explained below (see *infra*, section 2.7.), the ruling neither reveals how many nor which judges voted in favour of or against the decision.

The double parity rule was one of the core elements of the political agreement that created the BeCC,[375] and received strong support from the executive as well as Parliament.[376] The Council of State also supported this part of the agreement.[377] This rule was meant to protect consociational agreements. When establishing the BeCC, government officials realised that the Court would not only have to judge technical juridical questions, but also political issues. The latter cases would require an evaluation of opportunity elements.[378] The idea was to avoid a BeCC that would limit itself to a restrictive juridical reasoning devoid of political sensitivities, against the general will of the political representatives.[379] On the contrary, the interpretation of the competence allocating rules had to be executed in a dynamic way,[380] which was considered impossible should the Court be exclusively composed of lawyers.[381] Parliamentary and political experience would give the Court insight into the balance between the different

---

372 For example, on the Indian Supreme Court, bench size is underscored by specific (constitutional) rules. See C Chandrachud, 'Measuring Constitutional Case Salience in the Indian Supreme Court' (2014) 42 Journal of Law and Society, 42, 45.

373 For example, several guiding criteria are published on the website of the UK Supreme Court, including cases of public importance and cases that raise a point in relation to the European Convention of Human Rights. For more information, see https://www.supremecourt.uk/procedures/panel-numbers-criteria.html.

374 In comparison with other European countries, these rules are particularly detailed. See M De Visser, *Constitutional Review in Europe: A Comparative Analysis* (Hart Publishing 2014), 214.

375 Advisory opinion of the Council of State to the draft of 23 May 1980 of the law on the institutional reform, *Parl Doc* Senate no 435/1, 50 (*"een van de sleutelbepalingen"*).

376 Report of 30 March 1983 from the commission on constitutional and institutional reform, about the draft law on the composition, competence and functioning of the constitutional court, *Parl Doc* Senate no 246/2, 143.

377 Advisory opinion of the Council of State to the draft of 23 May 1980 of the law on the institutional reform, *Parl Doc* Senate no 435/1, 51: *"nuttige waarborg"*.

378 Report of 30 March 1983, ibid., 144, 146.

379 Explanatory memorandum of 23 May 1980 to the draft of the law on the institutional reform, *Parl Doc* Senate no 435/1, 12.

380 Explanatory memorandum of 9 July 1981 to the draft of the law on the composition, competence and functioning of the constitutional court, *Parl Doc* Senate no 704/1, 12.

381 Report of 30 March 1983, ibid., 144, and explanatory memorandum of 9 July 1981, ibid.,12.

political authorities, which was to be preserved.[382] The government expected interplay between the lawyers and politicians.[383]

Nonetheless, not all politicians agreed upon this parity rule. Some opposition members preferred an exclusive composition of lawyers to avoid political pressure on the judges. These opponents argued that, because of the principle of separation of powers, the BeCC should not engage in political issues nor opportunity considerations. They did not believe that former members of Parliament, who were inevitably connected to a certain political party and/or language area, could disassociate themselves from their political environment.[384] Nevertheless, the proposition was accepted by the majority in Parliament as a part of the large package deal concerning the state reform.

During the negotiations on the extension of the BeCC's competences in 1988, some politicians seized the chance to question (once more) the Court's composition.[385] Considering the presence of former politicians and the balance between Dutch-speaking and French-speaking judges, several members of the commission on institutional reform expressed their fear that other issues than legal accuracy would prevail. Therefore, they argued that the judiciary was more suitable to judge constitutional issues.[386] Nonetheless, the government repeated that this composition had been an essential condition for granting a judicial institution the competence to review legislation approved by a parliamentary majority.[387] Government officials specified that this composition continued to be a guarantee for "a balanced case law, mindful of the political as well as the legal aspects of the delicate community conflicts with which the BeCC will be confronted."[388] Furthermore, they added that, only if the BeCC acted prudently and thus showed itself a 'reliable' partner, would the government (re)consider additional extensions of the its competences.[389]

Further, the appointment process also reflects that each judge needs to be acceptable to the political branch. First, a list of two candidates is adopted by a two-thirds majority vote of alternately the House of Representatives and the Senate. Then, one of the two candidates is chosen by 'the King', which actually

382 Report of 30 March 1983, ibid., 145, and report of 25 November 1988 from the commission on constitutional and institutional reform by Lallemand and Baert, *Parl Doc* no 483/2, 2.
383 Report of 30 March 1983, ibid., 145.
384 Amendment of 30 March 1983 by De Clippele on the draft law on the composition, competence and functioning of the constitutional court, *Parl Doc* Senate no 246/3.
385 Report of the plenary session of 14 June 1988, *Parl Doc* Senate, no 22, 473.
386 Report of 8 June 1988 from the commission on constitutional and institutional reform by Lallemand and Leemans, about the reform of article 107*ter* of the Constitution, *Parl Doc* Senate no 100-3/2, 2–11.
387 Ibid., 12.
388 Ibid., 2.
389 Ibid., 12.

means that the government needs to approve the final decision.[390] When a new judge needs to be chosen, it is the custom to take into account the results of the most recent elections. Hence, the main political ideologies are represented in the Court. During the inauguration speech of the recently nominated judge Riet Leysen, president Alen called this custom 'quasi-constitutional' and added that the 'balanced and representative' composition of the BeCC is meant to increase its democratic legitimacy.[391]

Nonetheless, other measures were taken to limit political influence. For example, contrary to a former system in the Law of 3 July 1971,[392] any legislative interference in the judicial procedure is excluded.[393] Also, the judges were to be appointed for life, instead of a renewable term of eight years, as was initially suggested.[394] This was considered a guarantee for the independence of the court, because the judges would not be dependent on possible re-election by the Senate.[395] The former Dutch-speaking president of the Court, André Alen, also considers these rules as a guarantee for the Court's independence.[396]

2.3.2. EVALUATION

Like in many other countries in the European Union, the selection procedure for the constitutional judges envisages the involvement of Parliament.[397] Although this can enhance the democratic legitimacy of the Court, it is also said to present the risk of partisanship.[398] Yet the appointment is conditional on the approval by a

390 Report of 30 March 1983 from the commission on constitutional and institutional reform, about the draft law on the composition, competence and functioning of the constitutional court, *Parl Doc* Senate no 246/2, 142, and advisory opinion of the Council of State to the draft of 23 May 1980 of the law on the institutional reform, *Parl Doc* Senate no 435/1, 60, 142.

391 Speech by president André Alen during the formal hearing on the occasion of the inauguration of judge Riet Leysen, 19 March 2014.

392 Articles 20 and 21 of the Special Act: procedure to prevent and regulate conflicts between the law and decrees, and between decrees.

393 Explanatory memorandum of 23 May 1980 to the draft of the law on the institutional reform, *Parl Doc* Senate no 435/1, 14.

394 Yet judges can be dismissed for 'serious misconduct': see article 49 of the Special Act, and M De Visser, *Constitutional Review in Europe: A Comparative Analysis* (Hart Publishing 2014), 222.

395 Report of 30 March 1983 from the commission on constitutional and institutional reform, about the draft law on the composition, competence and functioning of the constitutional court, *Parl Doc* Senate no 246/2, 138.

396 Speech by president André Alen during the formal hearing on the occasion of his inauguration, 5 February 2013. To confirm this statement, president Alen refers to BeCC case no 157/2009, 13 October 2009, B.6.

397 M De Visser, *Constitutional Review in Europe: A Comparative Analysis* (Hart Publishing 2014), 209.

398 Ibid.

special majority of Parliament, which means the candidate needs to be acceptable to representatives across the political spectrum. Therefore, supermajority appointment methods, as well as life tenure, are said to be joint mechanisms to tackle the risk of partisanship[399] and other deliberative failures.[400] In contrast, appointment methods that are less consensual are associated more strongly with political influence. For example, the US Supreme Court appointment mechanism – judges are nominated by the President and appointed by a majority of the Senate – is often criticised for being partisan.[401] In particular, political alignment with the nominating President is a dominant selection criterion.[402] Judicial elections, especially when the judicial tenure is limited and renewable, make judges even more vulnerable to political incentives. An alternative to the supermajoritarian method are the 'judicial appointment commissions'. A combination of both may also occur, as in South Africa for example. Appointments to the SACC are made by the President, after consultation with the Judicial Service Commission (JSC) and the leaders of the political parties. For all positions other than the Chief Justice and Deputy Chief Justice, the JSC prepares the list of nominees. If the president refuses all proposed candidates, the JSC may provide a supplemental list.[403] This system was set in place to provide for a measure of minority party influence. If not, the dominance of one political party (ANC) would have been too strong.[404] In any case, the designer of the constitutional court should choose an appointment method that increases the chances of an 'optimal' composition of the court.

Under the condition of maintaining a certain collegial culture amongst the judges, diversity within a constitutional court is said to improve its deliberative potential immensely. An ideologically diverse institution has the capacity to amplify the arguments and information on the table.[405] Hence, it ensures that different perspectives are incorporated into the decision-making process.[406] In a heterogeneous society like Belgium, a plural court symbolises the recognition

399 "A judge is acting in a more partisan manner when he or she applies a neutral legal rule in a manner that demonstrates greater deference to members of a particular political party": see CR Yung, 'A Typology of Judging Styles' (2015) 107 Northwestern University Law Review, 1757, 1776.

400 CH Mendes, *Constitutional Courts and Deliberative Democracy* (Oxford University Press 2013), 156–9.

401 Ibid., 157.

402 HJ Abraham, *Justices and Presidents: a Political History of Appointments to the Supreme Court* (Oxford University Press 1974), 54.

403 H Klug, *The Constitution of South Africa: a Contextual Analysis* (Hart Publishing 2010), 233.

404 T Roux, *The Politics of Principle: the First South African Constitutional Court, 1995–2005* (Cambridge University Press 2013), 167.

405 CH Mendes, *Constitutional Courts and Deliberative Democracy* (Oxford University Press 2013), 45.

406 VF Comella, *Constitutional Courts and Democratic Values* (Yale University Press 2009), 39–43. For empirical evidence, see A Vermeule, 'Should We Have Lay Justices?' (2006) 134 Harvard Public Law Working Paper, 1.

that constitutional review is an enterprise that needs to include different voices.[407] Although the presence of legal specialists is vital for the court to understand and solve each specific case within the available constitutional framework,[408] including judges with different professional backgrounds can offer additional viewpoints and give a concrete meaning to fundamental legal principles.[409] It would be especially helpful to add a judge capable of interpreting statistical causal interdependencies. This would ensure that this relevant knowledge is present in the Court, where it cannot be compensated by the conventional case-by-case mechanisms for the incorporation of expertise (like amicus briefs, expert witnesses and so on).[410] Having this judge participating in all stages of the decision-making process provides an institutional foundation for non-legal expertise. If needed, the expert judge can aid his or her colleagues to recognise the force of the 'better argument'.[411] The second parity, between Dutch-speaking and French-speaking judges, reflects the linguistic heterogeneity of Belgian society. The presence of judges – and law clerks – from both linguistic groups ensures that their respective opinions are integrated. Therefore, although this may not be the initial reason for the double parity rule, it enhances the deliberative potential of the BeCC.

Compared to other courts, the qualifications that the judges on the BeCC must possess are particularly detailed.[412] In some countries, such as France and the US for example, there are no legal or constitutional requirements to become a constitutional judge. Yet many of the judges that were active on the French *Conseil Constitutionnel* to date were either formerly active in politics or held a law degree.[413] In the US, it is an unwritten prerequisite that judges should have a law degree and preferably some prior judicial experience. Naturally, the need to win the approval of the appointing institution leads to the selection of nominees

---

407 Not all former politicians are necessarily lawyers. For example, one of the current judges, Jean-Paul Snappe, was a former school teacher.

408 VF Comella, *Constitutional Courts and Democratic Values* (Yale University Press 2009), 40; and M De Visser, *Constitutional Review in Europe: A Comparative Analysis* (Hart Publishing 2014), 216.

409 Professional diversity would alleviate the 'like-mindedness' that arises from common professional training. See: A Vermeule, 'Should We Have Lay Justices?' (2006) 134 Harvard Public Law Working Paper, 1; and CH Mendes, *Constitutional Courts and Deliberative Democracy* (Oxford University Press 2013), 155.

410 Vermeule argues that a constitutional court should contain more than one lay justice, and that there should be a diversity of non-legal expertise. Also, there is a middle ground between appointing experts to the Court and soliciting views from the Court, particularly by hiring law clerks with joint degrees or with other non-legal expertise. See A Vermeule, *Law and the Limits of Reason* (Oxford University Press 2009), 138, 153.

411 Ibid., 152 and further.

412 For an overview of the required qualifications on constitutional courts in the European Union, see M De Visser, *Constitutional Review in Europe: A Comparative Analysis* (Hart Publishing 2014), 211 and further.

413 Ibid., 212.

with distinguished legal, judicial or political careers. In most countries, being legally trained is a strict eligibility criterion – although there is some variety in the threshold to be crossed.[414] Other than legal qualifications and judicial experience, which are also the prominent criteria in many other countries in the EU, in some other countries eligibility rules state that the constitutional court must reflect societal sub-divisions. For example, the Constitution of South Africa stipulates that consideration must be given to the "need for the judiciary to reflect broadly the racial and gender composition of South Africa".[415] Several former judges on the SACC have a history as anti-apartheid fighters.[416] Although it is not as strictly regulated as for the BeCC, this requirement guarantees that at least some societal heterogeneity is reflected in the composition of the Court. In conclusion, diversity protects constitutional adjudication against the deliberative perils of homogeneity.

In addition to this diverse composition, the BeCC – like most other European courts – is engaged in a cooperative enterprise which, notwithstanding the majority rule, needs to result in a collective outcome. Hence, the judge in charge of writing the opinion must be careful to take into consideration the comments and concerns of fellow judges in order to reach a majority. Also, it has been noted that when judicial appointments are negotiated within a broader coalition, individual judges are faithful to the consensual mode rather than their strict ideological preferences or a political party.[417] Hence, this procedural environment is believed to reinforce the collegial dynamic of the judicial decision-making process.[418] Such a process maximises information and might lead to a creative solution that would not be possible without extensive internal debate.[419] Hence, courts like the BeCC are believed to produce decisions that are more deliberative than those courts with more limited collegial dynamics. This is in contrast to courts where each judge is also allowed to publish separate opinions (see *infra*, section 2.7.). This would create an environment favouring individualistic behaviour rather than cooperation among the justices.[420]

---

414 Ibid., 215.

415 Article 174(1) and (2) of the Constitution of South Africa.

416 Specifically, Justices Sachs and Yacoob.

417 V Grembi and N Garoupa, 'Judicial Review and Political Partisanship: Moving from Consensual to Majoritarian Democracy' (2015) 43 International Review of Law and Economics, 133–5.

418 A Dyevre, 'Unifying the Field of Comparative Judicial Politics: Towards a General Theory on Judicial Behaviour (2010) 2 European Political Science Review, 297, 319.

419 CH Mendes, *Constitutional Courts and Deliberative Democracy* (Oxford University Press 2013), 66.

420 Although some of the institutional factors favouring individualistic behaviour can also be found in European courts, not one has all of them simultaneously. See A Dyevre, 'Unifying the Field of Comparative Judicial Politics: Towards a General Theory on Judicial Behaviour' (2010) 2 European Political Science Review, 297, 319.

However, in the absence of collegial cooperation between the judges, the strict parity rule may also prevent the Court from transcending political preferences. Especially when the legislation under review is the result of a supermajoritarian agreement, political pressure to respect the negotiated outcome may be high. Thus, finding a compromise within the court – where most political parties that agreed upon the compromise are indirectly 'represented' – might then prevail on other minority viewpoints outside the scope of the agreement. Although the expectation that the BeCC acts as a 'guardian of consociationalism' is less pronounced, it is still present. For example, in preparatory documents on the reform of the BeCC in 2003, a government official made a comment about existing legislation related to the language border. He suggested that the BeCC was not expected to declare this legislation unconstitutional (through a preliminary procedure), considering the presence of former politicians in the BeCC, who "understand the intricacies of political negotiations".[421]

2.4. ACCESS ROUTES AND AGENDA-SETTING

2.4.1. FROM A LIMITED TO AN OPEN-ACCESS POLICY

When the BeCC was established, access possibilities were very limited. The legislator installed two access routes: preliminary questions and annulment actions. Both procedures could be initiated after the legislation had been promulgated (*a posteriori*).[422] First, the preliminary procedures are referred to the BeCC by other judges or courts when a constitutional question arises in a concrete case (the procedure *a quo*), and may concern recent as well as old legislation. Legislation which has been applied without any problems for years may come under siege when, for example, it becomes applicable to a new phenomenon. The referring judge should then turn to the BeCC for a conclusive answer about the constitutionality of the applicable legislative provision(s). Although the final decision is left to the judge, the litigants can request to put this preliminary procedure in motion.

Second, within six months after its promulgation, legislation can be challenged *in abstracto* via the annulment procedure before the BeCC.[423]

[421] Report of 17 January 2003 from the commission on constitutional and institutional reform, about the draft law on the composition, competence and functioning of the constitutional court, *Parl Doc* Chamber no 2099/003, 7.

[422] In several other countries in continental Europe, the constitutional validity of laws can be questioned before they are promulgated (a priori). See M De Visser, *Constitutional Review in Europe: A Comparative Analysis* (Hart Publishing 2014), 99–111.

[423] Yet, in exceptional circumstances (e.g. after a declaration of unconstitutionality in a preliminary proceeding) this term can reopen. See articles 4 and 2° of the Special Act on the Constitutional Court.

When initiating this procedure, litigants aim to remove unconstitutional provisions from the legal order. Initially, the right to start an annulment procedure was exclusively reserved for executives of the federal and subnational levels.[424] Although the initial idea was that this access would be conditional on the demonstration of a legitimate interest, this condition was quickly dropped. Government officials realised that it is in every government's interest to enforce respect for competence allocating rules.[425] The access via annulment procedure was also quickly extended to the presidents of each legislative chamber, under the condition that two thirds (initially one third) of its representatives demanded the lodging of a petition before the BeCC.[426] This special majority threshold was introduced in an amendment, to protect minority rights as well as majority rights.[427] On the one hand, it allowed for parliamentary assemblies, as opposed to executives, to act against other entities suspected of overstepping their competences. At the same time, it excluded the possibility of the opposition challenging legislation approved by a majority of representatives in their own legislative chamber, because this might be inspired by "considerations, particular for temporary political coalitions"; for the same reason, a regular majority for triggering constitutional procedures was also considered undesirable.[428] It was therefore only possible for parliamentary representatives to act against other entities, but not against legislation that colleagues in their own legislative chamber had approved. Apart from these institutional entities, no other actors – e.g. individuals, business organisations or interest groups – were initially allowed to initiate an annulment procedure before the BeCC.

Once the procedure is initiated, other individuals or legal entities are allowed to introduce additional memorandums. However, they were initially not considered a real 'party' in the procedure.[429] Institutional actors were explicitly invited, by means of an automatic communication, to participate in the procedure. The presidents of each legislative chamber could intervene without a request from the members of this chamber because it was considered necessary that they could act when the legislation of their respective Parliament was challenged.[430] In annulment procedures, if the challenged provision had

424 The Council of Ministers or the Government of a Community or Region (this also applies to the Joint Board of the Common Community Commission and the Board of the French Community Commission).

425 Report of 30 March 1983 from the commission on constitutional and institutional reform, about the draft law on the composition, competence and functioning of the constitutional court, *Parl Doc* Senate no 246/2, 51.

426 Subamendment of R Gijs and D André of 27 April 1983 of the draft law on the composition, competence and functioning of the constitutional court, *Parl Doc* Senate no 246/13, 1–2.

427 Ibid., 2.

428 Ibid.

429 BeCC case no 1, 28 June 1985.

430 J Velaers, *Van Arbitragehof tot Grondwettelijk Hof* (Maklu 1990), 498–9.

already been reviewed in a preliminary procedure, the registry of the BeCC also notified those actors that participated in the preliminary procedure. When an ordinary court asked a preliminary question to the BeCC, it was the registry of that court that notified the actors in the procedure *a quo*.[431]

The Belgian state reform in 1988 lead to an expansion of the access possibilities. Considering that the enforcement of educational freedom and equality was an essential element of this reform, politicians agreed that additional institutional guarantees had to be installed. In particular, not only institutional actors, but also students, parents and employees of educational establishments should become able to initiate an annulment procedure before the BeCC.[432] More generally, from then on all individuals and legal entities with a justifiable interest could lodge a petition before the Court. This was a radical modification, since the review shifted from resolving conflict between institutional actors to the protection of individual rights.[433] Unlike institutional actors, who are presumed to have a legitimate interest, individuals and legal entities are obliged to demonstrate their interest in the case. The legislator deliberately chose not to specify how this 'interest' should be understood. The responsibility was passed to the BeCC to further develop the concept and to give it a concrete meaning.[434]

The following guidelines can be found in the BeCC's case law: the challenged legislation should harm the situation of the applicant directly;[435] the interest in the application should be personal,[436] topical[437] and lawful,[438] and not merely hypothetical.[439,440] An *actio popularis* – which means the applicant acts in

431 Currently, these rules are still applicable. Annulment procedure: automatic notification of the institutional actors and, if the legislation under review was the subject of a prior procedure, of the parties in that case (articles 76 §1-4 and 78 of the Special Act). Preliminary procedure: automatic notification of the institutional actors and parties before the referral court (article 77 of the Special Act).

432 Report of the plenary session of 14 June 1988, *Parl Doc* Senate no 23, 492.

433 Ibid., 470.

434 Report of 25 November 1988 from the commission on constitutional and institutional reform by Lallemand and Baert, *Parl Doc* Senate 1988–89 no 483/2, 5, 46–7, 62–3.

435 Recent examples: BeCC case no 27/2013, 28 February 2013, B.2; BeCC case no 58/2013, 25 April 2013, B.5.1; and BeCC case no 72/2013, 22 May 2013.

436 For example, BeCC case no 157/2014, 23 October 2014, B.4. This does not mean that the BeCC has to accept the interest of each party separately. The BeCC accepts that parties can introduce a memorandum together, showing that they each have a similar interest in the case: see BeCC case no 166/2002, 13 November 2002.

437 For example, BeCC case no 58/2013, 25 April 2013, B.5.2.

438 However, the defending party only exceptionally argues that the interest in the case is not lawful. And even so, the BeCC does not easily reject a memorandum for this reason. See BeCC case no 127/2000, 6 December 2000, A.3 and B.3.1 (in which the interest was considered lawful).

439 For example, BeCC case no 171/2001, 10 November 2011, B.4.2.

440 For an in-depth evaluation of these conditions, see P Popelier, *Procederen voor het Grondwettelijk Hof* (Intersentia 2008), 183.

name of the whole population – is not allowed.[441] The interest of legal entities, including those of public institutions,[442] should be linked to the organisation's objectives, as defined in the law or their official statutes. Associations, such as political parties, can only act against legislation that may harm their specific prerogatives.[443] Notwithstanding these conditions, cases are only rarely declared inadmissible for a lack of interest.[444] On the contrary, the BeCC seems to apply an open access policy.

Once a case is declared admissible, the BeCC is expected to answer questions of constitutionality. Hence, in principle, there is no docket control limiting the Court's case load. However, the Court is allowed to opt for a 'limited procedure' when one of the following situations occur. First, when the case is manifestly inadmissible or the court is manifestly incompetent, the court may declare this in the ruling without investigating the constitutional question itself. The second situation applies when the case is manifestly unfounded, evidently calls for a negative reply, or is relatively straightforward. Without any further judicial procedure, the Court may then settle the case by declaring the action well-founded or unfounded, or by giving a positive or negative reply to the constitutional question. This does not give the Court actual agenda-setting powers, but does function as a filter to reduce some of the work load.

2.4.2. EVALUATION

In principle, constitutional cases are brought before a court by external provocation and not by internal initiative. The power to act *ex officio*, for want of a litigant willing to raise the right legal question, would introduce the risk of biased judgments.[445] Hence, in order to guarantee the inclusiveness of the review procedure, wide access must be guaranteed. In Belgium, governmental as well as private actors may file a claim or memorandum, in *ex post* annulments as well as preliminary procedures. Although most countries in the European Union have adopted similar *a posteriori* access routes, this particularly wide accessibility is unique to Belgium.[446] Although the private actors need to

---

441 For example, BeCC case no 146/2013, 7 November 2013, B.5.3; and BeCC case no 157/2014, 23 October 2014, B.4.

442 For example, BeCC case no 196/2004, 8 December 2004, B.3.2.

443 For example, BeCC case no 72/2016, 25 May 2016, B.2.1-B.2.3.

444 Yet, the Court exceptionally makes strategic use of the interest requirement to limit its involvement in politically controversial cases. See M De Visser, *Constitutional Review in Europe: A Comparative Analysis* (Hart Publishing 2014), 129, discussing BeCC case no 76/94, 18 October 1994, as an example.

445 CH Mendes, *Constitutional Courts and Deliberative Democracy* (Oxford University Press 2013), 74.

446 M De Visser, *Constitutional Review in Europe: A Comparative Analysis* (Hart Publishing 2014), 99, 128–30. Other countries have installed 'constitutional complaint procedures'

demonstrate a legitimate interest, this condition is interpreted broadly. In addition, initiating and intervening in a review procedure is, in principle, free of charge. This wide accessibility increases the range of perspectives that can be addressed by or incorporated into the court proceedings.[447] The quantity of the information, presented as competing views and arguments, increases the probability of reaching correct decisions.[448]

Yet, when evaluating these access possibilities from a comparative perspective, they remain restricted. In particular, in some countries, access is also granted to so-called *amicus curiae* (friends of the court). This ancient practice, which dates back to the Roman period, offers access to "a bystander, who without having an interest in the cause, of his own knowledge makes a suggestion on a point of law or of fact for the information of the presiding judge".[449] In other words, these actors do not necessarily have a direct stake in the outcome of the case, but are nonetheless allowed to provide arguments and recommendations on how the case should be decided.[450] The amici system was first incorporated in the common law systems as an alternative for third-party interventions. Hence there is a substantive overlap between the access possibilities of *amici curiae* (common law system) and/or a third-party intervention (civil law system). Comparing them, however, shows that the *amici curiae* system actually guarantees broader access facilities. In particular, it opens up the constitutional review procedure for experts, academic scholars or other actors with specific and useful knowledge. The objective of their participation might be, for example, to protect unrepresented actors (e.g. detainees, refugees) or the public interest, or to point out an error to the Court.[451] Other judicial institutions, such as the USSC,[452] the SACC[453] and the ECtHR[454] already offer this opportunity, albeit under the condition of acceptance by the involved parties and/or the court itself.

---

that can be initiated by private actors. Yet this procedure is not oriented towards objective constitutional control of legal norms, but rather serves a remedial function in relation to specific infringements committed by the regular judiciary or administration.

447 CH Mendes, *Constitutional Courts and Deliberative Democracy* (Oxford University Press 2013), 162.

448 LB Tremblay, 'The Legitimacy of Judicial Review: The Limits of Dialogue between Courts and Legislatures' ¾ 2005 ICON, 617, 636.

449 S Krislov, 'The Amicus Curiae Brief: From Friendschip to Advocacy' (1963) 72 Yale Law Journal, 694.

450 A Maamouri, 'L'Amicus Curiae et la Motivation des Décisions des Cours Suprêmes Américaine et Canadienne' in F Hourquebie and MC Pontoreau (eds.), *La Motivation des Decisions des Cours Suprêmes et Cours Constitutionelles* (Bruylant 2012), 118–19.

451 D Shelton, 'The Participation of Nongovernmental Organizations in International Judicial Proceedings' (1994) 88 The American Journal of International Law, 611–12.

452 Rule 37 of the USSC statutes defines an amicus curiae brief as a document "that brings to the attention of the Court relevant matter not already brought to its attention by the parties".

453 Rule 10 of the SACC statutes, promulgated on 31 October 2003.

454 Article 36 §2 ECHR: "The President of the Court may, in the interest of the proper administration of justice, invite any High Contracting Party which is not a party to the

A system with *amicus curiae* allows a court to enhance its role as a deliberative forum and can contribute to the quality of its reasoning. Notwithstanding the specific knowledge and experience of the judges, they cannot have expertise on each issue that is treated.[455] Although wide access possibilities are guaranteed, the involved parties might equally lack the knowledge or resources to gather evidence or to formulate legal arguments.[456] The absence of sufficient correct information may cause judicial errors that undermine confidence in the courts and the legal system.[457] For example, the lack of a sufficient background in interferential statistics makes it difficult to evaluate the assumed causalities underlying legislative decisions. *Amici curiae* can fill in the gaps and address issues that the parties did not include, either purposefully or inadvertently, in their memoranda. Importantly, they may present scientific evidence to the Court.[458] Also, *amici curiae* can offer perspectives on the broader implications of the decision, beyond the particular interests of the parties.[459] If the arguments brought forward by the *amicus curiae* are considered valuable, the Court can use this additional information to underpin its judgment.[460] Empirical research on the USSC has repeatedly shown that this external input has a significant effect on the court's case law.[461] Research on the *amicus briefs* before the ECtHR confirms that this court also systematically makes use of this information and expertise to underpin its judgments.[462] For example, *amici curiae* in ECtHR proceedings

---

proceedings or any person concerned who is not the applicant to submit written comments or take part in hearings."

455 PM Collins, 'Lobbyist before the U.S. Supreme Court: Investigating the influence of Amicus Curiae Briefs' (2007) 60 Political Research Quarterly, 55, 58: "they operate in an environment of incomplete information."

456 D Shelton, 'The Participation of Nongovernmental Organizations in International Judicial Proceedings' (1994) 88 The American Journal of International Law, 611, 615; and A Maamouri, 'L'Amicus Curiae et la Motivation des Décisions des Cours Suprêmes Américaine et Canadienne' in F Hourquebie and MC Pontoreau (eds.), *La Motivation des Decisions des Cours Suprêmes et Cours Constitutionelles* (Bruylant 2012), 129.

457 D Shelton, ibid., 616.

458 PM Collins, *Friends of the Supreme Court: Interest Groups and Judicial Decision Making* (Oxford University Press 2008), 27: "Unlike the direct parties to litigation, amicus participants may be policy specialists, equipped with an intimate knowledge of a particular policy arena."

459 D Shelton, ibid., 611, 618; and PM Collins, *Friends of the Supreme Court: Interest Groups and Judicial Decision Making* (Oxford University Press 2008), 27.

460 CH Mendes, *Constitutional Courts and Deliberative Democracy* (Oxford University Press 2013), 105, 161–2.

461 For example: GA Caldeira and JR Wright, 'Amici Curiae before the Supreme Court: Who Participates, When and How Much?' (1990) 52 The Journal of Politics, 782; JF Spriggs and PJ Wahlbeck 'Amici Curiae and the Role of Information at the Supreme Court' (1997) 50 Political Research Quartely, 365; and PM Collins, 'Lobbyist before the U.S. Supreme Court: Investigating the Influence of Amicus Curiae Briefs' (2007) 60 Political Research Quarterly, 55.

462 RA Cichowski, 'Civil Society and the European Convention of Human Rights' in J Christoffersen and MR Madsen, *The European Court of Human Rights between Law and Politics* (Oxford University Press 2011), 96.

frequently provide comparative legal analyses, which can give the case before the court a different perspective.[463]

Next to the access conditions, there are other elements to be taken into account when evaluating the inclusive potential of the review procedure. In particular, agenda-setting powers may limit the case load presented to the Court. The BeCC has only limited control over its agenda. There is no docket control to select and thus limit the case load presented to the judges. Only manifestly (un)founded or straightforward cases might not be scrutinised to the fullest extent. Conversely, other courts have complete discretion to select the cases that will be given a full hearing. In the US, for example, fewer than 5% of the several thousand petitions survive this docket control.[464] The same can be said for Germany, where the German Federal Constitutional Court only grants review in less than 1% of the constitutional complaints it receives.[465] Hence, although the first threshold for litigants may seem lower (considering the access to *amici curiae*), most of their claims are rejected without a substantive review procedure. Prior research on the USSC has shown that individual claims have less chance of surviving the docket than, for example, those of states or organised groups.[466]

From a deliberative point of view, docket control mechanisms may have benefits and drawbacks.[467] First, an overload of cases would diminish the quality of the rulings, since judges may not have time to investigate and discuss cases thoroughly. Next, judges may waste time reviewing trivial cases that are neither relevant nor opportune in the current democratic debate. Also, mandatory review would make it more difficult for judges to decide when the time is ripe and the political climate favourable to take a stance on a sensitive issue.[468] On the other hand, agenda-setting powers may equally present risks. More specifically, courts may be biased, denying unprivileged actors the opportunity

---

463 N Bürli, 'Amicus Curiae as a Means to Reinforce the Legitimacy of the European Court of Human Rights' in S Flogaitis, T Zwart and J Fraser (eds.), *The European Court of Human Rights and its Discontents* (Edward Elgar 2013), 139–40.

464 See: the US Judiciary Act of 1925 (43 Stat. 936); D Fontana, 'Docket Control and the Success of Constitutional Courts' in T Ginsburg and R Dixon (eds.), *Comparative Constitutional Law* (Edward Elgar 2011), 631; and M Rosenfeld, 'The United States of America' in J Bell and M-L Paris (eds.), *Right-Based Constitutional Review: Constitutional Courts in a Changing Landscape* (Edward Elgar 2016).

465 D Fontana, ibid., 627.

466 HW Perry, *Deciding to Decide: Agenda Setting in the United States Supreme Court* (Harvard University Press 1991), 136.

467 For an overview, see D Fontana, 'Docket Control and the Success of Constitutional Courts' in T Ginsburg and R Dixon (eds.), *Comparative Constitutional Law* (Edward Elgar 2011), 624–41.

468 A Dyevre, 'Unifying the Field of Comparative Judicial Politics: Towards a General Theory on Judicial Behaviour (2010) 2 European Political Science Review, 297, 319; CH Mendes, *Constitutional Courts and Deliberative Democracy* (Oxford University Press 2013), 160–1; and T Roux, *The Politics of Principle: the First South African Constitutional Court, 1995–2005* (Cambridge University Press 2013), 366.

to raise constitutional issues. Also, the court may avoid scrutinising politically controversial cases, while the system of checks and balances might necessitate a more intense review in those cases. In Belgium, not as many cases are brought before the BeCC as compared, for example, with the USSC.[469] Hence, a distribution of temporal resources is currently not necessary to guarantee the quality of the review procedure. In conclusion, in the Belgian context, the arguments against docket control currently prevail over its potential benefits.

2.5. INVESTIGATIVE POSSIBILITIES

2.5.1. THE 'BROADEST' INVESTIGATIVE POSSIBILITIES

From 1983 onwards, the BeCC has possessed the 'broadest' investigative possibilities.[470] More specifically, the BeCC is allowed: to exchange correspondence with the Prime Minister of the federal level and the Minister-President of the subnational entities or any other public entity; to demand documents or information from the parties or public entities; to hear any person who may have useful information; to make on-site observations; and to appoint experts. Moreover, in the preparatory documents, it was argued that the Court's competences are not limited to these 'examples'. In principle, anything is possible, except for actions that are contrary to the law (e.g. organising a referendum).[471] These competences belong to the Court itself and, in principle, not to individual judges, although delegations are allowed. In practice, the judge-rapporteur, who writes the first draft, may suggest actions to the Court. After these have been executed, the rapporteur should report on them to the Court.[472] Without much further debate between government officials, the article introducing these competences was adopted unanimously.[473]

The BeCC has stated it can only use these competences when they are necessary to answer the legal questions in a particular case. Also, it considers taking such measures only useful for the collection of factual information that is relevant to the case.[474] It has been argued that this excludes the collection

469 The US Supreme Court gets about 7000 requests to hear cases per year (from which around 80 are decided by full opinion), while the BeCC handles all cases brought before the court, an average of 100 per year (although this has increased over the years).

470 Article 74 of the Special Act.

471 Report of 30 March 1983 from the commission on constitutional and institutional reform, about the draft law on the composition, competence and functioning of the constitutional court, *Parl Doc* Senate no 246/2, 215.

472 Ibid., 210.

473 Ibid., 215.

474 BeCC case no 29/2010, 18 March 2010, B.4.

of information from experts and academics.[475] Except for certain questions requiring further clarification or documentation,[476] the BeCC rarely makes use of these possibilities.[477]

2.5.2. EVALUATION

In general, it is said that constitutional courts should take some position between an adversarial and inquisitorial procedure.[478] An adversarial procedure – where courts simply mediate between the information brought forward by the involved parties – guarantees that all cases are dealt with fairly. However, the specific nature of constitutional questions may require a more active approach. Instead of distributing rights and duties in a bilateral dispute, constitutional courts need to answer more complex questions with potentially far-reaching consequences. Many normative assumptions (underlying the challenged legislation) need empirical clarification.[479] The judges usually do not possess specialised knowledge in all the issues brought before them.[480] Therefore, specific mechanisms to challenge arguments and invite further response enhance its deliberative potential immensely.[481]

In Belgium, appropriate rules exist that make the Court able to collect such information from the parties and through its own motion. Such an inquisitorial procedure is believed to be more likely to produce the correct decision.[482] Conversely, if the Court functions in an adversarial rather than an open-ended and interactive way, its deliberative potential would decline considerably.[483] Yet the BeCC rarely uses its inquisitorial competences. A possible reason is

---

475 E Maes, *De Rol van een Grondwettelijk Hof in Rechtsstatelijk Perspectief* (KULeuven, Institute for Constitutional Law 2016), 513.

476 For example: BeCC case no 29/1996, 15 May 1996; and BeCC case no 89/2011, 31 May 2011.

477 For a discussion, see E Maes, *De Rol van een Grondwettelijk Hof in Rechtsstatelijk Perspectief* (KULeuven, Institute for Constitutional Law 2016), 512.

478 CH Mendes, *Constitutional Courts and Deliberative Democracy* (Oxford University Press 2013), 163; and K Möller, *The Global Model of Constitutional Rights* (Oxford University Press 2012), 131.

479 See *supra*, section 1.3.2.4. on 'rational justification' as a key ingredient of deliberative performance.

480 JK Staton and G Vanberg, 'The Value of Vagueness: Delegation, Defiance and Judicial Opinions' (2008) 52 American Journal of Political Science, 504, 506.

481 CH Mendes, *Constitutional Courts and Deliberative Democracy* (Oxford University Press 2013), 163; and K Möller, *The Global Model of Constitutional Rights* (Oxford University Press 2012), 131.

482 G Cumming, *Expert Evidence Deficiencies in the Judgments of the Court of the European Union and the European Court of Human Rights* (Kluwer 2014), 22; and A Vermeule, *Law and the Limits of Reason* (Oxford University Press 2009), 152.

483 CH Mendes, *Constitutional Courts and Deliberative Democracy* (Oxford University Press 2013), 163.

that judges might fear that inviting certain experts would indicate prejudice. Also, evaluating expert evidence may be a difficult exercise because the judges are usually not familiar with the statistical language used in such documents (see *supra*, section 1.3.2.4.). Yet without asking for expert advice, there is a risk that the Court may not always produce well-informed and well-reasoned judgments. This does not only impede the Court from fulfilling its deliberative role, some even argue that it may lead to a breach in effective judicial protection.[484]

Another court that has similar inquisitorial competences, but does not hesitate to use them, is the German Constitutional Court. In particular, if useful, this court invites statements from experts (e.g. the Statistical Bureau) or societal groups. The parties involved in the procedure are given the opportunity to express their opinion on these statements.[485] Not all courts are allowed to question witnesses or hear evidence. Yet, when cases are argued up from lower courts – as is the case in South Africa and the US – the supreme court can consider the record of the evidence of the original court that heard the matter.[486] This allows the constitutional conversation to develop over time.[487] In addition, both the SACC and USSC allow *amici curiae* to present evidence to the court. Hence, further investigative possibilities may be less necessary when the system also ensures that a variety of arguments can be heard by the court.

2.6. SANCTIONING POSSIBILITIES

2.6.1. A LIMITED SET OF LEGAL SANCTIONING POSSIBILITIES

In principle, the Special Act only allows the BeCC to either (partially) annul or uphold legislation in response to an annulment request, or declare it (un)constitutional in response to a preliminary reference.[488]

As of their publication in the 'Official Belgian Journal' (*Belgisch Staatsblad*), the annulment judgments have final and binding effect. When the actions for annulment are accepted, the annulled legislation disappears retroactively from the legal system. By adopting this as the rule, the Belgian legislator granted

---

484 In the European context, Cumming adds that it may also lead to a violation of article 6(1) ECHR: see G Cumming, *Expert Evidence Deficiencies in the Judgments of the Court of the Europeion Union and the European Court of Human Rights* (Kluwer 2014), 73.

485 D Grimm, 'Proportionality in Canadian and German Constitutional Jurisprudence' (2007) 57 University of Toronto Law Review, 383, 391.

486 Rule 19 of the SACC statute explicitly states that "the appeal record shall consist of the judgment of the court from which the appeal is noted, together with all the documentation lodged by the parties in that court and all the evidence which may have been led in the proceedings and which may be relevant to the issues that are to be determined."

487 VF Comella, *Constitutional Courts and Democratic Values* (Yale University Press 2009), 58.

488 Article 8 (annulment procedure) and 26 §1 (preliminary question) of the Special Act.

priority to the principle of legality.[489] However, when appropriate, the Court can moderate the retroactive effect of an annulment.[490] Such outcomes can be identified as 'temporal modulations'. In particular, the Court can either give its decision an effect *ex nunc*, thus maintaining the validity of the legislation until the date of the publication of the annulment, or impose an effect *pro future*, thus provisionally maintaining the validity of the legislation.[491] The latter outcome gives the legislator a delay to 'repair' unconstitutional legislation. When the challenges are dismissed, the judgment is nevertheless binding on the courts with respect to the points of law settled by the Court. Yet this does not exclude the possibility of the legislation being challenged anew through a preliminary reference.[492]

A preliminary ruling does not have the same *erga omnes* effect as annulment judgments.[493] According to the Special Act, the referring court and any other court of law passing judgment in the same case should comply with the ruling.[494] Nevertheless, the preliminary rulings do have a 'reinforced authority'. Ordinary courts can dispense of their obligation to refer a constitutional question to the BeCC when there has already been a similar judgment, under the condition of compliance with that judgment.[495] A similar possibility of moderating a declaration of unconstitutionality in time was, until recently, not legally provided in preliminary procedures. Despite the lack of legal basis, the BeCC assumed, for the first time in case no 125/2011,[496] that in exceptional circumstances it has the power to proclaim a temporal modulation in a preliminary ruling. This judicially-created sanctioning possibility was validated by the legislator.[497]

2.6.2. EVALUATION

A deliberative court is expected to engage with a variety of strategies to communicate its rulings to other actors, such as the legislator, ordinary courts

---

489 S Verstraelen, 'The Temporal Limitation of Judicial Decisions: The Need for Flexibility Versus the Quest for Uniformity' (2013) 14 German Law Journal, 1687, 1693.

490 Article 8 of the Special Act: "Where the Court so deems necessary, it shall, by a general ruling, specify which effects of the nullified provisions are to be considered maintained or be provisionally maintained for the period appointed by the Court."

491 S Verstraelen, ibid., 1697.

492 MF Rigaux and B Renauld, *La Cour Constitutionelle* (Bruylant 2009), 228.

493 M De Visser, who studied the framework of a variety of European constitutional courts, states that Belgium is the only court where the invalidation of legislation does not always have *erga omnes* effect: M De Visser, *Constitutional Review in Europe: A Comparative Analysis* (Hart Publishing 2014), 309, 312.

494 Article 28 of the Special Act.

495 MF Rigaux and B Renauld, *La Cour Constitutionelle* (Bruylant 2009), 257.

496 BeCC case no 125/2011, 7 July 2015.

497 In particular, the law of 25 December 2016 introduced a second paragraph in article 28 of the Special Act on the Constitutional Court.

and the public in general. A diverse set of sanctioning modalities provides the opportunity to improve the deliberative quality of future legislative decisions. Shapiro and Stone Sweet call this the 'pedagogical authority' of past jurisprudence. In that regard, the sanctioning possibilities available to the BeCC are rather limited. In particular, by simply disapproving of the challenged legislation, the Court does not always provide a 'road map' on how to enact a new statute in conformity with the Constitution.[498]

Yet, as will be discussed in chapter 5, the BeCC has created an extensive set of 'modulated outcomes' to communicate with its audience. Constitutional courts in many other countries have developed similar methods. For instance, courts across continental Europe have embraced the technique of 'constitution-conforming interpretation'.[499] Generally, this means that if legislation can be interpreted in different ways, only the one which ensures its compatibility with the Constitution must be followed. Yet sometimes these courts stretch the meaning of a 'conciliatory interpretation' and use it as a tool to modify the actual content of legislation in order to avoid an overruling of the legislation. In particular, they use this technique to extend or limit the reach of the law.[500] Some courts also formulate substantive requirements in their rulings, with which the new statute must comply.[501] Outside Europe, there are also courts that take refuge in creative sanctioning modalities in between the simple acceptation or overruling of legislation. In the US, for instance, the technique of 'constitution-conforming interpretation' is known as the 'avoidance canon', because the court would avoid addressing the actual constitutional question.[502] Yet this disguises the fact that, by using this canon, judges may creatively change the law.[503] In addition, the USSC is known to apply methods such as 'levelling up' or 'levelling

[498] E Luna, 'Constitutional Road Maps' (2000) 90 Journal of Criminal Law and Criminology, 1125, 1128. Yet, the BeCC may offer some guidance in the motivational part of the ruling.

[499] For European countries, see: M De Visser, *Constitutional Review in Europe: a Comparative Analysis* (Hart Publishing 2014), 281 and further (e.g. chapter 6: Testing and Remedying Unconstitutionality); VF Comella, *Constitutional Courts and Democratic Values* (Yale University Press 2009), 74; M Shapiro and A Stone Sweet, *On Law, Politics and Judicialization* (Oxford University Press 2002), 63, 71–3; and A Kavanagh, *Constitutional Review under the UK Human Rights Act* (Cambridge University Press 2009), chapters 4 and 5.

[500] M De Visser, *Constitutional Review in Europe: A Comparative Analysis* (Hart Publishing 2014), 291–3.

[501] In particular, the Italian Constitutional Court proclaims '*sentenze additive di principio*': ibid., 317.

[502] For example, *Ashwander v. Tenn. Valley Auth*, 197 U.S. 288, 348 (1936). For a discussion see ES Fish, 'Choosing Constitutional Remedies' (2016) 63 UCLA Law Review, 322, 356 and further.

[503] RA Posner, 'Statutory Interpretation – in the Classroom and in the Courtroom' (1983) 50 University of Chicago Law Review, 800; EA Young, 'The Continuity of Statutory and Constitutional Interpretation: an Essay for Phil Frickey' (2010) 98 California Law Review, 1371, 1376; and ES Fish, 'Choosing Constitutional Remedies' (2016) 63 UCLA Law Review, 322, 357.

down' to modify legislation towards conformity with the Constitution.[504] The SACC equally avoids declaring legislation invalid by adopting certain 'reading strategies' that, respectively, interpret or alter the challenged legislation in a restrictive or extensive manner.[505] The SACC is also allowed to proclaim certain constitutional remedies that explicitly require specific actions. For example, it may install judicial oversight, require the engagement of the parties to discuss the case between them and report back within a certain period of time,[506] or require the government to report back on its compliance (a structural interdict).[507] These creative outcomes have a remedial function, seeking to ensure that legislation is applied in a constitutional manner. Hence, by proclaiming such outcomes, courts aim to maximise the protection of fundamental rights in each individual case. Therefore, Shapiro and Stone Sweet argue that, by using these techniques, courts can strengthen judicial control over policy outcomes.[508]

In addition to substantive modulations, the BeCC can add a temporal modulation to the ruling. When this is a modulation *pro future*, requiring that the legislator should act within a certain time limit, this sends the signal that *some* action should be taken. Other courts within Europe are also known to instruct the legislator to act within a 'reasonable time', or even set a specific deadline.[509] The USSC can equally make its judgment non-retroactive and set a time limit to give Congress the opportunity to enact new legislation (although it uses this competence rarely).[510] The SACC may also suspend its orders of invalidity to allow the legislature to repair the unconstitutional provision(s).[511] From a deliberative perspective, setting specific time limits may have benefits as well as downsides. First, they potentially increase the consequential character of the ruling by explicitly enquiring action from the legislator. By addressing the

---

504 ES Fish, ibid., 322, 348 and further.

505 L Du Plessis, 'The Status and Role of Legislation in South Africa as a Constitutional Democracy: Some Exploratory Observation' (2011) 14 Potchefstroom Electronic Law Journal, 92, 94–5.

506 Cameron argues that such orders "indicate a shift from the traditional view of adversarial litigation, in which one party 'wins' and the other party 'loses'. Forcing the parties to engage can result in beneficial compromise and reduce conflict and tension." See E Cameron, 'A South African Perspective on the Judicial Development of Socio-Economic Rights' in L Lazarus, C McCrudden and N Bowles (eds.), *Reasoning Rights: Comparative Judicial Engagement* (Hart Publishing 2014).

507 For other examples, see M Swart, 'Left out in the Cold? Crafting Constitutional Remedies for the Poorest of the Poor' (2005) 21 South African Journal on Human Rights, 215.

508 M Shapiro and A Stone Sweet, *On Law, Politics and Judicialization* (Oxford University Press 2002), 187–9.

509 M De Visser, *Constitutional Review in Europe: A Comparative Analysis* (Hart Publishing 2014), 315–16; P Popelier, S Verstraelen, D Vanheule and B Vanlerberghe, 'The Effect of Judicial Decisions in Time: Comparative Notes' in P Popelier et al. (eds.), *The Effects of Judicial Decisions in Time* (Intersentia 2014), 10.

510 ES Fish, 'Choosing Constitutional Remedies' (2016) 63 UCLA Law Review 322, 332–3, 360.

511 H Klug, *The Constitution of South Africa: a Contextual Analysis* (Hart Publishing 2010), 183.

legislator explicitly, the court engages in dialogue. Giving a set period in which to enact new legislation facilitates oversight by the public at large, making it more difficult for the legislator not to comply with the ruling. Without a specific time frame, the court leaves room for the legislator to argue that a (long) delay for compliance is reasonable.[512] However, public scrutiny after a temporal modulation may also cause problems for the court. When the strict deadline is surpassed without (a convincing) justification, this may decrease the court's authority and, in the long run, its legitimacy. Therefore, some authors argue that setting a vaguer time limit may be a better strategy to simultaneously encourage compliance and decrease the risk of the loss of authority.[513]

2.7. TRANSPARENCY

2.7.1. PUBLICATION OF AN *EX ANTE* NOTICE AND THE *EX POST* COLLECTIVE OUTCOME

The Belgian Constitutional Court guarantees the publicity of its case law, both at the beginning of the review procedure and when the final ruling is pronounced. First, when a case is lodged before the Court, the registrar arranges the publication of a notice in the Belgian Official Journal (*Belgisch Staatsblad – Moniteur Belge)*, which is accessible to all Belgian citizens. In this publication, the initiator and the subject of the action for annulment or the preliminary question are indicated. Then, when the Court has reached its final decision, the ruling – including information about the parties and their arguments – is published in the same Official Journal and on the website of the BeCC (www.const-court.be). Translation is provided in four languages: the three official Belgian languages – Dutch, French and German[514] – and recently a selection of rulings have also become available in English.[515] This therefore allows citizens to consult the Court's case law online.

Other than making public the outcome of the case, the Court is not legally obliged to follow a certain argumentative framework or make public the sources that served to develop the Court's reasoning. Yet, as will be discussed

---

512 D Hausman, 'Government Noncompliance with Constitutional Court Orders in South Africa' in L Bartels and CW Bonneau, *Making Law and Courts Research Relevant* (Routledge 2014), 184.

513 JK Staton and G Vanberg, 'The Value of Vagueness: Delegation, Defiance and Judicial Opinions' (2008) 52 American Journal of Political Science, 504.

514 However, judgments following preliminary questions are no longer translated into German (except if the question was raised in German).

515 More precisely, a complete English translation is available for two cases from 2015. In addition, the BeCC has published a summary of a selection of cases from 1985–2014, for the purpose of the CODICES database of the Venice Commission.

in chapters 6 and 7, the Court usually does underpin its rulings with extensive reasons. Also, the BeCC publishes other relevant information on its website. This effort facilitates the accessibility of its case law. For example, the Court publishes a yearly report with the important cases and some general statistics, press communiqués, academic studies, etc. In addition, it is possible to search the whole body of opinions based on certain tracking words. Finally, the BeCC regularly sends out (electronic) newsletters to anyone who subscribes to them. In these letters, an overview is given of recent rulings, together with some basic information on the case, such as the procedure, subject and outcome. This allows citizens, legal entities, politicians or other interested actors to filter through the Court's case law. Several previous presidents of the BeCC have emphasised during their inauguration speeches that they wished to improve communication with Belgian citizens and the press. Concerning the yearly reports, they said that the aim was to inform the legislator about constitutional problems. They also wanted to make the justification of their rulings as explicit and clear as possible. The aim was to strengthen the legitimacy of the BeCC and the social acceptability of its rulings.[516]

Notwithstanding the publication of the majority opinion and additional information online, it remains difficult to evaluate how the decision is made. Deliberations and the voting processes among the judges are kept secret, and decisions are expressed in a single voice without dissenting opinions. The ruling includes the names of all judges who deliberated on the case (the number of which depends on panel size, see *supra*, section 2.3.), but not their individual votes. Hence, there is no means to know whether the decision was adopted with a simple majority or rather with unanimity.

However, when the BeCC was established, the Council of State suggested introducing concurring opinions if there was an agreement on the final dictum, but not on the substantiating motives. In its advisory opinion on the law establishing the Court, the Council of State argued that this might make it easier for the judges to agree on the dictum and referred to the common law system, the German Constitutional Court and the ECtHR, where this practice was already accepted.[517] An amendment was suggested to introduce such minority opinions, with the intention of avoiding the risk that judges would vote collectively, without taking responsibility by clarifying the justificatory ground for the decision. It was argued that, should an individual judge be able to write a separate opinion, this would force the majority to argue more extensively why they do not agree

516 The speech by president Jean Spreutels during the formal hearing on the occasion of his inauguration, 26 June 2013, and the speech by president André Alen during the formal hearing on the occasion of his inauguration, 5 February 2013.

517 Advisory opinion of the Council of State of 25 March 1981 on the draft of the law concerning the composition, competence and functioning of the Court of Arbitration, *Parl Doc* Senate no 704/1, 53.

with this minority opinion. Nonetheless, the government official responsible for the institutional reform replied that the concept was not suitable for the BeCC. It would be dangerous to allow such opinions, considering the delicate nature of the cases brought before the Court (at the time, only conflicts between national and subnational entities). It was additionally argued that separate opinions would conflict with the Belgian legal tradition. Also, the government official argued that this would threaten the objective of the constitutional debate, since judges would be more concerned about how their functioning is perceived by their linguistic community or the politicians that supported their nomination.[518] The amendment was not adopted and the system introduced was such as still exists today: rulings are published as a single majority opinion with no further information on the judges' individual preferences.

2.7.2. EVALUATION

In principle, all the BeCC's rulings are accessible online to any Belgian citizen (and anyone who understands one of the three official Belgian languages). This allows them to evaluate which pleas were raised by the involved parties, and whether these claims were accepted and why. Nonetheless, other constitutional or supreme courts allow for an even wider accessibility regarding their jurisprudence. More specifically, preparatory or other documents may be added to the online publication. On the website of the USSC, for example, one can find transcripts and audio fragments of the oral arguments before the court.[519] The SACC, in turn, prepares a media summary before the oral arguments and another for distribution after pronouncing its decision. The press may attend hearings and cameras in fixed positions are usually allowed in court throughout a hearing.[520] However, placing a great amount of information online does not necessarily enhance transparency, particularly when it diminishes the clarity of what has actually been decided by the court.[521]

Another institutional facilitator that is believed to increase transparency on constitutional case law is the publishing of separate opinions. Next to the majority opinion, many systems allow judges to write either a dissenting opinion (when they do not agree with the majority outcome) or a concurring

518 Report of 30 March 1983 from the commission on constitutional and institutional reform, about the draft law on the composition, competence and functioning of the constitutional court, *Parl Doc* Senate no 246/2, 194 and further.

519 For more information, see http://www.supremecourt.gov/.

520 For more information, see http://www.constitutionalcourt.org.za/site/thecourt/role.htm.

521 P Popelier and AA Patiño Álvarez, 'Deliberative Practices of Constitutional Courts in Consolidated and Non-Consolidated Democracies' in P Popelier, A Mazmanyan and W Vandenbruwaene (eds.), *The Role of Constitutional Courts in Multilevel Governance* (Intersentia 2013), 221.

opinion (when they do agree with the outcome but on different grounds). In continental Europe, only some countries have accepted this practice, and even then judges seem reluctant to actually write individual opinions.[522] Principles of collegiality and secrecy of deliberation seem especially strongly rooted in this legal tradition. Separate opinions are also allowed and somewhat more frequent in the SACC.[523] Yet this practice appears most frequently in countries with a common law tradition. The USSC judges, for instance, rarely publish judgments that are unanimously accepted by all nine judges.[524]

Some authors argue that more transparency on the reasoning process of the BeCC would further enhance the BeCC's deliberative potential.[525] Currently, the secrecy surrounding the internal deliberation process and the prohibition of separate opinions make it difficult to evaluate how the BeCC's opinions come about. Some argue that allowing separate opinions would lead to a better understanding of the judgment and would raise the legal consciousness of society. The dissenting opinion helps to integrate society by showing respect to minority opinions. The dissent reflects that a plurality of opinions exists in a democratic society. Moreover, this would promote public debate by opening dialogue among the judges, between the judges and legal scholars, and between the commentators of court judgments and the legislator, etc. In that sense, dissenting opinions can enrich democratic conversation by signalling that there is room for evolution and reconsideration.[526] Hence, they may serve as inspiration in future legislative or judicial discussions.[527] In addition to the public dialogue dimension, dissenting opinions are also instruments of the

522 A Dyevre, 'Unifying the Field of Comparative Judicial Politics: Towards a General Theory on Judicial Behaviour (2010) European Political Science Review, 297, 301.

523 JL Gibson and GA Caldeira, 'Defenders of Democracy? Legitimacy, Popular Acceptance, and the South African Constitutional Court' (2003) 65 The Journal of Politics, 1, 6.

524 This has always been the case: see LM Friedman et al., 'State Supreme Courts: A Century of Citation' (1981) 33 Stanford Law Review, 773, 786. More recent information can be found at https://www.supremecourt.gov/opinions/opinions.aspx.

525 P Popelier and AA Patiño Álvarez, 'Deliberative Practices of Constitutional Courts in Consolidated and Non-Consolidated Democracies' in P Popelier, A Mazmanyan and W Vandenbruwaene (eds.), *The Role of Constitutional Courts in Multilevel Governance* (Intersentia 2013), 219. For a discussion on separate opinions within the Belgian context, see: B Nelissen, 'Judicial Loyalty Through Dissent or Why The Timing is Perfect for Belgium to Embrace Separate Opinions' (2011) 15 EJCL; S Feyen, 'Afwijkende Meningsuitingen in het Belgische Grondwettelijk Hof: Mensenrechtelijk Beschermd, Wenselijk of Gevaarlijk?' in A Alen and J Theunis, *Leuvense Staatsrechtelijke Standpunten* (die Keure 2012), 229–88; and E Maes, *De rol van een Grondwettelijk Hof in Rechtsstatelijk Perspectief* (KULeuven, Institute for Constitutional Law 2016).

526 VF Comella, *Constitutional Courts and Democratic Values* (Yale University Press 2009), 49; CA White and I Boussiakou, 'Separate Opinions in the European Court of Human Rights' (2009) 9 Human Rights Law Review, 37; and K Kelemen, 'Dissenting Opinions in Constitutional Courts' (2013) German Law Journal, 14, 1345, 1352.

527 E Maes, *De Rol van een Grondwettelijk Hof in Rechtsstatelijk Perspectief* (KULeuven, Institute for Constitutional Law 2016), 545.

deliberative ideal in the sense that they can increase the intensity of the internal debate. Judges would try to persuade each other in order to form a majority on the court, increasing the quality of their reason-giving.[528]

Yet dissenting opinions may also result in deliberative failures. It is argued that the presence of separate opinions leads to rulings that are opaque and ambiguous, and therefore hinder the development of the law.[529] Dissenting opinions would, contradicting the argument above, cause unnecessary confusion in understanding the judgment and reduce its persuasiveness.[530] For example, suggestions on how future legislation should be altered have limited instrumental value when published in a dissenting opinion.[531] These suggestions offer little encouragement to law-makers as they lack the support of the majority of the judges. Therefore, when implementing these suggestions in new legislation, the law-makers would not even be sure that this legislation would survive a new challenge before the constitutional court.[532] Separate opinions suggest that decisions are the product of each judge's personal predilection, rather than a rational deduction based on the facts and 'the law'.[533] If the ruling does not have (enough) consequential potential, dissenting opinions may undercut legal certainty and predictability. In the long run, this might cause a problem for the legitimacy of the Court itself. In addition, allowing separate opinions would create an environment favouring individualistic behaviour rather than cooperation among the justices.[534] Instead of stimulating judicial discussion, allowing dissent would incite judges to stubbornly concentrate on their own arguments. Conversely, a collegial dynamic is needed to guarantee the quality of the internal deliberation process and, therefore, of the outcome of this process.

---

528 Ibid., 552; and W Mastor, 'L'Effet Performative des Opinions Séparées sur la Motivation des Decisions Constitutionnelles Majoritaires' in F Hourquebie and MC Pontoreau (eds.), *La Motivation des Decisions des Cours Suprêmes et Cours Constitutionelles* (Bruylant 2012), 89–90.

529 CH Mendes, *Constitutional Courts and Deliberative Democracy* (Oxford University Press 2013), 171; and MC Ponthoreau, 'L'Énigme de la Motivation Encore et Toujours L'Éclairage Comparatif' in F Hourquebie and MC Pontoreau (eds.), *La Motivation des Decisions des Cours Suprêmes et Cours Constitutionelles* (Bruylant 2012), 20.

530 W Mastor, 'L'Effet Performative des Opinions Séparées sur la Motivation des Decisions Constitutionnelles Majoritaires' in F Hourquebie and MC Pontoreau (eds.), *La Motivation des Decisions des Cours Suprêmes et Cours Constitutionelles* (Bruylant 2012), 92.

531 RC Black et al., *US Supreme Court Opinions and Their Audiences* (Cambridge University Press 2016), 22.

532 E Luna, 'Constitutional Road Maps' (2000) 90 Journal of Criminal Law and Criminology, 1125, 1207.

533 LM Friedman et al., 'State Supreme Courts: A Century of Citation' (1981) 33 Stanford Law Review, 773, 785; FB Cross et al., 'Citations in the U.S. Supreme Court: an Empirical Study of their Use and Significance' (2010) 2 University of Illinois Law Review, 533, 546; and S Dothan, *Reputation and Judicial Tactics* (Cambridge University Press 2015), 39.

534 A Dyevre, 'Unifying the Field of Comparative Judicial Politics: Towards a General Theory on Judicial Behaviour' (2010) European Political Science Review, 297, 319.

In Belgium, it is additionally argued that the existence of dissenting opinions would conflict with the Court's consensual composition and functioning. Dissenting opinions would potentially threaten the acceptance of the Court's decisions in both linguistic communities.[535] In controversial cases, courts are believed to have an interest in projecting unity by avoiding dissent.[536] Although this risk may not be overestimated, a dissenting opinion may add fuel to political or public conflicts. Recently, the current Dutch-speaking and French-speaking presidents of the BeCC confirmed that they agree with the arguments of opponents of separate opinions. More specifically, they stated that they understand and support the legislator's choice to exclude these possibilities.[537]

Since dissenting opinions remain a very difficult issue in Belgium, Maes has recently suggested an 'in between' solution. To decrease the possibility of political tension as a reaction to the dissenting opinion, she argues that judges should be allowed to publish their separate opinions anonymously.[538] This would allow the Court to continue to play its 'pacifying' role, without ignoring the existence of a plurality of opinions in a society like Belgium. However, this author is not convinced that the Court's public would be unable to attribute the opinions to a specific judge or, maybe more importantly, a judicial sub-group, even if the anonymity rule is strictly respected. In a country where little is needed to incentivise political conflict, a majority opinion – provided it is well-reasoned – may calm public opinion and bring together those who would otherwise continue to disagree. Also, the collegial dynamics within the court encourage the judges to transcend their individual preferences in search of a reasonable compromise. This does not mean that minority arguments should be set aside, but that they should be integrated and addressed by the Court, instead of being discussed separately. As mentioned before, the circle of arguments that characterises the deliberative exercise is believed to produce high quality outcomes.

2.8. THE PROSPECTS OF DELIBERATION

With an understanding of the institutional devices of the Belgian Constitutional Court, it becomes clear which 'judicial good practices' related to the key

[535] P Popelier and AA Patiño Álvarez, 'Deliberative Practices of Constitutional Courts in Consolidated and Non-Consolidated Democracies' in P Popelier, A Mazmanyan and W Vandenbruwaene (eds.), *The Role of Constitutional Courts in Multilevel Governance* (Intersentia 2013), 221.

[536] S Dothan, *Reputation and Judicial Tactics* (Cambridge University Press 2015), 39.

[537] The speech by president Jean Spreutels during the formal hearing on the occasion of his inauguration, 26 June 2013, and the speech by president André Alen during the formal hearing on the occasion of his inauguration, 5 February 2013.

[538] E Maes, *De Rol van een Grondwettelijk Hof in Rechtsstatelijk Perspectief* (KULeuven, Institute for Constitutional Law 2016), 569.

ingredients of deliberative performance are within reach and which are not. Yet, some of the institutional rules discussed above may limit the possibility of evaluating these 'good practices'. Hence, this section explains which aspects of the Court's case law can be scrutinised from a deliberative angle in the empirical part of this book.

First, the requirement of an external initiative and the lack of agenda-setting powers make it difficult for the BeCC to control the inclusiveness of the procedure. An internal initiative by the Court or a mobilisation of others to challenge legislation is not allowed because this would introduce the risk of partiality. Hence, the range of viewpoints that reach the Court ultimately depends on who is willing to participate in the review procedure. As mentioned before, the requirement to demonstrate an interest in the case is interpreted broadly. In addition, the Court can demand further information or documentation from those already involved in the procedure, or may hear experts, but it rarely uses these competences. Finally, the BeCC has very limited control over its docket. Except for the 'limited procedure' for specific situations, the BeCC has no control over its case load. In conclusion, it is the shared responsibility of all participants involved to provide input for the forthcoming decision.

This does not mean that a study of the actors involved in the Court's review procedures is without interest. First, the participation of different types of initiating and intervening parties reflects how the Court's role is perceived, and how this may have evolved over the years. Also, the normative ideal of inclusiveness does not only relate to the active inclusion of a wide range of perspectives, but also implies an equal responsiveness to all those involved. Hence, an alternative approach could be to analyse how participation is linked with other aspects of the ruling (see chapters 5, 6 and 7).

The second key ingredient relates to the internal deliberation process, which should be defined by a collegial exchange of arguments. It is likely that the Court's decisions reflect negotiations that have occurred during different stages of the decision-making process.[539] However, it is difficult to investigate directly how the judges interact with each other, considering the secrecy of deliberation and the absence of dissenting opinions. Although the written decision may be considered as the embellished re-articulation of this internal phase, it should be noted that making statements about the deliberation process based on patterns that seem to appear in the Court's case law remains speculative.

The transparency and rationality of the justification form the third and fourth key ingredients. The evaluation of the institutional framework shows that the BeCC has a wide discretion to formulate the justificatory ground

[539] TH Hammond, CW Bonneau and RS Sheehan, *Strategic Behavior and Policy Choice on the U.S. Supreme Court* (Stanford University Press 2005), 39; and L Baum, *Judges and Their Audiences: a Perspective on Judicial Behaviour* (Princeton University Press 2006), 51.

for its rulings. As mentioned, courts may enhance the quality of this justification by the consistent application of a fixed argumentative framework and by citing persuasive and relevant authorities to underpin the judgment. Ultimately, the ruling should clarify whether and why the challenged legislation is compatible with the Constitution or not. An evaluation of the transparency and rationality of the justification will involve a citation analysis (chapter 6), as well as an examination of the Court's use of the proportionality analysis (chapter 7).

Finally, the fifth ingredient relates to the dialogue dimension of constitutional adjudication. The BeCC has wide discretionary powers to address the legislator. More specifically, the BeCC has developed – within the boundaries of the institutional framework – diverse methods of formulating an answer to a question of constitutionality. In addition, the justificatory ground may prompt the legislator to react to the ruling, or to improve the quality of legislation more generally. For instance, the BeCC can point out that a deficiency in the parliamentary procedure has led to constitutional infringement. Hence, the evaluation of the dialogue dimension of the Court's case law should include an analysis of the variety of sanctioning modalities (chapter 5), as well as of specific aspects of the justificatory ground (chapters 6 and 7).

2.9. CONCLUSION: A VENUE FOR DELIBERATION IN A CONSOCIATIONAL SETTING

When analysing the institutional design of the Belgian Constitutional Court, the conclusion is that it has developed into a fully-fledged human rights court with considerable deliberative potential. Important features of a deliberative institution are: composition rules that reflect societal heterogeneity, wide access possibilities, a collegial internal decision-making process, a broad set of reference norms and a variety of communication strategies to stimulate constitutional dialogue with other actors in the democratic polity.

Considering the wide accessibility of the Court, extrajudicial actors, who may be frustrated with failed attempts of the legislator, have the opportunity to bring their claim before the Court. Hence, it is likely that the Court will be asked to adjudicate on politically charged or otherwise controversial matters.[540] When it does, it has considerable potential to fulfil the deliberative expectations mentioned in the normative framework. Importantly, it has the right tools at hand in order to act as a deliberative institution. Moreover, the fact that

540 I Unah and AM Hancock, 'U.S. Supreme Court Decision Making, Case Salience and the Attitudinal Model' (2006) 28 Law & Policy, 295, 299–300; F Maltzman, JE Spriggs and PJ Wahlbeck, *Crafting Law on the Supreme Court: The Collegial Game* (Cambridge University Press, 2000), throughout.

it interprets some of its competences broadly suggests that it is willing to be responsive to these constitutional claims.

However, further improvements would enhance its deliberative potential. As explained above, allowing for the possibility for *amici curiae* – without a direct interest in the case, but with useful information and particularly expert evidence – to participate would enable a more in-depth evaluation of the constitutional question.

Notwithstanding that the continuing expansion of the BeCC's competences demonstrates the trust of the legislator in the added value of constitutional review, the preparatory parliamentary documents equally reflect the ambiguous relation between consociationalism and constitutional adjudication. In particular, politicians were initially reluctant to create a fully-fledged constitutional court because this could threaten their policy freedom, especially regarding consociational package deals.[541] The legislator's concern that review procedures may impact on (super)majoritarian compromises is reflected in the Court's institutional design. When the Court was established, government officials stated that only if the BeCC showed itself trustworthy when executing this delicate task could it grow into a genuine constitutional court.[542] The legislator installed a court with a restricted set of reference norms, introduced limited access possibilities and established the double parity rule. The first two elements were repeatedly loosened in several reforms, but the composition rules remained untouched, even though several politicians criticised them in the run-up to these reforms. Hence, the decision-making process of the BeCC – as with many other European constitutional courts – is constrained by a collegial dynamic between judges with various backgrounds. This should guarantee that the BeCC takes into account policy considerations during its decision-making process. Importantly, the rationale behind this evolution and the double parity balance may still weigh on the BeCC. In the next chapter, it is discussed in more detail how such external factors may affect the Court's decision-making.

541 This protection of the legislator's prerogatives was one of the main purposes of the BeCC's limited competences: see the report of the plenary session of 14 June 1988, *Parl Doc* Senate no 22, 470.

542 For example: the report of 8 June 1988 from the commission on constitutional and institutional reform by Lallemand and Leemans, about the reform of article 107*ter* of the Constitution, *Parl Doc* Senate no 100-3/2, 11–12; and the report of the plenary session of 14 June 1988, *Parl Doc* Senate no 22, 470–1.

CHAPTER 3

VARIATION OF JUDICIAL BEHAVIOUR WITHIN THE INSTITUTIONAL BOUNDARIES

3.1. INTRODUCTION

In the previous chapter, the institutional contours of the BeCC's judicial behaviour were discussed. A few important conclusions could be drawn. On the one hand, the BeCC has considerable potential to fulfil the deliberative expectations that weigh on it. However, the parliamentary documents also demonstrated that the Court's competences could only be expanded if the BeCC showed itself to be a 'reliable' partner. The rationale behind this evolution, in particular that the BeCC is expected to act prudently when a judicial outcome would impact upon political prerogatives, may still weigh on the Court. To fully comprehend the role of the Court within the Belgian democratic polity, it should be elucidated to what extent expectations such as these might still weigh on the Court's decision-making process. The Court might attain or frustrate those expectations in different cases, revealing which incentives surround its decision-making process.

Each judicial decision is the transformation of inputs – challenging or supportive of the legislation under review – into outputs. More specifically, it is said that "judges' decisions are a function of what they prefer to do, tempered by what they think they ought to do, but constrained by what they perceive is feasible to do".[543] There is a large body of scholarship, especially in the US, aiming to explain the choices justices make.[544] The basic assumption of these scholars is that justices are committed to a vision on public policy, and that the desire to maximise their effectiveness drives their actions.[545]

---

543 JL Gibson, 'From Simplicity to Complexity: The Development of Theory in the Study of Judicial Behavior' (1983) 5 Political Behavior, 7, 9.

544 See *supra*, footnotes 2 and 3. Although US scholars are still dominant in this field, in the last few years there has been more and more studies on law and courts in other countries. For example, see T Roux, *The Politics of Principle: the First South African Constitutional Court, 1995–2005* (Cambridge University Press 2013).

545 L Baum, *Judges and Their Audiences: a Perspective on Judicial Behaviour* (Princeton University Press 2006), 5–11; and A Dyevre, 'Unifying the Field of Comparative Judicial Politics: Towards a General Theory on Judicial Behaviour' (2010) 2 European Political Science Review, 297, 311.

Through empirically analysing judicial behaviour, of the US Supreme Court in particular, they have amassed evidence indicating that justices actually seek to achieve, and strategically act to secure, this particular goal. The envisioned judicial target is believed to be centred on law or politics, or a combination of both.[546] The traditionally dominant models of judicial behaviour – labelled legal, attitudinal and strategic – each emphasise one aspect of these targets.

This chapter, drawing upon these theories on judicial behaviour, explains why strategic actions may be expected from the BeCC. In particular, it is argued that in salient cases, the formulation of the ruling – the outcome as well as the justificatory ground – is likely to be affected by strategic considerations regarding the anticipated behaviour of other actors involved in the broader policy arena. Although the Court's decision-making is undoubtedly affected by a blend of factors (legal, ideological, etc),[547] the incorporation of the logic of the strategic model can significantly enhance our understanding of the BeCC's behaviour and of the behaviour of constitutional courts in continental Europe in general.

3.2. MODELLING JUDICIAL BEHAVIOUR

3.2.1. THE LEGAL, ATTITUDINAL AND STRATEGIC MODELS

Although the literature on judicial behaviour is diverse and continuously evolving,[548] scholars usually adhere to one of three *traditional* models – legal, attitudinal or strategic – to explain the choices judges make.[549] All three models are based on the general assumption that judges (micro level) or courts (macro level) aim to contribute to 'good policy', although the focus in each model is different with regard to what such policy entails and how this shapes judicial behaviour.

First, according to the strictly legal model, judges aim to accurately interpret and apply the law, without taking into account other considerations. As a sort

546 As Mendes stated, "Courts are empowered by the normative directives of law and constrained by the forces of politics." CH Mendes, *Constitutional Courts and Deliberative Democracy* (Oxford University Press 2013), 104.

547 Grossman and Wells summarise these factors as: "the value preferences of justices, the type, feasibility and potential consequences of demands made on the Court, the state of the law in a particular area, the dynamic of the collegial decision-making process, pressures from the environment and other factors": JB Grossman and RS Wells, 'Constitutional Law and Judicial Policy Making' (John Wiley & Sons 1972), 45.

548 For alternative approaches to (individual) judicial behaviour, see for example D Klein and G Mitchell (eds.), *The Psychology of Judicial Decision-Making* (Oxford University Press 2010).

549 Nonetheless, no claim to universality is attributed to one of the traditional models of judicial behaviour: A Dyevre, 'Unifying the Field of Comparative Judicial Politics: Towards a General Theory on Judicial Behaviour' (2010) 2 European Political Science Review, 297, 314. Also, all approaches have the potential to provide us with important insights into the law and courts: L Epstein and J Knight, 'Toward a Strategic Revolution in Judicial Politics: a Look Back, a Look Ahead' (2000) 53 Political Research Quarterly, 625.

of 'mechanical jurisprudence', decisions are then a function of the facts of that case in light of the meaning of statutes and the Constitution.[550] Although legal boundaries necessarily narrow the range of options the judges may select,[551] few scholars fully accept this as a *single* explanation.[552] In constitutional adjudication, such as in Belgium, many cases leave room for interpretation. Hence constitutional courts have some degree of discretion to decide how to formulate their opinions.[553]

Next, the attitudinal model puts forward a judge who acts according to his ideological preferences.[554] Proponents of this model have focused largely on the last stage of decision-making, analysing how individual justices (micro level) vote on the final opinion or write dissenting opinions. For instance, scholars studying the US Supreme Court have shown that the preponderance of judges with either a liberal or conservative background can largely explain the case outcomes during a certain period of time (as long as there is no shift in this preponderance).[555] Similarly, these judges prefer to write a separate opinion when the majority of the court is ideologically too distant from his or her personal preference.[556] However, as in many countries in continental Europe, the composition of the BeCC is strictly balanced in each case, and the decision procedure is collegial (see *supra*, sections 2.3. and 2.7.). This makes it less likely that variation between cases, on the macro level, can be accounted for by attitudinal factors.[557] Moreover, all decisions are presented to the public as

---

550 JA Segal and HJ Spaeth, *The Supreme Court and the Attitudinal Model Revisited* (Cambridge University Press 2002), 48.

551 FB Cross and BJ Nelson, 'Strategic Institutional Effects on Supreme Court Decision-making' (2001) 95 Northwestern University Law Review, 1437, 1443: "The notion that judges place some value on legal accuracy is almost inescapable." Hence, few scholars positively claim the law does *not* matter: B Friedman, 'The Politics of Judicial Review' (2005) 84 Texas Law Review, 257, 275.

552 Cross and Nelson call this the 'naïve legal model': see FB Cross and BJ Nelson, 'Strategic Institutional Effects on Supreme Court Decisionmaking' (2001) 95 Northwestern University Law Review, 1437.

553 L Baum, *Judges and Their Audiences: a Perspective on Judicial Behaviour* (Princeton University Press 2006), 8; and A Dyevre, 'Unifying the Field of Comparative Judicial Politics: Towards a General Theory on Judicial Behaviour (2010) 2 European Political Science Review, 297, 312–3.

554 JA Segal and HJ Spaeth, *The Supreme Court and the Attitudinal Model Revisited* (Cambridge University Press 2002); and I Unah and AM Hancock, 'U.S. Supreme Court Decision Making, Case Salience and the Attitudinal Model' (2006) 28 Law & Policy, 295.

555 JA Segal and HJ Spaeth, *The Supreme Court and the Attitudinal Model Revisited* (Cambridge University Press 2002).

556 A Dyevre, 'Unifying the Field of Comparative Judicial Politics: Towards a General Theory on Judicial Behaviour' (2010) 2 European Political Science Review, 297, 319.

557 Ibid., 319–20: "institutional meso variables provide an explanation for why studies of European judicial politics based on the attitudinal approach have found statistical correlations between attitudes and behaviour that are weaker than those found in research on the US Supreme Court".

a unanimous majority opinion. Hence, even though individual ideology may play a role during the internal deliberation process, it is difficult to evaluate how it affects the Court's decision-making at the aggregated macro level.[558]

Third, the strategic model suggests that judges are goal-directed actors that operate in a strategic or interdependent decision-making context. Hence, judges focus on the effects of their decisions within the context of their own court and the broader policy arena.[559] At the micro level, it is believed that judges act strategically in order to produce majority opinions as close as possible to the one they desire.[560] For instance, they will try to persuade colleagues, or even bargain with them, in order to gain support for their own views. At the macro level, the court needs the support of other (political, administrative, etc) actors to enforce its decisions. The main idea is that only by recognising their interdependency can courts maximise their effectiveness as a policy-maker, both within the context of a single case and in the long term.

One the one hand, without legal incentives to generate compliance,[561] courts need to rely on other strategies to stimulate the implementation of a particular decision.[562] To be successful in shaping policy, they need to move within a set of possible alternatives – the 'tolerance interval'[563] – acceptable to other relevant

558 Ibid., 302: "only when seperate opinions are both allowed and fairly common can researchers paint a more accurate picture of the ideological positions of individual judges".

559 Here is a selection of examples of scholars who adhere to the strategic model: MA Bailey and F Maltzman, *The Constrained Court* (Princeton University Press 2011); L Epstein, J Knight and WF Murphy, 'The Interactive Nature of Judicial Decision Making' in N Maveety (ed.), *The Pioneers of Judicial Behaviour* (University of Michigan Press 2003); WN Eskridge and PP Frickey, 'Foreword: Law as Equilibrium' (1994) Harvard Law Review, 26; JL Gibson, 'From Simplicity to Complexity: The Development of Theory in the Study of Judicial Behavior' (1983) 5 Political Behavior, 7; B Friedman, 'The Politics of Judicial Review' (2005) 84 Texas Law Review, 257, 273–4; and PT Spiller and R Gely, 'Strategic Judicial Decision Making' in GA Caldeira, RD Keleman and KE Whittington (eds.), *The Oxford Handbook of Law and Politics* (Oxford University Press 2008).

560 Baum criticises the micro level version of this model, in particular because – in his opinion – personal motives are insufficiently taken into account. See L Baum, *Judges and Their Audiences: a Perspective on Judicial Behaviour* (Princeton University Press 2006), 14 and further.

561 For this reason, many countries have adopted special mechanisms that are responsible for monitoring these opinions. For example: SS Abrahamson and G Lessard, 'Interbranch Communications: The Next Generation' in F Magnum (ed.), *Conference on Assessing the Effects of Legislation on the Workload of the Courts: Papers and Proceedings* (Diane Publishing 1995), 20; and D Hausman, 'Government Noncompliance with Constitutional Court Orders in South Africa' in L Bartels and CW Bonneau, *Making Law and Courts Research Relevant* (Routledge 2014), 184.

562 G Vanberg, *The Politics of Constitutional Review in Germany* (Cambridge University Press 2005), 177; and RC Black et al., *US Supreme Court Opinions and Their Audiences* (Cambridge University Press 2016).

563 T Roux, *The Politics of Principle: the First South African Constitutional Court, 1995–2005* (Cambridge University Press 2013), 113.

actors that play a role in the ultimate policy choice.[564] More specifically, they must think ahead to prospective consequences and anticipate the probable reactions of their audience (the legislature, other courts, litigants or the general public).[565] If they do not modify their decision accordingly, they risk seeing non-compliance with their rulings.[566] In particular, it is impossible to confidently rule out the risk of legislative override.[567] Hence, by adjusting its ruling to anticipated reactions, the court may actually enhance the consequential character of its case law, meaning its rulings have an impact on public policy.

On the other hand, the strategic model equally assumes that courts are concerned with the long-term effects of their decisions. Courts may become irrelevant for policy-making if their decisions are regularly overruled or ignored.[568] Therefore, a court will avoid overstepping the boundaries of the tolerance interval because this may weaken its legitimacy and narrow the interval for future cases. Even when a court's institutional security is relatively strong, such as in Belgium,[569] there is always a risk that the institutional framework that shapes the court's deliberative potential is modified by the legislator. By acting strategically, the court enhances its capacity to continue its institutional role over the long run.[570] Indeed, although such behaviour may partly be based on institutional self-interest, it is also based on the (moral) concern to preserve the reputation of constitutional courts and the Constitution they uphold.[571]

---

564 B Friedman 'The Politics of Judicial Review' (2005) 84 Texas Law Review, 257, 311; T Roux, *The Politics of Principle: the First South African Constitutional Court, 1995-2005* (Cambridge University Press 2013), 29, 31, 67.

565 KE Whittington, 'Once More Unto the Breach: Postbehavioralist Approaches to Judicial Politics' (2000) Law and Social Enquiry, 601, 612; G Vanberg, *The Politics of Constitutional Review in Germany* (Cambridge University Press 2005), 177; and L Epstein and J Knight, *The Choices Justices Make* (CQ Press 1998), 79–88.

566 L Epstein and J Knight, *The Choices Justices Make* (CQ Press 1998), 82; and F Maltzman, FJ Spriggs and PJ Wahlbeck, 'Strategy and Judicial Choice: New Institutionalist Approaches to Supreme Court Decision Making' in CW Clayton and H Gillman (eds.), *Supreme Court Decision-Making: New Institutional Approaches* (University of Chicago Press 1999), 46–63.

567 O Larsson and D Naurin, 'Judicial Independence and Political Uncertainty: How the Risk of Override Affects the Court of Justice of the EU' (2016) 70 International Organization, 377, 384.

568 Ibid., 384.

569 Altering the institutional framework of the BeCC would mean altering the Constitution and/or the Special Act on the Constitutional Court. Both would require a special majority in Parliament.

570 T Roux, *The Politics of Principle: the First South African Constitutional Court, 1995-2005* (Cambridge University Press 2013), 24, 29, 67, 365, 371. Roux argues that this is an especially viable strategy for constitutional courts in new democracies, such as South Africa. In a mature constitutional democracy, courts have built the capacity to decide politically controversial cases in a legally principled way without sacrificing their institutional independence.

571 A Kavanagh, *Constitutional Review under the UK Human Rights Act* (Cambridge University Press 2009), 201.

Within the context of this book, the strategic model is particularly interesting for the following reasons. First, the model is not only used to describe individual judicial behaviour (micro level) but is also suitable for analysing collegial court activities (macro level).[572] In other words, building on this theory, hypotheses can be formulated with regard to how particular case characteristics may affect different aspects of the majority opinion in that case, and not only individual judicial behaviour. Next, the model incorporates some features from the other models, since it presupposes that judicial behaviour is shaped by the audiences that the court addresses. In particular, legal accuracy is believed to play a role in the judicial decision-making process because courts care about how they are perceived by the legal community.[573] Political constraints, on the other hand, also find their way into this theory because courts are believed to adapt their behaviour to induce compliance by the legislative branch. Although the model remains a simplification of reality, its conception of judicial behaviour may produce important insights and advance our understanding of how courts make their decisions. The next section explains in more detail why the strategic model might offer an explanation for the behaviour of the Belgian Constitutional Court.

3.2.2. WHY THE STRATEGIC MODEL FITS THE BELGIAN CASE

Although the Belgian Constitutional Court's behaviour is inescapably affected by a variety of factors, there are reasons to believe that its case law will reflect strategic behaviour. A core argument of the proponents of the strategic model is that judicial behaviour is structured by the institutional framework and the political context in which it functions.[574] Below, three main arguments are put forward, linked to these contextual factors, that may explain why the strategic model fits the Belgian case. In short, notwithstanding the (reinforced) authority of constitutional rulings in the legal order, the BeCC lacks mechanisms to prompt others to implement its rulings, or to prevent them from making decisions that conflict with them. Further, an analysis of parliamentary documents showed that the legislator's concern that review procedures may impact on (super)majoritarian compromises determined the Court's institutional design. In particular, collegial constraints oblige the judges to take into account the

---

572 F Maltzman, JE Spriggs and PJ Wahlbeck, *Crafting Law on the Supreme Court: The Collegial Game* (Cambridge University Press, 2000), 15.

573 L Baum, *Judges and Their Audiences: a Perspective on Judicial Behaviour* (Princeton University Press 2006), 47.

574 L Epstein, J Knight and WF Murphy, 'The Interactive Nature of Judicial Decision Making' in N Maveety (ed.), *The Pioneers of Judicial Behaviour* (University of Michigan Press 2003), 204.

views of the different sub-groups represented in the Court. Finally, considering the ambiguous relation between consociationalism and constitutional review, the political environment wherein the Court functions is likely to induce the Court to act prudently.

First, to a certain degree, the BeCC needs to rely on the goodwill of other actors in the policy arena to implement its decisions. An important player to be taken into account is the legislative branch.[575] The Court itself cannot do much more than facilitate the accessibility of its case law (see *supra*, section 2.7.1.) In addition, the Special Act on the BeCC also proclaims that a communication of its rulings must be made to all parliamentary assemblies.[576] Also, in 2007, the federal legislator established a 'Special Committee for Legal Evaluation' that has to, among other things, monitor the BeCC's case law.[577] This was intended to meet the concern that many rulings of the BeCC did not receive appropriate legislative follow-up.[578] In the meantime, the federal Special Committee has published several reports on the Court's case law,[579] including specific legislative propositions. However, too few initiatives have made it into actual legal text, and those that have did not really respond properly to the case law of the Court.[580] Moreover, there are no similar institutions at the sub-national levels responsible for monitoring the Court's case law regarding their legislation. Other actors to be taken into account are the litigants, the general public and the news media. In particular, if the BeCC confirms the legislator's policy choices, its ruling should be justified by arguments that can reasonably be embraced by those who

575 Note also that executive actions may repair unconstitutional legislation, in particular through executive decrees or circulars. For examples see S Verstraelen, 'Constitutionele dialoog als een lens: onderzoek naar het wetgevend optreden na de vaststelling van een ongrondwettige lacune door het Grondwettelijk Hof' (2016) 1 Tijdschrift Voor Wetgeving, 19.

576 Article 113, 2° of the Special Law of 6 January 1989 on the Constitutional Court.

577 Law of 25 April 2007 establishing a parliamentary committee for the evaluation of legislative acts. On the benefits and risks of locating this monitoring function within the legislative branch, see SS Abrahamson and G Lessard, 'Interbranch Communications: The Next Generation' in F Magnum (ed.), *Conference on Assessing the Effects of Legislation on the Workload of the Courts: Papers and Proceedings* (Diane Publishing 1995), 23.

578 In the scholarship that advanced this criticism, it was argued that the lack of legislative responses could mainly be attributed to the busy schedule and other priorities of the parliamentary committees (e.g. on finances or social issues). See for example: H Decroo, 'De invloed van de arresten van het Arbitragehof op het parlementaire werk' (2001) Rechtskundig Weekblad, 259; and A Goris, K Muylle, and M Van Der Hulst, 'Twintig jaar Arbitragehof v. wetgever: van vertrouwen naar dialoog' in A Alen (ed.), *Twintig jaar Arbitragehof* (Kluwer 2005), 51.

579 The most recent report dates from April 2014: see the report of activities of the parliamentary committee for the evaluation of legislative acts, *Parl Doc* Senate no 5-1407/3 and *Parl Doc* Chamber no 53-1969/3.

580 Ibid., 2. Yet without systematic data on the legislative responses, it is difficult to evaluate whether there is a genuine, positive inter-branch dialogue.

opposed the legislation. The news media can function as an intermediate actor between the Court and its audience, including the legislator as well as individual citizens.[581] For instance, in order to induce legislative change, what may be needed more than judicial guidelines is a groundswell of national opinion on the subject.[582] Essentially, non-compliance reduces the Court's legitimacy and its effectiveness as a policymaker.[583]

Without mechanisms to impose binding obligations upon its audience, the Court must rely on other strategies to ensure the acceptance and implementation of its case law. The strategic model emphasises that, when estimating their zone of discretion, judges must be aware of the preferences of other key actors involved, as well as the process by which they are aggregated.[584] When compliance difficulties are expected, courts may prudently modify their decisions according to the anticipated reaction of these other actors, tempering it so as not to exceed their tolerance threshold.[585] This is intended to reduce the chances that they will limit or reverse those decisions or, more generally, to minimise the extent of criticism of the Court's ruling.[586] Traditionally, scholars concentrate on the strategic 'separation-of-powers game', in which judges formulate their ruling in such a way as to avoid the possibility that it will be overturned by legislation.[587] Yet, in order to improve the effectiveness of its case law, the Court should be aware of how its decision will be received in the broad policy arena. In particular, heavy criticism, even when this does not result in an actual legislative override, can decrease

581 C Bateup, 'Expanding the Conversation: American and Canadian Experiences of Constitutional Dialogue in Comparative Perspective' (2006) 44 New York University Public Law and Legal Theory Working Papers, 6, 21.

582 E Luna, 'Constitutional Road Maps' (2000) 90 Journal of Criminal Law and Criminology, 1125, 1221; and DP Haider-Markel, MD Allen and M Johansen, 'Understanding Variations in Media Coverage of U.S. Supreme Court decisions' (2006) 11 The International Journal of Press/Politics, 209.

583 FB Cross and BJ Nelson, 'Strategic Institutional Effects on Supreme Court Decisionmaking' (2001) 95 Northwestern University Law Review, 1437, 1470: "failure to implement drains the court's decision of meaning, may eliminate any policy benefit that the court hoped to achieve, and may incidentally undermine the future significance of judicial decisions."

584 O Larsson and D Naurin, 'Judicial Independence and Political Uncertainty: How the Risk of Override Affects the Court of Justice of the EU' (2016) 70 International Organization, 377, 383.

585 G Vanberg, *The Politics of Constitutional Review in Germany* (Cambridge University Press 2005), 14; PT Spiller and R Gely, 'Strategic Judicial Decision Making' in GA Caldeira, RD Keleman and KE Whittington (eds.), *The Oxford Handbook of Law and Politics* (Oxford University Press 2008), 36; and B Friedman, 'The Politics of Judicial Review' (2005) 84 Texas Law Review, 257, 312.

586 L Baum, *Judges and Their Audiences: a Perspective on Judicial Behaviour* (Princeton University Press 2006), 63.

587 For example: B Friedman, 'The Politics of Judicial Review' (2005) 84 Texas Law Review, 257, 308–20; G Vanberg, *The Politics of Constitutional Review in Germany* (Cambridge University Press 2005); and T Roux, *The Politics of Principle: the First South African Constitutional Court, 1995–2005* (Cambridge University Press 2013), 22.

the Court's institutional standing. Under the strategic model, it is assumed that courts are able to make a risk assessment. In particular, judges are believed to be able to predict political responses given their sophisticated understanding of the legislative process and of policy preferences.[588] This understanding enables them to anticipate probable reactions and modify the decision accordingly. In Belgium, prior political experience gives the judges insight into what is feasible considering the existing political climate.[589] The better informed the Court is, the more able it will be to make a more sophisticated strategic choice.[590]

A second important reason to expect in the BeCC a propensity to act strategically is because of the consensual constraints that weigh on it. Scholars studying the strategic model acknowledge that the constraints weighing on judicial behaviour primarily stem from intra-institutional rules.[591] The BeCC's balanced composition, and the collegial pressures that follow from it, temper what the court can decide.[592] Its rulings are not, as the attitudinal model would suggest, simply the aggregate of what individual justices independently choose to do, since the final decision will need to be balanced. Judges on collegial courts must necessarily moderate their views to reach a single opinion.[593] In particular, they must win the support of their colleagues to mobilise a majority.[594] In Belgium, this majority opinion should be acceptable to each sub-group of judges whose preferences are protected by the double parity rule. Support is needed from the Dutch-speaking as well as the French-speaking judges, and the professional judges will not be able to push through their opinion without taking into consideration those of the judges with political experience. Instead of making sure that the ruling resembles as closely as possible a personal policy preference,[595] judges on the BeCC are likely to have internalised the need to take into account the opinions of all sub-groups within the Court. Hence, the collegial dynamics within the BeCC are expected to be stronger than in countries where

588 PT Spiller and R Gely, 'Strategic Judicial Decision Making' in GA Caldeira, RD Keleman and KE Whittington (eds.), *The Oxford Handbook of Law and Politics* (Oxford University Press 2008), 36.

589 VF Comella, *Constitutional Courts and Democratic Values*, (Yale University Press 2009), 45.

590 O Larsson and D Naurin, 'Judicial Independence and Political Uncertainty: How the Risk of Override Affects the Court of Justice of the EU' (2016) 70 International Organization, 377, 385.

591 F Maltzman, JE Spriggs and PJ Wahlbeck, *Crafting Law on the Supreme Court: The Collegial Game* (Cambridge University Press, 2000), 149.

592 B Friedman, 'The Politics of Judicial Review' (2005) 84 Texas Law Review, 257, 280.

593 L Baum, *Judges and Their Audiences: a Perspective on Judicial Behaviour* (Princeton University Press 2006), 51.

594 JB Grossman and RS Wells, 'Constitutional Law and Judicial Policy Making' (John Wiley & Sons 1972), 235; and F Maltzman, JE Spriggs and PJ Wahlbeck, *Crafting Law on the Supreme Court: The Collegial Game* (Cambridge University Press, 2000).

595 F Maltzman, JE Spriggs and PJ Wahlbeck, ibid., 25.

only a simple majority is required, and where judges are allowed to express their individual opinions.

The double parity rule also ensures that the opinions of the different audiences are known to the Court. For example, a judge whose career has been entirely within the legal community is likely to identify with that community, while the same can be said for judges who were previously connected to the political community.[596] The strategic model assumes that judges care about how their decisions are perceived by the audience they address. Also, judicial identification with sub-groups enhances the competition within the Court, which fosters strategic behaviour in order to reach a collective outcome. In short, these formal and informal rules permanently guarantee a certain judicial equilibrium which is likely to be reflected in a strategically drafted majority opinion.

A final argument is that the political climate in a consociational polity like Belgium induces a constitutional court to act prudently. In general, overturning legislation is believed to be difficult when there is strong legislative-executive cohesion.[597] Courts have little room for manoeuvre when the legislative parties operate within a strong coalition government. Overruling legislation that originates in consensual decision-making is (even) more difficult than when it has its basis in simple majority decision-making.[598] When judicial appointments bring the judiciary in line with the elected branches (in that same consensual structure), it is considered even more difficult to oppose them.[599] When challenged provisions are part of a supermajoritarian compromise on which the political partners have negotiated extensively, judicial review is a delicate endeavour. When specific pieces of legislation are declared null or void, this can constitute a serious setback for political actors. Eliminating one small element from a package deal can jeopardise the delicate balance that was achieved between the different segments that constitute a consociation. Even worse, it might be necessary to reopen time-consuming and costly negotiations between the political partners.[600] Hence, in an attempt to avoid confrontation with the legislature, the Court may adjust its ruling in light of this anticipated behaviour. As such, in some cases, the consensual character of the Belgian policy process may narrow down the boundaries of the Court's judicial discretion.

---

596 L Baum, *Judges and Their Audiences: a Perspective on Judicial Behaviour* (Princeton University Press 2006), 48.

597 BR Weingast, 'Rational-Choice Institutionalism' in I Katznelson and HV Milners (eds.), *Political Science: The State of the Discipline* (WW Norton & Company 2002), 676.

598 T-I Harbo, 'The Function of the Proportionality Principle in EU Law' (2010) 16 European Law Journal, 158, 170.

599 On the political independence of the judiciary, see J Ferejohn, F Rosenbluth and CR Shipan, 'Comparative Judicial Politics' in C Boix and SC Stokes (eds.), *The Oxford Handbook of Comparative Politics* (Oxford University Press 2009), 733–35.

600 P Popelier, 'The Belgian Constitutional Court: Guardian of Consensus Democracy or Venue for Deliberation?' in A Alen et al., *Liber Amicorum Marc Bossuyt* (Intersentia 2013), 483.

In conclusion, prudent behaviour may be the appropriate strategy for the BeCC to ensure short-term compliance and long-term support. It is likely that, over time, even the judges will no longer view this as a constraint because they have internalised the image that the legislator has of them.[601] This was recently recognised by the Court itself, in the words of the current Dutch-speaking president, Prof. Dr. André Alen. He confirmed that, while the Court is a guardian of fundamental rights, it also needs to take into account the balances achieved in consociational agreements.[602]

However, there are occasions in which the Court may feel prompted to act strategically. Judicial behaviour is believed to be shaped, at least in part, by the anticipated reactions of other relevant actors. In turn, estimating which reactions are possible or probable depends on who is judging on the Court. Hence, more strategic actions may be expected in cases that are perceived as salient,[603] either by the judges themselves or by other actors in the larger decision-making arena.[604] In what follows, it is discussed in more detail why case salience can be considered a trigger of strategic behaviour.

3.2.3. CASE SALIENCE AS A TRIGGER OF STRATEGIC BEHAVIOUR

In principle, salient cases are believed to have higher visibility and to potentially raise major policy questions. In judicial behaviour studies, typically two types of salience are identified. A case is *politically salient* when it touches upon a difficult or controversial question due to the issues or actors involved, or to the political context in which the case needs to be decided. When the Court faces a novel or unique legal question, a case can be considered *legally salient*. These cases influence the development of the law regardless of whether this

---

601 I Venzke, 'Judicial Authority and Styles of Reasoning: The Self-presentation between Legalism and Deliberation' (2016) 4 Amsterdam Law School Legal Studies Research Paper, 1, 16.

602 The speech by president André Alen during the formal hearing on the occasion of his inauguration, 5 February 2013.

603 Salience also plays a role in studies on the attitudinal approach or individual judicial behaviour. See: I Unah and AM Hancock, 'U.S. Supreme Court Decision Making, Case Salience and the Attitudinal Model' (2006) 28 Law & Policy, 295; and B Bartels, *Heterogeneity in Supreme Court Decision Making: How Situational Factors Shape Preference-Based Behavior* (PhD dissertation, Ohio State University 2006).

604 For example: F Maltzman, FJ Spriggs and PJ Wahlbeck, 'Strategy and Judicial Choice: New Institutionalist Approaches to Supreme Court Decision Making' in CW Clayton and H Gillman (eds.), *Supreme Court Decision-Making: New Institutional Approaches* (University of Chicago Press 1999), 57; RL Vining Jr and T Wilhelm, 'Measuring Case Salience in State Courts of Last Resort' (2011) 64 Political Research Quartely, 559; and D Klein and G Mitchell, *The Psychology of Judicial Decision Making* (Oxford University Press 2010), 10–22.

is known to the public.[605] These categories of salience are not strictly defined and may overlap.[606] For the purpose of this research, the conceptualisation of salience should be closely linked to strategic judicial behaviour. Therefore, case salience is here understood as the pressure weighing on the Court to adapt its decisions in order to ensure the acceptance of and compliance with its decisions. In other words, a measure of contemporaneous salience should indicate "how important the case is to the Court at the time it was making the decision".[607]

Salience is a latent characteristic that we cannot directly observe. Rather, we observe certain manifestations of the underlying salience.[608] Hence, in order to evaluate whether case salience is correlated to judicial behaviour, several measures need to be identified. Various measures of salience have already been selected and discussed to that effect in political science scholarship.[609] In particular, scholars usually rely on one[610] of the following measures: media attention, the participation of a large and/or diverse group of litigants or a larger panel size. While the first two indicate how external actors (the public in general and the litigants) perceive case salience,[611] the last measure focuses on the internal perspective (the judges). Instead of relying on one operationalisation of case salience, this research integrates all three measures in the analysis of the BeCC's behaviour. In this way, more refined interferences can be drawn about the ways in which different types of salience are related to the choices judges make. The three measures of salience will be discussed in more depth in chapter 4, where they are linked to the BeCC database. Nonetheless, in order to explain why strategic behaviour is expected in cases where these measures are present rather than absent, they are briefly introduced in section 3.2.3.1.

The following section (3.2.3.2.) discusses which strategic actions may generally be expected in salient cases. Traditionally, scholars concentrate on the strategic adjustment of the final outcome – is the challenged legislation

605 TA Collins and CA Cooper, 'Case Salience and Media Coverage of Supreme Court Decisions: Toward a New Measure' (2012) 65 Political Research Quartely, 396–7.

606 C Chandrachud, 'Measuring Constitutional Case Salience in the Indian Supreme Court' (2014) 42 Journal of Law and Society, 42, 45.

607 TS Clark et al., 'Measuring the Political Salience of Supreme Court Cases' (2015) Journal of Law and Courts, 37, 40.

608 Ibid., 44.

609 Examples include complexity, subject, *amici* participation and printing in constitutional law books or law reviews. See: L Epstein and JA Segal, 'Measuring Issue Salience' (2000) 44 Amercian Journal of Political Science, 66; and TS Clark et al., ibid., 37.

610 Therefore, the extent to which different conceptualisations of case salience are correlated with each other is unclear. See TS Clark et al., ibid.

611 A measure based on the behaviour of others is the leading approach in the literature. See RC Black, MW Sorenson and TR Johnson, 'Toward an Actor-Based Measure of Supreme Court Case Salience: Information-Seeking and Engagement During Oral Arguments' (2012) 66 Political Research Quartely, 804.

overruled or not? – and particularly on the individual judicial votes.[612] In Belgium, however, voting behaviour is not only concealed from the public – making it difficult to study – but the judicial outcome is also believed to be the result of a collegial effort. In addition, scholars nowadays acknowledge that an exclusive focus on the judicial outcome may be too narrow.[613] Instead, there is a range of judicial behaviour that might reflect strategic calculations. I explore which actions are institutionally available to the BeCC and why others are not. Instead of first listing the actions that might suit the BeCC and then those that may not, they are discussed in the 'chronological' order of the judicial process – from docket control to the final voting stage. The idea behind this section is not to sum up hypotheses regarding the BeCC's behaviour, which will be developed in the next chapters, but to explore how the Belgian case might fit within the current state of knowledge on strategic judicial behaviour.

3.2.3.1. Case Salience Measures

Firstly, media attention is the dominant measure in studies focusing on the influence of political salience on judicial behaviour.[614] The reason for this choice is not only because it is believed that the media reports on important cases but equally because the media influences public perception of the importance of issues.[615] In that sense, the news media acts as an intermediary between judges and other audiences they care about.[616] Previous research showed that the 'news values' that tend to drive newspaper journalists to cover constitutional cases are conflict, controversy and impact.[617] In contrast, a simple, non-controversial case

612 For example, A Bustos and T Jacobi, 'Strategic Judicial Preference Revelation' (2014) 57 The Journal of Law and Economics, 113.

613 For example: KE Whittington, 'Once More Unto the Breach: Postbehavioralist Approaches to Judicial Politics' (2000) Law and Social Enquiry, 601; B Friedman, 'Taking Law Seriously' (2006) 4 Perspectives on Politics, 261, 265; and F Maltzman, FJ Spriggs and PJ Wahlbeck, 'Strategy and Judicial Choice: New Institutionalist Approaches to Supreme Court Decision Making' in CW Clayton and H Gillman (eds.), *Supreme Court Decision-Making: New Institutional Approaches* (University of Chicago Press 1999), 61.

614 The first innovative approach was introduced by Epstein and Segal (see *supra*, footnote 609), who measured salience based on the coverage on the front page (yes/no) of the New York Times the day after the decision. Collins and Cooper (see *supra*, footnote 605) incorporated coverage across the entirety of multiple newspapers, generating an additive index. TS Clark et al., (see *supra*, footnote 609) added that coverage should be measured across each stage of the case, including before the decision was taken.

615 L Epstein and JA Segal, ibid., 66; TA Collins and CA Cooper, ibid., 396.

616 L Baum, *Judges and Their Audiences: a Perspective on Judicial Behaviour* (Princeton University Press 2006), 135.

617 On the relation between certain news values – such as impact, conflict, controversy and prominence – and case characteristics of the US Supreme Court, see: MD Allen and DP Haider-Markel, 'Connecting Supreme Court Decisions, Media Coverage and

is unlikely to have generated any publicity before the petition is submitted.[618] When the Court expects that its ruling will be under closer public scrutiny, in particular when the case has received media attention during the decision-making procedure, it needs to be careful not to overstep the boundaries of the 'tolerance interval' created by other actors who are responsible for implementation. In other words, when the case is covered by the news media, chances that the Court will employ a long-term strategy increase.[619] The influence of political salience can be expected to increase when judges have prior experience in electoral politics, such as in Belgium.[620]

Next, the involvement of a large group of petitioning and intervening parties equally signals the importance of a case.[621] It demonstrates that a broad set of interests are at stake and that the impact of the case is potentially stronger.[622] Courts may be incited to act prudently when a broad set of interests is at stake. A ruling that goes against the expectations of a large group of litigants may result in the loss of public support. This support is considered essential for constitutional courts, such as the BeCC, that lack binding mechanisms to ensure compliance with their decisions. A large group of participants may equally be a measure of case strength, since a flagrant constitutional violation is likely to attract more participants. It is believed that constitutional courts stand in a stronger position when the number of separate parties and the mix of party types increases.[623] However, intensive participation may be less influential when the case is highly politically salient.[624]

Public Opinion: The Case of Lawrence v. Texas' (2006) 27 The American Review of Politics, 209–10; and K Sill et al., 'Media coverage of the U.S. Supreme Court: How Do Journalists Assess the Importance of Court Decisions?' (2013) 20 Political Communication, 1, 13.

618 LS Wrightsman, 'Persuasion in the Decision Making of US Supreme Court Judges' in D Klein and G Mitchell (eds.), *The Psychology of Judicial Decision Making* (Oxford University Press 2010), 29.

619 S Dothan, *Reputation and Judicial Tactics* (Cambridge University Press 2015) 58.

620 L Baum, *Judges and Their Audiences: a Perspective on Judicial Behaviour* (Princeton University Press 2006), 72.

621 I Unah and AM Hancock, 'U.S. Supreme Court Decision Making, Case Salience and the Attitudinal Model' (2006) 28 Law & Policy, 295, 299; JF Spriggs and PJ Wahlbeck, 'Amici Curiae and the Role of Information at the Supreme Court' (1997) 50 Political Research Quartely, 365; GA Caldeira and JR Wright, 'Amici Curiae before the Supreme Court: Who participates, When and How Much?' (1990) 52 The Journal of Politics, 782; and F Maltzman, JE Spriggs and PJ Wahlbeck, *Crafting Law on the Supreme Court: The Collegial Game* (Cambridge University Press 2000), throughout.

622 K Sill et al., 'Media Coverage of the U.S. Supreme Court: How Do Journalists Assess the Importance of Court Decisions?' (2013) 20 Political Communication, 1, 15–17.

623 P Harris, 'Difficult Cases and the Display of Authority' (1985) 1 Journal of Law, Economics and Organization, 209, 213. Harris argues that this increases the probability of a reversal of a precedent.

624 I Unah and AM Hancock, 'U.S. Supreme Court Decision Making, Case Salience and the Attitudinal Model' (2006) 28 Law & Policy, 295, 301.

Finally, panel size can also serve as a measure of case salience.[625] While 'media attention' and 'participation' operationalise salience based on the behaviour of others, this measure starts from the perspective of the justices themselves.[626] It is believed that individuals display higher levels of engagement with a topic that is salient to them.[627] Hence, the propensity to request a plenary session is likely to relate to how salient a given case is considered.[628] Given the criteria determining the composition of the Court, panel size can be a measure of political salience, legal salience or both.[629] Hence, this measure adds another layer to the measurement of case salience because it goes beyond the assumption that cases deemed salient by actors beyond the Court – such as the media or litigants – must also be salient from a justice's personal perspective. It is expected that more efforts are invested in the judicial opinion when panel size increases. In addition, a larger panel size increases the number of different perspectives to be taken into account, which provides an enriching variety of experiences and insights. The judges need to confer with each other in order to reach a majority opinion.[630] In sum, a judicial outcome cannot be understood without acknowledging the collective nature of the decision-making process that undergirds it.[631]

3.2.3.2. Strategic Actions in Salient Cases

Prior research has shown that justices act differently when deciding salient cases. Justices act with greater interest, intensity and motivation than they

625 C Chandrachud, 'Measuring Constitutional Case Salience in the Indian Supreme Court' (2014) 42 Journal of Indian Law and Society, 42, 45.

626 An alternative is to rely on transcripts of oral arguments, but this measure cannot be used when the internal documents are not published (such as in Belgium). See RC Black, MW Sorenson and TR Johnson, 'Toward an Actor-Based Measure of Supreme Court Case Salience: Information-Seeking and Engagement During Oral Arguments' (2012) 66 Political Research Quartely, 804.

627 This idea stems from social psychology research: ibid., 804. See also F Maltzman, JE Spriggs and PJ Wahlbeck, *Crafting Law on the Supreme Court: The Collegial Game* (Cambridge University Press 2000), 83.

628 This was, for example, acknowledged during interviews with justices on the Canadian Supreme Court who said that it was expected that the whole court would sit for a particularly important or controversial issue. See DR Songer, SW Johnson, CL Ostberg and MA Wetstein, *Law, Ideology and Collegiality: Judicial Behaviour in the Supreme Court of Canada* (McGill Queen's University Press 2012), 161.

629 C Chandrachud, 'Measuring Constitutional Case Salience in the Indian Supreme Court' (2014) 42 Journal of Law and Society, 42, 46.

630 In that sense, a diversified panel is an antidote to the tendency of collective deliberation to drive the like-minded to extreme conclusions. See R Posner, *How Judges Think* (Harvard University Press 2008), 31.

631 L Epstein and J Knight, 'Toward a Strategic Revolution in Judicial Politics: a Look Back, a Look Ahead' (2000) 53 Political Research Quarterly, 643.

otherwise would.[632] Next, the variety of considerations that shape the decision tend to increase with case saliency.[633] Finally, it may affect other relevant actors' preferences, and thus potentially change the way judges anticipate their response. Depending on the case circumstances, the ideas concerning what is expected from the Court may change.[634] Therefore, salience may significantly affect the different stages of the judicial decision-making process: from the initial docket control, through the writing process, to the final voting stage.[635] In addition, strategic behaviour is not necessarily linked to one individual case, but may also be reflected in the development of case law over time. In what follows, the judicial decision-making process is scrutinised in a chronological order, and it is pointed out which strategic actions are available to the Belgian Constitutional Court and why others are not.

First, deciding which cases to accept for closer scrutiny or who can present arguments before the court may reflect strategic considerations.[636] If institutionally possible, courts can avoid confrontation with the legislature by simply deciding not to hear a case. Or, conversely, they may postpone accepting politically controversial cases into their docket until the time is ripe. Such agenda-setting actions may be an important strategy for courts that have control of their docket such as the USSC[637] or the SACC,[638] but is difficult for the BeCC.[639] As mentioned before, the latter court is required to formulate an opinion once the case is declared admissible. Courts may equally act strategically when deciding who may present their arguments. Although access to the BeCC requires a legitimate interest in the case, it has been established that the Court interprets this condition broadly. Moreover, if a request is not accepted, this should be

632 D Klein and G Mitchell, *The Psychology of Judicial Decision Making* (Oxford University Press 2010), 22.

633 I Unah and AM Hancock, 'U.S. Supreme Court Decision Making, Case Salience and the Attitudinal Model' (2006) 28 Law & Policy, 295, 299.

634 This is also a weakness of the strategic model. Scholars have identified strategies that might be pursued under certain circumstances, often immediately followed by a disclaimer that the contrary strategy might be more appropriate in some circumstances. See L Epstein, J Knight and WF Murphy, 'The Interactive Nature of Judicial Decision Making' in N Maveety (ed.), *The Pioneers of Judicial Behaviour* (University of Michigan Press 2003), 208.

635 F Maltzman, JE Spriggs and PJ Wahlbeck, *Crafting Law on the Supreme Court: The Collegial Game* (Cambridge University Press 2000), 12.

636 B Friedman, 'The Politics of Judicial Review' (2005) 84 Texas Law Review, 257, 292–5.

637 For example: L Epstein and J Knight, *The Choices Justices Make* (CQ Press 1998), 88–94; and V Baird, 'The Effect of Politically Salient Decisions on the U.S. Supreme Court's Agenda' (2004) 66 The Journal of Politics, 755–72.

638 For example, T Roux, *The Politics of Principle: the First South African Constitutional Court, 1995-2005* (Cambridge University Press 2013), 377.

639 L Baum, 'Motivation and Judicial Behavior' (2007), a paper prepared for the *Workshop on Exploring the Judicial Mind*, University of Virginia, 16: "their ability to choose cases [...] does not eliminate variation in case salience, it reduces that variation: cases that the justices see as very unimportant will not be accepted for full consideration".

explicitly justified in the ruling itself, making it difficult to arbitrarily exclude litigants from the case. In conclusion, it is unlikely that highly controversial cases are filtered out before the actual decision-making stage.[640] Instead, when the BeCC handles a political hot potato, strategic behaviour is likely to manifest itself in how a case is treated.

Another strategy to influence the final ruling is opinion assignment to specific judges. When there are no strict rules, as for example in the US, it has been noticed that chief justices and other majority opinion assigners typically reserve high salience cases either for themselves, or for the justice(s) to whom they are closest ideologically.[641] This would result in opinions that would best reflect directly their own set of values and preferences on the case while maintaining the majority coalition.[642] In Belgium, however, the registrar appoints the cases chronologically to a judge-rapporteur following a certain fixed list.[643] Also, even if these rules could be circumvented, strategic opinion assignment may not have a direct effect on the ruling because this is always the result of a collegial effort. The judge-rapporteur has to take into account other judges' preferences if he or she wants to persuade a majority to accept the opinion draft.

The next step concerns the internal decision-making and opinion-writing process. Since (individual) strategic behaviour by the BeCC judges before this stage is unlikely, one can expect a propensity in the Court to put more energy in this step. In general, justices are believed to have stronger opinions on salient issues. This means that they will want to participate in the drafting process, and will have to negotiate more intensively if they want to reach a unanimous opinion.[644] Hence, more time and energy is expended in shaping the content of

---

640 Yet the Court does exceptionally make strategic use of the interest requirement to limit its involvement in politically controversial cases. See M De Visser, *Constitutional Review in Europe: A Comparative Analysis* (Hart Publishing 2014), 129, discussing BeCC case no 76/94, 18 October 1994, as an example. Also, the Court can, strategically, postpone publishing its ruling in a politically sensitive case, for example to wait for a ruling of the ECtHR.

641 F Maltzman, JE Spriggs and PJ Wahlbeck, *Crafting Law on the Supreme Court: The Collegial Game* (Cambridge University Press 2000), 29–59; and L Baum, *Judges and Their Audiences: a Perspective on Judicial Behaviour* (Princeton University Press 2006), 110.

642 I Unah and AM Hancock, 'U.S. Supreme Court Decision Making, Case Salience and the Attitudinal Model' (2006) 28 Law & Policy, 295, 299.

643 Articles 59 and 67 of the Special Act.

644 Bargaining is a type of behaviour typically associated with strategic decision making: L Epstein and J Knight, *The Choices Justices Make* (CQ Press 1998), 57–79; TH Hammond, CW Bonneau and RS Sheehan, *Strategic Behavior and Policy Choice on the U.S. Supreme Court* (Stanford University Press 2005), 39; RC Black, MW Sorenson and TR Johnson, 'Toward an Actor-Based Measure of Supreme Court Case Salience: Information-Seeking and Engagement During Oral Arguments' (2012) 66 Political Research Quartely, 804, 810–11; and PT Spiller and R Gely, 'Strategic Judicial Decision Making' in GA Caldeira, RD Keleman and KE Whittington (eds.), *The Oxford Handbook of Law and Politics* (Oxford University Press 2008), 83.

the majority opinion than in relatively trivial disputes.[645] Research on the USSC shows that more than an average number of drafts are written in salient cases, which suggests that these rulings are formulated more carefully than others.[646] On the one hand, this would expose the judges to a broader range of rationales for each possible outcome, requiring a more fully elaborated discussion on their consequences[647] and resulting in judgments that are lengthier and more carefully reasoned.[648] On the other hand, a closer scrutiny of the internal drafts on the USSC showed that virtually all changes made reflected strategic calculations by the opinion writers about the preferences of other relevant actors.[649]

Strategic behaviour may find various expressions in the majority opinion. Instead of simply overruling legislation, the court may include explicit or implicit signals in the justificatory ground of the ruling. For example, it can highlight which substantive boundaries should be taken into account, or criticise the legislative procedure, both of which are meant to influence future legislation. Signalling is believed to be a less confrontational way to communicate.[650] Also, courts have the discretion to select the authorities to which they refer in a particular ruling (chapter 6). Courts may try to avoid taking a stand on a politically sensitive issue by taking refuge in external 'sources of authority', for example by referencing international (case) law or scientific studies.[651] Finally, judges can write opinions that are more vague or more precise, depending on which strategy better serves the purpose of stimulating implementation (chapter 7). In particular, instead of explicitly pointing out how to remedy the constitutional fault, the Court may

---

645 L Epstein and JA Segal, 'Measuring Issue Salience' (2000) 44 Amercian Journal of Political Science, 66; and TS Clark et al., 'Measuring the Political Salience of Supreme Court Cases' (2015) 3 Journal of Law and Courts, 37, 59.

646 For 'sophisticated opinion writing', see: L Epstein and J Knight, *The Choices Justices Make* (CQ Press 1998), 94–107; F Maltzman, JE Spriggs and PJ Wahlbeck, *Crafting Law on the Supreme Court: the Collegial Game* (Cambridge University Press 2000), 6 and further; and PT Spiller and R Gely, 'Strategic Judicial Decision Making' in GA Caldeira, RD Keleman and KE Whittington (eds.), *The Oxford Handbook of Law and Politics* (Oxford University Press 2008), 122.

647 B Friedman, 'The Politics of Judicial Review' (2005) 84 Texas Law Review, 257, 284.

648 On the 'elaborate display of reasoning from authority', see P Harris, 'Difficult Cases and the Display of Authority' (1985) 1 Journal of Law, Economics and Organization, 209–10. This is especially the case "when [judges] risk being perceived as agents of a political minority trying to impose its policy preferences on democratically elected legislators." See A Dyevre, 'Unifying the Field of Comparative Judicial Politics: Towards a General Theory on Judicial Behaviour' (2010) 2 European Political Science Review, 297, 321. Lax and Cameron argue that justices invest more strongly in the quality of their opinions in salient cases: JR Lax and CM Cameron, 'Bargaining and Opinion Assignment on the US Supreme Court' 23 The Journal of Law, Economics & Organization, 292.

649 L Epstein and J Knight, *The Choices Justices Make* (CQ Press 1998), 98.

650 WN Eskridge and PP Frickey, 'Foreword: Law as Equilibrium' (1994) Harvard Law Review, 26, 40.

651 P Popelier, 'The Belgian Constitutional Court: Guardian of Consensus Democracy or Venue for Deliberation?' in A Alen et al., *Liber Amicorum Marc Bossuyt* (Intersentia 2013), 496.

prefer to write an opinion that is vague enough to allow the legislator to keep the status quo policy.[652]

As previously mentioned, many scholars concentrate on the judicial outcome and more particularly on whether the challenged legislation is overruled or not. However, the use of various other sanctioning modalities may equally reflect strategic considerations (chapter 5). As mentioned before (2.6.1.), many courts have developed more creative outcomes in order to communicate with their audience. Such 'modulated outcomes' indicate how legislation should be understood or altered in order for it to be applied in a constitutional manner. Such modulations may serve as a strategic compromise when a violation has been found but a simple invalidation would exceed the threshold of acceptance. Second, providing deadlines for legislative revision of unconstitutional statutes would also suggest that the court is concerned about future legislative evasion of its decision.[653] Shapiro and Stone Sweet argue that such creative techniques strenghten the court's dominance over policy outcomes.[654] Hence, while at the same time acting prudently in order not to overstep the legislator's acceptance threshold, courts may actually maximise their effectiveness as a policy-maker.

Next, researchers have noted that more dissenting opinions are published in salient cases. The reason for this is the higher visibility in salient cases, which causes the hardening of the justices' ideology and, therefore, more division within the court.[655] However, as explained in section 2.7., separate opinions are not allowed in Belgium, and the majority opinion does not include any information on the judges' individual voting behaviour. With no means to express their individual opinions, judges are enquired to discuss the case more intensely in search of a ruling that satisfies the required majority of the judges. Hence, it is the majority opinion and not the number or nature of separate opinions, that may reflect the internal negotiations that have occurred during different stages of the decision-making process. In other words, in countries where the internal collegial dynamics between the judges are stronger, case salience may rather affect both the outcome and the justificatory ground of the majority opinion.

In conclusion, constitutional courts potentially have a wide range of possibilities to strategically anticipate the reactions of other relevant actors.

---

652 JK Staton and G Vanberg, 'The Value of Vagueness: Delegation, Defiance and Judicial Opinions' (2008) 52 American Journal of Political Science, 504, 516.

653 G Vanberg, 'Legislative-Judicial Relations: A Game-Theoretic Approach to Constitutional Review' (2001) 45 Amercian Journal of Political Science, 346, 348.

654 M Shapiro and A Stone Sweet, *On Law, Politics and Judicialization* (Oxford University Press 2002), 187–89.

655 RL Vining Jr and T Wilhelm, 'Measuring Case Salience in State Courts of Last Resort' (2011) 64 Political Research Quartely, 559, 567–8; and TA Collins and CA Cooper, 'Case Salience and Media Coverage of Supreme Court Decisions: Toward a New Measure' (2012) 65 Political Research Quartely, 396–7.

Yet, considering the absence of docket control, the small degree of discretion to grant access and strict rules for opinion assignment, the BeCC cannot rely on the same tools as other courts to filter the cases and actors it wants to hear. Therefore, it can be expected that strategic considerations will rather affect the next stage of the decision-making process: writing the majority opinion. Accordingly, in what follows, the analysis should concentrate on the relation between case salience, on the one hand, and case outcome and the justificatory ground, on the other.

3.3. PRELIMINARY CONCLUSION: LAUNCHING THE CASE LAW ANALYSIS

In the first part of this book, a normative framework was set out to evaluate the deliberative performance of constitutional courts, centred on the key concepts of inclusiveness, rationality, transparency and dialogue. In this second part, a bridge was built between the deliberative expectations weighing on constitutional courts and the forthcoming case law analysis. The main argument was that, in order to fully comprehend the role of constitutional courts in a democratic society, the institutional and contextual contours of judicial decision-making must be recognised.

The analysis of the BeCC's institutional framework showed that it has grown into a fully-fledged constitutional court. When the Court was established in 1983, its competences were limited and served to protect consociational bargains and deal-making. The composition of the court, with a strict parity between French-speaking and Dutch-speaking judges, and between 'professional' judges and ex-politicians, reflects these concerns. Over the years, the legislator has repeatedly extended the Court's competences. Although there are some options for further improvement, the Court has the procedural equipment to enhance the deliberative quality of democratic policy-making. Moreover, the flexible approach of the Court, extending its competences if needed, shows that it is willing to provide a deliberative forum to those seeking an alternative route when the legislative branch falls short. Yet the strict double parity rule has remained in place. Hence, the decision-making process of the BeCC – as with many other European constitutional courts – is constrained by a collegial dynamic between judges with various backgrounds. Also, the preparatory parliamentary documents to these reforms reflect the legislator's concern that review procedures could impact on (super)majoritarian compromises. This rationale behind the Court's establishment and further development may still weigh on the Court.

Although judicial behaviour may be fuelled by the willingness to maximise impact on the legitimacy and quality of democratic policy-making, it is also constrained by what is (politically) feasible. In chapter 2, building on judicial behaviour scholarship, it was argued that the strategic model may offer an explanation for the BeCC's behaviour. The strategic model puts forward a constitutional court that balances its decisions between principled decision-making and a degree of pragmatism. The 'principled' aspect of the decision-making process ensures that judges have the common good in mind[656] and that legal constraints determine the nature and quality of the reasons judges can offer in support of a decision.[657] The pragmatic approach would result in strategic calculations of how to prevent non-compliance or loss of institutional security, taking into account the anticipated reactions from the legislature, litigants or other judges. It was argued that, considering the institutional and political context in which the BeCC functions, its case law can be expected to reflect such strategic considerations. More specifically, case salience – indicated by increased media attention for the case, more participation and larger panel size – is expected to function as a trigger of strategic behaviour. The easier it is to involve the constitutional court (broad access possibilities, a large set of reference norms), the more issues will be referred to it and the more likely it will be that the court is asked to adjudicate salient cases. Considering that the BeCC cannot strategically filter out controversial cases or refuse to hear certain actors, strategic considerations will rather be reflected in how the ruling is formulated. To ascertain this main hypothesis, the BeCC's case law – and in particular the case outcomes, citation practices and the Court's approach to the proportionality analysis – will be scrutinised in the third part of this book.

---

656 CH Mendes, *Constitutional Courts and Deliberative Democracy* (Oxford University Press 2013), 27.

657 T Roux, *The politics of principle: the first South African Constitutional Court, 1995–2005* (Cambridge University Press 2013), 75.

PART III

EMPIRICAL ANALYSIS OF THE BELGIAN CONSTITUTIONAL COURT'S CASE LAW

While the previous part of the book concentrated on the potential relation between the deliberative expectations weighing on the Court and the behaviour it exhibits, this third part includes an extensive case law analysis aiming to explain the Court's behaviour. This analysis combines normative and empirical elements, an interdisciplinary approach that is often lacking in studies on judicial behaviour.

For this purpose, an extensive database on the case law of the BeCC has been produced, including all cases – annulment procedures as well as preliminary references – since its inception in 1985 until 2015 (n=3145).[658] A total of 55 variables were coded, which can be divided into four variable groups related to: (1) the key features of the procedure, (e.g. annulment/preliminary procedure); (2) the participants involved (defending, initiating and intervening parties); (3) the Court's reasoning process (reference norms, citations, etc); and (4) case outcome. An overview of all variables can be found in the Annex to this book. In addition, data measuring the number of newspaper articles published on each case is relied upon, provided by the library and documentation office of the Belgian Constitutional Court for academic purposes.

In chapter 4, the salient cases will be identified within the Court's case law. It will be explained how the salience measures can be translated into explanatory variables, which will be integrated into the regression models in the following three chapters. Each of these chapters is centred on a particular judicial practice (case outcome, citation patterns, the proportionality analysis). In particular, in the chapter 5, it is argued that modulated outcomes may serve as a strategic compromise when a violation has been found but a 'simple' declaration of unconstitutionality would exceed the 'tolerance interval' acceptable to political actors. Although these outcomes are not necessarily more deferential towards legislative majorities, they do not confront the legislature in the same way as

658 These include all judgments in which the Court proclaimed a final decision on the substance of the case. Other rulings, for example when the Court decided on a request for suspension, declared the request inadmissible or sent a preliminary reference to the Court of Justice, are not included in the dataset.

a declaration of unconstitutionality. However, the study of judicial behaviour should go beyond binary codings of case outcomes and look into the justificatory ground of constitutional rulings. Therefore, chapter 6 explores how the Court embeds citations of external authorities in its rulings. An extensive study of citation practices provides a window into judicial preferences and performance. It is argued that the Court may base its rulings more strongly on citations of external authorities in order to ensure compliance with its decisions. Finally, in the last chapter, the focus is the application of the proportionality analysis as an argumentative framework in fundamental rights adjudication. It is argued that the Court may be less clear on the grounds for establishing a violation when it estimates a vague opinion may better serve the purpose of ensuring implementation. In particular, the Court may opt not to apply the proportionality analysis to its full extent as a strategy to protect itself against institutional challenges while striking down a policy to which it objects.

Methodologically, each of these chapters follows the same structure. First, it is discussed how the Court should shape its case law in light of the deliberative expectations that weigh on it. Special attention will be paid to the reason-giving requirement and the engagement in dialogue. Next, a descriptive analysis is carried out to reveal certain patterns in the Court's case law. When there is some evolution over time, this is illustrated by graphs. In addition, the correlations are explored between each judicial practice and other case characteristics. Next, a statistical analysis aims to lay bare which factors may influence the Court's behaviour. A number of hypotheses are tested with regard to strategic actions in salient cases. Although other explanations cannot be entirely excluded, if the analysis reveals a strong significant relation between the salience variables and each dependent variable, this supports the main hypothesis that the strategic model suits the Belgian case. Throughout these chapters, particular (salient) cases brought before the BeCC will be discussed, providing the opportunity to illustrate causal patterns with factual arguments. In particular, these cases can illuminate how the BeCC manages constraints impacting on its decisions, leading to a strategic equilibrium. Finally, comparative references show how the Court's case law can be situated within the broader literature on judicial behaviour. Numerous studies already exist on the behaviour of courts in specific countries, mostly with a common law tradition. The analysis of the BeCC – which shares many features with other European Courts – may reveal certain differences in behaviour that allow for further reflection on the effect of institutional (composition, procedure, etc) or political (majoritarian, consociational) settings on judicial behaviour. This empirical analysis contributes to fundamental discussions about the appropriate role for judicial institutions to play in a democratic society.

CHAPTER 4

TRANSLATING CASE SALIENCE INTO MEASURABLE EXPLANATORY VARIABLES

4.1. INTRODUCTION

In the previous chapter, building on judicial behaviour theories, general expectations were set forth about the Belgian Constitutional Court's behaviour. In particular, it was argued that strategic behaviour can be expected in salient cases. But how to identify these salient cases? While in the US context a case is often considered salient simply because it has survived the docket control,[659] this cannot be said for cases before the BeCC where similar selection mechanisms do not exist. Moreover, considering the broad access possibilities and large set of reference norms, it is easier to trigger the involvement of the Court, which increases the probability it will be asked to adjudicate salient cases. When identifying appropriate salience measures, the specific setting in which a Court functions should be taken into account.

In this chapter, the selection of salience measures that can be reasonably integrated as explanatory variables in the statistical analysis of the Court's case law is explained. Importantly, these measures should be determined by objective, measurable facts instead of relying on some subjective evaluation.[660] In addition, they should indicate contemporaneous salience, meaning that the case was salient at the time the judges were resolving it, regardless of retrospective considerations.[661] Also, while the traditional approach in judicial

[659] See TS Clark et al., 'Measuring the Political Salience of Supreme Court Cases' (2015) 3 Journal of Law and Courts, 37.

[660] Other measures used in the literature, such as subject matter or case complexity, partially rely on an evaluation of the researcher (e.g. whether he or she considers cases on criminal law to be more salient than family law, or whether fiscal matters would be more complex than questions of immigration law). For a short evaluation of these measures, see RL Vining Jr and T Wilhelm, 'Measuring Case Salience in State Courts of Last Resort' (2011) 64 Political Research Quartely, 559, 561–2.

[661] L Epstein and JA Segal, 'Measuring Issue Salience' (2000) 44 Amercian Journal of Political Science 66–7.

behaviour studies is to rely on one operationalisation of case salience, in this book various measures are combined. Hence, more refined inferences can be drawn about the ways in which different aspects of case salience are related to the choices judges make.

Three potential measures of case salience were already put forward: (1) the participation of a large, diverse group of litigants; (2) media coverage during the decision-making procedure; and (3) a deliberation in plenary session.

Essentially, the Belgian database includes a range of information containing variables measuring who participated in the procedure, the number of newspaper articles published on each case and the composition of the Court (see Annex). In what follows, an overview is given of these variables and how they relate with each other and with other case features. For instance, newspaper journalists and the judges may be guided by the participation patterns in a specific case. And vice versa, a case that garners media attention may equally attract additional participations. The news media sometimes even reports on the possibility that a case may be lodged before the Court, prior to the official petition being introduced. As discussed below, the findings indeed suggest that cases where a larger group of participants was involved are also covered in more newspaper articles (section 4.3.), and are more likely to be settled in plenary session (section 4.4.). In short, this descriptive analysis allows the reader to better assess why strategic behaviour may be expected in cases where these salience measures are present, rather than absent.

One can assume that a case is simple and non-controversial when there is little participation, no media coverage and the case is settled in a restricted session. Conversely, although strategic behaviour may be activated by each of the salience measures, this is especially to be expected when all three are present. Therefore, the chapter ends with an overview of these 'highly salient cases' (n=57). Drawing on parliamentary preparatory documents and newspaper articles, it is explained why these cases can be considered highly controversial. These judgments are excellent candidates for an in-depth study in the following empirical chapters. In particular, by linking the case's background to the final ruling, one can designate the relevant explanatory factors for the observed strategic behaviour.

4.2. PARTICIPATION

A first measure of case salience relates to who participated in the review procedure. In short, a large, diverse group of litigants indicates that the consequences of the case may be wide-ranging, or at least more so than in simple routine cases. Also, more participation may equally be an indicator of case strength, since a flagrant constitutional violation is likely to attract more participants. Under the strategic model, it is assumed that judicial behaviour is partly determined by the anticipated consequences of the review procedure.

More specifically, it is believed that constitutional courts stand in a stronger position as the number of separate parties and the mix of party types increase.[662]

To estimate how *litigant salience* is correlated to the Court's case law, it should first be clarified which situations are considered distinctive and may therefore trigger strategic actions. For instance, studies on the USSC have concentrated on the effect of interest group participation through the *amici curiae* system,[663] or the participation of the solicitor general.[664] Yet, as established in chapter two on the institutional contours of judicial decision-making, other access rules apply in Belgium. Therefore, other measures should be selected to measure litigant salience in Belgian constitutional review cases.

In this section, an overview is given of the participation patterns in the BeCC's case law. First, it is explained which data were collected related to the number and capacity of the participants (section 4.2.1.). Next, the general trends are discussed, differentiating between annulment and preliminary procedures (section 4.2.2.). Finally, based on these results, two explanatory variables measuring litigant salience are selected (section 4.2.3.). In particular, it is argued that the size of the group of individuals and participation diversity can reasonably be integrated as explanatory variables in a statistical analysis of the Court's case law. This analysis aims to reveal significant relations between these explanatory variables and the Court's behaviour.

4.2.1. MEASURING PARTICIPATION IN CONSTITUTIONAL REVIEW PROCEDURES

As discussed before (see *supra*, section 2.4.) the Belgian Constitutional Court is widely accessible for a broad set of actors. In particular, any citizen or legal entity can initiate, or intervene in, an annulment procedure, under the condition that he or she can demonstrate a legitimate interest in the case ('private actors'). In addition, federal and sub-national governments have the same rights, and do not have to establish a specific interest in the case. The presidents of each parliamentary assembly may also lodge a case before the Court, at the request

662 P Harris, 'Difficult Cases and the Display of Authority' (1985) 1 Journal of Law, Economics and Organization, 209, 213. Harris argues that this increases the probability of a reversal of a precedent.

663 For example: GA Caldeira and JR Wright, 'Amici Curiae before the Supreme Court: Who participates, When and How Much?' (1990) 52 The Journal of Politics, 782; and F Maltzman, JE Spriggs and PJ Wahlbeck, *Crafting Law on the Supreme Court: The Collegial Game* (Cambridge University Press 2000), throughout.

664 The solicitor general is the office responsible for representing the US Government in Supreme Court cases. See K Sill et al., 'Media coverage of the U.S. Supreme Court: How Do Journalists Assess the Importance of Court Decisions?' (2013) 20 Political Communication, 1, 15–17.

of two thirds of the representatives in their assembly or they may intervene in a procedure without such request. The latter three categories can be defined as 'institutional actors'. In preliminary procedures, it is technically the referring judge who lodges the case before the Court. Nonetheless, the litigants involved in the procedure before this judge (also called the procedure *a quo*) may have provoked this initiative. In addition, these litigants, as well as any other actor, can introduce a memorandum during a later stage of the preliminary procedure, under the same access conditions as in annulment procedures. Table 4.1 includes an overview of all ten types of 'private' or 'institutional' actors.

Table 4.1. Overview of the different categories of litigants participating in review procedures before the Belgian Constitutional Court

'Private' actors who need to demonstrate an interest in the case	Individuals
	Interest groups
	Companies
	Local governments
	Public entities/private entities with a public objective
	Political actors
Institutional actors	The federal government
	Regional governments
	Presidents of the parliamentary assemblies

Interest groups are usually non-profit associations, acting against legislation that can negatively affect their members (e.g. trade unions) or other vulnerable persons (e.g. refugees, children). 'Companies' were coded as private legal entities with a commercial objective (Belgian NVs, BVBAs, insurance companies). A local government can be a local community (*gemeente*, *stad*), the bench of Mayor and Aldermen, social services organised at community level (OCMW) or representatives of local communities (e.g. in tax issues). Examples of public entities or private entities with a public objective are the administrative entities in charge of social services or environmental issues, but also schools and universities, public transport agencies, the national lottery, etc. A 'political actor', finally, may be a political party or an individual politician. A political party can participate in a review procedure as a legal entity – if it can demonstrate that its objectives are affected by the legislation under review – or as an association if the legislation deals with the rights, duties or characteristics of political parties as such.[665] Individual politicians can participate in two situations: if their status

[665] For example: BeCC case no 146/2007 (NVA), 28 November 2007; and BeCC case no 86/2012, 28 June 2012, B.4.2.2-B.4.6 (Groen!).

as a representative is negatively and directly affected by the legislation under review,[666] or as an individual citizen, when their personal situation may be affected.[667]

In each case before the Court, any combination of these types of litigants can be involved. Therefore, instead of creating one participation variable, several variables were created with categories according to the litigant's capacity (initiating and/or intervening party). In the preliminary procedure, a litigant was registered as the initiating party when he or she provoked the preliminary question. Considering that the intervening parties in the preliminary procedure were not necessarily involved in the procedure before the referring judge, additional nominal categories were included to indicate whether such 'new' actors participated. Table 4.2 includes an overview of the nominal categories that could be coded for each type of litigant (except individuals, see *infra*).

Table 4.2. Overview of the different codes for each litigant variable (see Annex, variables VAR10–VAR17)

0	None
1	Initiating party
2	Intervening party
3	Initiating and intervening party
	(Only in preliminary procedures)
4	The litigant involved in the procedure before the referring judge raised the preliminary question and intervenes in the procedure before the BeCC
5	The litigant involved in the procedure before the referring judge raised the preliminary question and, together with another litigant from that category, intervenes in the procedure before the BeCC
6	The litigant involved in the procedure before the referring judge did not raise the preliminary question but intervenes in the procedure before the BeCC
7	The litigant involved in the procedure before the referring judge did not raise the preliminary question but, together with another litigant from that category, intervenes in the procedure before the BeCC

Individual litigants dominate both the annulment and preliminary procedures. Also, in contrast to the other types of litigants, there is considerable variety in the number of individuals involved. Moreover, the participation of a larger group of individuals indicates that the case potentially has a broader impact than other cases. Therefore, instead of creating one nominal variable for individuals (such as presented in table 2), several variables were created to allow for differentiation in the size of the group involved. In particular, two nominal variables were

666 For example, BeCC case no 10/2001, 7 February 2001, B.2.3.

667 For example, BeCC case no 39/2013, 14 March 2013.

created for individuals as initiating or intervening party, each comprising three categories (0=1–5, 1=5–20 and 2=more than 20 individuals involved). An additional dichotomous variable was included for preliminary procedures, to track whether or not these individuals were involved in the procedure before the referring judge. An overview of the variables used to code the involvement of individuals can be found in table 4.3.

Table 4.3. Overview of the variables for individual litigants (see Annex, variables VAR9a–c)

Individual: initiating party	0 = none
	1 = between 1–5 individuals
	2 = between 5–20 individuals
	3 = more than 20 individuals
Individual: intervening party	Idem to above
Individual: new intervening party in preliminary procedure	0 = no / 1=yes

4.2.2. DATA ANALYSIS

4.2.2.1. Annulment Procedures (n=1027)

(1) Private Actors

Tables 4.4. and 4.5. Overview of the involvement of private actors in annulment procedures

Individuals		**n**
As initiating party	1–5 individuals	348
	5–20 individuals	115
	<20 individuals	76
As intervening party	1–5 individuals	55
	5–20 individuals	8
	<20 individuals	8

	Initiating party	**Intervening party**	**Both**
Interest groups	380	24	45
Business organisations	187	14	22
Local governments	56	14	6
Public entities	58	18	4
Political actors	26	1	/

With an overall involvement in 54% of the annulment actions, the results as presented in tables 4.4 and 4.5 confirm that individuals dominate these procedures.[668] Moreover, since the reform of 1989, when participating in review procedures was no longer an exclusive competence of the institutional actors, this percentage has remained relatively stable. Although individuals also participate in competence conflict cases, they are certainly more active in fundamental right cases (31% vs 61%). In particular, they are more interested in cases related to educational law (71%) and judicial organisation (90%), but more reluctant when the case deals with tax law (37%). Usually, it is a single individual or small group of individuals who initiates the procedure. In a smaller number of cases, a group of more than five or even more than twenty individuals took the initiative. Interventions by individuals are mostly made in cases where their peers already lodged the case before the Court.[669] Larger groups of individuals (>5) are more likely to connect their claim to the ECHR and other international human rights treaties.[670] Conversely, smaller groups usually invoke the equality principle without seeking additional support under supranational or international treaties.

Interest groups are the second most active group of litigants in annulment procedures (45%). Similar to individuals, they are more drawn to fundamental rights cases rather than competence conflict cases (48% vs 19%). They do not only regularly initiate the action, but in a significant number of cases interest groups also join in to strengthen the claim. Overall, there is no trend toward more or less participation of interest groups over the years. Rather, they are drawn to certain subject areas, in particular to migration issues (84%) and criminal legislation (65%). The results also suggest that interest groups attempt to build stronger claims by connecting their pleas to the ECHR and other international human rights treaties.[671]

Third, companies were involved in 22% of the annulment procedures, mostly as the initiating party. In order to protect their commercial interests, these actors usually act in fundamental rights cases related to tax law (47%), commercial

668 There is no category 'both' for individuals, since in almost *all* cases where an individual was involved as intervening party, another individual (or more) initiated the procedure. For example, of the 55 cases where 1–5 individuals intervened, there were 50 in which individuals were already involved as the initiating party (22 cases with 1–5, 18 with 5–20 and 10 with more than 20 individuals involved).

669 Only in 2% of the cases, (a group of) individuals intervened without their peers being already involved as initiating party.

670 In particular, when less than five individuals are involved, the ECHR or other international treaties are invoked in 31% and 15% of the cases, respectively, while this increases to 46% and 28% when more than five are involved (independent samples t-test; equal variance not assumed; p=0.000).

671 In particular, the ECHR and international human rights treaties were invoked in 44% and 26% of the cases, respectively, when interest groups were involved. This percentage drops to 24% and 10% when they were not involved (independent samples t-tests; equal variance not assumed; p=0.000).

or financial law (45%) and environmental or energy law (42%). More than any other type of litigant, companies link their claims to European law.[672] Except for a spike in 1995,[673] the data do not indicate an upward or downward trend in their involvement.

Finally, public entities (8%) and local governments (7%) are less active in annulment procedures. Considering that teaching institutions are registered as public entities, it is not surprising that their involvement correlates with the subject area of educational law (25%). Local governments, in turn, are drawn to cases related to the organisation of the state (31%). On rare occasions, a political actor participates in the procedure (2%), also usually in cases related to the organisation of the state (63%).

(2) Institutional Actors

Table 4.6. Overview of the involvement of institutional actors in annulment procedures

	Initiating party	Intervening party	Both
Federal government	54	34	/
Regional governments	46	151	30
Presidents of the parliamentary assemblies	9	10	/

Before the reform in 1989, which widened the Court's accessibility extensively, institutional actors had the exclusive right to initiate or intervene in an annulment procedure. During these first years, the federal and regional government(s) were involved in, respectively, 62% and 82% of the cases. While the federal level usually initiated the procedure to act against a breach of the competence allocating rules by regional entities, the activities of the latter consisted primarily of interventions. After the reform, the average participation rate of the institutional actors declined dramatically. Between 1989–2015, the federal government was involved in 7% of the cases, and regional entities in 20%. This decrease is mainly due to the fact that, since 1989, only a small proportion of the cases brought before the Court deals with competence conflicts.[674] In fundamental rights cases, institutional actors are rarely involved.[675]

672 In particular, European legislation was invoked in 26% of the cases in which a business group was involved, while this drops to 12% when they were not involved (independent samples t-test; equal variance not assumed; p=0.000).

673 This spike can be explained by the adoption of an environment tax (law of 16 July 1993 completing the federal state structure, published in the Official Belgian Journal on 20 July 1993). The Court stated that individuals who feared that the tax costs would be passed on to consumers did not have a legitimate interest to participate in the review procedure.

674 During this period, the federal government participated in 40% and regional entities in 70% of the competence conflict cases.

675 Both the federal government and the regional entities participated in only 1% of the fundamental rights annulment procedures.

The results demonstrate that regional entities remain especially active as interveners.[676] On the one hand, the regions are triggered to act when they have adopted or want to adopt legislation with similar content to the legislation under review.[677] By participating in the review procedure, they can indirectly defend their (future) policy decisions and avoid the possibility that a similar annulment action will be introduced. On the other hand, regional interventions can also be aligned with the initial claim, usually when the legislation under review is adopted in breach of the competence allocating rules.[678]

Finally, the presidents of parliamentary assemblies rarely participate in constitutional review cases. In nine cases they initiated the annulment action, at the request of two thirds of their assembly. Usually, the cause for this request is the adoption of legislation by another parliamentary assembly in breach of the competence allocating rules.[679] In another ten procedures, the presidents intervened (without such official request from the representatives), usually to defend legislation adopted by their own assembly.[680]

4.2.2.2. Preliminary Procedures (n=2118)

(1) Private Actors

Tables 4.7. and 4.8. Overview of the involvement of private actors in preliminary procedures

Individuals		
As initiating party	1–5 individuals	729
	5–20 individuals	18
	<20 individuals	6
As intervening party	1–5 individuals	1130
As 'new' intervening party	1–5 individuals	18

	Raised the preliminary question	**Involved in the procedure *a quo* but did not raise the preliminary question**	**'New' party**
Interest groups	42	66	30
Business organisations	229	232	23
Local governments	49	114	13
Public entities	44	155	15
Political actors	3	2	2

676 For the period 1985–2015: as initiating party (4.2%), intervening party (13.7%) or both (2.1%).
677 For example, BeCC case no 81/2012, 28 June 2012.
678 For example, BeCC case no 184/2011, 8 December 2011.
679 For example, BeCC case no 60/2011, 5 May 2011.
680 For example, BeCC case no 91/2010, 29 July 2010.

As demonstrated in tables 4.7 and 4.8, individual litigants dominate preliminary procedures even more strongly than annulment procedures. Overall, they participated in 61% of the preliminary cases. Usually, a single individual, or a small group (<5) raises the preliminary question. Moreover, even when they did not raise the question, 53% of the individual litigants that were involved in the procedure *a quo* participate in the preliminary procedure. In exceptional cases, other individuals, who were not involved in the procedure *a quo*, intervene in the review procedure. The involvement of individual actors is especially concentrated in preliminary procedures related to migration law (78%) or the law of persons or family law (75%).

Next, companies are equally active in preliminary procedures as in annulment actions (22%). Yet, it is unusual for these litigants to get involved in a review procedure when they did not participate in the procedure *a quo*. The findings confirm the propensity to participate in procedures that may affect their commercial interests, in particular in cases related to environmental or energy law (56%), commercial or financial law (43%) or tax law (32%).

Conversely, interest groups are not as prominent in preliminary procedures. Overall, they participated in 6% of these cases, and usually they were already involved in the procedure *a quo*. There is somewhat more activity of interest groups in cases related to labour or social security law (10%), but this is the exception. These results suggest that interest groups primarily act through annulment actions as a strategy to affect policy decisions. Once legislation has been in place for a while, but is challenged during a particular judicial procedure, they do not seem interested in intervening in the case before the BeCC and assisting others in building their claim.

Further, the results indicate that local governments are usually, in the procedure before the referring judge, the party opposing the one that raised the preliminary question. In particular, they participated in 8% of the preliminary procedures but mainly in the capacity of intervener. These actors are particularly drawn to review procedures that may affect the institutional framework or competences of local entities or affect the situation of their employees. In particular, the findings show that their participation significantly relates to the subject area of administrative law (39%).

A similar pattern appears in the results for public entities (10%). Although these actors occasionally do raise a preliminary question, they usually introduce their memorandum once the case has already been initiated. There is a wide range of different public entities. Nonetheless, the results indicate that teaching institutions, on the one hand, and the national authorities responsible for employment and the payment of benefits, on the other hand, are most active. In particular, there is a significant relation between the participation of public entities and the subject areas of education law (33%) and labour and social security law (19%).

In only seven cases, a political actor was involved (0.3%). Similar to the annulment procedure, cases related to the organisation of the state primarily attract their attention (20%).[681]

(2) Institutional Actors

Table 4.9. Overview of the involvement of institutional actors in preliminary procedures

	Raised the preliminary question	Involved in the procedure *a quo* but did not raise the preliminary question	'New' party
Federal government	13	4	41
Regional governments	19	53	196
Presidents of the parliamentary assemblies	1	2	3

Table 4.9 shows that institutional actors are less active in preliminary procedures compared to annulment procedures (overall federal government 3%, regional governments 12%). The involvement of the presidents of parliamentary assemblies (in five cases) is negligible. This is mainly due to the fact that the vast majority of the preliminary questions can be categorised as fundamental rights cases (94%). Both the federal government and the regional entities are more active in competence conflict cases.[682] The results indicate that, in contrast with all other types of litigants discussed above, they were usually not involved in the procedure before the referring judge, but introduced their memorandum during a later stage. In particular, these actors get involved when the legislation under review, adopted by another entity, conflicts with the competences that were allocated to them.

4.2.3. CONCLUSION: TWO EXPLANATORY VARIABLES RELATED TO LITIGANT SALIENCE

4.2.3.1. Size of the Group of Individuals

As demonstrated in the above discussed data analyses, both annulment and preliminary procedures are dominated by individual litigants. Moreover, taking

681 Yet, this difference is not significant (independent samples t-test; equal variance not assumed; p=0.172).

682 The federal government was involved in 22% of the competence conflict cases, and in only 0.7% of the fundamental rights cases. Similarly, regional governments were involved in 46% of the competence conflicts vs 9% of the fundamental right cases.

into account that the diversity within the group of participants is often limited (see *infra*, section 4.2.3.2.), in many cases *only* individuals are involved. At the same time, the data shows that there is considerable variety in the size of the group of individuals involved. As mentioned before, a larger group of individuals may indicate that the case potentially has a broader impact. Hence a reasonable measure for litigant salience would be a single explanatory variable capturing the size of the group of individuals involved.

To create such an explanatory variable, the collected data were recoded into the variable 'size of the group of individuals'. As discussed in section 4.2.1., the involvement of individuals in annulment and preliminary procedures was initially measured through three variables, differentiating between their involvement as initiating and intervening party (see Annex, *VAR9a–c*). Next, the results for these variables were added up, taking into account possible overlap (e.g. a case where 15 individuals initiated the procedure, followed by an intervention of another 10 individuals – hence a total of more than 20 individuals were involved). This resulted in a variable with four values: none (0), 1–5 (1), 5–20 (2) or more than 20 (3) individuals involved. In table 4.10, the results for this variable are presented on the left. As the right column shows, the last two values were merged into one category, creating the explanatory variable 'size of the group of individuals' with three categories which will be integrated in the regression models in chapters 5, 6 and 7. The value 'no individuals were involved' will serve as the reference category (REF).

Table 4.10. Overview of the results for the explanatory variable 'size of the group of involved individuals'

Count variable	Number of cases (percentage)	Categories of the explanatory variable 'size of the group of individuals'
0	1299 (41%)	No individuals involved (REF)
1–5	1625 (52%)	One to five individuals involved
5–20	135 (4%)	More than five individuals involved
>20	86 (3%)	

4.2.3.2. Participation Diversity

As mentioned before, the involvement of a large, diverse group of petitioning and intervening parties signals the importance of a case. Hence, there are reasons to believe that the Court's behaviour is affected by the extent of diversity within the group of litigants.

To measure the diversity within a group of litigants, the collected data were recoded into a single variable measuring 'participating diversity'. In particular, first, the above discussed variables for each type of litigant (see Annex, *VAR9–17*) were recoded into nine dichotomous variables. Then, these dummies were added up into a count variable with nine values (min 0, max 9). In table 4.11, the results for this count variable are presented on the left. Finally, as the right column shows, the last four values were merged into one category, resulting in the explanatory variable 'participation diversity' which will be integrated in the regression models in chapters 5, 6 and 7. The category with the most registrations will serve as the reference category (REF).

Table 4.11. Overview of the results for the explanatory variable 'participation diversity'

Count variable	Number of cases (percentage)	Categories of the explanatory variable 'participation diversity'
0	319 (10%)	No initiating or intervening parties involved (only in preliminary procedures)
1	1640 (52%)	One type of litigant involved (REF)
2	910 (29%)	Two types of litigants involved
3	221 (7%)	A diverse group of litigants (>2)
4	48 (2%)	
5	6	
7	1	

In addition to the data analysis of each of the separate types of litigants (4.2.2.), it is interesting to discuss the variety in participation diversity. Table 4.11 shows that, in the majority of cases, one type of litigant is involved (52%). If it is an annulment action, the case is most likely to be initiated by individuals or interest groups.[683] In preliminary procedures, a memorandum is usually introduced by an individual who was involved in the procedure before the referring judge.[684] Further, the results indicate that a significant proportion (10%) of the preliminary questions are drawn up by the referring judge, without any request or involvement at a later stage by the litigants from the procedure *a quo*. Only in these cases can participation diversity be equal to zero.[685] Next, the findings show that in 29% of the procedures there was cooperation between two different types of litigants. Lastly, the findings show that cases rarely attract a wide variety (>2) of litigants. As will be discussed below, such a diverse group of participants attracts more media attention (section 4.3.) and is more likely to be settled in plenary session (section 4.4.). In preliminary procedures, additional memoranda are usually introduced by other private actors who equally participated in the procedure *a quo*, or institutional actors who did not. In annulment actions,

683 In the majority of these cases where only one type of litigant was involved, it was an individual (42%) or interest group (23%).

684 In the majority (69%) of these cases where only one type of litigant was involved, it was an individual.

685 In annulment procedures, there is always at least one initiating party (if not, the procedure is inadmissible).

there is overall more diversity within the group of litigants.[686] For, instance, in fundamental rights cases interest groups often act together with individuals or business groups.[687] Also, competence conflict cases usually draw the attention of a combination of different institutional actors.[688]

A noteworthy 'outlier' with seven types of litigants involved[689] was case no 110/99.[690] The challenged Flemish decree introduced an assistance mechanism for persons whose financial security was at risk due to war circumstances. The regulation was particularly delicate because the assistance would also be provided to individuals who were first condemned for crimes during the war, but were given a certain level of redemption afterwards. For this reason, some perceived the mechanism as an allocation benefiting 'collaborators of the Nazis'. Certain war victims argued that it was disgraceful that they would be treated similarly to those individuals who made them victims in the first place.[691] These actors also expressed their criticism through the news media and announced that they would initiate a constitutional review procedure should the legislation be adopted.[692] In addition, in its advisory opinion, the Council of State stated that, by adopting this decree, the Flemish legislator had acted in contravention of the competence allocating rules.[693] Several institutional actors had also stated their concerns about the proposal.[694] Notwithstanding these protests, the law was adopted by the Flemish Parliament at the end of June 1998. Both the private and institutional actors who had announced judicial action initiated a procedure before the BeCC. Hence, the context in which the Court had to examine the legislation was one of overwhelming resistance, as discussed extensively by the news media.[695,696]

686 Participation diversity mean of 1.7 vs 1.2 (independent samples t-test; equal variance not assumed; p=0.000).

687 The first combination occurred in 24%, and the second in 10% of these cases.

688 In 22% of these cases, both the federal government and at least one of the regional entities was involved.

689 In particular, the federal government, regional governments, individuals, interest groups, local governments, several presidents of parliamentary assemblies and political actors.

690 BeCC case no 110/1999, 14 October 1999.

691 This opinion was expressed during the decision-making procedure, in particular in an advice by the High Council of (disabled) war victims and former members of the army, *Parl Doc* 1995–1996, no 298/8.

692 For example: Het Laatste Nieuws, 12 June 1998, *"Erg, zo'n vernedering op onze leeftijd. Oud-strijders boos om toelage voor Vlaamse collaborateurs"*; Le Matin, 12 June 1998, *"Indemniser les collabos? Tirs de barrages democrats"*.

693 Advisory opinion of the Council of State, *Parl Doc* 1995–1996, no 298/2.

694 For example: De Standaard, 12 June 1998, *"Franstalig België vecht tegen repressiedecreet"*; De Morgen, 12 June 1998, *"Dehaene start procedure bij Arbitragehof. Decreet -Suykerbuyk veroorzaakt emotionele reacties in Wallonië"*.

695 For example: Grens Echo, 3 August 1998, *"Flahaut beantragt beim Schiedshof Annullierung des Suykerbuyk-Dekrets. Text im Staatsblatt erschienen"*; De Standaard, 16 December 1998, *"Oorlogsslachtoffers trekken naar Arbitragehof tegen decreet-Suykerbuyk"*; Le Matin, 3 February 1999, *"130 requêtes en annulation: le décret Suykerbuyk fait l'unanimité contre lui"*.

696 As will be discussed below (section 5.5.4.2.), this case resulted in a simple invalidation.

4.3. MEDIA ATTENTION

Rulings proclaimed by a constitutional court potentially have a strong impact on democratic policy-making and on citizens' day-to-day life. Therefore, when a constitutional case is lodged before the court, this is likely to draw the attention of the news media. The nature and extent of coverage is expected to vary between different cases. Newspaper journalists usually look for certain cues (such as the subject area and participants) indicating that the public audience will find their story appealing and important. Previous research showed that the 'news values' that tend to drive newspaper journalists are conflict, controversy and impact.[697] The extent of media attention for a case is usually considered as a manifestation of its underlying political salience.[698]

In what follows, an overview is given of the news media coverage of the BeCC's constitutional review cases. First, it is discussed how these data were collected and why the data can be used as a reliable, objective measurement of contemporaneous political salience. Next, which case features (e.g. certain subject areas, participants, etc) function as cues for journalists to cover a certain case is examined.

4.3.1. MEASURING MEDIA ATTENTION FOR CONSTITUTIONAL REVIEW PROCEDURES

To evaluate a case's newsworthiness, journalists must rely on information available in the public forum. First, the Court informs the general public of each case brought before it. In particular, the registrar arranges the publication of a notice in the Belgian Official Journal (*Belgisch Staatsblad – Moniteur Belge*), which is accessible to all Belgian citizens. In this publication, the initiator and the subject of the action for annulment or the preliminary question are indicated. In addition, the actors involved in the procedure may actively seek the attention of the news media. By drawing this attention, they can make their claim heard and possibly persuade others to join the review proceedings.

---

697 On the relation between certain news values – such as impact, conflict, controversy and prominence – and case characteristics of the US Supreme Court, see: MD Allen and DP Haider-Markel, 'Connecting Supreme Court Decisions, Media Coverage and Public Opinion: The Case of Lawrence v. Texas' (2006) 27 The American Review of Politics, 209–10; and K Sill et al., 'Media coverage of the U.S. Supreme Court: How Do Journalists Assess the Importance of Court Decisions?' (2013) 20 Political Communication, 1, 13.

698 TS Clark et al., 'Measuring the Political Salience of Supreme Court Cases' (2015) 3 Journal of Law and Courts, 37, 44; and DP Haider-Markel, MD Allen and M Johansen, 'Understanding Variations in Media Coverage of U.S. Supreme Court decisions' (2006) 11 The International Journal of Press/Politics, 64.

To measure the level of media attention paid to the BeCC's judgments, data collected by the library and documentation office of the Constitutional Court (last updated in January 2017) is relied upon.[699] In particular, by looking for specific catchwords, such as 'constitutional court' and 'judicial review', this office registered how many articles were published on each individual case in the most-circulated newspapers.[700] A sub-division was made between articles that where published before and after the pronunciation of the ruling.

This unique dataset presents several advantages, which are emphasised in recent literature on salience measurements. First, separating the articles published prior to, from the coverage after, the decision, allows for a more refined analysis of the effect of case salience on judicial behaviour. Coverage after the decision is systematically influenced by characteristics of the decisions themselves, which are often consequences of salience and not causes.[701] As confirmed by the data, there is only a moderate correlation between media attention before and after the ruling.[702] Hence, using this after-measure would flip causal chronology and creates a risk of post-treatment bias.[703] Next, it is considered more accurate to employ the number of articles about a case rather than a dichotomous measure of coverage.[704] This does not only indicate whether but also to what extent a case can be considered salient. Further, while some scholars only take into account front page coverage, articles may appear in any section of the paper. Hence, the Belgian media dataset is not influenced by what else is going on across the news universe – which could lead to the improper categorisation of otherwise salient cases.[705] Finally, instead of analysing only one newspaper, the dataset includes articles published in various newspapers. Hence, the risk of ideological or geographical bias is reduced and the data instead present a more balanced image of case salience.[706]

However, the measure is not flawless. The news media does not always pick up every salient issue, certainly not prior to the ruling. It's possible that litigants

699 A special thank you to Luc Théry and Kris van Put for providing me the data (including regular updates).

700 For example: De Standaard, De Morgen (Flemish Region); Le Soir, La Libre Belgique (Walloon Region). For an overview, see L Théry, 'Markante arresten uit twinting jaar rechtspraak van het Arbitragehof: een vergelijking tussen de commentaren in de rechtsleer en de weerklank in de geschreven pers' (2006) 7 TBP, 387, 394.

701 This is identified as post-treatment bias: see TS Clark et al., 'Measuring the Political Salience of Supreme Court Cases' (2015) 3 Journal of Law and Courts, 37.

702 Pearson correlation= 0.358, p=0.000.

703 RC Black, MW Sorenson and TR Johnson, 'Toward an Actor-Based Measure of Supreme Court Case Salience: Information-Seeking and Engagement During Oral Arguments' (2012) 66 Political Research Quartely, 804–5; and TS Clark et al., 'Measuring the Political Salience of Supreme Court Cases' (2015) 3 Journal of Law and Courts, 37, 41.

704 TS Clark et al., ibid., 46.

705 RC Black, MW Sorenson and TR Johnson, ibid., 805; and TA Collins and CA Cooper, 'Case Salience and Media Coverage of Supreme Court Decisions: Toward a New Measure' (2012) 65 Political Research Quartely, 396, 398.

706 TA Collins and CA Cooper, ibid., 398.

with limited political or social visibility or few resources may not succeed in attracting media attention.[707] Journalists are then left to their own devices in determining which cases to write about, which does not necessarily guarantee coverage of (all) salient cases. In addition, as an explanatory factor of judicial behaviour, this measure assumes that cases deemed salient by the media must necessarily be salient from the justices' perspective, which may not always be the case. Finally, the data only include paper articles, whereas online media is becoming more and more prominent. Nonetheless, as a reasonable measure for case salience, integrating media attention in the models explaining judicial behaviour should yield significant results.

4.3.2. DATA ANALYSIS

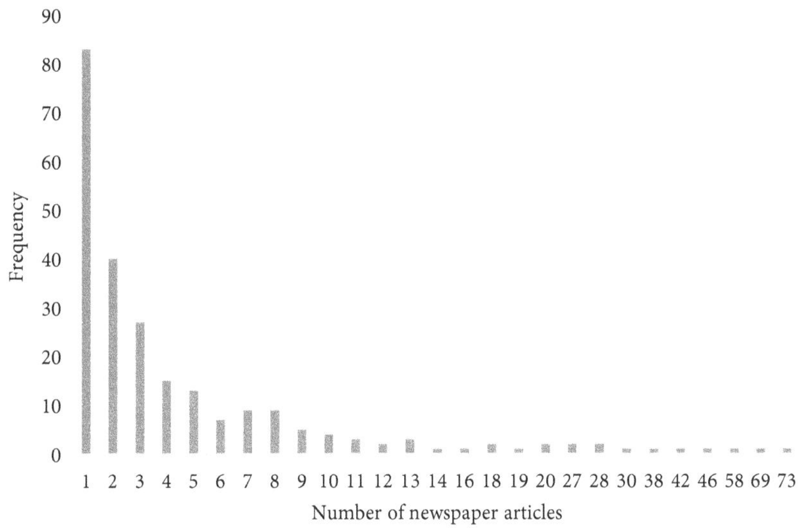

Figure 4.1. Media coverage >1

Overall, there is very little news media attention for constitutional cases during the judicial procedure. The vast majority of cases fall into obscurity (92%).[708] Therefore, a case can be considered newsworthy once it is covered in at least one newspaper article. Yet, the long tail at the right in figure 4.1 shows that there is considerable spread within the group of newsworthy cases. Some cases have the propensity to be covered extensively (max: 73).[709] Rather than having

707 K Sill et al., 'Media Coverage of the U.S. Supreme Court: How Do Journalists Assess the Importance of Court Decisions?' (2013) 20 Political Communication, 1, 6.

708 Conversely, the news media are more interested in a constitutional review case once the decision is taken. In particular, 27% of all rulings received at least some media attention.

709 Within the group of cases that is covered in at least one article (n=238), the mean is 5.53 and standard deviation 9.62.

increased generally over the years, news media attention seems instead to be pushed upwards by certain case features. Therefore, the question that arises is to what extent media coverage is affected by the type of procedure, the litigants and the legislation under review.

First, annulment procedures receive significantly more attention than preliminary questions.[710] Annulment actions are directed towards legislation that has recently been adopted by the Parliament, and may therefore be considered more topical by newspaper journalists. Also, an annulment procedure can lead to retroactive removal of the unconstitutional (part of the) legislation from the Belgian legal order. By delivering a decision to strike down legislation, the Court confronts the parliamentary majority and news media tend to be driven by (the prospect of) such conflict.[711] Preliminary procedures, on the other hand, usually result from a judicial disagreement between individuals. They may be considered less newsworthy if the question concerns legislation that has already been applied for several years. Also, the consequence of an invalidation proclaimed in a preliminary procedure is different. As explained above (section 2.6.), this does not have the same *erga omnes* effect as an annulment. Although the judiciary and administration are expected to declare unconstitutional provisions inapplicable, the legal text remains untouched. Hence, although a legislative response to these rulings is appropriate, they do not confront the legislative branch in the same way as an annulment outcome.

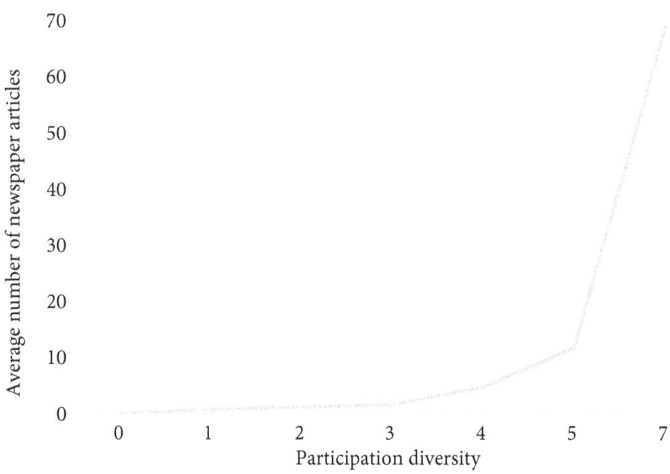

Figure 4.2. Average number of newspaper articles published during the procedure in relation to participation diversity

---

710 Average of 1.1 vs 0.08 articles (independent samples t-test; equal variance not assumed; p=0.000).

711 It should be noted that, at the moment the ruling is proclaimed, the power ratio between the political parties may have shifted and a new majority coalition may be formed.

The relation between media coverage and participation has already been mentioned. As demonstrated by figure 4.2, the higher the participation diversity, the larger the extent of media coverage for a case during the judicial procedure.[712] It should be noted, however, that this relation can be understood as a two-way process. On the one hand, journalists are prompted to cover cases that potentially affect a larger number of people because these articles may attract a broader audience.[713] On the other hand, by bringing constitutional cases into the public forum, citizens without any legal expertise may learn about certain procedures that would otherwise remain in obscurity. More informed citizens are able to express themselves and make their causes heard.[714] Hence, more and more actors may join a particular case (within a certain time limit) due to coverage during the Court's decision-making process. The interplay between media coverage and participation can be illustrated by case no 102/1999.[715] In this case, federal legislation related to tobacco advertising was challenged by both private and institutional actors, since the ban was not only considered discriminatory and harmful to certain commercial interests but was also considered in conflict with the competence allocating rules. Even before the legislation was approved by Parliament (in December 1997), the news media reported that proceedings before the Court were likely to be initiated.[716] In April 1998, the annulment action was lodged before the Court by an interest group, followed in August by more interest groups, business organisations, local governments and the Walloon government. These petitions were quickly picked up by newspaper journalists, resulting in additional coverage.[717] A few months later, a considerable number of memoranda were introduced by 'new' intervening parties, which was again covered extensively in the newspapers.[718] Afterwards, the media attention quietened down until the hearing before the Court, which was held at the end

---

712 In particular, the mean per category of participation diversity is: 0=0.02; 1=0.22; 2=0.53; 3=0.83; 4=2.88; 5=11.67; 7=69. As shown in table 4.11, there is no category 6 for participation diversity.

713 For instance, prior research on the USSC has shown that more participation (*amici curiae*) does signal newsworthiness. See K Sill et al., 'Media Coverage of the U.S. Supreme Court: How Do Journalists Assess the Importance of Court Decisions?' (2013) 20 Political Communication, 1, 11.

714 M Schudson, *The Power of News* (Harvard University Press 1995), 204 and further.

715 BeCC case no 102/99, 30 September 1999.

716 For example: La Libre Belgique, 2 December 1997, "*Toute la Wallonie s'essouffle pour contrer la loi anti-tabac*"; and Vers L'Avenir, 5 December 1997, "*Tabac: Collignon ne lâche pas prise. Le gouvernement wallon va demander à la Cour d'arbitrage d'annuler la loi qui interdit la publicité pour les produits du tabac*".

717 De Standaard, 6 August 1998, "*Gebroers naar Arbitragehof tegen verbod tabaksreclame*"; De Morgen, 7 August 1998, "*Professor Blanpain laakt poging vernietiging verbod op reclame*"; and Le Matin, 27 November 1998, "*Collignon confirme le recours à la Cour d'arbitrage. Guerre du tabac: Dehaene n'a pas convaincu les siens*".

718 De Morgen, 22 December 1998, "*Uitgevers vragen om vernietiging tabakswet*".

of June 1999.[719] As indicated by this succession of events, media coverage can trigger more participation and vice versa.

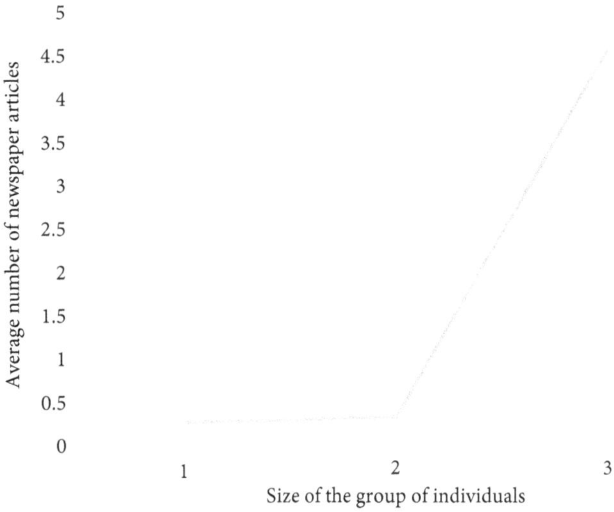

Figure 4.3. Average number of newspaper articles in relation to the size of the group of individuals

In addition, as suggested by figure 4.3, there is also a (two-way) relation between the size of the group of individuals involved and the extent of news coverage.[720] In case no 124/2010,[721] for example, an impressive number of almost 700 individuals (together with several local governments) brought the case before the Court. In the months leading up to the official petition (in February 2010), the possibility of an annulment action and the potential consequences of a review procedure had been widely discussed in several newspapers.[722] The size of the group would probably not have been as extensive if the news media had paid no attention to the issue. Both the official petition and the outcome in the preliminary suspension procedure received considerable attention in the newspapers.[723]

---

719 Le Matin, 30 June 1999, *"Pub tabac: ça va fumer ... Santé (Etat) ou économie (Région wallonne)? La Cour d'arbitrage se prépare à trancher"*.

720 In particular, the mean per category is: 1=0.26; 2=0.33; 3=4.56.

721 BeCC case no 124/2010, 28 October 2010.

722 For example: De Morgen, 22 October 2009, *"Communautaire rel over Vlaams inpectie in Franstalige scholen"*; L'Echo, 22 October 2009, *"Inspections: recours probable devant le Cour constitutionnelle"*; Le Soir, 22 October 2009, *"Périphérie. Ecole: la flandre passe en force. Les francophones veulent saisir la Cour constitutionnelle"*; De Morgen, 29 October 2009, *"Franstaligen naar Grondwettelijk Hof over faciliteitenscholen"*; and La Libre Belgique, 28 January 2010, *"Communautaire. Recours adopté contre le décret «inspection»"*.

723 Le Soir, 6 March 2010, *"Périphérie. Recours contre l'inspection scolaire"*; De Morgen, 30 July 2010, *"Vlaamse inspectie in Franstalige scholen van Brusselse rand geschorst"*; and L'Echo, 30 July 2010, *"L'inspection francophone rétablie dans ses droits. La Cour constitutionnelle balise le décret flamand sur l'enseignement dans la périphérie"*.

With regard to the relation between media coverage and participation, the results equally indicate that the involvement of a political actor is a cue for newspaper journalists. Although the number of cases in which these actors were involved is very limited, there is a considerable and significant mean difference in the average media coverage that these cases receive.[724] Several reasons can explain this result. First, the involvement of political actors signals that there may be a growing or ongoing political conflict. An example is case no 72/2005,[725] relating to fiscal legislation providing a one-off amnesty for fiscal fraud. Even before the legislation was adopted, members of the opposition announced they would challenge the legislation before the Court.[726] The news media equally reported on the sceptical advisory opinion of the Council of State, which was refuted by the legislative majority.[727] The opposition acted upon their intention and lodged a case before the Court. This open conflict between the legislative majority and minority triggered additional news media attention. In the newspapers, both the opinions of the proponents and opponents of the law were addressed.[728] Moreover, politicians are likely to actively seek the attention of news media, leading to increased coverage.[729] For instance, in case no 39/2013,[730] the Court dealt with a preliminary question relating to fiscal legislation that was raised by a prominent politician. The politician, who had been requested to disclose personal financial information as part of an investigation into fiscal fraud, challenged this request in court. During this procedure, the politician argued that lifting banking secrecy was contrary to the right to privacy and requested to refer a preliminary question related to that issue to the BeCC. At the same time, he gave several interviews to newspaper journalists, during which he announced his request. This resulted in extensive news coverage, even before the question was officially referred to the Court.[731]

---

724 Eight newspaper articles vs 0.3 (independent samples t-test; equal variance not assumed; $p=0.008$).

725 BeCC case no 72/2005, 20 April 2005.

726 De Standaard, 14 October 2003, "*Fiscale amnestie ook zonder repatriëring*"; L'Echo, 20 December 2003, "*Les livrets d'épargne et les terrains seront exclus du champ de le DLU*"; and De Tijd, 19 December, "*Meerderheid sleutelt niet meer aan EBA. CD&V vecht fiscale amnestie aan bij Arbitragehof*".

727 Financieel Ekonomische Tijd, 11 October 2003, "*Raad van State ziet graten in fiscale amnestie. Wetsontwerp loopt voor Arbitragehof risico op vernietiging*"; and De Standaard, 19 December 2003, "*Regering verwerpt kritiek Raad van State op fiscale amnestie*".

728 L'Echo, 26 February 2004, "*Fiscalité: l'oppostion CD&V attaque la DLU devant la Cour d'arbitrage*"; Cash, 25 March 2004, "*Finances personelles. Amnistie fiscale. DLU: questions au spécialiste*"; and La Libre Belgique, 13 October, 2004, "*Fiscalité: la DLU ne sera pas un échec*".

729 K Sill et al., 'Media Coverage of the U.S. Supreme Court: How Do Journalists Assess the Importance of Court Decisions?' (2013) 20 Political Communication, 1, 11–18.

730 BeCC case no 39/2013, 14 March 2013.

731 De Tijd, 3 December 2012, "*«Deze wet is gevaar voor de democratie»*"; L'Echo, 3 December 2012, "*Les services des impôts visent Karel De Gucht*"; De Morgen, 5 December 2012, "*«Ik word gepest door de fiscus». Karel De Gucht, Europees commissaris voor Handel, verzet zich*

Finally, a case may garner attention due to the subject area of the legislation under review. The subject-wise distribution of covered cases demonstrates that a variety of issues can be picked up by newspapers. Yet there is one that stands out. In particular, a constitutional challenge against legislation dealing with the 'the organisation of the state' (n=46) is considered more newsworthy than any other subject area.[732] This category includes cases related to the attribution of competences between the federal and subnational entities[733] or electoral organisation.[734] These pieces of legislation are usually adopted after a process of intense political negotiations, where Dutch-speaking and French-speaking politicians had to overcome their opposing views. When a constitutional review procedure is initiated, this may give rise to a new political conflict. For instance, in case no 35/2003,[735] three laws were challenged that implemented the institutional reform agreement 'Lambermont'. This agreement was reached by the Dutch-speaking and French-speaking coalition partners, but strongly criticised by the political opposition. Again, the open conflict between the legislative majority and minority was an incentive for newspaper journalists, resulting in a large number of articles covering the case.[736] In many 'state organisation' cases, like in this example, there was a political actor involved. Unsurprisingly, the news media attention peaks in cases where this combination occurs.[737]

More generally, competence conflict cases receive somewhat more attention than fundamental right cases.[738] Nonetheless, more attention is given to

tegen opheffen van zijn bankgeheim"; and Het Nieuwsblad, 5 December 2012, *"Karel De Gucht: «Fiscus gaat te ver»"*. The preliminary question was lodged before the BeCC on 3 April 2012: see De Standaard, 4 April 2012, *"Belastingen. Bankgeheim De Gucht naar Grondwettelijk Hof"*.

732 Average of 3.6 newspaper articles vs for example fundamental rights and freedoms (1.4) tax law (0.6), criminal law (0.3), law of persons and family law (0.09) or migration law (0.06).

733 For example, BeCC case no 169/2015, 26 November 2015.

734 For example, BeCC case no 161/2015, 19 November.

735 BeCC case no 35/2003, 25 March 2003.

736 Financieel Ekonomische Tijd, 1 June 2001, *"CVP: meerderheid manipuleert grondwet om tweederde te halen. Christen-democraten trekken naar Arbitragehof"*; Le Soir, 6 August 2001, *"Un retour de manivelle pour Polycarpe? La Cour d'arbitrage dira si l'accord du Lombard est inconstitutionnel"*; L'Echo 22 January 2002, *"Politique: devant la Cour d'arbitrage : les communes à facilités attaquent le Lambermont"*; and De Standaard, 1 February 2002, *"Lambermont: N-VA en FDF naar Arbitragehof"*.

737 In particular, these cases (n=18) were covered in an average of 7 newspaper articles. Yet, even when no political actor was involved (n=28), these cases receive more attention than any other subject area (1.65).

738 Fundamental rights cases (average 0.3); competence conflict cases (1). Yet, this mean difference is not significant (independent samples t-test; equal variance not assumed p=0.058).

the latter type of case when either the ECHR or EU law is invoked.[739] Yet 'mixed' cases, wherein both types of reference norms are invoked, are covered most extensively.[740] This may, however, be largely due to the fact that mixed cases also have the highest participation diversity, considering that both private (e.g. individuals) and institutional actors (e.g. regional governments) usually have an interest in the case.[741]

4.3.3. CONCLUSION: AN EXPLANATORY VARIABLE RELATED TO POLITICAL SALIENCE

The data analysis confirms that newspaper journalists are interested in cases that are controversial and/or potentially have a large impact on democratic policy-making. In particular, they are drawn to annulment actions introduced by a large or diverse group of litigants or by a political actor. More generally, cases that revolve around a political conflict are considered particularly newsworthy. Therefore, media attention is a reasonable indicator of political salience and should yield significant results when used to evaluate the strategic behaviour of the Court.

However, including an overly dispersed continuous variable in a regression model may distort the results. Therefore, based on the results discussed above, the count variable 'media attention' was recoded as a categorical variable, with three categories: no attention (0 articles), little media attention (1–5 articles) and extensive media attention (<5 articles). The category 'no attention' will serve as the reference category.

Table 4.12. Overview of the results for the explanatory variable 'media attention'

Categories of the explanatory variable 'media attention'	Number of cases (percentage)
No attention (REF)	2907 (92%)
Little attention (1–5 articles)	178 (6%)
Extensive attention (>5 articles)	60 (2%)

[739] In particular, the average media coverage increases to 1 when the ECHR is invoked and 1.8 when EU law is.

[740] Mixed cases (1.3) (independent samples t-test between fundamental rights and mixed cases; equal variance not assumed; p=0.008).

[741] Fundamental rights cases (average 1.3); competence conflict cases (1.8); and mixed cases (2.1) (independent samples t-test between first two categories: equal variance not assumed; p=0.000; and between the last two categories: equal variance assumed p=0.001).

4.4. PANEL SIZE

Finally, the size of the panel of judges deciding the case may also be reflected in strategic behaviour. While the variables relating to 'media attention' and 'participation' measure the behaviour of others, the variable 'panel size' starts from the perspective of the justices themselves. Scholars have argued that higher levels of activity by the justices indicate that a case is more salient to the Court as a whole as well as to individual justices.[742] Whether panel size measures political salience, legal salience, or both, depends on the criteria determining the composition of the Court.[743]

In what follows, an explanation for which data were collected, and why panel size can be used as a reliable, objective measurement of case salience is provided. Next, drawing on a descriptive data analysis, it is discussed how panel size has evolved over time, and the case features to which a deliberation in plenary session is primarily linked.

4.4.1. MEASURING PANEL SIZE

In Belgium, each case is, in principle, submitted to seven judges. When the case is relatively straightforward, the judges-rapporteurs may suggest submitting it to a 'limited procedure'.[744] If so, the case is similarly submitted to a panel of seven judges but within a more limited time frame. However, one of the two presidents may submit a case to the Court in plenary session, and they are obliged to do where this is requested by at least two judges.[745] In those cases, there are at least ten judges and a maximum of twelve judges involved. When the Court deliberates in plenary session, the double parity rule is strictly applied.

---

742 RC Black, MW Sorenson and TR Johnson, 'Toward an Actor-Based Measure of Supreme Court Case Salience: Information-Seeking and Engagement During Oral Arguments' (2012) 66 Political Research Quartely, 804–5.

743 C Chandrachud, 'Measuring Constitutional Case Salience in the Indian Supreme Court' (2014) 42 Journal of Law and Society, 42, 46; RC Black, MW Sorenson and TR Johnson, 'Toward an Actor-Based Measure of Supreme Court Case Salience: Information-Seeking and Engagement During Oral Arguments' (2012) 66 Political Research Quartely, 804; and F Maltzman, JE Spriggs and PJ Wahlbeck, *Crafting Law on the Supreme Court: the Collegial Game* (Cambridge University Press 2000), 83.

744 In particular, article 72 of the Special Act states: "If the judges-rapporteurs consider that the action for annulment is manifestly unfounded, the preliminary question evidently calls for a negative reply, or the case, owing to its very nature or the relatively straightforward nature of the issues raised therein, can be settled with a judgment delivered after a preliminary procedure".

745 Article 56 of the Special Act on the Constitutional Court.

Measuring panel size in Belgium is relatively straightforward. A categorical variable was created with the following categories: (1) seven judges (the procedure as per article 71); (2) seven judges (limited procedure as per article 72); and (3) plenary session (see Annex, *VAR18*).

Table 4.13. Overview of the results for the variable 'panel size' (see Annex, VAR18)

Panel size	Number of cases (percentage)
Seven judges (procedure article 71)	1782 (57%)
Seven judges (limited procedure article 72)	190 (6%)
Plenary session	1172 (37%)

Because there are no rules determining,[746] or guiding,[747] the decision to refer a case to plenary session, this relies solely on a request from the judges. When an annulment action or preliminary question is brought before the Court, a range of information is already available for the judges to guide them in that decision. In particular, the judges obtain information about the actors who initiated the procedure, the legislation under review and the constitutional grounds on which the legislation is challenged.

The propensity to request a plenary session relates to how salient the case is perceived to be by the judges, who are either legal specialists or former politicians, and either Dutch-speaking or French-speaking. On the one hand, a judge may request a plenary session because the case touches upon a controversial issue, for instance because the Dutch-speaking and French-speaking community have opposing views. Hence, a plenary session may reflect that the president or a group of judges preferred that all sub-groups were equally represented during the deliberations. In addition, one can assume that the professional judges wish to be included in the drafting process when the case deals with a novel or unique legal question. Therefore, in the Belgian situation, a plenary session may indicate that a case is legally or politically salient, or a combination of both.

746 For example, on the Indian Supreme Court, bench size is underscored by specific (constitutional) rules. See C Chandrachud, 'Measuring Constitutional Case Salience in the Indian Supreme Court' (2014) 42 Journal of Law and Society, 42, 45.

747 For example, several guiding criteria are published on the website of the UK Supreme Court, including cases of public importance, and cases that raise a point in relation to the European Convention of Human Rights: see https://www.supremecourt.uk/procedures/panel-numbers-criteria.html.

4.4.2. DATA ANALYSIS

Figure 4.4. Evolution in time for the variable 'panel size'

First, the results show that, overall, most cases were decided in restricted session with seven judges involved (63%). Yet, from 2000 onwards, and especially during the last ten years, requests for plenary session have become more and more common. With the exception of 1987 – when 8 out of 11 rulings were proclaimed in plenary session – cases before 2007 were mostly settled in restricted session. Nowadays, this situation is inverted: a plenary session has become the preferred panel size to review constitutional cases.

A first, remarkable result is the relation between media attention and panel size. In particular, 34% of the cases that were not covered in the newspaper were decided in plenary session. In the group of cases that received some attention, this percentage increases to 67%. Finally, almost all cases that were intensively covered were dealt with in plenary session (92%). There are several explanations for this result. On the one hand, the decision of newspaper journalists to cover a certain issue and the Court's decision to treat a case in plenary session are often taken simultaneously. In that case, this result suggests that the judges and newspaper journalists are driven by the same case characteristics. As will be demonstrated below, there is considerable overlap between the two measures with regard to the correlation with the type of procedure, participation and subject issues. On the other hand, it is plausible that the judges are more likely to request a plenary session when they anticipate that their decision will be under public scrutiny.

Further, panel size is partly determined by the type of procedure. While two thirds of the preliminary questions are settled in restricted session (32%), the probability that an action for annulment is decided in plenary session is almost 50:50 (47%). This suggests that judges want to be included in the drafting process when the potential impact of the case is stronger. As mentioned before, when the annulment procedure results in striking down (part of) the challenged legislation, this has more dramatic consequences for the legislative branch. Nonetheless, considering that the number of preliminary questions has increased more sharply than the number of annulment actions, the evolution towards more plenary sessions must be affected by other factors than the type of procedure.

The subject area of the legislation under review may equally trigger a request for a plenary session. The results show that, of all legal domains, there are two which stand out. More cases related to the 'organisation of the state' (65%) or 'migration' (58%) were settled in plenary session.[748] Because the cases from both areas are evenly spread in time,[749] these differences are not due to their concentration in more recent years. The relation between 'state organisation' legislation and panel size suggests that the judges are sensitive to political considerations. Because these cases are usually politically controversial, the results suggest that the judges consider it important that the review is carried out by a panel where both the Dutch-speaking and French-speaking judges and the legal specialists and former politicians are equally represented. Also, since the case outcome can give rise to a political conflict, the Court may want to address its audience in the largest coalition possible. Research on the US Supreme Court has shown that the larger the majority of judges who voted in favour of the decision, the greater the appearance of certainty and the more likely it is that the decision will be accepted.[750] In addition, the judges pay special attention to 'migration' issues, notwithstanding that these cases are seldom covered by the news media[751] and usually do not attract a large group of participants.[752,753] Hence, it can be assumed that these cases are not politically controversial, but rather are considered relevant from a legal perspective. Many of these cases have a supranational or international dimension.[754] Hence, the cases may require

---

748 In all other legal domains (for an overview, see the Coding Book in the Annex), there were as many cases decided in restricted session as in plenary session.

749 In particular, 53% of the 'migration' issues and even 65% of the 'state organisation' cases were decided before 2007.

750 WF Murphy, *Elements of Judicial Strategy* (University of Chicago Press 1964); and RC Black et al., *US Supreme Court Opinions and Their Audiences* (Cambridge University Press 2016). Yet it should be noted that this argument was based on research conducted in the context of the USSC, where individual opinions are allowed. Therefore, in the Belgian setting, where all decisions (even when discussed by a lower number of judges) are presented as consensual, a decision in plenary session may be less influential.

751 Only four of these cases were covered in the news media.

752 Average participation diversity of 1.2 vs overall diversity of 1.4 (independent samples t-test; equal variance not assumed; $p=0.002$). In only two cases, a large group of individuals was involved.

753 For example, BeCC case no 133/2015, 1 October 2015.

754 In particular, the ECHR is invoked in 53% of these migration cases (vs average 21%) and EU law in 15% (average 6%) (independent samples t-test; equal variance not assumed; $p=0.000$ and $p=0.004$).

a more extensive legal analysis (e.g. scrutiny of the case law of the ECtHR or the European Court of Justice) and therefore prompt the professional judges to request a plenary session.

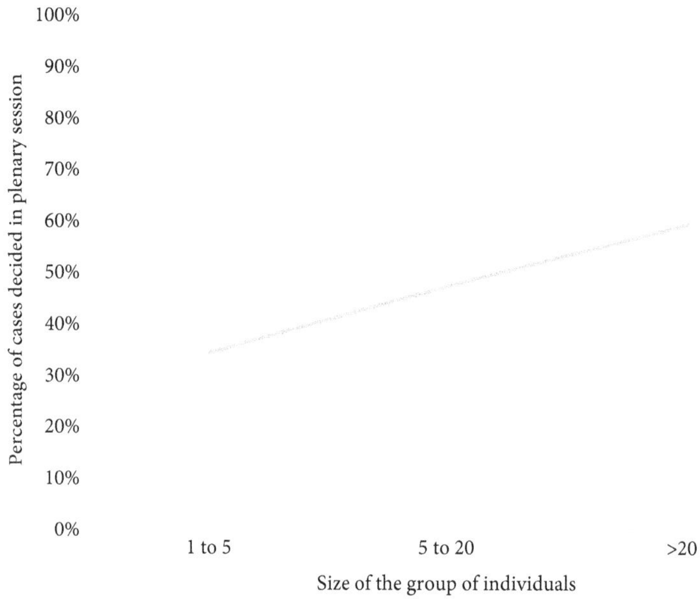

Figure 4.5. Panel size in relation to the size of the group of individuals

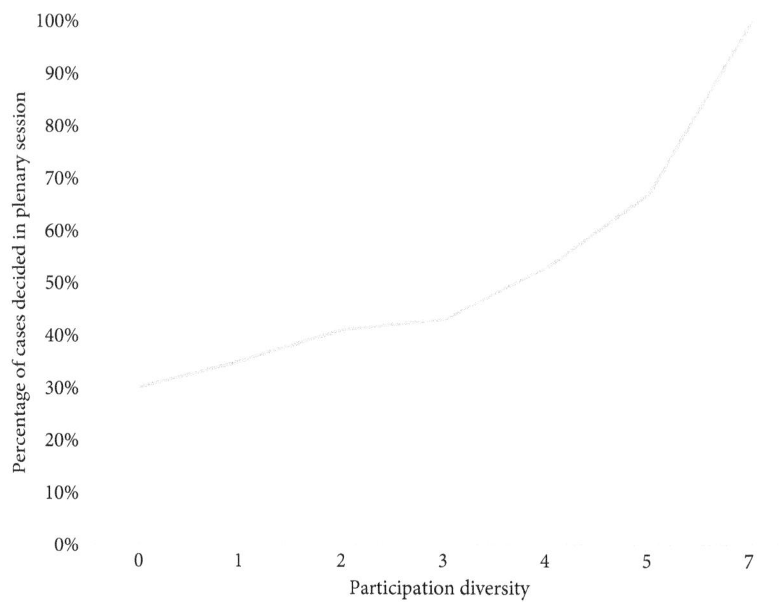

Figure 4.6. Panel size in relation to participation diversity

Further, panel size may also be affected by the type or number of participants involved in the review procedure.[755] First, the results indicate that more efforts are spent on cases that involve a broader set of interests. In particular, the judges deliberate more regularly in plenary session when an interest group is involved (50%). Also, as figures 9–10 indicate, the larger the group of individuals,[756] and especially the more diverse the group of litigants,[757] the more likely the case is to be settled in plenary session. Hence, cases that potentially affect a larger group of citizens are perceived as more salient by the judges on the BeCC. Finally, in most cases where a political actor was involved, a restricted session was considered inadequate.[758]

The petitioners should not only indicate which piece of legislation they wish to challenge, but also on which constitutional grounds. The data demonstrate that fundamental rights cases (36%) and competence conflict cases (39%) receive, on average, equal attention from the BeCC judges. Nonetheless, mixed cases, where the Court is requested to review legislation against both reference norms, are more likely to be settled in plenary session (54%).[759] In addition, more plenary sessions occur when the Court is requested to review against the ECHR (58%) or EU law (62%). Petitions that raise a variety of pleas or pleas based on supranational law are not necessarily more controversial, but may require a more extensive legal analysis. Therefore, this may prompt judges, especially those with a legal background, to request a plenary session.

There are additional indications that panel size is affected by a case's legal relevance. For instance, the Court deliberates more often in plenary session when the legislation under review is an implementation of a European directive (58%). In principle, this implementation process requires the Belgian government to adopt legislation in accordance with the principles determined at the European level. When this legislation is challenged on constitutional grounds, this may indicate that the European directive conflicts with the Belgian Constitution. Also, cases following a preliminary reference to the European Court of Justice (ECJ) are also more frequently settled in plenary session (83%). Notwithstanding that these cases with a European connotation are usually neglected by the news media, their legal relevance pushes the judges to request a plenary session.

755 PT Spiller and R Gely, 'Strategic Judicial Decision Making' in GA Caldeira, RD Keleman and KE Whittington (eds.), *The Oxford Handbook of Law and Politics* (Oxford University Press 2008), 89: "the cases that attract the most attention from those outside of the Court also attract the most attention from the justices themselves".

756 In particular, the mean per category is: 0=30%; 1=35%; 2=0,53; 3=41%; 4=53%; 5=67%; and 7=100%.

757 In particular, the mean per category is: 1=34%; 2=47%; 3=59%.

758 62% of these cases (n=32) were decided in plenary session.

759 54% (n=198) (independent samples t-test; equal variance not assumed; p=0.000).

4.4.3. CONCLUSION: AN EXPLANATORY VARIABLE RELATED TO POLITICAL AND LEGAL SALIENCE

In conclusion, the above findings suggest that judges wish to discuss a case more elaborately with their colleagues when the case potentially has a strong impact, when they consider there should be a strict balance between all sub-groups within the Court and/or when the case requires a more extensive legal analysis. A plenary session is thus linked to a case's politically controversial nature, its legal relevance or a combination of both. In order to investigate the relation between a plenary session and the Court's behaviour, the variable 'panel size' was recoded into an explanatory variable with only two categories: (0) restricted session, and (1) plenary session.

Table 4.14. Overview of the results for the explanatory variable 'panel size'

Categories of the explanatory variable 'panel size'	Number of cases (percentage)
Restricted session (REF)	1973 (63%)
Plenary session	1172 (37%)

4.5. HIGHLY SALIENT CASES (N=57)

In conclusion, the selected measures are objective and reflect salience at the time the case is lodged before the Court. In particular, the information was either drawn from the online published rulings (participation, panel size) or, based on certain determined catchwords, from a variety of publicly accessible newspapers. Although the results indicate that there is a level of congruence between the measures, they do not overlap. It is possible that different judicial practices are related more or less strongly to one of the separate measures. For instance, judicial salience may dictate the Court's citation practices, but litigant salience may be more strongly linked to the case outcome. Therefore, instead of creating a single variable that merges the different measures,[760] they will serve as separate explanatory variables. When the results indicate a significant relation between these variables and various aspects of the BeCC's case law, this suggests that strategic considerations are inherent to the BeCC's decision-making process.

Although strategic behaviour may thus be activated by each of the salience indicators, this is particularly to be expected in highly salient cases – where each of these indicators is present rather than absent. To deepen the empirical findings, each regression analysis will be completed with some highly

[760] Such as the measure developed in TS Clark et al., 'Measuring the Political Salience of Supreme Court Cases' (2015) 3 Journal of Law and Courts, 37.

salient case examples. In particular, a detailed analysis of these case examples can illustrate how the BeCC manages constraints impacting its decision-making process, leading to a strategic equilibrium reflected in the final decision. In addition, the in-depth study serves to interpret the empirical results from a deliberative perspective.

As shown in table 4.15, the majority of cases (53%) do not score on any of the indicators and can be considered *non-salient*. The second largest group (36%) are the cases of *low salience*, where only one indicator is present. The findings indicate that the BeCC often deliberates in plenary session, without the case being covered in the newspapers *or* the participation of a large or diverse group of participants or of political actors (such as with migration issues). Conversely, not many cases are picked up by the news media without any sign of litigant salience or a request for plenary session. Next, a smaller group of cases (9%) can be categorised as *moderately salient*, with two of the three indicators present. A noteworthy result is that the Court rarely deliberates in restricted session when a large or diverse group of participants or a political actor was involved *and* the case received some media attention. Finally, only a limited number of cases (n=57) can be considered *highly salient*, since they received at least some media attention, there was either a large group of individuals or a diverse group of litigants or political actors involved, and they were decided in plenary session.

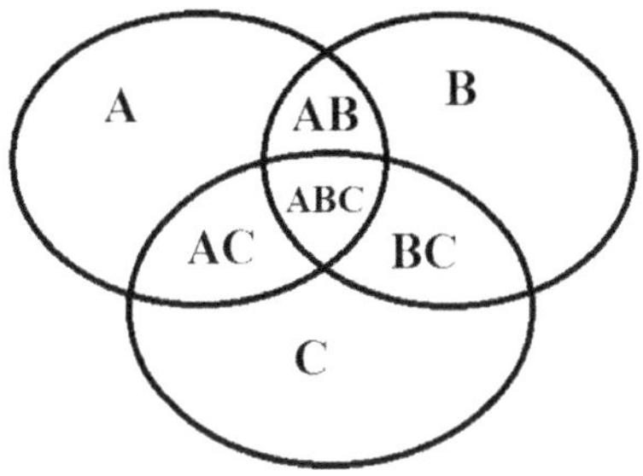

SALIENCE?	Indicator	N=
Non-salient		1683
Low salience	A	226
	B	48
	C	843
Moderate salience	AC	155
	AB	15
	BC	118
High salience	ABC	57
TOTAL		3145

Figure 4.7. and Table 4.15. Overview of the overall results for the variable 'case salience'

A=participation of a large group of individuals (>5), a diverse group of litigants (>2) or a political actor (yes/no); B=media attention (>1); C=plenary session (yes/no)

An overview of the *highly salient* cases can be found below (table 4.16). As mentioned before, these cases are excellent candidates for an in-depth study, and particularly to illustrate causal patterns with factual arguments. Therefore, this section ends with a discussion of a selection of these highly salient cases,[761] focusing on the political process leading up to the challenged legislation and the news media coverage prior to the petition. How the BeCC manages the impact of the case's underlying salience on its decision will be scrutinised in the following empirical chapters.

Many highly salient cases revolve around a political conflict. Several of these politically charged cases dealt with the division of the so-called 'BHV' constituency – a particularly sensitive issue on which Dutch-speaking and French-speaking politicians (and the general public) were divided. A brief historical overview can clarify why this can be considered a highly salient issue within the Belgian polity. Until 2012, this constituency was comprised of the Brussels Region (B) and part of the Flemish region (Halle Vilvoorde). While, in principle, citizens within the Flemish region can only vote for Dutch-speaking politicians, inhabitants in BHV could also vote for French-speaking politicians. The division into two separate constituencies, which was requested by the Flemish parties, was strongly opposed by the French-speaking politicians. Although Halle and Vilvoorde were part of the Flemish region, many of their inhabitants were actually French-speaking. Disintegrating BHV could have caused a considerable loss of votes for the French-speaking political parties in the HV constituency. When a 1993 law relating to the federal state structure confirmed the existence of the BHV constituency, a large group of Flemish individuals challenged these provisions before the BeCC.[762] Although in this case different provisions of the law were challenged by other actors,[763] the news media showed particular interest in the 'BHV dimension' of the case.[764] When, in 2003, electoral legislation was adopted that again did not fulfil the Flemish request for a division, the political opposition was very critical and publicly announced that it would seek judicial redress.[765] The whole procedure before the

---

761 Some of these cases were in discussed in the previous sections, in particular: BeCC case no 102/99, 30 September 1999; BeCC case no 110/1999, 14 October 1999; BeCC case no 35/2003, 25 March 2003; BeCC case no 124/2010, 28 October 2010; BeCC case no 72/2005, 20 April 2005; and BeCC case no 39/2013, 14 March 2013.

762 BeCC case no 90/94, 22 December 1994.

763 For example, the German-speaking community challenged the fact that they were under-represented at the federal level (with no permanent representation on the executive level) while the decisions taken at this level also apply to their community. Also, to elect the 'directly elected senators', French-speaking and Dutch-speaking constituencies were created, but no separate German-speaking one.

764 For example: La Wallonie, 21 January 1994, *"Francophones de la périphérie. Recours introduit devant la Cour d'arbitrage"*; and De Standaard, 7 October 1994, *"Arbitragehof buigt zich over klacht niet-splitsing Brussel-Halle-Vilvoorde"*.

765 For example: Financieel Ekonomische Tijd, 29 May 2002, *"Oppositie met kieshervorming naar Arbitragehof. CD&V kondigt politieke actie aan in Vlaams-Brabant"*; L'Echo, 29 May 2002,

BeCC received considerable attention in the news media.[766] Finally, as a corollary of the division of the BHV constituency in 2012, an arrangement was adopted for the BHV judicial district. Yet this reform was challenged by members of the Flemish judiciary, together with a political party in opposition.[767] Because the outcome of this procedure could potentially re-escalate the political conflict, the news media paid considerable attention to the case.[768] These examples show that political parties outside the majority coalition sometimes pass on a political 'hot potato' to the Court. Considering the balanced composition of the Court, it can be expected that the final ruling will reflect a judicial decision-making process centred on finding a compromise between the different sub-groups within the Court.

While the BHV issue mainly resulted from a political conflict between the parties north and south from the Belgian language border, other highly salient cases revolve around a conflict between members of the political majority and minority. In particular, in two cases related to party funding, the challenge was introduced by members of a political party in opposition. First, a law adopted in 1999 introduced a strict condition for becoming eligible for party funding, in particular to respect and comply with the fundamental rights and freedoms protected by the ECHR. During the legislative decision-making procedure, politicians from one specific party ('Vlaams Blok') argued that the law targeted their party and aimed to reduce or eliminate their funding.[769] Yet, as part of the parliamentary minority, they were not able to prevent the adoption of the legislation. Therefore, a group of leading figures of 'Vlaams Blok' resorted to the BeCC and initiated an annulment procedure.[770] This political conflict was quickly picked up by the news media.[771]

"Réformes: le CD&V attaquera la loi électorale devant la Cour d'arbitrage. Conforté par l'avis du Conseil d'Etat"; and De Morgen, 13 September 2002, *"Laatste woord over kieswet voor Arbitragehof. Oppositie geeft verzet tegen nieuw kiesstelsel nog juridisch verlengstuk"*.

766 BeCC case no 73/2003, 26 May 2003.

767 BeCC case no 96/2014, 30 June 2014.

768 For example: De Standaard, 1 September 2012, *"N-VA tackelt BHV juridisch. Partij moet bewijzen dat splitsing «discriminerend» is"*; La Libre Belgique, 26 September 2012, *"Recours contre l'autre BHV. Magistrats et avocats flamands"*; De Tijd, 26 February 2013, *"68 magistraten vechten BHV-hervorming aan"*; and Le Soir, 7 August 2013, *"BHV: ne tentons pas le diable, il est dans les détails"*.

769 For example: the report of the Commission for Internal Affairs, published on 10 July 1998, *Parl Doc* Chamber no 1084/6-96/97, throughout; the additional report of the Commission for Internal Affairs, published on 4 December 1998, *Parl Doc* Chamber no 1084/22-96/97, throughout; and the report of the Commission for Internal Affairs, published on 26 January 1999, *Parl Doc* 1-1197/3-98/99, throughout.

770 BeCC case no 10/2001, 7 February 2001.

771 For example: De Morgen, 24 August 1999, *"Vlaams Blok brengt beknotting racistische partijen voor Arbitragehof"*; and Le Soir, 24 August 1999, *"Le Blok en justice pour conserver sa dotation. Recours à la Cour d'arbitrage en annulation de la loi sur le financement des partis"*.

A few years later, a new law was adopted to clarify the funding withdrawal procedure. In particular, the Council of State was made competent to judge on such withdrawals. Before, a lack of clarity had in practice impeded the application of the law of 1999. Again, several 'Vlaams Blok' politicians made clear that they felt targeted and strongly criticised the legislative proposal, but their effort was to no avail.[772] One year after the law's adoption, a group of parliamentary representatives initiated a funding withdrawal procedure against 'Vlaams Blok'. Within the context of this procedure before the Council of State, the litigants requested to refer several preliminary questions to the BeCC.[773] The requesting litigants, who defended the interests of 'Vlaams Blok', announced their action through the news media.[774] Once referred to the BeCC, the case continued to receive considerable attention in the newspapers.[775] In conclusion, in these cases the opposition tried to reverse a policy decision they had not been able to avert at the legislative level. Indirectly, the Court was called upon to judge their rights as members of the political minority.

However, not all highly salient cases result from a political conflict. An example is case no 154/2007,[776] in which the Court dealt with legislation introducing regulations for carrying and trading arms. The challenged legislation, whose main purpose was to protect citizens against firearms crimes, was adopted shortly after a major shooting incident in Antwerp. At the time, the incident dominated the news, which had accelerated the legislative decision-making process.[777] In order to avoid any impulsive purchases of firearms, a new licencing system was set up. Also, a central registration point was created, aiming to facilitate the traceability of all firearms within Belgium.[778] At the time, the law

---

772 For example: the report of the Commission for Internal Affairs, published on 3 February 2004, *Parl Doc* Chamber no 51/0217, throughout; and the report of the plenary session in the parliamentary assembly on 12 February 2004, 25–44.

773 BeCC case no 195/2009, 3 December 2009.

774 Gazet van Antwerpen, 9 July 2008, *"Proces tegen Vlaams Belang moet naar Grondwettelijk Hof"*; and De Standaard, 10 July 2008, *"Proces Vlaams Belang waarschijnlijk naar Grondwettelijk Hof"* (published while the procedure was pending, but before the preliminary questions were referred to the BeCC).

775 For example: De Tijd, 15 January 2009, *"Partijfinanciering. Uitspraak over Vlaams Belang wellicht niet voor verkiezingen"*; La Libre Belgique, 15 January 2009, *"Partis. Financement du Belang à la Cour constitutionnelle"*; and Het Laatste Nieuws, 22 September 2009, *"Vlaams belang wraakt vijf rechters"*.

776 BeCC case no 154/2007, 19 December 2007.

777 A first draft of the legislation was submitted in 2001 (*Parl St* Chamber no 50-1598/001) but expired. On 7 February 2006, a new draft was submitted (*Parl St* Chamber no 51-2263/001). A few days after the incident (May 2006), several amendments were discussed (*Parl St* Chamber no 51-2263/002) followed by a report of the Special Committee on Justice (*Parl St* Chamber no 51-2263/003). The law was adopted on 8 June 2006. For a discussion, see V Verlinden, *De Hoeders van de Wet* (Die Keure 2010), 222–4.

778 Explanatory memorandum to the draft of 7 February 2006 of the law regulating economical and individual activities with firearms, *Parl St* Chamber no 51-2263/001.

was considered amongst the strictest arms regulations in the world. The main points of the law met with broad political support and were adopted without extensive discussion. Yet, due to the acceleration, some argued that the quality of the decision-making process left much to be desired.[779] Shortly after its adoption, a petition was lodged before the Court by several individual firearm owners, a business buying and selling firearms, and associations acting in the interest of one or both. In short, these actors argued they were treated unreasonably by the new regulations, considering they owned a firearm for recreational, sporting or historical reasons without any intention to commit a crime with it. One of these associations was consulted during the legislative procedure, but its concerns had been neglected.[780] The judicial action was discussed in the newspapers.[781] In this case, the Court was requested to evaluate the interest of firearm owners, in a context of broad political and public support for the legislative decision.

Finally, a case can also be considered highly salient because it deals with a morally controversial issue, such as same-sex marriage.[782] During the decision-making process in preparation of a law allowing same-sex marriage, several politicians emphasised the delicate nature of this issue.[783] In its advisory opinion, the Council of State had shown itself sceptical towards the proposal because it conflicted with the traditional understanding of marriage. In addition, the Council argued that it would not be discriminatory to reserve the marriage statute for heterosexual couples.[784] Nonetheless, these arguments were considered outdated and the legislation was adopted with a broad majority. Yet the law was challenged before the BeCC by a group of heterosexual couples, whose complaints were covered in the news media.[785] The married couples argued that, due to the new law, their marriage did not represent anymore what they wanted it to be at the moment they were wed. The non-married couples argued that the new law obliged them, before joining in marriage in accordance with their religious beliefs, to accede to a marital status conflicting with these beliefs. Hence, the Court was called upon to judge in this delicate matter.

---

779 V Verlinden, *De Hoeders van de Wet* (Die Keure 2010), 223.

780 See *Parl St* Chamber no 51-2263/002, 78 and further.

781 For example: De Morgen, 25 July 2006, "*Wapenliefhebbers naar Arbitragehof tegen wapenwet*"; and Le Soir, 26 July 2006, "*Armes. La Cour d'arbitrage saisie d'une requête en annulation. Les armuriers flinguent la loi*".

782 BeCC case no 159/2004, 20 October 2004.

783 See the report of the Commission of Justice, *Parl Doc* no 50-2165/002, 7–19.

784 Ibid., 5.

785 De Standaard, 6 November 2003, "*Klacht tegen homohuwelijk bij Arbitragehof*".

Table 4.16. Overview of the highly salient cases (n=57)

Case no	Short description *FRC = fundamental rights case* *CCC = competence conflict case* *MC = mixed case*	Annulment procedure	Participation Diversity	Large group of individuals	No of newspaper articles published before the ruling
1990/018	MC – electoral legislation applicable to the local level	X	3		7
1990/026	MC – electoral legislation applicable to the European level	X	3	X	1
1994/090	MC – structure of the federal state (e.g. BHV constituency)	X	(2)	X	3
1998/128	MC – inheritance tax	X	5	X	4
1999/090	FRC – religious freedom in education	X	(2)	X	1
1999/102	MC – tobacco advertising case	X	4		46
1999/110	CCC – assistance mechanism for war victims	X	7	X	69
2000/020	FRC – financial allocations to political parties		3		2
2000/040	FRC – criminal procedure related to customs and excise taxes		3	X	1
2001/010	FRC – financial allocations to political parties	X	3		3
2001/102	FRC – health insurance		3		4
2003/014	FRC – access conditions (exams) for attorneys to the magistracy	X	(1)	X	1
2003/035	MC – federal structure, elections, joining of lists, municipalities with special language facilities	X	5	X	38
2003/036	FRC – federal structure, the allocation of seats in the Brussels regional parliament	X	(2)	X	27

(continued)

Table 4.16 *continued*

Case no	**Short description** *FRC = fundamental rights case* *CCC = competence conflict case* *MC = mixed case*	**Annulment procedure**	**Participation Diversity**	**Large group of individuals**	**No of newspaper articles published before the ruling**
2003/050	MC – night flights, noise pollution	X	3	X	3
2003/051	MC – night flights, noise pollution	X	3	X	3
2003/073	FRC – BHV case	X	(2)	X	30
2003/094	MC – building permit granted by a regional decree (parliamentary ratification)	X	(2)	X	1
2003/160	FRC – supervision of financial actors and services	X	(2)	X	20
2004/111	FRC – corporate income tax	X	(1)	X	2
2004/146	MC – anti-discrimination law	X	3		1
2004/159	FRC – same-sex marriage	X	(1)	X	2
2005/044	MC – restructuring higher education in Flanders	X	3		2
2005/148	FRC – appointments to the Muslim executive	X	(2)	X	11
2007/154	MC – weapon regulations	X	3	X	9
2008/182	FRC – court fees payable by the losing party	X	3	X	3
2009/002	MC – protection of the environment against cell phone radiation	X	4		3
2009/009	FRC – social elections	X	(2)	X	4
2009/121	FRC – enrolment system for schools in the Brussels Region	X	3	X	9
2009/195	FRC – financial allocation to political parties		3	X	8

(continued)

Table 4.16 *continued*

Case no	**Short description** *FRC = fundamental rights case* *CCC = competence conflict case* *MC = mixed case*	**Annulment procedure**	**Participation Diversity**	**Large group of individuals**	**No of newspaper articles published before the ruling**
2010/074	FRC – military discipline	X	(2)	X	10
2010/124	CCC – school inspections in municipalities with special language facilities	X	4	X	73
2010/151	FRC – noise pollution of flights		4		2
2011/004	FRC – enrolment system for schools in the French-speaking Community	X	(2)	X	10
2011/009	MC – supervision of auditors on public institutions	X	5		4
2011/037	FRC – tobacco ban in restaurants and bars	X	3		20
2011/040	FRC – Islamic headscarfs in schools		3		13
2011/050	MC – planning and housing policy in the Flemish Region	X	3		4
2011/089	FRC – quota for foreign students in medical education	X	(1)	X	8
2011/188	FRC – spatial planning, large landowners	X	(2)	X	3
2012/073	FRC – funding for education in the French-speaking Community	X	3	X	2
2012/144	FRC – building permit granted by a regional decree (parliamentary ratification)	X	5	X	28
2012/145	FRC – prohibition of the full-face veil	X	3		19
2013/117	MC – Energy transport	X	3		5

(continued)

Table 4.16 *continued*

Case no	**Short description** *FRC = fundamental rights case* *CCC = competence conflict case* *MC = mixed case*	**Annulment procedure**	**Participation Diversity**	**Large group of individuals**	**No of newspaper articles published before the ruling**
2013/121	MC – family reunification for migrants	X	(2)	X	4
2013/141	MC – fiscal fraud	X	4	X	3
2013/144	FRC – planning and housing policy in the Flemish Region	X	3		1
2013/170	CCC – tax on savings account	X	4		1
2014/073	MC – competences of the local government within the Brussels Region	X	4		5
2014/080	FRC – private education	X	(2)	X	1
2014/096	FRC – division of the BHV judicial district	X	3	X	18
2014/103	FRC – law enforcement reform (police)	X	(2)	X	1
2014/162	FRC – corporate income tax	X	3	X	11
2015/070	FRC – fees for judicial procedures		3		2
2015/105	CCC – tax on cell phone pylons	X	3		8
2015/116	FRC – differential treatment of employees and workmen	X	(2)	X	1
2015/131	FRC – urgent medical care for migrants	X	3		1

CHAPTER 5
CASE OUTCOMES

5.1. INTRODUCTION

Each case brought before the Court leads to a final dictum, which is the concluding part of the judgment and answers the raised constitutional question(s) ('pleas'). Traditionally, empirical judicial behaviour studies focus on case outcomes, and in particular on the extent to which the ideological preferences of the individual judges determine whether challenged legislation is invalidated or not.[786] Yet, for two reasons, the approach in this chapter is different.

First, in Belgium voting behaviour is not only concealed from the public, but the judicial outcome is also believed to be the result of a collegial effort. The BeCC, like most other European constitutional courts, needs to function within an institutional environment that is believed to reinforce the collegial dynamic of judicial decision-making. In particular, no dissenting opinions are allowed and the double parity rule prevents judges from pushing through their opinion without taking into consideration the concerns of other judges.[787]

Second, a binary categorisation of case outcomes (invalidated or not) is too limited.[788] Like in many other countries,[789] the BeCC has developed diverse

---

786 For example: JA Segal and HJ Spaeth, *The Supreme Court and the Attitudinal Model Revisited* (Cambridge University Press 2002); and A Bustos and T Jacobi, 'Strategic Judicial Preference Revelation' (2014) 57 The Journal of Law and Economics, 113.

787 Although some of the institutional factors favouring individualistic behaviour can also be found in European courts, not one has all of them simultaneously: A Dyevre, 'Unifying the Field of Comparative Judicial Politics: Towards a General Theory on Judicial Behaviour' (2010) 2 European Political Science Review, 297, 319.

788 M De Visser, *Constitutional Review in Europe: A Comparative Analysis* (Hart Publishing 2014), 301.

789 For European countries, see: M De Visser, *Constitutional Review in Europe: A Comparative Analysis* (Hart Publishing 2014), 281 and further (Chapter 6: Testing and Remedying Unconstitutionality); VF Comella, *Constitutional Courts and Democratic Values* (Yale University Press 2009), 74; and M Shapiro and A Stone Sweet, *On Law, Politics and Judicialization* (Oxford University Press 2002), 63, 71–3. For the US, Canada and UK, see: ES Fish, 'Choosing Constitutional Remedies' (2016) 63 UCLA Law Review, 322; and A Kavanagh, *Constitutional Review under the UK Human Rights Act* (Cambridge University Press 2009), 186. For South Africa, see L Du Plessis, 'The Status and Role of Legislation in South Africa as a Constitutional Democracy: some Exploratory Observations' (2011) 14 Potchefstroom Electronic Law Journal, 92, 94–5.

methods for answering a question of constitutionality. As mentioned before (section 2.6.) the law only allows the BeCC to reject the challenge or (partially) invalidate the unconstitutional provision(s). If legislation is invalidated, the Court can also temper the retroactive effect of this decision.[790] However, the Court also proclaims 'modulated outcomes'.[791] In general, such creative outcomes indicate how the legislation should be interpreted or altered in order for it to be applied in a constitutional way.

Importantly, there are no (internal) rules determining whether the finding of a violation should lead to either a simple invalidation or a modulated outcome.[792] Also, the Court holds a discretionary power to decide whether it is appropriate to temper the retroactive effect of its decision.[793] Therefore, a study of case outcomes provides insights into how the Court addresses its audience, how this has developed over time, and why in some cases a particular outcome is considered more suitable than others.

The plan of this chapter is as follows. In section 5.2., the case outcomes are studied from a deliberative perspective. More specifically, how case dicta can be used as a vehicle for dialogue about constitutional meanings and responsibility is explored.[794] In short, by proclaiming clear and constructive dicta, courts may catalyse deliberation outside of their own scope. The role of the news media is also discussed, because journalists share some responsibility in raising awareness about and drawing attention to relevant cases.

Next, in section 5.3. the various possible case outcomes are discussed in more detail, illustrating how the case law was coded with examples from the Court's rulings. Following this, two analyses are carried out on the case outcomes – the first with a descriptive and the second with an explanatory focus.

The first analysis makes up section 5.4. and aims to *describe* which case outcomes appear in different types of cases and how this has evolved over time. The section is centred on the following question: has the BeCC, over time, made

790 See articles 8 (annulment procedure) and 26§1 (preliminary question) of the Special Act.

791 C Behrendt, *Le juge constitutionnel, un législateur-cadre positif: Les normes juridictionnelles relatives à la production et au contenu de norms législatives futures – une analyse comparative en droit français, belge et allemand* (doctoral thesis at the University Paris I Panthéon-Sorbonne 2005); and J De Jaegere, 'Actieve rechtsvorming door het Grondwettelijk Hof: waar ligt de grens?' (2014) 1 Tijdschrift voor Bestuurskunde en Publiek Recht, 22.

792 The Court's rulings have developed on a case-by-case basis. See M Verdussen, 'La responsabilité civile du fait de légiférer en violation de la constitution' in D Renders (ed.), *La responsabilité des pouvoirs publics* (Bruylant 2016), 420. More generally, modulated outcomes are "not usually envisaged by the legal framework governing constitutional adjudicatory processes, but instead embraced by those courts in their case law." See M De Visser, *Constitutional Review in Europe: A Comparative Analysis* (Hart Publishing 2014), 309.

793 S Verstraelen, 'The Temporal Limitation of Judicial Decisions: The Need for Flexibility Versus the Quest for Uniformity' (2013) 14 German Law Journal, 1687, 1699.

794 M De Visser, *Constitutional Review in Europe: A Comparative Analysis* (Hart Publishing 2014), 331–2.

more use of techniques that leave room for or prompt a legislative response? The signalling strength of each dictum is discussed, and the legislative consequences that may or should follow from these dicta. In addition, it is taken into account how the news media responds to different judicial outcomes.

The second analysis, in section 5.5., is focused on *explaining* case outcomes. Although legal rules and values are principally expected to determine whether legislation is found unconstitutional or not, strategic considerations may also affect the case outcome. Essentially, the Court must think ahead to the prospective consequences and anticipate the probable reactions of other actors (in)directly involved in the review procedure. In this chapter, hypotheses are developed in two steps. In the first, the relation between case salience and the finding of a violation is explored. In particular, it is hypothesised that in cases that are perceived as salient by the litigants, the news media and the Court itself, a violation is more likely to be established. Importantly, if so, this relation does not necessarily reflect strategic behaviour by the Court, but may be simply due to the fact that cases receive more attention when the legislator has acted in contravention of the Constitution. The second step concentrates on the subset of cases where a violation was found, and explore the relation between case salience and the specific type of outcome: invalidation or modulation. In particular, it is hypothesised that, *if* a violation has been found, increased case salience will prompt the Court to act more prudently by proclaiming a modulated outcome instead of a blunt invalidation. The two sets of hypotheses are tested through two logistic regression models. The results indicate that the establishment of a violation is mainly determined by the procedural traits of the case, but that strategic considerations dictate whether the Court opts for a modulated outcome over an invalidation.

5.2. A DELIBERATIVE PERSPECTIVE: ENGAGING IN DIALOGUE THROUGH CONSTRUCTIVE CASE OUTCOMES

Through their rulings, constitutional courts indicate the boundaries of what is constitutionally acceptable. Although the giving of reasons is also an essential medium of communication, the case dictum is considered the pre-eminent vehicle for engaging in dialogue. As explained in the normative framework, the dicta should leave room for and initiate an interactive engagement with other actors: citizens, the legislator and regular courts.[795] First, a clear case dictum

[795] See P Popelier and AA Patiño Álvarez, 'Deliberative Practices of Constitutional Courts in Consolidated and Non-Consolidated Democracies' in P Popelier, A Mazmanyan and W Vandenbruwaene (eds.), *The Role of Constitutional Courts in Multilevel Governance* (Intersentia 2013), 223.

can stimulate the acceptance of approved legislation or, conversely, give citizens reason to request legislative change if a violation has been found. Next, the case dicta can assist the political branches in amending current legislation or drafting new legislation, so that it will survive future constitutional challenges.[796] Finally, through the dicta, the Court can instruct the regular courts on how legislation should be interpreted or applied in conformity with the Constitution.

In general, the outcomes in a constitutional review procedure fall into three categories: an acceptation, invalidation or modulation. Without going into detail on the practical consequences of these different outcomes in the Belgian context, which will be discussed below, this section explores their value within an ongoing process of constitutional dialogue.

ACCEPTATION – First, when the Court establishes that no constitutional violation is found, this consolidates the legislative outcome.[797] Although an acceptation does not exclude the possibility that the same legislative provisions are challenged anew on other grounds, until then no legislative reaction is required. In addition, it signals to the judiciary and general public that the legislation can and should be applied without any problems.

INVALIDATION – Next, when legislation is invalidated, this signals that the decision made at the political level conflicts with the Constitution. Depending on the procedural characteristics of the case, an invalidation results in the removal of the provision from the legal order (annulment procedure) or, while leaving the legal text untouched, its inapplicability in concrete judicial procedures (preliminary procedure).[798] Although these outcomes aim to solve the constitutional infringement, they may also create new difficulties. For instance, a partial invalidation may render the legislation unclear or shift its meaning. Also, it may create an unwanted legislative gap, for example where the invalidated provision includes a criminal offence. In that case, striking down the statute altogether may disrupt the legislative intention to criminalise particular behaviour.[799] Therefore, a legislative reaction may remain appropriate.

---

796 C Bateup, 'The Dialogic Promise: Assessing the Normative Potential of Theories of Constitutional Dialogue' (2006) 71 Brooklyn Law Review, 17, 19.

797 Because they simply validate what the democratic process has produced, Sunstein calls them "democracy-permitting outcomes": C Sunstein, *One Case at a Time: Judicial Minimalism on the Supreme Court* (Harvard University Press 1999), 26.

798 De Visser, who studied the institutional framework of a large selection of European constitutional courts, states that the BeCC is the only court where the invalidation of legislation does not always have *erga omnes* effect: M De Visser, *Constitutional Review in Europe: A Comparative Analysis* (Hart Publishing 2014), 309, 312.

799 For example, the incrimination of rape, but excluding the situation when the victim is married to the perpetrator, or striking down anti-discrimination law in order to remedy a discriminatory exclusion of one category from that law. See ES Fish, 'Choosing Constitutional Remedies' (2016) 63 UCLA Law Review, 322, 324, 343.

However, a simple invalidation often leaves the lawmaker in the lurch on how exactly to respond. Although the Court can include additional instructions in the justificatory ground for the ruling, the invalidation *as such* does not provide a 'road map' on how to enact a statute in conformity with the Constitution.[800]

Modulation – An alternative can be to address the audience through more creative case dicta. All modulated outcomes are best understood as a strategy for communicating how the statute should go forward. In particular, they indicate how the challenged legislation should be interpreted or altered for it to be applied in a constitutional manner.[801] By doing so, the Court can actually preserve the validity of the legislation.[802] Such communication is addressed to both the judiciary and the legislator.

First, these outcomes provide instructions to the judiciary on how to apply the law fairly and equitably in the context of each individual case. Hence, for the litigants who initiated the review procedure, a modulated outcome creates a more favourable situation than where the court simply invalidates the challenged legislation.[803] For instance, the litigants probably prefer to see constructively altered (e.g. broadened) legislation being applied to the case, instead of it being invalidated altogether. In addition, for the initial addressees of challenged legislation, a simple invalidation means that (at least for the time being) they lose the rights or benefits whose denial to others was the cause of the review procedure.[804] Second, they offer a 'road map' for lawmakers on how to alter the legislation to conform with the Constitution.[805] Although it is not necessarily always the case, the Court may even stay closer to the legislative intent than

---

800 E Luna, 'Constitutional Road Maps' (2000) 90 Journal of Criminal Law and Criminology, 1125, 1128.

801 As Fish argues, all modulations involve the same basic action – changing the statute's meaning in order to fix a constitutional violation: ES Fish, 'Choosing Constitutional Remedies' (2016) 63 UCLA Law Review, 322, 365. Also see M De Visser, *Constitutional Review in Europe: A Comparative Analysis* (Hart Publishing 2014), 293: "[This] may entail the judicial rewriting of the legislation in question, which technically takes the form of adding words or phrases, substituting a portion of the text or removing particular expressions or complete sentences." Yet there is considerable conceptual confusion in academic scholarship on modulated outcomes. See D Pinard, 'A Plea for Conceptual Consistency in Constitutional Remedies' 18 National Journal of Constitutional Law, 105.

802 On the court as a 'constitutional cleaner', see AR Brewer-Carias, *Constitutional Courts as Positive Legislators: A Comparative Law Study* (Cambridge University Press 2011), 31–40, 73–191, 265–328.

803 A Kavanagh, *Constitutional Review under the UK Human Rights Act* (Cambridge University Press 2009), 119, 132.

804 M De Visser, *Constitutional Review in Europe: A Comparative Analysis* (Hart Publishing 2014), 303.

805 E Luna, 'Constitutional Road Maps' (2000) 90 Journal of Criminal Law and Criminology, 1125, 1126.

when the law is invalidated altogether.[806] If a new legislative process is generated, Parliament may consolidate the censured text in conformity with constitutional jurisprudence. Although this does not exclude other creative solutions, by following the Court's instructions the legislator can avoid courses of action that are "fraught with constitutional danger".[807] If not, the new legislation may be denounced for the same reasons. In that sense, by encouraging political actors to revise the challenged provision(s) in a particular way, courts strengthen their dominance over policy outcomes.[808] In conclusion, from a dialogue perspective, one can argue that modulated outcomes involve a more constructive strategy than invalidations. In particular, the lawmakers are given an *ex ante* 'road map', instead of largely unconstructive disapproval *ex post*.

Yet modulated outcomes can only lead to a constructive dialogue when there is clarity on what they entail. Courts should be consistent in phrasing the case dicta, in order for the judiciary and legislator to understand what is expected from them. Ambiguity will work against effective implementation in two ways: by leaving the court's audience uncertain as to the court's intent and by providing leeway to those who want to evade the court's ruling.[809] Also, the phrasing is equally important in the sense that the language used in describing the legislative road map may very well find its way into new legislation. An unclear or faultily formulated dictum may breed equally flawed law statutes.[810]

There is an additional downside to proclaiming modulated outcomes. In the absence of a legislative consolidation of the judgment or an alternative answer from the legislator, the text of the unconstitutional provisions remains untouched. Legal certainty may suffer in the sense that other actors can no longer content themselves with scrutinising the text of a given statute, but are required to examine the body of constitutional case law.[811] This may not cause any difficulties when the ruling only indicates which interpretation should be given to the text, but is problematic when the modulation constructively alters the text. It is not evident that the judiciary or administration should apply this legislation in a manner that conflicts with its explicit text. Courts do not have

---

806 For example, the problem may concern an issue that the legislature simply overlooked: M De Visser, ibid., 303. Also see ES Fish, 'Choosing Constitutional Remedies' (2016) 63 UCLA Law Review, 322, 324–6.

807 C Bateup, 'The Dialogic Promise: Assessing the Normative Potential of Theories of Constitutional Dialogue' (2006) 71 Brooklyn Law Review, 18.

808 M Shapiro and A Stone Sweet, *On Law, Politics and Judicialization* (Oxford University Press 2002), 189.

809 L Baum, 'Implementation of Judicial Decisions' (1976) 4 American Politics Research, 86, 92.

810 E Luna, 'Constitutional Road Maps' (2000) 90 Journal of Criminal Law and Criminology, 1125, 1208.

811 M De Visser, *Constitutional Review in Europe: A Comparative Analysis* (Hart Publishing 2014), 304.

the competence to alter legislation passed by Parliament. Therefore, modulated outcomes are associated with judicial activism,[812] or even the violation of the separation of powers principle.[813]

Even when the court's decision is publicly accessible and the case outcome sends a clear signal, such legislative consolidation is not inevitable. Notwithstanding the authority of their decisions, constitutional courts usually lack mechanisms to ensure their implementation. In order to induce legislative change, what may be needed more than judicial guidelines is a groundswell of national opinion on the subject.[814] The news media can function as an intermediate actor between the court and society at large, including the legislator as well as individual citizens.[815] By reporting more elaborately on some cases than on others, the news media stimulates the dispersion of information, raises awareness and increases the rulings' signalling strength.[816] When bringing constitutional review outcomes into the public forum, citizens without any legal expertise may learn about decisions that would otherwise remain in obscurity. More informed citizens are able to express themselves and make their causes heard.[817] Involving the citizenry in the ongoing public debate can put pressure on the political branch. The public outcry can be such that the legislator is mobilised to address the issue. In addition, citizens have the capability to hold the legislative branch accountable, by electing representatives in Parliament. The costs that elected officials must potentially bear if they defy a judicial decision depend on how easy it is for others to consider that it has not been properly implemented.[818] The public is only able to monitor compliance, and to impose these costs on politicians, when it is informed about the decisions it is indirectly

812 Ibid., 303–4.

813 AR Brewer-Carias, *Constitutional Courts as Positive Legislators: A Comparative Law Study*, (Cambridge University Press 2011), 38–40.

814 E Luna, 'Constitutional Road Maps' (2000) 90 Journal of Criminal Law and Criminology, 1125, 1221; DP Haider-Markel, MD Allen and M Johansen, 'Understanding Variations in Media Coverage of U.S. Supreme Court Decisions' (2006) 11 The International Journal of Press/Politics, 209.

815 C Bateup, 'Expanding the Conversation: American and Canadian Experiences of Constitutional Dialogue in Comparative Perspective' (2006) 44 New York University Public Law and Legal Theory Working Papers, 6, 21.

816 SS Abrahamson and G Lessard, 'Interbranch Communications: The Next Generation' in F Magnum (ed.), *Conference on Assessing the Effects of Legislation on the Workload of the Courts: Papers and Proceedings* (Diane Publishing 1995), 20. On the 'agenda-setting role' of the news media, see: K Sill et al., 'Media Coverage of the U.S. Supreme Court: How Do Journalists Assess the Importance of Court Decisions?' (2013) 20 Political Communication, 1, 3; and L Baum, *Judges and Their Audiences: a Perspective on Judicial Behaviour* (Princeton University Press 2006) 135.

817 M Schudson, *The Power of News* (Harvard University Press 1995), 204 and further.

818 JK Staton and G Vanberg, 'The Value of Vagueness: Delegation, Defiance and Judicial Opinions' (2008) 52 American Journal of Political Science, 504, 507.

enforcing.[819] In conclusion, without public awareness, the outcome risks lacking any instrumental value.

Hence, examining the coverage of judicial decisions is central to developing an understanding of how the Court's audience comes to learn about and comprehend constitutional decisions. Moreover, if the Court aims to strengthen the signalling power of its rulings, it should recognise the role of news dissemination. An awareness of which factors trigger attention would allow the Court to reinforce its role in the democratic policy-making arena.

5.3. A VARIETY OF SANCTIONING POSSIBILITIES: CODING CASE OUTCOMES

Each ruling proclaimed by the Court ends with a concluding part which comprises the Court's answers to the constitutional question(s) raised ('pleas'). In a single ruling, the Court usually addresses several pleas, with an average of two pleas per case. In the concluding part of the ruling, it sums up how many and which pleas were found (un)convincing. When a plea is found convincing, this means that the challenged legislation is – at least to some extent – unconstitutional. Such pleas result in (partial) invalidation or modulation. An unconvincing plea, on the other hand, will be dismissed by the Court, resulting in a (partial) acceptation of the law. Only when all pleas are rejected by the Court is the challenged legislation upheld as a whole (full acceptation).

Table 5.1 includes a typology of all possible answers the Court can give to an individual plea (a–f), either in an annulment or preliminary procedure. A more detailed description of these answers can be found below.

For each individual case, how many pleas led to one of these six options, each option being a count variable, has been coded. For example, a case in which the BeCC addresses seven pleas may end in three invalidations, one modulation and three acceptations. In addition, whether the case led to a temporal modulation (dichotomous variable) has also been coded.

The last column in table 5.1 demonstrates the overall results for these variables. In particular, for the count variables, it shows which proportion of the *total* number of pleas raised in *all* 3145 cases (n=6543) led to each type of outcome. For the dichotomous variable, the last column includes the number of cases in which a temporal modulation was registered.

[819] JK Staton, 'Constitutional Review and the Selective Promotion of Case Results' (2006) 50 American Journal of Political Salience, 99; and G Vanberg, 'Legislative-Judicial Relations: A Game-Theoretic Approach to Constitutional Review' (2001) 45 Amercian Journal of Political Science, 346.

Table 5.1. Overview of the different sanctioning possibilities

		Variables	Percentage
Acceptation	(a)	Declaration of constitutionality	75
Invalidation	(b)	Declaration of unconstitutionality	11
Substantive modulation	(c)	Modulated declaration of unconstitutionality	6
	(d)	Modulated declaration of constitutionality	4
	(e)	Establishment of an unconstitutional 'extrinsic lacuna'	1
	(f)	'double interpretation' = unconstitutional when interpreted in one way, but constitutional when interpreted in another way (only in preliminary procedures)	3
			No of cases
Temporal modulation	(g)	Modulation of the retroactive effect of the proclaimed invalidation	99

The first variable (a) represents the situation where the BeCC simply rejects the plea, without any further reservations.[820] These outcomes can usually be recognised by the short statement that the plea is not well-founded.[821] If all pleas related to a challenged provision are rejected, this provision is – at least temporarily – accepted as constitutional. Therefore, this type of outcome is also referred to as an 'acceptation'. The consequences of an acceptation outcome depend on the type of procedure. In an annulment ruling, the Court then concludes that '(apart from the above), the request is rejected'.[822] Although such an outcome does not exclude the possibility that the legislative provision(s) may be challenged anew on other grounds,[823] until then the legislation can be applied without any difficulties.[824] In the case dictum of a preliminary ruling, the Court then concludes that 'the challenged provision(s) do(es) not violate

820 Very rarely, the BeCC points out a problem of unconstitutionality in the justificatory ground, but nevertheless rejects the plea. This outcome was coded separately, but later merged with (a) because this situation only occurred in a handful of cases. For example: BeCC case no 35/93, 6 May 1993, B.5.2; and BeCC case no 27/2005, 2 February 2005. There was a similar ruling in BeCC case no 137/2005, 19 July 2005.

821 For example, BeCC case no 89/2016, 9 June 2016, B.3.3, B.4.2.4 and further.

822 For example, see BeCC case no 89/2016, 9 June 2016.

823 Once the ruling is published, the time limit of six months to initiate an annulment procedure most likely will have passed. Yet a new challenge can be brought before the Court through a preliminary question.

824 G Rosoux and F Tulkens, 'Considérations théoriques et pratiques sur la portée des arrêts de la Cour d'arbitrage' in V Thiry, B Renauld and JT Debry (eds.), *La Cour d'arbitrage: un juge comme les autres?* (Éditions du jeune barreau de Liège 2004), 103.

the Constitution'.[825] The actors involved in the specific case, as well as any other judge seeking to apply this legislation, are expected to accept this outcome.[826]

When the second variable (b) was coded, this means that the plea was well-founded and the challenged provision(s) was/were invalidated.[827] The consequences of such an outcome depend on the type of procedure. In an annulment ruling, the case dictum indicates which part of the legislation should be removed from the Belgian legal order.[828] Unless the *ex tunc* or *pro future* impact of this annulment is tempered (see *infra*), the annulled provisions can no longer yield any effects. In a preliminary ruling, the case dictum concludes that 'the challenged provision(s) violate(s) the Constitution'.[829] Unlike in other countries, such an invalidation does not have the same *erga omnes* effect as an annulment.[830] Although it does open a new six-month period in which actors may institute an action for annulment, this kind of follow-up procedure is rarely initiated. Hence, in practice, the legal text usually remains untouched. Nonetheless, the referring judge – as well as any other judge who wishes to apply the reviewed legislation in another case – should abide by the outcome. In particular, they should declare the unconstitutional provision(s) inapplicable.[831]

In between an acceptation and an invalidation are the substantive modulations. With these outcomes, the Court indicates how the legislation should be interpreted or altered in order for it to be applied in a constitutional way. If the legislation under review can be interpreted in several ways, the BeCC should indicate which interpretation is 'Constitution-conforming'.[832] Such an *interpretative* modulation should stay within the boundaries of the legal text, and remain close to the intentions of the legislator as set out in the preparatory documents.[833] When a certain legal provision is unconstitutional in every

---

[825] For example BeCC case no 88/2016, 2 June 2016.

[826] G Rosoux and F Tulkens, 'Considérations théoriques et pratiques sur la portée des arrêts de la Cour d'arbitrage' in V Thiry, B Renauld and JT Debry (eds.), *La Cour d'arbitrage: un juge comme les autres?* (Éditions du jeune barreau de Liège 2004), 116.

[827] For example BeCC case no 89/2016, 9 June 2016, B.9.3.5, B.11.5.

[828] For example, BeCC case no 63/2016, 11 May 2016.

[829] For example, BeCC case no 84/2016, 2 June 2016.

[830] M De Visser, *Constitutional Review in Europe: A Comparative Analysis* (Hart Publishing 2014), 309, 312.

[831] As confirmed by the Court itself in BeCC case no 39/2008, 4 March 2008, B.2.3. and BeCC case no 20/2009, 12 February 2009, B.4. Yet only a full a radical removal of the provision provides the necessary legal certainty. See the opinion of advocate-general Cruz Villalòn: "the legal position regarding provisions that have been found to be unconstitutional is characterised by an element of doubt that is incompatible with legal certainty and is unacceptable in the context of assessing whether national law fully meets the requirements of the transposition of a European Directive". This was confirmed by the European Court of Justice in C-421/12.

[832] This is called the 'Waleffe doctrine', based on a judgment of the Court of Cassation, 20 April 1950, Arr. Verbr. 1950, 517–519, Pas. 1950, I, 560.

[833] Other constitutional courts have adopted the same conditions. See AR Brewer-Carias, *Constitutional Courts as Positive Legislators: A Comparative Law Study* (Cambridge University Press 2011), 77.

possible interpretation, the Court sometimes resorts to more activist outcomes, such as straining the legal text in a particular way. Such *constructive* modulations can fill in a legislative gap but can also serve to limit the scope of the legislation. Yet there is no sharp line between a genuine interpretative modulation, which is respectful of legislative intentions, and a constructive modulation, which actually rewrites the statute afresh. Not only is the Court itself not always clear on which type of outcome it proclaims,[834] Belgian legal scholars interpreting these rulings also sometimes disagree on how to categorise them. Therefore, instead of creating variables that differentiate between an interpretative and a constructive modulation, the decision was taken to code the outcomes in relation to how the dictum was phrased. In particular, four types of modulations can be discerned.

To begin with, the Court can proclaim a modulated declaration of unconstitutionality (c) or constitutionality (d). In the first, the legislation is declared *unconstitutional* to the extent that a certain situation does (not) fall within its scope,[835] while the latter concludes that the legislation is *constitutional* in so far as a situation does (not) fall within its scope.[836] Although the first outcome suggests there is a graver constitutional infringement ('unconstitutional unless' vs 'constitutional but'), substantially both outcomes may alter the challenged legislation in a similar direction. In particular, both can interpretatively or constructively broaden or limit the scope of the challenged legislation. Whether the modulation has a broadening or limiting effect ('levelling up' or 'levelling down') often depends on how the law was initially drafted.[837]

Essentially, such a modulated declaration of (un)constitutionality indicates that only if modulated in that direction can the reviewed legislation be applied

834 For instance, in BeCC case no 178/2011, 17 November 2011, the Court argued that the challenged provision did not violate the Constitution "if interpreted as if it introduced a rebuttable presumption", while the preparatory documents showed that the legislator considered the unrebuttable character of the presumption necessary to reach its purpose. See *Parl Doc* Chamber no 51-1437/1, 23 and *Parl Doc* Chamber no 51-1437/25, 71–2. Also see the examples in footnote 842.

835 In the final dictum of an annulment procedure, this is formulated as "the legislation is annulled to the extent that ..." (e.g. BeCC case no 89/2016, 9 June 2016, B.9.5.6) and in a preliminary procedure as "the legislation violates ... to the extent that ..." (e.g. BeCC case no 91/2016, 9 June 2016, B.11).

836 In an annulment procedure, the BeCC concludes that "the request is rejected with the reservation that ..." (e.g. BeCC case no 89/2016, 9 June 2016, B.9.4.5) and in a preliminary procedure as "under the reservation that the legislation does not violate ..." (e.g. BeCC case no 81/2016, 2 June 2016, B.17).

837 For example, BeCC case no 137/2011, 27 July 2011, where the Court broadened the scope of the application of the legislation but at the same time introduced a limiting exception. Treating inclusively and exclusively worded statutes differently is said to be an arbitrary distinction because the style of drafting would be the single critical factor in the determination of the outcome: see ES Fish, 'Choosing Constitutional Remedies' (2016) UCLA Law Review (63), 322–386. For criticism on this distinction within the Belgian context, see J De Jaegere, 'Actieve rechtsvorming door het Grondwettelijk Hof: waar ligt de grens?' (2014) 1 TBP 22.

in conformity with the Constitution. In some rulings, the BeCC explicitly states that the judiciary should apply the legislation in its broadened meaning, in anticipation of legislative action. This occurred the first time in case no 111/2008[838] and has been repeated many times since then. In these rulings, the BeCC specifies that the judiciary should apply the legislation in its modulated sense when the gap can be identified 'in the legislative text' (instead of in the legal system as a whole) and when it can be filled in a 'sufficiently precise and complete way' (in order to avoid any judicial creativity). The Court of Cassation, the highest court in civil and criminal proceedings, has confirmed that regular courts can fill in the gap under these conditions.[839] However, in many other modulated rulings where the case dictum is phrased in a similar way, the BeCC leaves out an explicit statement about the consequences for the judiciary.[840] Therefore, there is considerable confusion on these modulated outcomes and many practitioners remain puzzled as to the specific consequences of these different types of modulated outcomes (see *infra*, section 5.4.).

Another modulated outcome is the 'extrinsic legislative gap' (e). In these cases, the BeCC declares the legislation under review constitutional *as such*, but identifies an unconstitutional gap in the legislative system as a whole.[841] The BeCC uses this kind of modulation when it considers that remedying this gap is an exclusive competence of the legislator. For instance, the Constitution determines that, in criminal and fiscal matters, only the legislator can alter legislation ('reinforced principle of legality'). Hence, these rulings should give an explicit incentive to the legislator to remedy the unconstitutionality, not necessarily by changing the challenged legislation but by creating or changing

---

838 BeCC case no 111/ 2008, 31 July 2008, B.8, B.10. The Court included this statement, with reference to ECtHR, 29 November 1991 (*Vermeire v. Belgium*), after a remark from the government that the Court could only establish not remedy a legislative gap. The ECtHR ruling stated that the judiciary is allowed to apply legislation in conformity with the equality clause, in anticipation of a legislative remedy.

839 Cass 14 October 2008 AR P081329N; Cass 3 November 2008, AR S070013N; and more recent judgments such as Cass 4 September 2015, AR F140128F and Cass 5 February 2016, AR C150011F.

840 In particular, all previous rulings before case no 111/2008. Moreover, even since this landmark ruling, there are cases in which a broadening modulation is proclaimed without this statement. See for example: BeCC case no 63/2009, 25 March 2009; BeCC case no 195/2011, 22 December 2011; and BeCC case no 96/2013, 9 July 2013. Also, when the modulation does not broaden, but instead limits the scope of the legislation, the Court does not make it explicit how the judiciary should respond. Yet such a 'levelling-down' modulation can alter the scope of legislation considerably. For example: BeCC case no 17/2009, 12 February 2009; and BeCC case no 40/2009, 11 March 2009.

841 For example: BeCC case no 112/2014, 17 July 2014, B.6.2 (preliminary procedure), "The discrimination is caused by the absence of ..." and dictum "The absence of ... violates"; and BeCC case no 121/2013, 26 September 2016, B.58.8 (annulment procedure), "The discrimination is cause by the absence of ..." and dictum "rejects the annulment action, under the reservation of the unconstitutionality established in in B.58.8".

other legislation.[842] Because this type of outcome makes it explicit which actions are required from the legislator (filling in the gap), they maximise the costs that a legislature must pay for non-complying with the ruling.[843] In principle, in anticipation of such legislative action, the judiciary is not allowed to apply the legislation in its modulated sense. However, the BeCC has acknowledged that the judiciary can, in exceptional circumstances.[844] Also, the regular courts sometimes broaden the scope of the reviewed legislation without this explicit permission.[845] Although it can be argued that such decisions offer a Constitution-conforming solution when the legislator does not respond, they are exceptionally delicate from a separation of powers perspective.

A last type of substantive modulation, which only occurs in the preliminary procedure, is the 'double interpretation' outcome (f). In these cases, the BeCC declares the challenged legislation unconstitutional if interpreted in one way, but constitutional if interpreted in another way.[846] Although the word 'interpretation' hides the fact that these outcomes can constructively alter legislation, usually they do stay close to the legislative text.[847] Moreover, this type of modulation is not quite as activist as the others because it leaves considerable room for manoeuvre to the regular courts. In particular, the referring judge may opt to apply the legislative provisions in conformity with the Constitution or, if he believes that the legislation should be interpreted as dismissed by the Court, he should declare it inapplicable to the case. There is no 'hierarchy' between the two interpretations.[848]

Finally, when actions for annulment are accepted, the BeCC can temper the retroactive effect of this invalidation (g).[849] In particular, the Court can

842 Yet, prior research has shown that the legislator often alters the content of challenged legislation instead of altering other legislation or creating a new law. See S Verstraelen, 'Constitutionele dialoog als een lens: onderzoek naar het wetgevend optreden na de vaststelling van een ongrondwettige lacune door het Grondwettelijk Hof' (2016) 1 Tijdschrift voor Wetgeving, 2, 14.

843 JK Staton and G Vanberg, 'The Value of Vagueness: Delegation, Defiance and Judicial Opinions' (2008) 52 American Journal of Political Science, 504, 508.

844 BeCC case no 1/2012, 11 January 2012. The Court did this statement because no legislative response had followed a ruling from 2009 (case no 198/2009) where it had declared the same provision unconstitutional.

845 For example, the Council of State, 17 December 1997, no 70.402, in conformity with BeCC case no 31/96, 15 May 1996. The Council of State even stated that this was a 'constitution-conforming interpretation'.

846 For example, BeCC case no 64/2016, 11 May 2016, B.6.3.

847 For example: BeCC case no 119/2010, 28 October 2010; and BeCC case no 13/2011, 27 January 2011. In the latter case, the BeCC acknowledges that the 'interpretation' constructively fills in an intrinsic gap (B.7.4).

848 B Lombart, 'Les techniques d'arrêts de la cour d'arbitrage' (1996) RBDC, 352; and P Popelier, 'De doorwerking van prejudiciële arresten van het Grondwettelijk Hof in de rechtspraak' (2010) CDPK, 393.

849 For example, BeCC case no 2/2016, 14 January 2016: "maintains the consequences of the annulled provision until ...".

give its decision an effect *ex nunc*, thus maintaining the effects until the date of the publication of the ruling or impose an effect *pro future*, thus provisionally maintaining the effects.[850] The latter temporal modulation calls upon the legislature to adopt a law that is in conformity with the Constitution within a certain period of time.[851] For a long time, the possibility of moderating a declaration of unconstitutionality in time was limited to annulment procedures. But despite the lack of legal basis, the Court considered that the opportunity offered by the Special Act on the Constitutional Court also applied to judgments delivered on a preliminary question. Hence, it assumed that, in exceptional circumstances, it had the power to maintain the effects of the unconstitutional provisions in a preliminary procedure.[852] Recently, this judicially-created sanctioning possibility was validated by the legislator.[853] Importantly, the Court holds a discretionary power to decide whether it is appropriate to proclaim a temporal modulation, in both annulment and preliminary procedures.[854]

5.4. CHOOSING A CASE DICTUM: DESCRIPTIVE TRENDS AND EVOLUTION IN TIME

5.4.1. INTRODUCTORY OVERVIEW

In this descriptive section, it is discussed the extent to which the BeCC uses constructive techniques to communicate with the legislator, and how this has evolved over time. For this purpose, the count variables discussed in the previous section have been transformed into outcome percentages, divided into three categories: acceptations, invalidations and substantive modulations. For each case, these percentages were calculated proportionally to the number of pleas raised by the litigants (which varies from case to case). For instance, a case where seven pleas were raised can end in three invalidations (43%), one modulation (14%) and three acceptations (43%). Hence, these percentages not only show whether but also to what extent the challenged legislation is found (un)constitutional in that particular case.

---

850 S Verstraelen, 'The Temporal Limitation of Judicial Decisions: The Need for Flexibility Versus the Quest for Uniformity' (2013) 14 German Law Journal, 1687, 1697.

851 M De Visser, *Constitutional Review in Europe: A Comparative Analysis* (Hart Publishing 2014), 313.

852 First in BeCC case no 125/2011, 7 July 2015: "the consequences of these provisions are maintained until ...".

853 In particular, the law of 25 December 2016 introduced a second paragraph in article 28 of the Special Act on the Constitutional Court.

854 S Verstraelen, 'The Temporal Limitation of Judicial Decisions: The Need for Flexibility Versus the Quest for Uniformity' (2013) 14 German Law Journal, 1687, 1699.

Figures 5.1–5.3 present the distributions of these different types of outcomes for the total number of cases (n=3145). In particular, they indicate the number of cases out of this total in which certain outcome percentages appeared. These figures clearly indicate that most rulings result in a full acceptation, invalidation or modulation (where the percentage equals 100). In particular, of all cases, approximately 1900 led to full acceptation, and smaller groups of cases uniquely lead to modulation (493) or invalidation (369). Hence, only in 383 cases was a combination of different types of outcomes registered. In other words, the large majority of cases could have been coded with a nominal variable with three categories: acceptation, invalidation or modulation. This remark will be particularly relevant in the next section, where the model is built to analyse the Court's strategic behaviour.

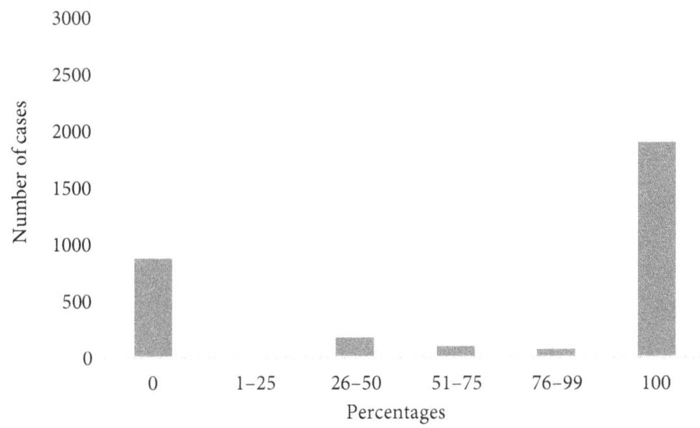

Figure 5.1. Acceptation

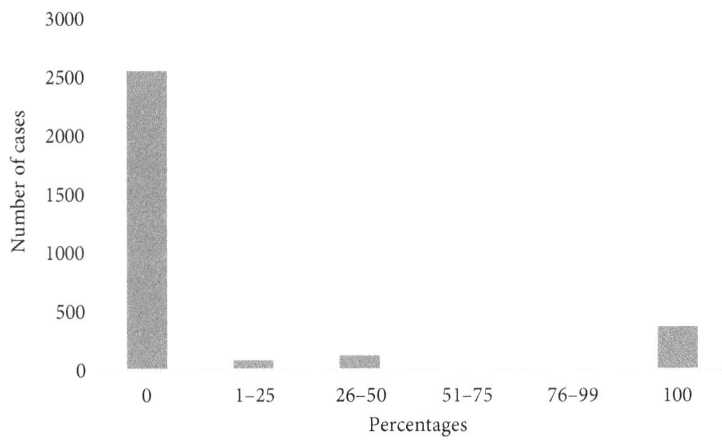

Figure 5.2. Invalidation

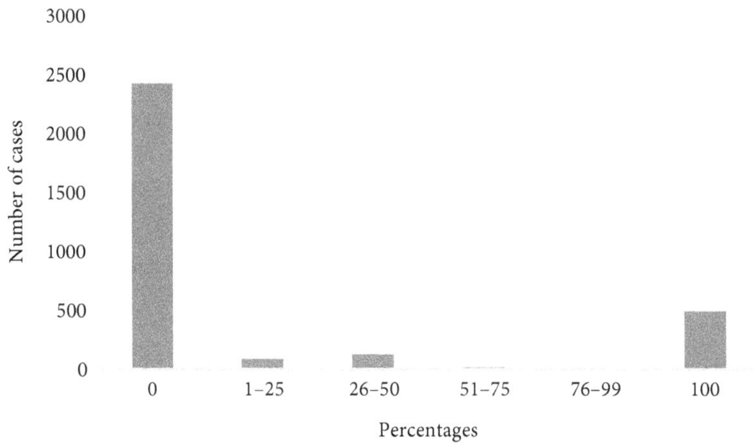

Figure 5.3. Modulation

A first exploration of the data suggested that the Court opts for different judicial outcomes depending on the type of procedure and the type of constitutional question(s) raised by the litigants.[855] In particular, the descriptive results showed that considerably more modulations were proclaimed in preliminary proceedings (average: 14.4%) than in annulment procedures (7.7%). In addition, more invalidations were proclaimed when the Court was requested to review against competence allocating rules (22.5%) than when it was not (12.7%). Considering these differences, the decision was taken to probe more deeply into the relation between the type of case and the outcomes.

Therefore, results are presented for six sub-groups: for both the annulment and preliminary procedures, three types of cases are discussed: (1) fundamental rights cases *sensu stricto*;[856] (2) competence conflict cases *sensu stricto*;[857] and (3) mixed cases, in which the Court reviewed against both types of reference norms (see figure 5.4).

The bulk of the cases are fundamental rights cases *sensu stricto*, especially in the group of preliminary questions. From 1989 onwards, when the BeCC became competent to review legislation against the equality clause (see *supra*, section 2.2.), the number of fundamental rights cases has been steadily increasing. Conversely, the number of cases that focus uniquely on a competence conflict

855 More information on the type of constitutional questions that can be raised before the BeCC can be found in chapter 2, section 2.2., on the reference norms.

856 Although in most of these cases, at least one plea was based on articles 10 and 11 of the Constitution (equality clause), some cases only involve other rights provisions such as articles 12 and 14 (the legality principle) or article 16 (concerning expropriation).

857 In these cases, all pleas raised were based on the competence allocating rules.

has slowly been declining since then. Review against both types of reference norms (so-called 'mixed' cases) is rare in preliminary procedures, but has grown more and more popular in annulment procedures. Moreover, as showed in the overview table of highly salient cases (section 4.5.), a significant proportion of these cases can be categorised as 'mixed'.[858]

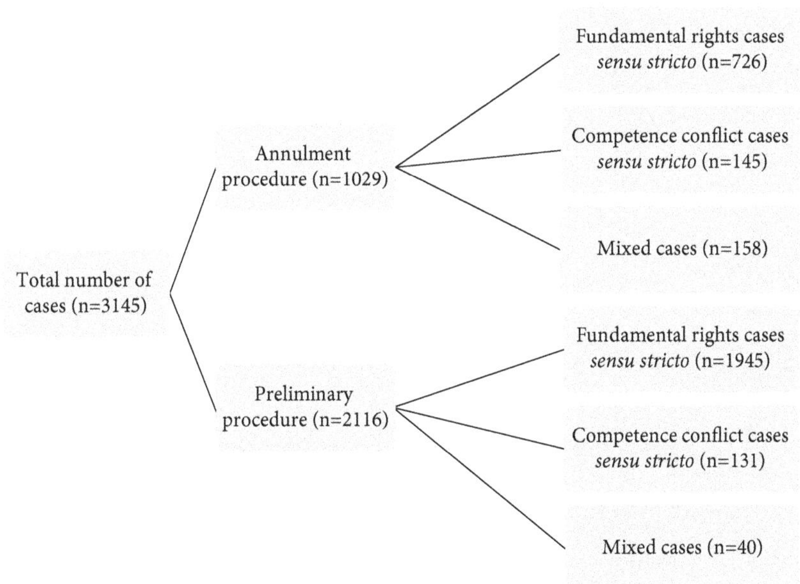

Figure 5.4. Overview of the sub-groups of cases

In what follows, for each of these six options, it is discussed how many acceptations, invalidations and modulations were registered, and how this has developed over time. In addition, it is also reported how many temporal modulations were registered in the annulment and preliminary procedures. The signalling strength of each dictum is explored, as well as the legislative consequences that may or should follow from it. Considering the deliberative value of constructive case outcomes, it is examined whether the BeCC, over time, has become more willing to use these techniques. Finally, it is explored how the news media responded to these different judicial outcomes. Because newspaper journalists have an important agenda-setting function, it is useful to examine which case outcomes draw their attention.

858 In particular, of the 57 cases labeled as 'highly salient', 14 are mixed, 2 are competence conflicts *sensu stricto* and 41 are fundamental rights cases *sensu stricto*.

5.4.2. ANNULMENT PROCEDURES

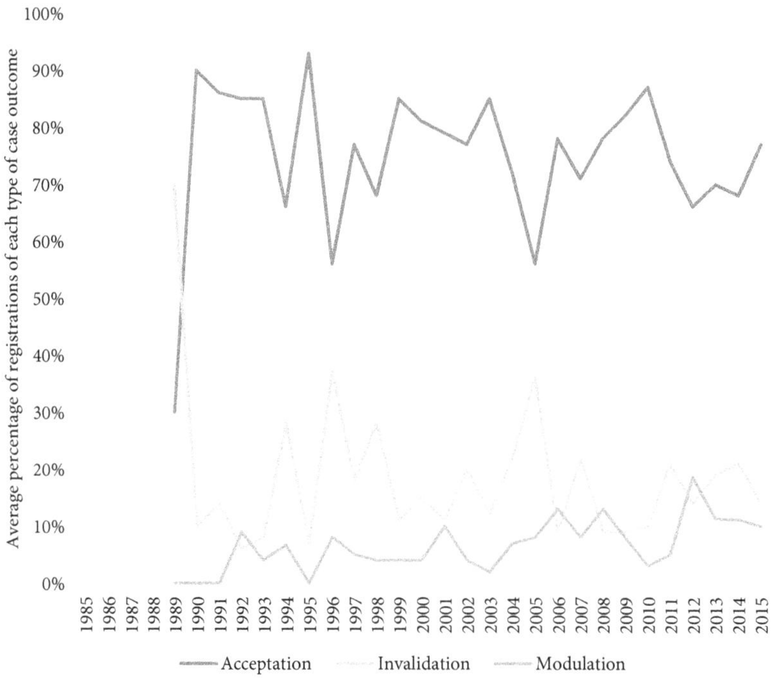

Figure 5.5. Case outcomes in fundamental rights annulment procedures

The upper line in figure 5.5 demonstrates that the BeCC rejects most annulment actions grounded on an alleged infringement of fundamental rights provisions (75% on average). Although the figure shows some fluctuation, there is no indication that the BeCC has become less or more deferential towards the legislator over the years.

In 38% of the cases, at least one constitutional infringement was found.[859] Overall, the BeCC seems to prefer to annul the unconstitutional provision (19% on average), rather than proclaim a modulation (7% on average). However, the results suggest a shift in the Court's case law since 2006. The average difference between annulments and modulations has become smaller, and there has even been a game of 'leapfrog' between both techniques. In particular, in 2006, 2008 and 2012, there were more modulations than invalidations. Finally, there has not been a significant increase in the use of temporal modulations in the fundamental rights cases. Over the years, the BeCC has tempered the retroactivity of approximately 30% of the proclaimed annulments.[860]

---

859 Conversely, in 62% of the cases all pleas were rejected.

860 In 195 (27%) fundamental rights cases, the BeCC (partially) annulled the challenged legislation. In 58 of these cases, the retroactive effect of the annulment was tempered for

These results suggest that the communication strategies of the Court have evolved over the years. Although an annulment may serve to emphasise the severity of a constitutional infringement, removing (part of) a law does not always provide a solution for the litigants who initiated the case. Modulated outcomes address the Court's audience, and in particular the legislator, in a more constructive way. With regard to the type of modulation, the BeCC prefers to proclaim modulated declarations of unconstitutionality ('annulment to the extent')[861] and constitutionality ('rejection under the reservation of').[862] Only rarely does the BeCC address the legislator explicitly by establishing an extrinsic gap and requesting that the gap be remedied.[863] Thus the Court seems to prefer giving concrete directions to judges on how to apply legislation in conformity with the Constitution, rather than stating they should anticipate a legislative remedy (extrinsic gap). By doing this, the Court aims to ensure that provisions are applied in conformity with the Constitution, in anticipation of legislative consolidation of its case law.

To illustrate this, it is interesting to compare cases no 157/2004[864] and no 64/2009,[865] both related to anti-discrimination legislation adopted to implement a European Directive.[866] Both laws included a list of the prohibited grounds of discrimination, such as religious beliefs and sexual orientation, thereby introducing a 'closed' system instead of a general ban on discrimination. Although the government initially stated that the aim was to combat any form of discrimination,[867] Parliament was reluctant to add other criteria to the list. In particular, the law of 2003 excluded 'political beliefs' and 'language', notwithstanding that amendments were introduced to include them.[868] The litigants, a group of political representatives, specifically challenged the exclusion

a certain period of time. For example: BeCC case no 132/2015, 1 October 2015; BeCC case no 138/2015, 15 October 2015; and BeCC case no 139/2015, 15 October 2015.

861 In 57 (8%) fundamental rights cases, a modulated declaration of unconstitutionality was proclaimed.

862 In 62 (9%) fundamental rights cases, a modulated declaration of constitutionality was proclaimed.

863 Only in 4 fundamental rights cases was an extrinsic gap established: BeCC case no 100/2007, 12 July 2007; BeCC case no 1/2011, 13 January 2011; BeCC case no 106/2013, 18 July 2013; and BeCC case no 2014/096.

864 BeCC case no 157/2004, 6 October 2004, on the anti-discrimination law of 25 February 2003.

865 BeCC case no 64/2009, 2 April 2009, on the anti-discrimination law of 10 May 2007.

866 Council Directive 2000/78/EC of 27 November 2000 establishing a general framework for equal treatment in employment and occupation.

867 "[T]he government wishes to combat any form of discrimination": see *Parl Doc* Senate 2001–2002, no 2-12/15, 52 and Chamber 2001–2002, 50-1407/005, 8–9,11.

868 On the exclusion of political beliefs, see *Parl Doc* Senate 2001–2002, no 2-12/15, 6, 17, 23, 55 and Chamber 2001–2002, 50-1407/005, 10 and on language, see *Parl Doc* Senate 2001–2002, no 2-10, 114.

of 'political beliefs'. As a result, the Court annulled the whole list of criteria because precluding specific grounds from the scope of the law was considered to conflict with the main purpose of combatting *any* form of discrimination. Moreover, in the Court's view, by doing so the law became applicable to all types of discrimination.[869] Considering that such an open system went against the EU Directive - an argument that was not given much attention to in this first ruling - the legislator needed to respond. The ruling was unclear with regard to whether a closed system would have been allowed if the legislator had given arguments to justify a limited approach, and if the list had included 'political beliefs' and 'language'.

The legislator responded by adopting a new law, which again introduced an exhaustive list but this time with the additional criteria 'political beliefs' and 'language'. In its advisory opinion on the second law, the Council of State argued that a closed system was not unconstitutional *in se*, but that it should include all 'important' criteria.[870] In the preparatory documents, the legislator clarified that the open system resulting from case no 157/2004 was unsatisfactory, particularly for reasons of transparency and legal certainty. Moreover, it was mentioned that the European Commission had sent an official notice of default to the Belgian State for not adopting the criteria from the EU Directive.[871] Yet the exhaustive character of the list again resulted in a constitutional challenge. The litigants, amongst them several associations of employees, objected that the preference of employees for a particular social union ('syndical belief') was not listed. In this ruling, however, the Court opted for a different outcome. It first confirmed that, considering that the legislation should be in line with the EU Directive, a closed system could be allowed.[872] Instead of annulling the list as a whole, the Court declared the provision unconstitutional "to the extent that 'syndical belief' was not included". Moreover, the Court stated that the civil judiciary, in anticipation of a legislative response, should apply the legislation as if it included 'syndical belief'.[873] In that sense, without claiming to have the last word, the BeCC gave instructions to the legislator to adapt the legislation in a particular way. In addition, the ruling gave concrete guidelines to the judiciary on how to apply the legislation in practice. Hence, the case illustrates well how the Court can engage in dialogue through constructive modulated outcomes.

---

869 BeCC case no 157/2004, 6 October 2004, B.13-15.

870 *Parl Doc* Chamber 2006/2007, no 51-2722/001, 112 and further.

871 *Parl Doc* Chamber 2006/2007, no 51-2722/001, 14–16.

872 BeCC case no 64/2009, 2 April 2009, B.7.7-8.

873 BeCC case no 64/2009, 2 April 2009, B.8.17. The Court added that, considering the reinforced principle of legality in criminal cases, judges on criminal courts cannot apply the legislation in its modulated sense but should wait for a modification of the legal text.

Nonetheless, considering that the legal text remains untouched after a substantive modulation,[874] it is not evident that the regular judiciary can apply the legislation as 'modulated' by the Court. Some argue that the absolute authority of annulment outcomes also applies when the Court annuls 'to the extent that'.[875] Similarly, when the Court rejects the annulment action under a certain condition, this is said to be a 'settled issue' that should be applied by the regular courts.[876] Yet it remains contested whether the judiciary and administration can apply legal provisions in a way that conflicts with the actual text of those provisions. Not all rulings where the Court proclaims a constructive modulation contain an explicit statement such as in the aforementioned case no 64/2009. An example is case no 131/2015[877] related to social services for foreigners. The challenged provision stated that public institutions for social services (OCMWs) do not owe their services, including urgent medical aid, to foreigners who are in a specific situation of employment in Belgium. In that sense, those foreigners were treated differently to foreigners who resided illegally in Belgium and who did get urgent medical aid if needed. The Court found that this difference in treatment could not be justified and annulled the provision "to the extent that OCMWs can refuse urgent medical aid to these employed foreigners". This outcome goes further than interpretation and changes the content of the challenged provision substantially, but leaves the legal text untouched.[878] In contrast to case no 64/2009, however, the Court did not include an explicit statement instructing the judiciary to either apply the legislation as such, or to anticipate a legislative response. More consistency in the Court's case law would at least create a clear framework for the regular courts and judiciary.

---

874 This is implied in the Court's case law since it can annul a whole law 'to the extent that', and continue to annul some provisions in that law 'to the extent that'. Also, the BeCC accepts preliminary questions with regard to legal provisions that were modulated in previous rulings, while it declares them 'without subject' if the questions relate to annulled legislation. See G Rosoux and F Tulkens, 'Considérations théoriques et pratiques sur la portée des arrêts de la Cour d'arbitrage' in V Thiry, B Renauld and JT Debry (eds.), *La Cour d'arbitrage: un juge comme les autres?* (Éditions du jeune barreau de Liège 2004), 111, 113.

875 See W Verrijdt, 'De plicht tot uitvoering van arresten van het Grondwettelijk Hof' in A Alen and S Sottiaux (eds.), *Leuvense staatsrechtelijke standpunten 2* (die Keure 2010), 347.

876 A 'settled issue', as meant in article 9§2, suggested by G Rosoux, 'Les réserves d'interprétation dans la jurisprudence de la cour d'arbitrage: une alternative à l'annulation' (2001) 3 RBDC, 403–404, and confirmed by BeCC case no 52/2006, 19 April 2006, and the Council of State 2 July 2010, no 206.397, 11.1.

877 BeCC case no 131/2015, 1 October 2015.

878 That the outcome did not remove the provision from the legal order can be deducted from a later preliminary ruling related to the same provision, which was not declared 'without subject' (BeCC case no 133/2015, 1 October 2015). This particular ruling concluded that the provision "violates the Constitution". This signals that the judiciary should declare it inapplicable, but still leaves unclear how the OCMWs should respond.

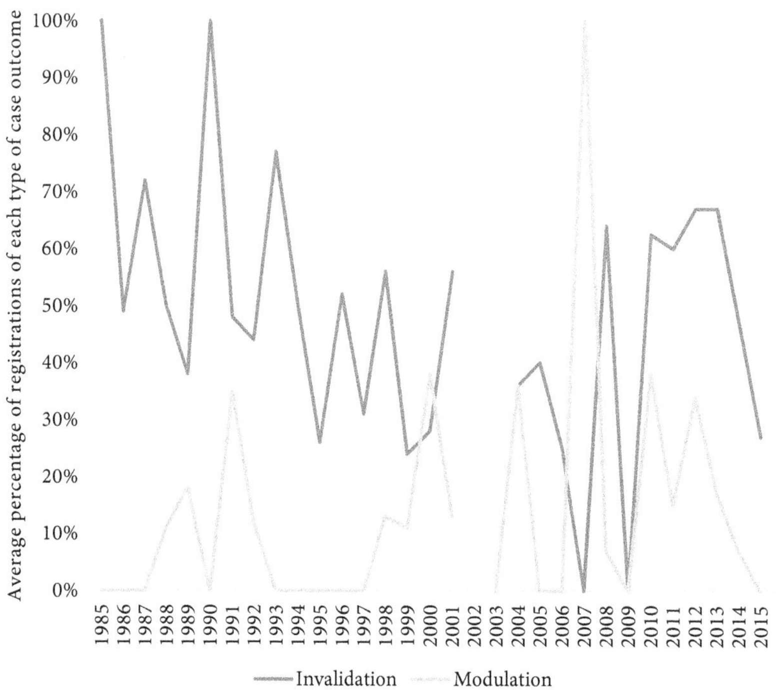

Figures 5.6. and 5.7. Case outcomes in competence conflict annulment procedures

Figures 5.6 and 5.7 demonstrate that there is less consistency in how the BeCC answers constitutional challenges in competence conflict cases. As mentioned before, there are not as many annulment actions that deal with a competence conflict compared to a fundamental rights challenge. In 2002, for example, there were none – which explains the 'gap' in figures 5.6 and 5.7. Also, when yearly percentages are calculated for only a handful of cases, they are subject to more fluctuation, which partly explains the many highs and lows in the figures. For example, the peaks in 2003 and 2007 can be explained by the fact that the Court dealt with only one annulment action based on the competence allocating rules.[879]

Overall, the results suggest that more constitutional infringements are found than in fundamental rights cases. In particular, in 72% of the competence conflict cases, the Court established at least one violation. Annulments in particular (average: 47%), but also modulations (average: 11%), appear more frequently.[880] However, in contrast with fundamental rights cases, figure 5.7 does not show a similar evolution towards more (or less) modulations. Hence, if a violation is found, the Court seems more reluctant to communicate through modulated outcomes than a simple annulment. A possible explanation is that, in contrast to the sometimes broadly formulated human rights provisions, the competence allocating rules are quite detailed. Moreover, when reviewing against the competence allocating rules, the Court can rely on a rich documentation indicating how these rules should be understood. This may prompt the Court to opt for a simple rejection or invalidation, and offers less leeway to a broad or restrictive interpretation of the challenged legislation. Finally, with regard to the temporal modulations, the BeCC has used this option in 29% of the cases in which an annulment was proclaimed.[881] Thus, although there are on average more annulments in the competence conflict cases, the proportion of those cases in which the BeCC has tempered its retroactive effect is similar to the fundamental rights cases.

These findings indicate that the BeCC acts more rigorously in competence conflict cases, especially in the first five years after its establishment. Yet, the fact that more violations are found in these cases may be due to a more targeted strategy of the litigants rather than a more aggressive reaction of the Court. Nowadays, very few cases deal with an alleged infringement of the competence

879 BeCC case no 92/2003, 24 June 2003 (100% rejection); and BeCC case no 48/2007, 21 March 2007 (100% modulation).

880 In 15 (10%) of the conflict competence cases, a modulated declaration of unconstitutionality was proclaimed; in 18 (12%) a modulated declaration of constitutionality; no extrinsic gaps.

881 In 90 out of 145 competence conflict cases, the BeCC proclaimed an annulment.

allocating rules. In the vast majority of these cases (75%), the initiating party is a government of another state level where the challenged legislation was adopted. Because such an initiation is often politically delicate, one can expect that these procedures are only pursued when a strong claim can be brought before the Court.

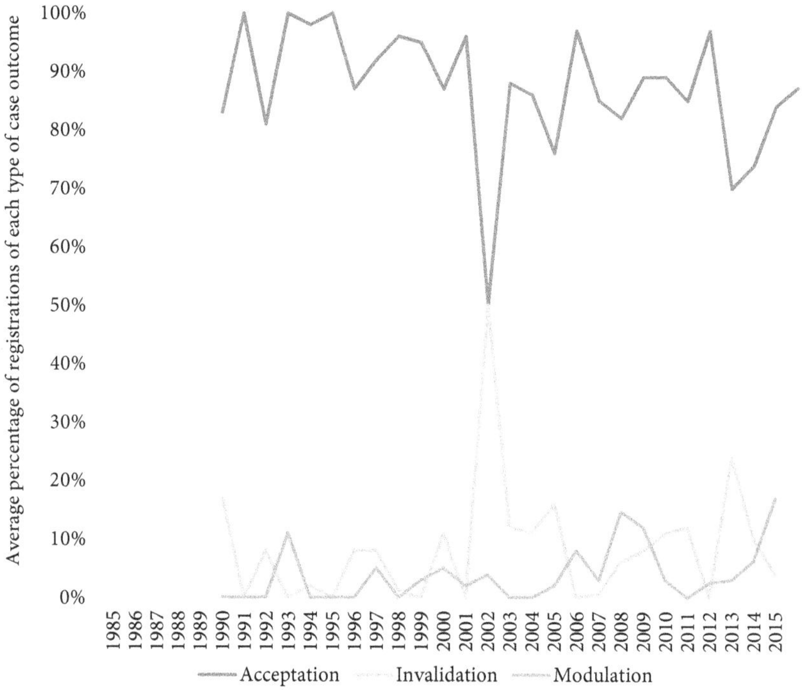

Figure 5.8. Case outcomes in mixed annulment procedures

In mixed cases, the BeCC needs to answer pleas based on competence allocating rules as well as on fundamental rights provisions. Hence, these rulings are usually longer and more complex than in the two other types of cases. As demonstrated in figure 5.8, most challenges in these cases are rejected (average: 87%). This result is counter-intuitive, because one would expect that when legislation is challengeable on multiple grounds, this leads to the finding of more violations. However, the *average* success percentage might appear lower simply because the litigants raise more pleas (average: 6),[882] of which only a few are accepted.

882 Conversely, in both fundamental rights and competence conflict cases, litigants invoke an average of 3 pleas.

This theory is confirmed by looking at the proportion of cases in which at least *one* of the pleas led to the finding of a violation. In particular, similar to the fundamental rights cases, in 39% of the mixed cases,[883] at least one constitutional infringement was established.

Nonetheless, the results demonstrate that requesting to review legislation against a variety of reference norms does not necessarily increase the chance that the BeCC will ascertain a constitutional infringement. This strategy does seem to have become somewhat more rewarding over the years, considering the slow decline in the average rejection rate after 2001.[884] With regard to the outcome when a violation is found, there is again a shift in the Court's case law from 2006 onwards. While at first the Court mostly preferred to proclaim an annulment, after 2006 more and more substantive modulated outcomes[885] appear in mixed cases, up to the point that their average number has jumped over that of annulments.[886] Temporal modulations appear less frequently in mixed cases than in the two other types of cases (21%).[887] Nonetheless, the majority of these temporal modulations were also proclaimed after 2006.

In conclusion, these results confirm that the Court has become more willing to offer instructions or guidelines on how to construe and apply legislation in conformity with the Constitution. In particular, over the last decade, and especially in annulment procedures that involve a fundamental rights component, more substantive and temporal modulations are proclaimed. Although this engagement in dialogue with both the legislator and the judiciary is promising, it should be recommended that the Court pays more attention to the phrasing of the modulated dicta. Without additional clarification, confusion will remain about the consequences of an annulment 'to the extent that' or rejection 'under the reservation that' for the judiciary and administration, which have to apply legislation in practice.

---

883 Hence, in 61 cases out of 158, at least one of the pleas was answered with a declaration of unconstitutionality or a modulation.

884 The steep fall in 2002 can be explained by the fact that only one mixed annulment action was lodged before the Court that year: BeCC case no 189/2002, 19 December 2002 (the plea based on the competence allocating rules was rejected, the plea based on the equality principle led to an annulment).

885 In 27 (17%) of the mixed cases, a modulated declaration of constitutionality was proclaimed; in 15 (10%) a modulated declaration of unconstitutionality; and one extrinsic gap (BeCC case no 121/2013, 26 September 2013, B.58.8).

886 In particular, there were on average more modulations than annulments in the years 2006, 2007, 2008, 2009, 2012 and 2015.

887 Of the 38 mixed cases where the BeCC has annulled legislation, in 8 a temporal modulation occurred (21%): BeCC case no 26/1990, 14 July 1990; BeCC case no 42/1997, 14 July 1997; BeCC case no 106/2004, 16 June 2004; BeCC case no 154/2007, 19 December 2007; BeCC case no 49/2008, 12 March 2008; BeCC case no 11/2009, 21 January 2009; BeCC case no 158/2013, 21 November 2013; BeCC case no 130/2014, 19 December 2014.

5.4.3. PRELIMINARY PROCEDURES

Figure 5.9. Case outcomes in fundamental rights preliminary procedures

Preliminary questions based on an alleged infringement of fundamental rights provisions form the largest group within the case law of the Court. Moreover, the number of such cases increased steeply until 2002, and has more or less stabilised since then. As demonstrated by figure 5.9, how the BeCC answers these questions has evolved over the years. While the average percentage of rejections has remained relatively stable (around 65%), there is an upward trend of modulated outcomes at the expense of simple invalidations. Similarly to the annulment actions based on fundamental rights, at least one violation was found in 38% of these cases. Yet, since 2001, there has not been a single year in which the BeCC preferred simply invalidating legislation over modulating it. Although there is an upward trend for all types of modulations, this is pre-eminently so for the modulated declarations of unconstitutionality ('unconstitutional unless').[888]

[888] In 267 (14%) of the fundamental rights cases, a modulated declaration of unconstitutionality was proclaimed; in 164 (8%) a double interpretation; in 47 (2%) a modulated declaration of constitutionality and in 35 (2%) an extrinsic gap.

Often, in these outcomes the BeCC broadens the scope of legislation and adds that the 'regular' courts should apply this legislation as understood in its broadened meaning (intrinsic gap).[889]

The explanation for this shift is twofold. On the one hand, by choosing modulated outcomes over a declaration of unconstitutionality, the BeCC may want to avoid practical difficulties. When legislation is simply declared unconstitutional, the referring judge should declare it inapplicable to the case. This may prompt the judge to resort to other creative solutions – not necessarily anticipated by the litigants. A modulation gives the referring court insight into how the reviewed legislation can be applied in conformity with the Constitution, in anticipation of legislative response. On the other hand, the BeCC may want to tighten its grip on judicial outcomes. In principle, the referring judge – as well as any other judge who has to apply the reviewed legislation – should abide by the ruling.[890] Hence, with a modulated outcome, the Court can point the judge in a particular direction.

The outcomes proclaimed in competence conflict cases differ noticeably between both types of procedure. While figures 5.10 and 5.11 showed that such cases mostly lead to annulments, in a preliminary procedure, most often no infringement is found at all (58%).[891] Moreover, on average 20% of these cases lead to a declaration of unconstitutionality, which is less than half of the average in annulment procedures. Yet more modulations appear than in annulment procedures (17%), mostly modulated declarations of (un)constitutionality.[892] Thus these results are consistent with those in the preliminary fundamental rights cases, which showed that the BeCC aims to communicate more directly with the judiciary through modulated outcomes. In other words, they do not necessarily demonstrate that the BeCC is less strict than in annulments procedures, but indicate that it prefers sanctioning modalities which suit the procedural characteristics of preliminary rulings.

---

889 For example: BeCC case no 94/2015, 25 June 2015; BeCC case no 149/2015, 22 October 2015.

890 When the Court proclaims a double interpretation, the judge can apply the legislation as interpreted in conformity with the Constitution, or should leave it aside it if he chooses the other interpretation. A modulated declaration of (un)constitutionality does not give alternatives: B Lombart, 'Les Techniques d'arrêts de la cour d'arbitrage' 1996 RBDC, 352; and H Boularbah, 'Interpretation ou qualification de la norme controlee et dessaisissement de juge a quo' in *Liber Amicorum Paul Martens* (Larcier 2007), 189–90.

891 Hence, in 42% of these cases, at least one violation was found (vs 72% for the annulment actions relating to a competence conflict).

892 In 13 (10%) of these cases, a modulated declaration of constitutionality was proclaimed; in 12 (9%) a modulated declaration of unconstitutionality; in 6 (5%) a double interpretation and no extrinsic gaps.

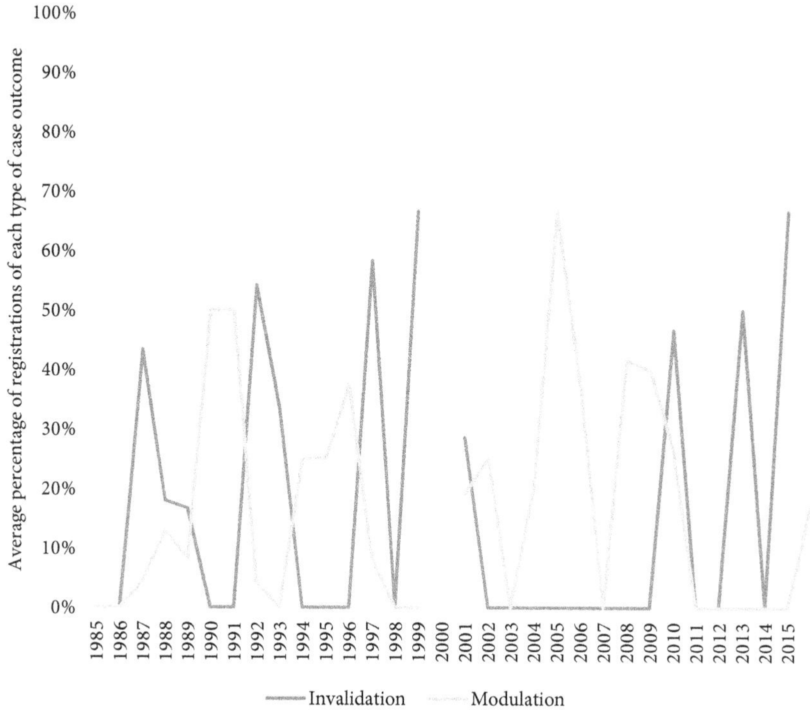

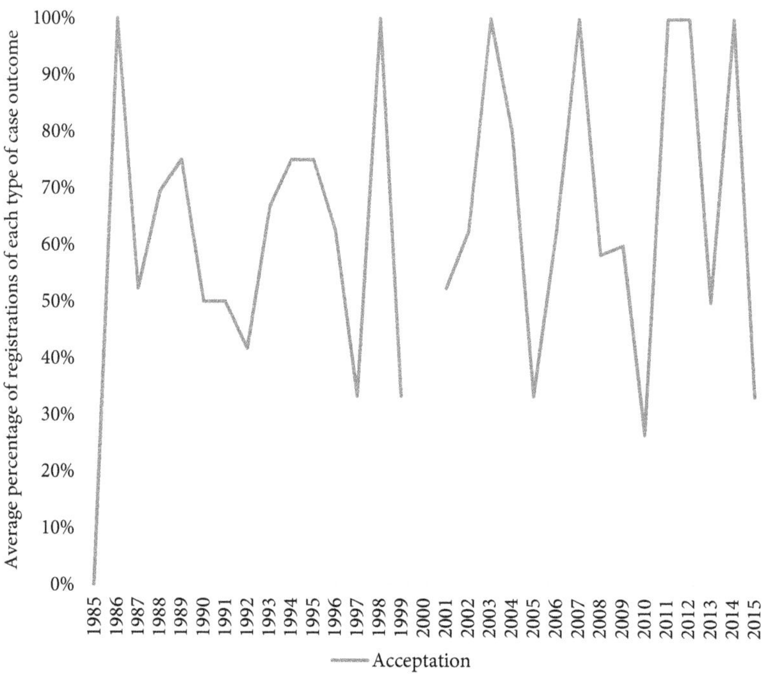

Figures 5.10. and 5.11. Case outcomes in competence conflict preliminary procedures

Finally, the results demonstrate that a referring judge who brings a mixed case before the Court usually receives the answer that no infringement could be found at all (77%). When a violation is found, the preferred remedy is a modulation (average: 10%).[893] Only rarely does the BeCC declare legislation unconstitutional (average: 4%).[894] Again, these results for the mixed cases are rather surprising. While one would expect that legislation which is challenged on multiple grounds deals with serious issues of unconstitutionality, not many are found by the Court. A plausible explanation for this result is that mixed cases are the results of a litigant strategy to challenge the legislation on as many grounds as possible while the case is actually not that strong.

After a long debate, the BeCC has accepted (in case no 125/2011)[895] that it can, in exceptional circumstances, modulate the temporal effect of a declaration of unconstitutionality in preliminary rulings.[896] In particular, the Court noted that a preliminary judgment has an effect that transcends the proceedings pending before the referring judge. Therefore, in light of the principles of legal certainty and legitimate expectation, the Court considered it necessary to analyse the extent to which the impact of its decision must be attenuated in time. It concluded that, notwithstanding that the law does not empower it to do so, it can provisionally retain the effects of unconstitutional provisions. Since then, the Court has only applied this in a few cases, although the data point to an upward trend.[897]

In conclusion, in preliminary procedures, the Court also increasingly engages in dialogue with the legislator and judiciary through modulated outcomes. Although the willingness to participate in this dialogic process should be encouraged, it should also be noted that modulated rulings can raise practical difficulties. If the outcome goes further than interpretation, and constructively alters the content of the legislation, it is not evident that the judiciary applies it as such. As long as the legal text remains untouched, the judiciary needs to base its decision in the Court's ruling and not in the law. Moreover, even though the results suggest that more 'intrinsic gap' and 'extrinsic gap' outcomes are proclaimed, many rulings still do not include such direct instructions. Therefore, it should be recommended that the Court develops a method with clear, verifiable

---

893 Out of 40 cases, there was 1 where a modulated declaration of unconstitutionality was proclaimed; 2 with a modulated declaration of constitutionality; 3 with a double interpretation and no extrinsic gaps.

894 BeCC case no 65/2001, 17 May 2001; BeCC case no 85/2002, 8 May 2002; and BeCC case no 113/2015, 17 September 2015. Only in the last case were all pleas accepted.

895 BeCC case no 125/2011, 7 July 2011.

896 Before, the Court sometimes rejected the plea in circumstances where there actually was a problem of unconstitutionality in order to avoid the practical problems that would arise from an invalidation without temporal modulation. In the justificatory ground, the Court then emphasised that there was an issue to be addressed by the legislator and that, if there was no legislative response, the Court would decide otherwise (invalidating the legislation) in a future case. See For example BeCC case no 27/2005, 2 February 2009.

897 Six out of 7 of these registered temporal modulations were proclaimed in 2014 and 2015.

conditions determining the outcome. In addition, the Court should display more consistency in the phrasing of its rulings, clarifying each time if it proclaims an interpretative or constructive modulation, and what the consequences are for the judiciary and legislator. The current ambiguity can actually constitute an obstacle for effective implementation of the Court's case law. More consistency would strengthen the signalling effect of the various types of outcomes, and improve the communication between the Court and its audience.

5.4.4. MEDIA ATTENTION ON THE COURT'S RULINGS, DEPENDING ON THE OUTCOME

The previous sections concentrated on how the Court communicates to its audience through the judgment dicta. Yet, without public awareness, the decision risks going unnoticed. The news media may draw attention to rulings that require a legislative response. When journalists face complex legal decisions that are difficult to interpret, they are likely to look for certain cues indicating that the public audience will find their story appealing.[898] The proclaimed dictum may function as an important cue to decide which case merits coverage. Hence, if the Court aims to strengthen the signalling power of its rulings, it is important to recognise which outcomes attract attention.

Table 5.2. Overview of the news media attention for the Belgian Constitutional Court's rulings

Type of procedure	Type of case	Type of outcome A = Acceptation I = Invalidation M = Modulation	Average number of articles
Annulment procedure (47%; 2.29)	Fundamental rights case (43%; 2.24)	A (32%)	0.76
		I (68%)	5.87
		M (54%)	2.56
	Competence conflict case (54%; 2.56)	A (40%)	1.05
		I (61%)	3.47
		M (52%)	2.07
	Mixed case (58%; 2.5)	A (44%)	1.14
		I (82%)	5.68
		M (77%)	3.44
	If invalidation: temporal modulation (73%; 9.15)		

(continued)

[898] In political science literature, markers of newsworthiness are known as 'news values': MD Allen and DP Haider-Markel, 'Connecting Supreme Court Decisions, Media Coverage and Public Opinion: The Case of Lawrence v. Texas' (2006) 27 The American Review of

Table 5.2 *continued*

Type of procedure	Type of case	Type of outcome A = Acceptation I = Invalidation M = Modulation	Average number of articles
Preliminary procedure (17%; 0.45)	Fundamental rights case (17%; 0.46)	A (10%)	0.21
		I (38%)	1.25
		M (25%)	0.67
	Competence conflict case (12%; 0.34)	A (4%)	0.08
		I (22%)	0.97
		M (24%)	0.41
	Mixed case (8%; 0.15)	A (7%)	0.16
		I (0%)	0
		M (14%)	0.14
	If invalidation: temporal modulation (29%; 8.86)		

Table 5.2 gives an overview of the news media attention for the Court's rulings, depending on the type of procedure, the invoked reference norms and the case outcome. The percentages denote the proportion of cases within each group that received at least some attention, meaning that they were discussed in at least one newspaper article. The numbers indicate how many articles, on average, were published on cases in this group.

Drawing from this overview, it is apparent that the news media are particularly drawn to cases where provisions are annulled. Removing provisions from the legal order potentially has a strong impact on a large group of citizens. In particular, all citizens who fall under the scope of application of the annulled provisions are affected. In addition, by annulling legislation, the Court openly confronts the majority in Parliament which approved the policy decision. Such judicial denunciation of political choices can be understood as a disagreement between different branches of power, and news media tends to be driven by such conflicts. Finally, annulling certain provisions from a specific statute may upset the balance in a political agreement by which the legislative majority ascended to power. Hence an invalidation may require that politicians renegotiate the terms of the agreement. For these reasons, it is not surprising that annulments draw the most attention. Although preliminary rulings generally receive far less attention, here also invalidations are covered most extensively. This result is in line with prior research on the USSC that identified the invalidation of legislation as

Politics, 209–10; and K Sill et al., 'Media Coverage of the U.S. Supreme Court: How Do Journalists Assess the Importance of Court Decisions?' (2013) 20 Political Communication, 1, 13.

one of the strongest factors driving media coverage.[899] Finally, cases where the Court has tempered the retroactivity of an invalidation receive additional attention. In sum, a ruling's newsworthiness is mainly determined by the (visible) impact it has on the democratic policy-making process.

A few examples can illustrate this finding. First, in case no 84/2015,[900] the Court dealt with federal legislation related to the collection and storing of private data, such as phone and e-mail conversations. Although the purpose of these measures was to fight serious crime and terrorism, no restrictions were placed on their scope of application. In particular, the government was allowed to collect and store any communication data from any person, without any indication of involvement in criminal activities, and without any time or geographical limit. For these reasons, the Court found that the measures were disproportional to the legislative purpose, and the entire law was annulled without tempering the retroactive effect of the ruling.[901] Newspaper journalists commented on the ruling, stating that problems would and did arise in concrete criminal proceedings. In particular, evidence that was collected under these provisions became invalid, which created the risk that some actual criminals could not be convicted.[902]

Another example is case no 105/2015,[903] related to a telecommunication tax introduced by a Walloon decree. Because this tax had previously been collected by local communities, the decree limited local fiscal autonomy. Yet the Court ruled that the competence to adopt such limitations was reserved to the federal legislator and annulled the challenged provisions. Considering the financial and legal difficulties caused by the annulment, however, the Court added that the effects of the provisions should be maintained.[904] The French-speaking news

899 K Sill et al., 'Media Coverage of the U.S. Supreme Court: How Do Journalists Assess the Importance of Court Decisions?' (2013) 20 Political Communication, 1, 20; and TS Clark et al., 'Measuring the Political Salience of Supreme Court Cases' (2015) Journal of Law and Courts 3(1), 57. It should be noted, however, that these articles do not elaborate on how the variable was coded (making it unclear whether modulated outcomes were considered constitutional or unconstitutional).

900 BeCC case no 84/2015, 11 June 2015. The law of 30 July 2013 implemented EU directive 2006/24/EC of 15 March 2006 on the retention of data generated or processed in connection with the provision of publicly available electronic communications services or of public communications networks.

901 Ibid., B.11-12.

902 De Standaard, 12 June 2015, "*Privacy-arrest bezorgt speurders kopzorgen. Grondwettelijk Hof vernietigt regels over bewaring communicatiegegevens*"; Le Soir 12 June 2015, "*Vie privée: les données seront mieux protégées*"; De Standaard, 13 June 2015 "*Grote onrust na vernietiging wet over bewaring communicatiegegevens. Vrijspraken dreigen door privacy-arrest*"; and Gazet van Antwerpen, "*Justitie. Arrest over telefonie al meteen gebruikt. Advocaten vragen vrijspraak omdat bewijs niet gebruikt mag worden*".

903 BeCC case no 105/2015, 16 July 2015.

904 Ibid., B.12-13.

media paid considerable attention to the ruling, concentrating on its practical consequences. In particular, due to the temporal modulation, the taxes which were already collected would not have to be reimbursed.[905]

Finally, in the preliminary ruling in case no 125/2011,[906] as discussed above, the unequal treatment with regard to the term of notice between 'workmen' and 'service employees' was declared unconstitutional, but the effects of the provision were provisionally maintained. More specifically, the legislator was given two years to remedy the constitutional infringement, during which the judiciary could continue to apply the discriminatory provision. The news media put pressure on the legislative branch by continuously referring to the ruling and reiterating that the legislator was obliged to respond within that time frame.[907]

Modulated outcomes are considered less newsworthy, both in annulment and preliminary procedures. Although modulations are not necessarily more deferential, they do not confront the legislative majority in the same way as a simple invalidation.[908] The absence of such a visible clash between the branches of power seems to deter newspaper journalists from paying attention to these rulings. Also, they may interpret these outcomes as mere instructions for the judiciary, while they are more interested in the consequences for the legislative branch. Only rulings with a modulated declaration of unconstitutionality ('violates to the extent that') receive somewhat more attention than other types of modulations.[909] A probable explanation is that the way these outcomes are

905 For example: La Libre Belgique, 17 July 2015, *"La Région recalée sur les pylônes GSM"*; Le Soir, 17 July 2015, *"Une taxe annulée mais pas interdite."*; Vers L'Avenir, 17 July 2015, *"Mâts et pylônes pas à l'abri; Région wallone. La taxe sur les mâts et pylônes annulée, mais ... Un arrêt de la Cour constitutionnelle annule les dispositions du décret «taxe sur les mâts et pylônes». Mais les effets sont maintenus"*.

906 BeCC case no 125/2011, 7 July 2011.

907 De Tijd, 8 July 2011, *"Nog twee jaar om arbeiders en bedienden gelijk te schakelen"*; L'écho, 8 July 2011, *"Vers un même préavis pour ouvriers et employés. Le législateur à deux ans pour harmoniser les durées des préavis des ouvriers et des employés, dit la Cour constitutionnelle"*; Knack, 11 January 2012, *"Economie. Arbeiders en bedienden. Klok tikt voor gelijk werknemersstatuut"*; La Libre Belgique, 21 March 2013, *"Concertation sociale. Statut unique: la balle dans le camp du gouvernement"*; Gazet van Antwerpen, 23 March 2013, *"Voor alle duidelijkheid. Eenheidsstatuut. Niemand geeft duimbreed toe. Regering moet tegen 8 juli oplossing presenteren voor probleem van halve eeuw oud"*; and La Libre Belgique, 6 June 2013, *"Statut unique: l'accord ou le saut dans l'inconnu. Le grand flou juridique de l'après-8 juillet"*.

908 M De Visser, *Constitutional Review in Europe: a Comparative Analysis* (Hart Publishing 2014), 303–304.

909 Rulings that included such an outcome are covered in, on average, one newspaper article. For example, BeCC case no 48/2012, 22 March 2012, where the Court found that a Flemish Decree violated the Constitution to the extent it did not, under certain circumstances, provide for a reimbursement of registration fees when buying a new house. See for example: De Standaard, 23 March 2012, *"Vlaamse registratierechten discrimineren. Vlaamse overheid moet registratierechten terugbetalen"*; and L'écho, 30 March 2012, *"Bonne nouvelle pour qui achète un bien neuf en Flandre"*.

phrased is most closely linked to a simple invalidation. Other types of modulation, such as the modulated declaration of constitutionality, double interpretations or even the extrinsic gap outcomes, are seldom covered in the news media. The limited newsworthiness of modulated outcomes is potentially problematic. Maybe even more than a clear-cut invalidation, they require a legislative response. Although there are other channels through which the legislator may be informed about the decision, the total lack of news media attention may be an important cause of legislative silence.

An example is preliminary ruling no 72/2012,[910] where the Court was requested to review a particular difference in protection between couples who were married or had concluded a legal partnership. In particular, the challenged provision limited the possibility for one of the married partners to sell part of their co-owned real estate, but the law did not provide a similar protection for legal partners. The Court ruled that this unequal treatment was discriminatory but added that this was not inherent to the challenged legislation, but was due to the absence of a similar rule for legal partners. Hence, the Court established an extrinsic gap that needed to be addressed by the legislator.[911] Although the ruling had consequences for a broad group of citizens, the news media did not pay attention to the outcome. Therefore, notwithstanding the Court's clear instructions, the legislator has yet to create a rule that eliminates the discrimination.[912]

In the above it has been argued that a constitutional court should engage in dialogue, with the aim of improving democratic policy-making. It is the responsibility of the Court to communicate effectively with the legislator through the case outcome (and justificatory ground). Yet the Court shares some responsibility with other institutions to produce an actual positive constitutional dialogue. The news media functions as an intermediate actor between the Court, legislator and citizenry. Because many modulations require legislative action, a lack of public attention is potentially problematic. For affected actors, legislative silence then means that their fundamental rights are not protected to the degree that is constitutionally required.[913] A legislator who is unwilling to take action may consider it convenient that citizens remain uninformed about the ruling. Without oversight by the public, the risk for the legislator of losing legitimacy by

---

910 BeCC case no 72/2010, 23 June 2010.

911 Ibid., B.10.1-2.

912 A legislative proposal to do so was rejected: see *Parl Doc* Kamer 2012–13, no 2998/1. For a detailed analysis of the legislative response to lacunae established by the BeCC, see S Verstraelen, 'Constitutionele dialoog als een lens: onderzoek naar het wetgevend optreden na de vaststelling van een ongrondwettige lacune door het Grondwettelijk Hof' (2016) 1 Tijdschrift voor Wetgeving, 2.

913 M De Visser, *Constitutional Review in Europe: A Comparative Analysis* (Hart Publishing 2014), 376.

ignoring judicial decisions is reduced. In conclusion, the role of the news media in shaping public perception cannot be underestimated.

5.5. STRATEGIC CONSIDERATIONS UNDERLYING THE CASE DICTUM

5.5.1. INTRODUCTION

When a constitutional complaint is lodged before the Court, the law clerks and judges are expected to scrutinise the case arguments carefully. Although the outcome is evidently to some extent dictated by legal rules and principles, there is also some room for judicial discretion. It is left to the Court to decide when an interpretative or constructive modulation is possible or when it is more appropriate for the legislature to remedy the rights violation.

Under the strategic model, it is assumed that courts adapt aspects of their decisions – including the outcome – in order to maximise their effectiveness. In particular, they must think ahead to prospective consequences and anticipate the probable reactions of other actors (in)directly involved in the review procedure, such as the legislature, other courts, litigants or the general public.[914] In order to ensure compliance with the judicial outcome, they must be careful not to overstep the boundaries of the 'tolerance interval' set out by these actors. Although the interplay between different expectations from different actors makes it hard to predict case outcomes,[915] there are reasons to believe that the Court, under certain circumstances, strategically adapts its case outcome. This decision necessarily involves an evaluation of which institution is best placed to determine how legislation should be understood and applied, and the question of whether the legislature is willing to carry out a legal reform.[916] In short, the hypothesis is put forth that salient cases may require a more prudent approach from the

---

914 KE Whittington, 'Once More Unto the Breach: Postbehavioralist Approaches to Judicial Politics' [2000] Law and Social Enquiry, 612; G Vanberg, *The Politics of Constitutional Review in Germany* (Cambridge University Press 2005), 177; and L Epstein and J Knight, *The Choices Justices Make* (CQ Press1998), 79–88.

915 Scholars have identified strategies that might be pursued under certain circumstances, often immediately followed by a disclaimer that the contrary strategy might be more appropriate in other circumstances. This is a weakness of the strategic model. See L Epstein, J Knight and WF Murphy, 'The Interactive Nature of Judicial Decision Making' in N Maveety (ed.), *The Pioneers of Judicial Behaviour* (University of Michigan Press 2003), 208. Moreover, anticipating the probable consequences of different outcomes is difficult, which means that the assessment of the court itself can be inaccurate: S Dothan, *Reputation and Judicial Tactics* (Cambridge University Press 2015), 119.

916 A Kavanagh, *Constitutional Review under the UK Human Rights Act* (Cambridge University Press 2009), 135.

Court, where it addresses the legislator through a modulated outcome instead of a simple invalidation.

In what follows, an empirical framework is developed in two steps to demonstrate that strategic considerations may (to some extent) explain the case outcomes of the BeCC.

In the first step, the odds on finding a violation are estimated within the whole range of data (n=3145). It is hypothesised that more violations are found in salient cases, in particular those that received considerable news media attention, attracted a large group of participants and/or were decided in plenary session. Yet, if the statistic model reveals significant results, this does not necessarily demonstrate that Court acts strategically, but can merely reflect that cases are more likely to be perceived as salient if the legislator acted in contravention of the Constitution.

In the second step, additional hypotheses are developed relating to the outcome *if* a violation has been established. The main hypothesis is that in (politically) salient cases, the Court is more inclined to act more prudently by opting for a substantive or temporal modulation instead of an invalidation. These hypotheses are tested for a subset of the data, in particular those cases in which a violation has been found (n=1244).

5.5.2. HYPOTHESES

5.5.2.1. *Finding a Violation (n=3145)*

The following three hypotheses concern the relation between case salience and the odds of finding of a violation within the whole range of data (n=3145). But it should be noted that this relation can be understood as a two-way process. It is likely that the severity of the infringement or, in other words, the likelihood that a violation will be found, affects the perception of case salience by the news media, the litigants and the Court itself. Hence, the finding of a violation may not be a function of the salience indicators, but simply of the fact that the legislation actually conflicts with constitutional requirements. Nonetheless, there are reasons to assume that the salience indicators additionally increase the odds on finding a violation. Prior research on the German Constitutional Court, for instance, has shown that the presence of outside support continues to exert a significant impact on the likelihood of more aggressive judicial behaviour, even when the model controls for the legal environment.[917]

[917] G Vanberg, *The Politics of Constitutional Review in Germany* (Cambridge University Press 2005), 109–10.

The first hypothesis relates to media coverage in the run-up to a particular case. Increased media attention does not only reflect the case's underlying salience, it also makes it more likely that the media will cover the case outcome. The data confirm that there is a significant positive relation between media attention before and after the Court's decision.[918] Intense media coverage increases the likelihood that citizens become aware of a legislative attempt to evade a certain case outcome. If those citizens value judicial authority, which is expected in advanced democracies such as Belgium,[919] resisting judicial decisions may result in the loss of electoral support.[920] The fear of such a backlash may induce the legislative branch to comply with judicial outcomes.[921] Anticipating this, the Court may feel less constrained to challenge public policies but, instead, may be willing to exercise its powers more aggressively.[922] In other words, the Court is in a strong position when legislative unwillingness to implement a judicial decision is likely to become public after the ruling, particularly when increased media attention is expected. Therefore, it is hypothesised that when a case is (intensively) covered by the media before or during the Court's decision-making procedure, it is more likely that the Court will establish a violation.

Hypothesis 1a: When more newspaper articles were published on the case prior to the judicial decision, it is more likely that a constitutional violation will be found.

Second, the case outcome presumably depends on the strength of the litigant's claim. Although this evidently does not mean that individual litigants cannot bring a strong claim before the Court, the involvement of a large group of participants can be considered as an indicator of case strength. In particular,

---

918 Pearson=0.358 (significant at the 0.01 level – two-tailed).

919 G Vanberg, *The Politics of Constitutional Review in Germany* (Cambridge University Press 2005), 21.

920 Vanberg mentions media coverage as one of the factors making it more difficult for legislative majorities to hide attempts at evasion: G Vanberg, *The Politics of Constitutional Review in Germany* (Cambridge University Press 2005), 22–3, 45–9. In addition, he argues that highly salient cases with greater public awareness create a more transparent environment: G Vanberg, 'Legislative-Judicial Relations: A Game-Theoretic Approach to Constitutional Review' (2001) 45 Amercian Journal of Political Science, 346, 355. In that sense, the news media ensures than the government is accountable to the public: K Sill et al., 'Media Coverage of the U.S. Supreme Court: How Do Journalists Assess the Importance of Court Decisions?' (2013) 20 Political Communication, 1–2.

921 S Dothan, *Reputation and Judicial Tactics* (Cambridge University Press 2015), 23: "Parties comply with the court when the reputational payoff is higher than the material cost of compliance".

922 JR Staton, 'Constitutional Review and the Selective Promotion of Case Results' (2006) 50 American Journal of Political Salience, 98; and G Vanberg, *The Politics of Constitutional Review in Germany* (Cambridge University Press 2005), 40.

it is said to be more probable that a larger group of actors will lodge a complaint before the Court when there is an actual constitutional infringement than when there is not.[923] Nonetheless, it is also believed that constitutional courts stand in a stronger position as the number of parties and the mix of party types increases.[924] In addition, when parties have an interest in seeing a decision implemented, they may engage in campaigns to raise awareness if the legislator fails to do so.[925] Hence, more intense participation may increase the threat to the legislator of losing public support after evading implementation, protecting the outcome from political reprisals. This would make the Court feel strongly mandated to challenge the legislator's views.[926] In sum, it is hypothesised that the participation of a larger and more diverse group of litigants will increase the likelihood that a violation is found.

Hypothesis 1b: As the number of individuals involved or the mix of party types increases, it becomes more likely that a constitutional violation will be found.

The third explanatory variable relates to the panel size. When a case is directed to a plenary session, all twelve (or, exceptionally, ten) judges should confer with each other to reach a decision. Possibly, judges anticipate the need to discuss a case more intensively with their colleagues when there are considerable doubts on the constitutionality of the challenged legislation. Hence, they will request a plenary session. Also, these outcomes have potentially strong consequences for the legislative branch. Considering that the case dictum and the reason-giving will be a road map for future legislation, the judges will want to be included in the drafting process. Only in plenary session can each judge contribute to the content of the ruling. In addition, if a violation is likely to be found, the Court

---

923 G Vanberg, *The Politics of Constitutional Review in Germany* (Cambridge University Press 2005), 109–10.

924 For example, it increases the probability that a precedent is reversed: P Harris, 'Difficult Cases and the Display of Authority' (1985) 1 Journal of Law, Economics and Organization, 209, 221. Also, Vanberg found that the German Constitutional Court is more aggressive when the number of amicus briefs increase: G Vanberg, *The Politics of Constitutional Review in Germany* (Cambridge University Press 2005), 103, 107.

925 Participants may act as *a posteriori* 'watchdogs', raising publicity and calling attention to evasive manoeuvres. Vanberg argues that interest groups especially have the resources and organisational capability to do so: G Vanberg, 'Legislative-Judicial Relations: A Game-Theoretic Approach to Constitutional Review' (2001) 45 Amercian Journal of Political Science, 346, 355; and G Vanberg, *The Politics of Constitutional Review in Germany* (Cambridge University Press 2005), 96.

926 C Bateup, 'Expanding the Conversation: American and Canadian Experiences of Constitutional Dialogue in Comparative Perspective' (2006) 44 New York University Public Law and Legal Theory Working Papers, 6, 45.

may want to address its audience in the largest coalition possible. Research has shown that the larger the majority, the greater the appearance of certainty and the more likely the decision is to be accepted.[927] Conversely, when finding a violation seems unlikely, a case can more easily be handled in limited session. Therefore, it is hypothesised that when a case is decided in plenary session, the Court is more likely to establish a violation.

Hypothesis 1c: When the Court deliberates in plenary session, it is more likely that a constitutional infringement will be found.

5.5.2.2. *Invalidation or Modulation: How to Interpret Judicial Preferences on Case Outcomes?*

When a constitutional violation is found, the BeCC can opt to invalidate the provision (with or without maintaining its effects) or opt for a substantial modulation. As explained before, the Court has considerable discretion to opt for the outcome that it considers most appropriate. Even when the finding of the violation itself is not or only scarcely affected by strategic considerations (but primarily by legal factors), it remains possible that the choice between these different outcomes does reflect such strategic behaviour. In particular, there are reasons to assume that the Court proclaims more substantive[928] and temporal modulations than invalidations in salient cases.

First, a substantive modulation may serve as a strategic compromise when a violation has been found but a 'simple' invalidation would exceed the threshold of acceptance. An invalidation leads to (retroactive) removal and/or the inapplicability of the unconstitutional provisions. Moreover, removing certain provisions from a specific statute may upset the balance in a particular political agreement by which a legislative majority ascended to power. Although modulated outcomes are not necessarily more deferential towards legislative majorities, they do not confront the parliamentary majority

---

927 WF Murphy, *Elements of Judicial Strategy* (University of Chicago Press 1964); and RC Black et al., *US Supreme Court Opinions and their Audiences* (Cambridge University Press 2016). Yet this argument was put forward in the context of the USSC, where individual opinions are allowed. This may be less influential in the Belgian setting, where all constitutional rulings are presented as consensual.

928 In particular, a modulated declaration of (un)constitutionality or extrinsic gap. Double interpretation outcomes were excluded because, in principle, they are not expected to reflect strategic considerations but rather follow from the way the preliminary question was formulated. Also, these types of outcomes only appear in preliminary procedures, which are almost always (96%) non-salient or of low salience.

in the same way as an invalidation.[929] They offer the legislator a road map on how to remedy the unconstitutional provision(s). Clearer instructions are believed to stimulate compliance.[930] In addition, instead of focusing on the impermissible, a modulated outcome offers more constructive guidelines to the judiciary. Sometimes, they even make it possible to bridge a period of legislative silence.[931] Finally, a substantive modulation is less likely to be covered by the news media, decreasing the risk that the Court's authority is undermined by a legislative evasion.[932] In other words, by modulating its decision, the Court circumvents the confrontation with the legislature that may damage its institutional standing, while at the same time offering constitutional protection for the litigants (or anyone falling under the scope of the challenged legislation). Moreover, Shapiro and Stone Sweet argue that such creative techniques strenghten the court's dominance over policy outcomes.[933] In conclusion, while at the same time acting prudently in order not to overstep the legislator's acceptance threshold, courts may actually maximise their effectiveness as a policy-maker.

Second, another judicial strategy in delicate cases consists in proclaiming a temporal modulation. Most of these modulations, both in annulment[934] and preliminary procedures,[935] grant the legislature a certain time period in which to change the unconstitutional rule. Such postponement of the invalidation is a way to bridge a period of legislative silence. This suggests that the Court is concerned about the effect of a simple invalidation, for example because it would disturb the balance in a political agreement.[936] An invalidation may require that politicians renegotiate the terms of the agreement. When the Court anticipates future non-compliance, it may want to send a clear signal that a legislative

929 M De Visser, *Constitutional Review in Europe: A Comparative Analysis* (Hart Publishing 2014), 303–4.

930 RC Black et al., *US Supreme Court Opinions and their Audiences* (Cambridge University Press 2016), 29.

931 Ibid., 304: "unless the legislature disagrees so strongly with the judicial modulation that it is willing to replace the existing provisions, the court's solution is likely to remain in place."

932 G Vanberg, *The Politics of Constitutional Review in Germany* (Cambridge University Press 2005), 27, 32: "a succesfull evasion [...] undermines the court's authority by challenging its role in the policymaking process and demonstrates its relative weakness."

933 M Shapiro and A Stone Sweet, *On Law, Politics and Judicialization* (Oxford University Press 2002), 187–9.

934 S Verstraelen, 'The Temporal Limitation of Judicial Decisions: The Need for Flexibility Versus the Quest for Uniformity' (2013) 14 German Law Journal, 1687, 1699.

935 Two exceptions (from the seven) are: BeCC case no 67/2014, 24 April 2014; and BeCC case no 57/2015, 7 May 2015.

936 G Vanberg, 'Legislative-Judicial Relations: A Game-Theoretic Approach to Constitutional Review' (2001) 45 Amercian Journal of Political Science, 346, 348.

revision is required. At the same time, because of the delicate nature of the case, the Court attenuates this signal by giving time to amend the unconstitutional provision(s). A temporal modulation *ex nunc*, only maintaining the effects already produced, can also be interpreted as a signal of goodwill towards the legislator. By tempering the retroactive effect, the practical difficulties that would otherwise arise can be avoided. Considering the Court has discretion to select the cases where these consequences should be avoided, delicate or controversial cases are excellent candidates for where the Court may want to accommodate the legislator's concerns.

The first hypothesis relates to the relation between media coverage and the case outcome. The results in chapter 4 indicated that a case that is intensely covered in the newspaper is likely to handle a politically controversial issue. More specifically, intense media attention suggests that the issue under review is central to the interests of relevant political actors. While public awareness makes legislative evasion more difficult, legislative majorities may remain willing to take the risk when they consider the issue of greater important.[937] When this risk is increasingly high or the adverse consequences relatively great, the Court may be prompted to adapt aspects of the ruling.[938] In particular, when a violation is found, but the BeCC has reasons to doubt the legislator's willingness to react to a simple invalidation of the law, a reasonable alternative is to opt for a substantive or temporal modulation.[939]

Hypothesis 2a: When more media articles are published on the case prior to the judicial decision, it is more likely that the case will lead to a modulated outcome.

A deliberation in plenary session may equally indicate that the case deals with a politically sensitive issue. When the Court deliberates in plenary session, the double parity rule is strictly applied. Hence, the sub-groups within the Court will need to negotiate intensely in order to reach a majority opinion.[940]

---

937 G Vanberg, *The Politics of Constitutional Review in Germany* (Cambridge University Press 2005), 29.

938 FB Cross and BJ Nelson, 'Strategic Institutional Effects on Supreme Court Decisionmaking' (2001) 95 Northwestern University Law Review, 1437, 1451.

939 Kavanagh argues that, similarly, the UK courts may be less likely to opt for a 'declaration of incompatibility' (and rather adjust the statutory text) when they feel that Parliament is not willing to reform the legislation: A Kavanagh, *Constitutional Review under the UK Human Rights Act* (Cambridge University Press 2009), 135.

940 Grossman and Wells argue that bargaining is one of the most common tactics used by justices to mobilise a majority. Compromises must be made to accomplish an institutional result. See JB Grossman and RS Wells, 'Constitutional Law and Judicial Policy Making' (John Wiley & Sons 1972), 235, 254.

Previous research has suggested that the tendency to bargain increases substantially when judges decide on a politically salient case.[941] At the aggregated level, this may result in less aggressive, more tempered behaviour. As mentioned above, a judicial compromise may be to proclaim a substantive or temporal modulation. While at the same time remedying the infringement and offering constitutional protection, the Court avoids a direct confrontation with the legislature. Therefore, it is hypothesised that cases which are treated in plenary session are more likely to result in a modulated outcome.

Hypothesis 2b: When the Court deliberates in plenary session, it is more likely that the case will lead to a modulated outcome.

5.5.3. OPERATIONALISATION

In what follows, the results are presented in two steps. First, six models are estimated to explore the odds on the finding of a constitutional violation. In this step, the whole range of data (n=3145) is scrutinised. The dependent variable tracks whether a violation was found, with value 0 representing a situation when all pleas were rejected, and value 1 when at least one violation was found. Hypotheses 1a–c refer to the salience measures (see chapter 4), which are integrated into the models as the explanatory variables. In addition, three additional factors were integrated as being linked to the procedural traits of the case. In particular, one relates to the type of procedure (0=preliminary ruling, 1=annulment ruling) and one to the type of case brought before the Court (0=fundamental rights case, 1=competence conflict case, 2=mixed case). Finally, an interaction between the above two variables was added to the model. The reason for integrating these variables is that the descriptive results demonstrated that, overall, some types of cases are likely to result in the finding of a violation than others. For instance, more are found in annulment procedures, and especially when they relate to a competence conflict. In total, six models are estimated: one for each salience indicator, one with all salience indicators combined, one with the 'control' procedural variables and a full model. An in-depth analysis of these models can demonstrate

941 F Maltzman, JE Spriggs and PJ Wahlbeck, *Crafting Law on the Supreme Court: The Collegial Game* (Cambridge University Press 2000), 6 and further; and PT Spiller and R Gely, 'Strategic Judicial Decision Making' in GA Caldeira, RD Keleman and KE Whittington (eds.), *The Oxford Handbook of Law and Politics* (Oxford University Press 2008), 83.

whether the finding of a violation is rather dictated by strategic considerations (hypotheses 1a–c), by the procedural traits of the case (control variables) or a combination of both.

In the second step, instances when the Court, *if* a violation is found, strategically adapts its outcome to a modulated declaration of (un)constitutionality, an extrinsic gap or a temporal modulation, instead of choosing an invalidation, are explored. Hence, these hypotheses are tested for a subset of the data, in particular those cases in which a violation has been found (n=1243). The dependent variable tracks whether at least one substantive or a temporal modulation was proclaimed (0=no, 1=yes).[942] As above, several models are estimated. In line with hypotheses 2a–b, news media attention and panel size were integrated as salience indicators. No hypotheses were formulated with regard to who participated in the procedure, making it redundant to integrate these salience measures in the models.[943] The analysis also controls for the type of procedure and invoked reference norm.[944] Hence, in total 5 models were estimated: one for each of the two salience indicators, one with these salience indicators combined, one with the 'control' procedural variables and a full model.

Given the binary nature of the dependent variable(s), a logit model is applied to analyse the relation between the different independent and control variables and the dependent variable(s). In principle, the intercept equals the odds that the dependent variable is coded as 1 when all other variables in the model are evaluated at 0. The other parameter estimates show the effect size of the independent variables, in relation to the outcome, when all other variables are held constant. A significant positive coefficient implies that an increase in the value of the particular variable raises the probability of that outcome. To facilitate the interpretation of the parameter estimates, a column with exponential estimates [Exp(B)] was added. These numbers indicate the multiplication of the odds that a particular outcome is proclaimed when a certain independent variable is present rather than absent.

---

942 In other words, the cases where both an invalidation and modulation was proclaimed (n=65) were integrated in the category modulation.

943 As a control, a model was estimated with the 'size of the group of individuals' and 'participation diversity' as explanatory variables. Yet the Omnibus Test of Model Coefficients confirmed that this model does not fit the data. Moreover, adding these variables to the full model did not increase its explanatory power.

944 Yet the interaction variable was left out the analysis because none of the interactions were significant, nor did it increase the explanatory power of the full model.

5.5.4. RESULTS

5.5.4.1. Hypotheses 1a–c with Regard to the Finding of a Violation (n=3145)

Table 5.3. Case outcomes – hypotheses 1a–c with regard to the finding of a violation (n=3145) – model effects (* = p<0.001; ** = p<0.01; * = p<0.05)**

	MODEL 1		MODEL 2		MODEL 3		MODEL 4		MODEL 5		FULL MODEL 6	
	B (standard error)	Exp (B)	B (standard error)	Exp (B)	B (standard error)	Exp (B)	B (standard error)	Exp (B)	B (standard error)	Exp (B)	B (standard error)	Exp (B)
Intercept	−0.460 *** (0.038)	0.631	−0.673*** (0.048)	0.510	−0.395*** (0.071)	0.674	−0.662 *** (0.079)	0.516	−0.500 *** (0.047)	0.606	−0.858 *** (0.093)	0.424
Explanatory Variables												
***Media attention**												
– No articles (REF)	/	/	/	/	/	/	/	/	/	/	/	/
– 1–5 articles	0.280 (0.155)	1.323					0.107 (0.160)	1.113			0.006 (0.168)	1.006
– >5 articles	0.935*** (0.268)	2.548					0.639* (0.275)	1.896			0.558* (0.283)	1.747
***Plenary session** (REF=0)			0.641 *** (0.075)	1.898			0.620 *** (0.078)	1.860			0.646*** (0.079)	1.907
***Participation diversity**												
– One type of litigant involved (REF)	/	/	/	/	/	/	/	/	/	/	/	/
– Only referring judge (preliminary procedures)					0.388** (0.133)	1.465	0.467*** (0.135)	1.595			0.651*** (0.143)	1.918
– 2 types of litigants involved					−0.018 (0.086)	0.983	−0.062 (0.087)	0.939			−0.091 (0.090)	0.913
– >2 types of litigants involved					−0.024	0.976	−0.118 (0.139)	0.888			−0.239 (0.148)	0.787
***Involvement of individuals**												
– No individual involved (REF)	/	/	/	/	/	/	/	/	/	/	/	/

– 1–5 individuals involved					–0.151 (0.083)	0.860	–0.098 (0.085)	0.906			0.094 (0.093)	1.099
– >5 individuals involved					0.181 (0.153)	1.198	0.103 (0.156)	1.109			0.336 * (0.165)	1.399
Control Variables												
***Type of procedure** (REF= preliminary procedure)									0.022 (0.090)	1.022	–0.019 (0.104)	0.982
***Type of Case**												
– Fundamental rights *sensu stricto* (REF)	/	/	/	/	/	/	/	/	/	/	/	/
– Competence conflict *sensu stricto*									0.177 (0.183)	1.193	0.322 (0.192)	1.380
– Mixed case									–0.598 (0.368)	0.550	–0.472 (0.375)	0.624
***Interaction type of procedure x type of case**												
– Annulment proc x fundamental rights case (REF)	/	/	/	/	/	/	/	/	/	/	/	/
– Annulment proc x competence conflict case									1.267*** (0.272)	3.550	1.290*** (0.280)	3.634
– Annulment proc x mixed case									0.613 (0.410)	1.846	0.483 (0.416)	1.621
Goodness of fit												
–2 Log likelihood	4205.382		4148.071		4198.256		4118.944		4149.221		4043.193	
Chi Square	15.399***		72.710***		22.525***		101.837***		71.560***		177.588***	
Hosmer & Lemeshow	0.000		0.000		1.576 (0.904)		4.956 (0.726)		0.000 (1.000)		7.553 (0.374)	
Nagelkerke R^2	0.007		0.031		0.010		0.043		0.030		0.074	

With regard to the model fit, the results indicate that the models accurately estimate the effects of the explanatory and control variables. In particular, the Omnibus Test of Model Coefficients shows that the Chi Square is significant, meaning that all models are better at estimating case outcomes than an intercept only model. Yet, the 'full' model fits the data best. The value of the log likelihood in this model shows that less unexplained observations remain than in the other models. Hence, the results indicate that case salience to some extent determines the case outcome. In particular, while the results for hypothesis 1b are mixed, hypotheses 1a and 1c are largely supported by the data.

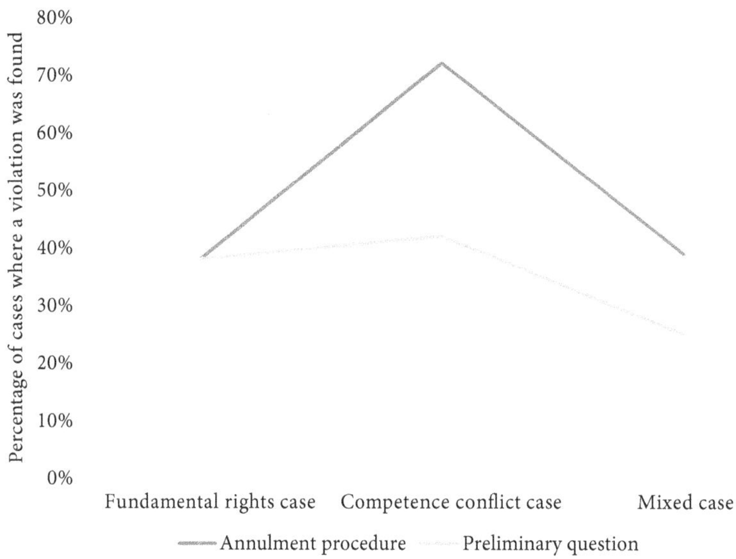

Figure 5.12. The finding of a violation in relation to the type of procedure and invoked reference norm

The results, such as visualised in figure 5.12, confirm the findings from the descriptive section. By adding the interaction variable to the model, the full model controls for the differences between all six sub-groups, depending on the type of procedure and type of invoked reference norm. The findings indicate that there is only one sub-group of cases where significantly more (or less) violations are found. In particular, when controlling for all other factors, the odds on finding a violation are 263% higher in annulment procedures dealing with a competence conflict case, compared to preliminary question related to fundamental rights question (=the reference category). Importantly, this effect has the largest explanatory power in the full model. The results equally confirm the descriptive results related to the differences between the reference category and other types of cases (see figure 5.12), but none of these effects are significant.

The first hypothesis related to media coverage can partly be confirmed. In particular, a violation is more likely to be established when a case has been intensively covered in the media prior to the decision. Even though adding variables to the model tempers the effect size of this variable, the full model shows that the odds on finding a violation continue to increase considerably (75%) when more than 5 articles have been published on the case. Conversely, when some attention has been given to the case (1–5 articles), this does not seem to affect the Court's decision. Even in model 1, where media coverage was included as a single explanatory variable, the model does not reveal a significant result. A possible explanation is that the Court is only prompted when it is increasingly likely that the ruling will be covered extensively in the newspapers. In other words, the Court's position may only be reinforced when there is a high probability that the legislator will be under public scrutiny. When the issue has attracted only a little attention prior to its decision, the Court may anticipate that this will not be the case. In conclusion, the positive relation between intense media coverage and case outcomes can be interpreted as a two-way process. In particular, when the legislator acts in contravention of the Constitution, this is likely to draw more attention from newspaper journalists.[945] Yet, only when the case has been covered extensively is the Court significantly more likely to establish a violation.

Next, the odds on finding a violation increase significantly when the Court deliberates in plenary session.[946] Particularly in the full model, these odds increase by 91%. Moreover, when controlling for the other factors, panel size seems to be one of the strongest determinants for the finding of a violation. This finding suggests that the request for a plenary session is triggered by a pre-emptive assessment by one or more judges that a violation will be established. A plenary session gives the opportunity to each individual judge to bring forward persuasive arguments and have a say in the drafting process. Conversely, if none of the judges estimates that the finding of a violation is probable, they are less keen to be included in the internal deliberation process. Importantly, this would mean that judges are aware that (some) constitutional cases leave room for

---

945 Violations were established in 39% of the cases that were not covered by the news media, in 46% of the cases that received a little attention and in 62% of the cases that were intensely covered.

946 In 49% of the cases where the Court deliberated in plenary session, a violation was found (vs 34%).

manoeuvre and that they aim to influence the justificatory ground and/or the outcome of the ruling. In addition, when establishing a violation, the Court may want to address its audience in the largest coalition possible. By doing so, they show that all opinions within the Court were heard and remove any doubt that a different composition could have led to another outcome.

The third 'participation' hypothesis can only partly be confirmed by the results. In particular, the involvement of a large group of individuals leads to more violations but only in the full model, and adding other categories of participants does not have a significant effect.

First, more violations are established in cases where more than five individuals participated.[947] In the full model, the odds on finding a violation significantly increase, by 40%, when such a large group was involved. Surprisingly, no significant result was found for this variable in the more limited models 3 (only participation) and 4 (combination of salience indicators). Only when the model controls for the type of procedure and reference norm does a significant result come forward. This may be explained by the considerable variation in the size of the group of individuals among different types of cases. The vast majority of cases where more than five individuals were involved are fundamental rights annulment procedures.[948] Hence the results suggest that, in these cases, the case outcome is related to the number of individuals supporting the claim. Yet another explanation can be that the numerical support in these cases increases more sharply when the legislator has acted in breach of the Constitution. Interestingly, only one category of the participation diversity variable is significant, and none go in the expected direction. In particular, the full model shows that 96% more violations are proclaimed in category 'zero', which are preliminary procedures initiated by the referring judge where no other litigants were involved.[949] In addition, a more diverse group of litigants, as compared to the reference category (one type of litigant involved), rather deters the Court from finding a constitutional infringement. A possible explanation is that more diversity does not necessarily mean that all participants oppose the provisions under review. Some may have intervened to support the legislation. Hence, instead of feeling strongly mandated to invalidate legislation, the Court may actually be persuaded by some litigants

947 A violation was found in 42% of the cases where no individual was involved, in 36% when 1–5 individuals and in 44% when more than 5 individuals were involved.

948 164 cases out of 221 (74%). In addition, there are also more individuals involved in mixed annulment procedures (31 cases). Conversely, there is rarely a large group of individuals involved in preliminary procedures, nor in competence conflict annulment procedures.

949 In particular, half of these cases lead to the finding of violation. This percentage drops to 36% in other preliminary procedures, and to 43% in annulment procedures.

to reject the challenge. Considering that no information was collected on the preferences of participants, additional research should clarify whether this explanation can be disproved.

Figure 5.13. The finding of a violation in relation to case salience

In addition to discussing the effects of the separate explanatory variables, figure 5.13 gives insight into the relation of (aggregated) case salience to the finding of a violation. As explained in chapter 4, highly salient cases are those that were deliberated in plenary session, received at least some media attention (>0) and involved a large and/or diverse group of litigants; while non-salient cases score on none of the salience measures. Figure 5.13 shows that the percentage of cases where a violation was established increases consistently from non-salient to highly salient cases. In line with the results discussed above, cases where all three salience indicators are present are logically the most likely candidates for finding a violation. In what follows, however, it is discussed whether these salience indicators equally determine how the Court responds to such a finding. In particular, it is explored whether the Court is more likely to establish a modulated outcome when these factors are present rather than absent.

5.5.4.2. Hypotheses 2a–b with Regard to Modulated Outcomes (n=1243)

Similar to what was concluded in the previous section, the Omnibus Test of Model Coefficients in table 5.4 shows that all models accurately estimate the effects of the explanatory and control variables, but the least unexplained observations remain in the full model.

Table 5.4. Case outcomes – hypotheses 1a–c with regard to the finding of a violation (n=3145) – model effects (* = p<0.001; ** = p<0.01; * = p<0.05)**

	MODEL 1		MODEL 2		MODEL 3		MODEL 4		FULL MODEL 5	
	B (standard error)	Exp (B)	B (standard error)	Exp (B)	B (standard error)	Exp (B)	B (standard error)	Exp (B)	B (standard error)	Exp (B)
Intercept	−0.048 (0.060)	0.953	−0.333*** (0.079)	0.716	−0.339*** (0.079)	0.712	−0.064 *** (0.072)	0.938	−0.331*** (0.087)	0.718
Explanatory Variables										
***Media attention**										
– No articles (REF)	/	/	/	/	/	/	/	/	/	/
– 1–5 articles	0.474* (0.240)	1.607			0.199 (0.242)	1.220			0.179 (0.252)	1.196
– >5 articles	1.336*** (0.404)	3.803			0.959* (0.410)	2.609			0.925* (0.417)	2.523
***Plenary session** (REF=0)			0.759*** (0.116)	2.136	0.690*** (0.120)	1.994			0.672*** (0.121)	1.959
Control Variables										
***Type of procedure** (REF= preliminary procedure)							0.322* (0.128)	1.380	0.130 (0.137)	1.138
***Type of Case**										
– Fundamental rights *sensu stricto* (REF)	/	/	/	/	/	/	/	/	/	/
– Competence conflict *sensu stricto*							−0.349 (0.179)	0.705	−0.345 (0.183)	0.708
– Mixed case							0.217 (0.262)	1.243	0.019 (0.270)	1.020
Goodness of fit										
−2 Log likelihood	1706.262		1679.349		1672.640		1711.902		1668.568	
Chi Square	16.804***		43.718***		50.426***		11.165*		54.498***	
Hosmer & Lemeshow	0.000		0.000		0.090 (0.956)		1.013 (0.603)		1.021 (0.961)	
Nagelkerke R^2	0.018		0.046		0.053		0.012		0.057	

The results show that neither the type of procedure nor the invoked reference norm dictates how the Court formulates its decision when a violation is found. Model 5 indicates that more modulations are proclaimed in annulment procedures, but the significance of this result disappears in the full model. This may be explained by the difference in the occurrence of substantive and temporal modulations in both types of procedure. While the first outcome appears somewhat more frequently in preliminary procedures,[950] the latter is logically more popular in annulment procedures.[951] Further, the model shows that the decrease in the number of modulations in competence conflict cases is almost significant at the standard acceptable level of 0.05 l.[952] Again, there is variation in the proclamation of substantive and temporal modulations in relation to the invoked reference norm. Substantive modulations are less popular in competence conflict cases, but more temporal modulations were registered in these cases.[953] In sum, the Court's propensity to act strategically by adapting the outcome does not depend on the type of procedure nor the invoked reference norm.

The results for the variable 'media attention', on the other hand, do reflect strategic considerations. In particular, the preferred outcome in intensively covered cases is clearly a modulation. Even when controlling for other factors, the odds on such an outcome continue to increase immensely (152%) when more than five articles were published on the case prior to the decision. This factor has the largest explanatory power in the full model. Conversely, a little bit of attention (1–5 articles) only comes forward as a significant result in the first model, where media attention was included as a single explanatory factor. When adding panel size (model 3), this significant result disappears. As discussed before, there is a positive relation between media attention and panel size: the more newspaper articles are published on a case, the more likely that case is to be decided in plenary session. Hence, the results indicate that extensive media attention continues to push the Court to act strategically irrespective of panel size.

---

950 47% of the cases where a violation was found, vs 40% for annulment procedures.

951 26% of the cases where an invalidation was proclaimed, vs 2% for preliminary procedures.

952 P-value in model 5=0.051 and in model 6=0.059.

953 Substantive modulations were registered in 46% of the fundamental rights cases, 32% of the competence conflict cases and 54% of the mixed cases where a violation was found. If the case led to an invalidation, its temporal effect was tempered in 14% of the fundamental rights cases, 20% of the competence conflict cases and 17% of the mixed cases.

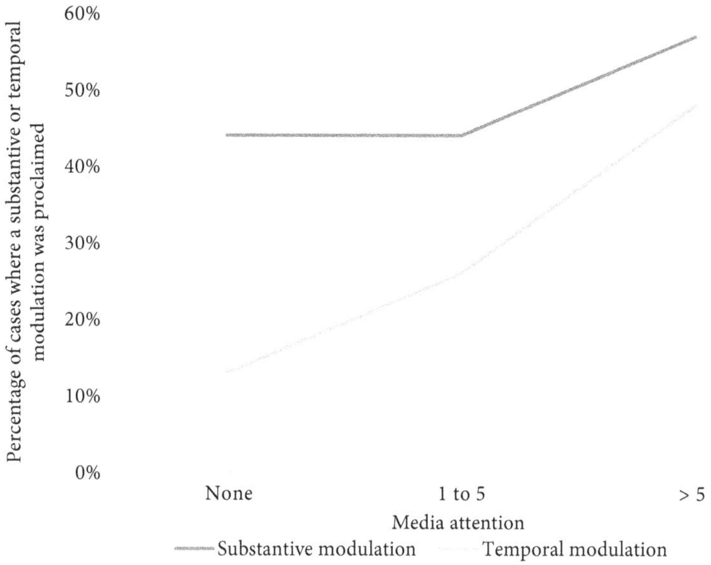

Figure 5.14. The percentage of modulations in relation to the extent of media attention

As demonstrated by figure 5.14, both substantive and temporal modulations appear more frequently in intensively covered cases.[954] An in-depth analysis of case outcomes demonstrates that the Court is especially likely to proclaim modulated declarations of constitutionality in intensively covered cases.[955] In these outcomes, the Court states that the legislation is constitutional 'with certain reservations' or 'in so far as'. The Court also proclaims somewhat more extrinsic gaps[956] but, remarkably, less modulated declarations of *un*constitutionality.[957] It was already argued above that the way the latter outcome is formulated suggests there is a graver constitutional infringement than when a modulated declaration of constitutionality is proclaimed ('unconstitutional unless' vs 'constitutional but'), although both outcomes can substantially alter the challenged legislation in a similar direction (see *supra*, section 5.3.). In particular, both can interpretatively or constructively broaden or limit the scope of the challenged legislation. Hence, the increase of the 'constitutional but'

954 The percentages in figure 5.14 were calculated as follows: (1) the number of cases where a substantive modulation was proclaimed compared to the number of cases where a violation was found, and (2) the number of cases where a temporal modulation was proclaimed compared to the number of cases where an invalidation was proclaimed.

955 The proportion of cases where a modulated declaration of constitutionality was proclaimed, compared to the total number of cases where a violation was found is: for no media attention (12%); 1–5 articles (25%); >5 articles (41%).

956 For extrinsic gaps, these percentages are 3%, 2% and 5%.

957 For modulation declarations of unconstitutionality these percentages are 30%, 22% and 24%.

and decrease of 'unconstitutional unless' outcomes indicate that when under public scrutiny, the Court considers it wiser to address its audience in *milder* terms. Finally, the Court is also considerably more likely to proclaim a temporal modulation when the case was covered in newspaper articles.[958] This can equally be understood as a strategy in delicate or controversial cases, in particular to attenuate the consequences of a simple invalidation.

The second hypothesis with regard to deliberation in plenary session is also largely supported by the data. In the full model, a deliberation in plenary session strongly pushes the odds on a modulation upwards (96%). Moreover, this result is significant at the 0.001 level, meaning the chances are very slim that this increase is a coincidence. Combining this result with those from hypotheses 1b, a certain pattern can be discerned in the Court's decision-making process. In particular, when considering that a violation is probable, judges are more inclined to request a plenary session. Given the impact of such rulings in the legal order, the judges will want to be included in the drafting process. Next, when a violation is in fact established during the internal deliberation process in plenary session, the Court prefers to answer the challenge with a modulated outcome.

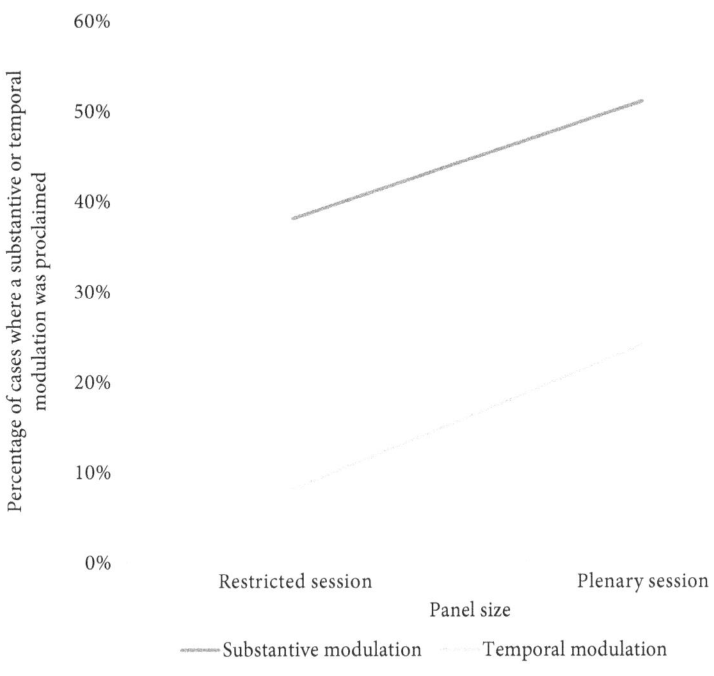

Figure 5.15. The percentage of modulations in relation to panel size

958 No media attention (13%); 1–5 articles (26%); >5 articles (48%).

With regard to the type of modulation in relation to panel size, figure 5.15 demonstrates that both more substantive and temporal modulations are registered in cases treated in plenary session.[959] Again, the results indicate that, in plenary session, the Court proclaims more modulated declarations of constitutionality and extrinsic gaps, but approximately the same number of declarations of unconstitutionality.[960] Moreover, three times more temporal modulations were registered in plenary session.[961] In sum, when a case is perceived as salient by the judges, they are inclined to proclaim an attenuated ruling rather than to bluntly disapprove of the challenged legislation. Nonetheless, it should be noted that extensive media attention is an even stronger incentive for the Court to use declarations of constitutionality and temporal modulations. This confirms that the Court acts prudently in cases that are under increased public scrutiny, independently of whether there has been a request for a plenary session.

An example of a case that was decided in plenary session and received extensive media attention is case no 44/2015, related to the 'municipal administrative sanctions'.[962] The challenged provisions expanded the possibilities for mayors and other specific local officers to impose these sanctions, even on minors. When several associations, including one defending children's rights, objected to the law before the Court, several critical articles were published in the newspapers.[963] The Court rejected their challenges, but included several restrictive interpretations in the ruling.

First, the law provided access to citizens' personal information (e.g. residence, license plate) to the person authorised to impose the administrative sanction, on condition of approbation by the administrators of these data. The law added that associations of local communities could submit, for their members, a general request for access. The litigants argued that such provision conflicted with the right to privacy. The Court found that this provision, notwithstanding the words

959 How these percentages were calculated is described in footnote 978.

960 The proportion of cases where a modulated declaration of constitutionality was proclaimed is: in restricted session (8%); plenary session (21%). For extrinsic gaps, these percentages are 2% and 5%. For modulated declarations of unconstitutionality these percentages are 30% and 29%.

961 In restricted session (8%); in plenary session (24%).

962 BeCC case no 44/2015, 23 April 2015, dealing with the law of 24 June 2013 related to the municipal administrative sanctions. This case can be considered 'moderately salient', because it does not score on the participation variable. Two types of participants were involved: interest groups and individuals (5 in total).

963 De Morgen, 21 November 2013, *"«Scholen straffen te streng». Wie vandaag jong is, heeft het niet onder de markt. We zijn streng, op straat en op school, en wie niet horen wil, moet voelen. Met GAS-boetes of schorsingen. Wat is er aan de hand?"*; De Standaard, 21 November 2013, *"Mama, papa en de GAS-ambtenaar. Opvoeding hoort geen kwestie van ambtenaren te zijn"*; Le Soir, 4 December 2013, *"Puis-je encore critiquer la police sans risquer d'amende?"* L'écho, 21 November 2013, *"Punissez votre enfant, ou payez!"*; and Gazet van Antwerpen, 18 January 2014, *"GAS-wet. «Iedereen wilde dat het snel ging». Politiek negeert negatieve adviezen hoogste magistraten"*.

'general access', cannot be understood as if such approbation would give access to *all* members of these local communities. Rather, in order to be in line with privacy rights, access can only be given to that authorised person and within the limited boundaries of his function.[964]

Another restrictive interpretation was given to a provision related to mixed offences, which can result in both criminal and administrative sanctions. The law provided that a specific agreement could be – or, for certain offences, had to be – negotiated between the local community and the Crown prosecutor. Such agreements specify in which cases the Crown prosecutor or the local officer can undertake action and make it possible to set up practical arrangements to exchange information. The Court declared the provision constitutional but added that the prosecutor should be able to request an amendment of the agreement at any time.[965] Hence, the Court built in a safeguard in order to protect the prosecutor's independence – which is guaranteed by the Constitution.

Notwithstanding these and other reservations,[966] the final dictum was that "the annulment action is rejected." The ruling was analysed by the news media, parts of which commented that the law 'barely' passed the test.[967] An alternative approach could have been to declare the provisions unconstitutional unless they were interpreted in a particular way, which would have been a more aggressive way to convey the same message. Hence, the case illustrates that when the Court is under public scrutiny, it is more inclined to address its audience in *milder* terms.

Another example is case no 158/2004, related to drugs regulations, also known as the 'marijuana law'.[968] The challenged provision stated that the police should not draw up a report, but rather merely record, in a case of possession of a given quantity of marijuana by a person of full age, if such possession is meant for personal use and does not involve a public nuisance or problematic use of the drug. The litigants challenged that several concepts in this provision, in particular 'personal use', 'public nuisance' and 'problematic use' were defined too vaguely. This criticism was repeated in several newspaper articles on the law.[969] Because of this vagueness, it was said, the provision conflicted with the

---

964 BeCC case no 44/2015, 23 April 2015, B.34.5.

965 Ibid., B.42.4.

966 44.3; 42.4; 44.3; 51.7; 57.5; 57.6.

967 De Morgen, 24 April 2015, *"GAS-boetes doorstaan test (net). Grondwettelijk Hof verwerpt beroep tegen gemeentelijke administratieve sancties"*; La Libre Belgique, 24 April 2015, *"Les sanctions communales ne voleront pas à la poubelle"*.

968 BeCC case no 158/2004, 20 October 2004, dealing with the law of 3 May 2003 on trafficking in poisonous, soporific, narcotic and other substances. This case can be considered 'moderately salient', because it does not score on the participation variable. Two types of participants were involved: interest groups and one individual.

969 La Meuse, 17 December 2003, *"Drogue: le loi 'cannabis' cause d'insécurité juridique ? Memorandum et recours"*; Vers L'Avenir, 17 December 2003, *"Drogue: le loi 'cannabis' cause d'insécurité juridique ? Memorandum et recours"*; Vers l'Avenir, *"Drogue: usage problématique*

constitutionally and internationally protected principle of legality in criminal matters, which involves requirements of precision, clarity and predictability. The Court followed these arguments, and stated that all three concepts were insufficiently specified to be in line with the Constitution.[970] Hence, it decided to strike down the provision but, simultaneously, made use of the faculty of retaining the effects of the provision, in particular until the date of publication of the ruling.[971] This was meant to avoid depriving a ground of defense for any person who was prosecuted on the basis of the annulled provision. Although this temporal modulation is justified for reasons of legal certainty in criminal proceedings, the Court only occasionally uses this possibility when invalidating criminal provisions.[972] Similarly, the Court sometimes retains the effects of annulled budget regulations to avoid financial difficulties,[973] but not always.[974] Hence, these examples show the Court is more likely to use its discretion and temper the retroactive effect of its decision when the case is perceived as salient by the news media and by the Court itself.

Figure 5.16. Type of outcome in relation to case salience

de la loi. Législation trop floue"; Le Soir 1 June 2004, "*Société: « Loi drogues »: un an de confusion. Douze mois après l'adoption de la nouvelle réglementation, le texte est difficilement applicable*".

970 BeCC case no 158/2004, 20 October 2004, B.6.4 (personal use), B.7.2-3 (problematic use), B.8.6 (public nuisance) and B.9 (conclusion).

971 Ibid., B.11.

972 In particular, the Court retained the effects of criminal provisions only in 15% of the cases where such provisions were invalidated.

973 For example, BeCC case no 13/2014, 19 January 2014, B.25.2, which was covered extensively prior to the decision.

974 For example, BeCC case no 30/2000, 21 March 2003, which was not covered by the news media (but decided in plenary session).

Finally, it is interesting to look at the relation between aggregated case salience and the outcome. On the one hand, as shown in figure 5.16, there is an increase of substantive modulations from non-salient to moderately salient cases, but little difference between moderately and highly salient cases. This result is in line with the hypotheses, considering that it was not expected that more participation would prompt the Court to opt for a modulated outcome. The findings do indicate there are somewhat more modulated declarations of constitutionality in highly salient cases, but this difference is less pronounced among cases of low to moderate saliency.[975] On the other hand, figure 5.16 suggests that the odds on a temporal modulation are additionally pushed upwards in highly salient cases, hence that more participation does play a role in that matter. Yet, this is contradicted by the descriptive results showing that only slightly more temporal modulations were proclaimed when a large group of individuals was involved,[976] and even fewer when a strongly diverse group of litigants was involved.[977] Hence, these results should be interpreted differently. In particular, in the group of moderately salient cases, the average number of temporal modulations is pushed downwards by the cases which had increased litigant diversity but which did not receive any media attention or were decided in restricted session. Conversely, all highly salient cases were covered in at least one newspaper article and decided in plenary session, which are the decisive factors pushing the Court to act more prudently.

A few additional examples can illustrate these results. First, in the highly salient case no 96/2014, the Court dealt with legislation related to the division of the BHV judicial district.[978] The challenged provisions were part of a larger political compromise on the sixth state reform, which also included the division of the BHV electoral constituency. Before the Court, the federal legislator emphasised the balanced character of the state reform and argued that invalidating some of the provisions would disrupt the peace between the different linguistic communities. The litigants on the other hand, argued first that protecting political peace was not a legitimate purpose, and second that the measures taken were disproportionate to this purpose. Many of the challenged provisions were considered 'essential elements' of the state reform,

[975] The proportion of cases where a modulated declaration of constitutionality was proclaimed is: in non-salient cases (7%); cases of low salience (15%); moderately salient (31%) highly salient (38%). Modulated declarations of unconstitutionality: 31%; 30%; 21%; 16%; and extrinsic gaps: 2%; 5%; 3%; 6%.

[976] In the context of annulment procedures where an invalidation was proclaimed: 26% when no individuals were involved; 24% when 1–5 individuals were involved; and 29% when more than 5 were involved.

[977] In the context of annulment procedures where an invalidation was proclaimed: 26% when one type of litigant was involved; 27% when 2 were involved; and 23% when 3 or more were involved.

[978] BeCC case no 96/2014, 30 June 2014.

approved by the *constitutional* legislator, making the Court incompetent to review them against the Constitution.[979] Other non-essential elements were also considered justified, even though some challenged provisions could result in certain practical problems.[980] Yet the Court acknowledged that the objective to protect a political balance cannot justify any unequal treatment. On one provision, related to the linguistic requirements for particular high-level judicial functions in the Brussels Region, the Court said it was not an essential part of the reform and could easily be replaced by an alternative measure achieving the same purpose.[981] The provision was invalidated but its effects were retained until the publication of the ruling. This was meant to ensure that persons already appointed under the unconstitutional system could remain in place. Another provision was declared constitutional under a restrictive interpretation. This provision introduced a system to regulate the shift of staff from the BHV district to the two newly created judicial districts. In principle, the law states that when a judge is appointed in a new function, he cannot apply for another function for a period of three years. Yet the Court argued that appointments made under the challenged provision cannot be understood as falling under this rule, meaning that the judges by compulsory appointments could immediately apply for another function if they wanted.[982]

Importantly, these findings should not be understood as a permanent reluctance of the Court to proclaim a simple invalidation in highly salient cases. In particular, in nine of these cases, the Court did declare the challenged provision(s) invalid, without tempering the effects of this ruling in time. A remarkable pattern appears when studying the salience indicators for these cases in detail. First, half of this group received only very little attention in the newspapers (1–5).[983] Yet the results indicate that a significant prompt for the Court to opt for a temporal modulation is the extensive coverage of the case prior to the ruling.[984] The other half of the group did receive such media attention, but also have another trait in common: a very large and especially diverse group of litigants.

Some of these cases have already been mentioned, in particular the school inspection case,[985] the Lambermont case,[986] and the case related to

---

979 Ibid., B.63.1-2, B.109.2.

980 Ibid., B.80.3-4.

981 Ibid., B.96, B.100.3, B.101.1 (explicitly proposing an alternative method to achieve the legislative purpose).

982 Ibid., B.125.3.

983 BeCC case no 90/94, 22 December 1994, (5); BeCC case no 128/98, 9 December 1998, (4); BeCC case no 51/2003, 30 April 2003, (3); BeCC case no 188/2011, 15 December 2011, (3); and BeCC case no 117/2013, 7 August 2013, (5).

984 In particular, of all highly salient cases where the Court opted for an invalidation (n=20), in 10 a temporal modulation was proclaimed. Of those 10, 7 were covered extensively in the newspapers.

985 BeCC case no 124/2010, 28 October 2010. See *supra*, section 4.3.2.

986 BeCC case no 35/2003, 25 March 2003. See *supra*, section 4.3.2.

the assistance mechanism for persons whose financial security was at risk due to war circumstances.[987] The fourth case is no 144/2012,[988] in which the BeCC dealt with a legislative act confirming an executive decision concerning certain environmental permits. Due to this homologation, the review of the permits was withdrawn from the Council of State (competent to review executive decisions) and given to the BeCC (legislative decisions). Several individuals and interest groups criticised the fact that the BeCC can only review the content of the decision, and not the procedural aspects. Some of those permits were, prior to this homologation, suspended or annulled by the Council of State because of errors committed during the executive decision-making procedure. The Court developed an extensive and complex reasoning to declare the law unconstitutional, in particular by first referring a preliminary question to the ECJ.[989] The ECJ stated that a complete review is not obligatory for legislative decisions, provided that all relevant information was taken into account in an in-depth preparatory procedure.[990] The Court objected that, although there was a parliamentary majority, not all interests were taken into account during the preparatory procedure, and annulled the provisions. Finally, in case no 89/2011,[991] a large group of individuals challenged the limited access, on the basis of nationality, to certain medical and para-medical programmes in higher education. Again, the Court first sent a preliminary question to the ECJ before making its final decision. The ECJ ruled that when Member States derogate from a principle of EU law, the reasons invoked to do so must be supported by solid and consistent evidence.[992] Subsequently, the BeCC requested the author of the challenged legislation to provide such accurate and evidential data. On the basis of this evidence it concluded that limitations were justified for some programmes, but not for all. Hence, the legislation was partly invalidated.

The context in which the Court had to examine each of these cases was one of overwhelming resistance. Not only the participation of a large or diverse group of litigants, but also a critical ruling of the ECJ, may give a strong incentive to the Court to invalidate the challenged legislation. Moreover, this resistance was covered extensively by the news media, which meant the Court could anticipate

987 BeCC case no 110/1999, 14 October 1999. See *supra*, section 4.2.2.3.

988 BeCC case no 144/2012, 22 November 2012. A similar reasoning was used in BeCC case no 29/2014, 13 February 2014.

989 BeCC 30 March 2010, case no 30/2010. The Court based its question on Council Directive 85/337/EEC of 27 June 1985 (now Directive 2011/92/EU of the European Parliament and of the Council of 13 December 2011) on the assessment of the effects of certain public and private projects on the environment.

990 ECJ, *Solvay e.a.*, C-182/10, 16 February 2012.

991 BeCC case no 89/2011, 31 May 2011.

992 ECJ (Grand Chamber), *Bressol and Chaverot*, C-37/08, 13 April 2010, paras 71–75.

that its final ruling would be under public scrutiny.[993] These findings indicate that, although the Court is inclined to act prudently in delicate cases, under certain circumstances – in particular when legislation is strongly, repeatedly and publicly criticised – more aggressive behaviour can be expected.

5.6. POSTSCRIPT AND PREVIEW OF THE FOLLOWING CHAPTERS

This first empirical chapter focused on the case outcomes in the Belgian Constitutional Court's case law. Drawing on the descriptive and regression data analyses, several conclusions can be drawn.

First, the Court has become more willing to offer instructions or guidelines on how to construe and apply legislation in conformity with the Constitution. Although this engagement in constitutional dialogue is promising, a reservation should be noted. In particular, the Court should pay more attention to the phrasing of the modulated dicta. Without additional clarification, confusion will remain about the consequences of modulated outcomes for the judiciary and administration, which have to apply legislation in practice.[994] In addition, in order to produce an actual positive dialogue with the legislator, the role of the news media cannot be underestimated. As an intermediate actor between the Court, legislator and citizenry, it has an important agenda-setting function. Because many modulations require legislative action, a lack of public attention for these outcomes is potentially problematic. Without public oversight, the legislator may be more likely to take the risk of ignoring the judicial decision.

Further, the logistic regression models indicated that the procedural traits of a case are the main determinants for the establishment of a constitutional infringement, but that strategic considerations mainly affect whether the Court

993 For example: (case no 110/1999) Le Matin, 12 June 1998, *"Un veto francophone unanime. Réactions indignées au décret Suykerbuyk"*; (case no 35/2003) L'écho, 6 February 2003, *"25 requêtes contre le Lambermont"*; (case no 124/2010) Le Soir, 29 March 2010, *"Périphérie. Parents, enseignants et communes ont plaidé pour leur inspection scolaire devant la Cour. Les francophones s'accrochent aux lois"*; (case no 89/2011) De Morgen, 14 April 2010, *"Europees Hof van Justitie keurt quota in Franstalig medisch hoger onderwijs af. Europa: «limiet op buitenlandse studenten is discriminerend»"*; and (case no 144/2012) Le Soir, 27 January 2009, *"Recours multiples contre le «DAR». Le décret d'autorisations régionales est attaqué par des associations de protection de l'environnement"*.

994 M De Visser, *Constitutional Review in Europe: A Comparative Analysis* (Hart Publishing 2014), 304: modulated outcomes place the citizens "at the mercy of the regular courts and the executive, as the State organs ... [apply] those clauses in the daily practice". Also see A Kavanagh, *Constitutional Review under the UK Human Rights Act* (Cambridge University Press 2009), 140, who argues that courts must balance their duty to do justice to the individual against values such as certainty and predictability in the law.

opts for a substantive or temporal modulation. In particular, the factor which has the largest effect size in relation to the odds on finding a violation is the combination of an annulment procedure with the invocation of the competence allocating rules. The relation to the participation variables was found to be limited. Nonetheless, the results demonstrated that more violations are found when the Court deliberated in plenary session and when the case received extensive media attention. Yet it is difficult to establish the direction of this correlation. When the legislator acts in contravention of the Constitution, this is likely to draw more attention from newspaper journalists and prompt judges to request a plenary session. Next, if a violation is found, the Court may opt to proclaim a substantive or temporal modulation. When pushback from politicians is expected, proclaiming a simple invalidation entails a risk for the Court. In particular, heavy criticism and/or non-compliance may threaten its institutional standing. The results show that the decision to opt for a modulated outcome is mainly prompted by the extent of media attention on the case. Together with a full panel size, the publication of more than five newspaper articles pushes the Court to proclaim a modulated declaration of constitutionality and, if it invalidates legislation, to moderate the effects of this invalidation in time. The procedural traits of the cases do not seem to affect the outcome in a similar way. In sum, this judicial practice can be understood as a strategy of the Court to address its audience in less aggressive terms when the case is particularly delicate.

Although these findings already provide considerable evidence that the Court is a strategic actor that takes into account external factors when drafting a ruling, focusing solely on case outcomes may underestimate the extent to which court can act strategically. A decision to reject, invalidate or modulate must be supported by a justification on grounds of principle. It is likely that this effect of case salience is reflected more in other stages of the decision-making process, in particular when drafting the justificatory ground for the ruling. Therefore, in the next chapters, more nuanced measures are explored, which represent the richer content of constitutional rulings.

CHAPTER 6

CITATION PRACTICES

6.1. INTRODUCTION

In principle, a constitutional ruling does not only include the final outcome, but also an (extensive) justification underpinning the decision. As explained in the normative framework, the requirement to give reasons is a special burden that weighs on courts. As a way to strengthen the justification, constitutional courts may document their judgments with citations of a variety of authorities. In each ruling, this reason-giving provides insight into the path of legal logic used to reach the judicial outcome. Citation patterns reveal where judges find their cues and what values they seek to promote. They are good indicators for understanding what arguments are considered legitimate for a given period of time.[995] Hence, an extensive study of citation practices provides a window into the legal culture and the performance of courts.

Although the study of judicial reason-giving has increased considerably in importance, empirical analyses of citation practices have been, until now, mostly territorially concentrated in the United States,[996] Canada,[997] Australia[998]

[995] On the value of empirical investigation into citation practices see for example: P McCormick 'The Supreme Court Cites the Supreme Court: Follow-up Citation on the Supreme Court of Canada, 1989–1993' (1995) 33 Osgoode Hall Law Journal, 453, 454; D Fausten, I Nielsen and R Smyth, 'A Century of Citation Practice on the Supreme Court of Victoria' (2007) 31 Melbourne University Law Review, 733, 735, 804.; and LM Friedman et al., 'State Supreme Courts: a Century of Citation' (1981) 33 Stanford Law Review, 773, 794, 818.

[996] For example: LM Friedman et al., 'State Supreme Courts: a Century of Citation' (1981) 33 Stanford Law Review, 773; JH Merryman, 'Toward a Theory of Citations: an Empirical Study of the Citation Practice of the California Supreme Court in 1950, 1960 and 1970' (1978) 50 Southern California Law Review, 381; I Nielsen and R Smyth, 'One Hundred Years of Citation of Authority on the Supreme Court of New South Wales' (2008) 31 University of New South Wales Law Journal, 189; and FB Cross et al., 'Citations in the U.S. Supreme Court: an Empirical Study of their Use and Significance' (2010) 2 University of Illinois Law Review, 489.

[997] For example: P McCormick, 'Judical Authority and the Provincial Courts of Appeal: a Statistical Investigation of Citation Practices' (1993) Manitoba Law Journal, 286; P McCormick, 'The Supreme Court Cites the Supreme Court: Follow-up Citation on the Supreme Court of Canada, 1989–1993' (1995) 33 Osgoode Hall Law Journal, 453; and V Black and N Richter, 'Did She Mention My Name?: Citation of Academic Authority by the Supreme Court of Canada' (1993) Dalhousie Law Journal, 377.

[998] For example: R Smyth, 'What do Intermediate Appellate Courts Cite? A Quantitative Study of the Citation Practice of Australian State Supreme Courts' (1999) 21 Adelaide Law Review, 51;

and New Zealand.[999,1000] In continental Europe, this field has been relatively unexplored.[1001] An analysis of judicial citations can improve our understanding of the judicial role within the European context. Therefore, this chapter aims to add to this knowledge by exploring the reason-giving practice of the BeCC.

The plan of this chapter is as follows. In section 6.2., it is explained how the proper use of citations enhances the Court's deliberative performance. In short, courts should underpin their rulings with citations of applicable, persuasive and relevant authorities. More specifically, this section reflects on the added value of precedents, (inter)national case law, legislative history documents and secondary authorities in constitutional adjudication.

Subsequently, in section 6.3., the ten most common authorities cited by the Court are presented. In addition, the concept of 'citation density' is introduced, which measures the number of different authorities cited per ruling and can serve as a reasonable proxy for the judicial effort put into a ruling.

In section 6.4., a descriptive analysis demonstrates how the grounding of the BeCC's judgments has developed over time and to what extent the different authorities are related to the issue under review. In particular, several figures display – for each type of citation – the yearly percentages of cases in which these citations were registered. To estimate the extent to which the legal substance of a case relates to referencing, correlations are calculated between the different authorities and (1) the domain in which the case is situated

R Smyth, 'Trends in the Citation Practice of the Supreme Court of Queensland over the Course of the Twenthieth Century' (2009) 28 The University of Queensland Review, 39; and D Fausten, I Nielsen and R Smyth, 'A Century of Citation Practice on the Supreme Court of Victoria' (2007) 31 Melbourne University Law Review, 733.

999 For example, R Smyth, 'Judicial Citations – an Empirical Study of Citation Practice in the New Zealand Court of Appeal' (2000) 31 Victoria University of Wellington Law Review.

1000 Moreover, most studies focus on citation practices within a single year or a few selected years: see M Heise, 'The Past, Present and Future of Empirical Legal Scholarship: Judicial Decision Making and the New Empiricism' (2002) 4 University of Illinois Law Review, 819, 826–9.

1001 Nonetheless, there have been recent contributions to fill in this gap. For example: S Lambrecht, 'The Attitude of Four Supreme Courts Towards the European Court of Human Rights: Strasbourg has Spoken …' in S Besson and AR Ziegler (eds.), *Le Juge en Droit International et Européen – The Judge in International and European Law* (Schulthess 2013); J Staben, 'Colourful Case Law: Citation Analysis of the German Constitutional Court's Jurisprudence', https://verfassungsblog.de/farbenfrohe-rechtsprechung-verweisungsanalyse-von-entscheidungen-des-bundesverfassungsgerichts (26 January 2015); T Agnoloni and U Pagallo, 'The Power Laws of the ICC, and their Relevance for Legal Scholars' in A Rotolo (ed.), *Legal Knowledge and Information Systems* (IOS Press 2015), 1–10; and P Popelier, 'Judicial Conversations in Multilevel Constitutionalism: the Belgian case' in M Claes et al. (eds.), *Constitutional Conversations in Europe* (Intersentia 2012), 73–99. Most studies on national European courts, however, are limited to the citation of foreign (case) law: see footnote 1024. In addition, there have been some studies on the citation practice of international courts, including the ECtHR: Y Lupu and E Voeten, 'Precedent in International Courts: A Network Analysis of Case Citations by the European Court of Human Right' (2012) British Journal of Political Science, 1.

(e.g. criminal law, administrative law) and (2) the reference norms against which the legislation is reviewed (e.g. equality clause, European legislation).

Section 6.5. focuses on explaining citation density. Importantly, some cases may require a more elaborate display of authorities than others. The main argument is that grounding a ruling more strongly in citations may serve as a strategy to stimulate compliance when pushback against the ruling is expected. In addition, opinion clarity can help monitor the implementation after the ruling, imposing costs for noncompliance.[1002] Therefore, it is hypothesised that increased media coverage, more participation and higher panel size – the case salience measures (see chapter 4) – push citation density upwards. Additionally, it is explained why cases in which the Court (partially) invalidates or modulates the challenged legislation are also more likely to include more citations. These hypotheses are tested through a regression analysis with citation density as dependent variable. Although other explanations cannot be excluded,[1003] a significant increase in citations when these factors are present indicates that the Court anticipates responses from external actors and that the desire to legitimate its decision prompts the Court to use more citations.

6.2. A DELIBERATIVE PERSPECTIVE: THE REASON-GIVING REQUIREMENT

At the centre of the deliberative ideal is the need to substantiate a decision with arguments. Judges must advance arguments to show that their conclusions are right, just or legitimate, and not simply to demonstrate that they have taken an available option.[1004] By avoiding making claims without support, the Court ensures the equal responsiveness of its decisions to all those affected. References to external sources show that the Court took the claim seriously and made the effort to explore the available information on the issue.[1005] Also, the quality of the judicial reason-giving affects the degree to which their decisions are perceived as legitimate.[1006] Hence, by invoking authorities, the Court stimulates the

---

1002 RC Black et al., *US Supreme Court Opinions and their Audiences* (Cambridge University Press 2016), 11.

1003 Such as case type (some areas may have more relevant authorities to cite), the law clerk who wrote the first draft, and case complexity. For more information see FB Cross et al., 'Citations in the U.S. Supreme Court: an Empirical Study of their Use and Significance' (2010) 2 University of Illinois Law Review, 489, 509.

1004 A Kavanagh, *Constitutional Review under the UK Human Rights Act* (Cambridge University Press 2009), 140.

1005 J Parkinson, *Deliberating in the Real World: Problems of Legitimacy in Deliberative Democracy* (Oxford University Press 2006), 99; M Bobek, *Comparative Reasoning in European Supreme Courts* (Oxford University Press 2013), 225.

1006 MC Ponthoreau, 'L'Énigme de la Motivation Encore et Toujours l'Éclairage Comparatif' in F Hourquebie and MC Pontoreau (eds.), *La Motivation des Décisions des Cours Suprêmes et*

understanding and acceptance of its decisions, even when there is no agreement on the grounds of the decision. Finally, when the judicial decision catalyses deliberation outside the Court, a clear justification can enhance the depth of this debate. The authorities cited may be particularly instructive, providing both substantial and procedural guidance, when a new legislative process is generated. In particular, some citations can be understood as a recommendation for a law reform,[1007] and other citations may expose the faults in the legislative policy-making process.[1008] This should make the legislator aware of the importance of a proper *ex ante* assessment of the legislative proposal. Consequently, the case law of the Court can affect the quality of the ensuing debate and the policy decisions following from this process. In conclusion, a proper use of citations strengthens the Court's deliberative performance.

For these reasons, it has been argued that courts should at least refer to *some* authority when solving a constitutional question.[1009] A judge that does not cite any authority may fail to convince the external audience of the accurate basis of the decision. Yet, there is no standard to guide a judge in *how much* authority is needed. What is 'enough' depends on the constitutional question, the available pool of authorities and the audience that the Court addresses.[1010] In general, the excessive citation of authorities, as well as oversimplification, should be avoided.[1011] Also, not every constitutional court is equally citation-intensive. Every legal system has its own rules and traditions relating to the proper presentation of a judicial decision. Courts in common law countries usually have a unified style of judicial reason-giving, providing a full account (possibly in footnotes)[1012] of all studied arguments and sources. Hence, the authorities consulted during the

Cours Constitutionelles (Bruylant 2012), 13, 17; and E Brems and L Lavrysen, 'Procedural Justice in Human Rights Adjudication: The European Court of Human Rights' (2013) 35 Human Rights Quarterly, 176, 180.

1007 I Nielsen and R Smyth, 'One Hundred Years of Citation of Authority on the Supreme Court of New South Wales' (2008) 31 University of New South Wales Law Journal, 189.

1008 For example, citations of scientific studies may show that the legislative inquiries were implemented in an unsatisfactory way, or that the legislative decision does not logically follow from the presented empirical results.

1009 HP Glenn, 'Persuasive Authority' (1987) 32 McGill Law Journal, 261, 264: "adherence to binding law may itself be perceived as highly arbitrary, in the absence of any elements of persuasion".

1010 JH Merryman, 'Toward a Theory of Citations: an Empirical Study of the Citation Practice of the California Supreme Court in 1950, 1960 and 1970' (1978) 50 Southern California Law Review, 381, 418–19.

1011 M Bobek, *Comparative Reasoning in European Supreme Courts* (Oxford University Press 2013), 236: "the solution to the tension between transparency and conciseness is [...] an evolving compromise." On the drawbacks of excessive citations, see: JH Merryman, 'Toward a Theory of Citations: an Empirical Study of the Citation Practice of the California Supreme Court in 1950, 1960 and 1970' (1978) 50 Southern California Law Review, 381, 419–22; and I Nielsen and R Smyth, 'One Hundred Years of Citation of Authority on the Supreme Court of New South Wales' (2008) 31 University of New South Wales Law Journal, 189, 194–5.

1012 LM Friedman et al., 'State Supreme Courts: A Century of Citation' (1981) 33 Stanford Law Review 773, 814.

judicial decision-making process overlap with the authorities cited in the ruling. This tradition is not fully shared on the European continent. It is believed that these courts have considerable institutional legitimacy and that societal trust can supplement the substantive reason-giving.[1013] Hence, low citation counts should not necessarily be interpreted as a lack of research, but might reflect a non-unified style of presentation.

The question rises as to *which* citations are appropriate in a specific case. In general, courts must justify their decisions in terms that can be universalised. For that purpose, they are restricted by pre-existing legal materials and factual information.[1014] Also, the cited authorities should be applicable[1015] and relevant to the case. Additionally, the cited authorities should be persuasive,[1016] by virtue of their institutional source (e.g. opinions of courts situated higher in the judicial hierarchy) and/or because of their content (e.g legislative history, academic scholarship, etc.).[1017] In general, four types of authorities appear in the case law of constitutional or supreme courts: precedents, foreign or (inter)national case law, legislative history documents and secondary authorities. The extent of their persuasiveness differs between legal systems. For instance, the cogency of precedents is considered stronger in the United States constitutional system than in Europe, while European scholars sometimes classify European (case) law as 'mandatory'.[1018]

First, courts may refer to their own decisions. By citing precedents, courts show they are self-reflective. It gives decisions historical depth, without wasting too much energy.[1019] Also, it improves the efficiency of the internal workings of the Court.[1020] By building on their precedents, courts develop an internally consistent body of case law and comply with the general principles of continuity and acknowledge the legal value of predictability in the law.[1021] Citing precedents

---

1013 M Bobek, *Comparative Reasoning in European Supreme Courts* (Oxford University Press 2013), 224, 230–3; and M Lasser, *Judicial Deliberation: a Comparative Analysis of Judical Transparancy and Legitimacy* (Oxford University Press 2004).

1014 C Guarniere and P Pederzoli, *The Power of Judges: a Comparative Study of Courts and Democracy* (Oxford University Press 2003), 10–11.

1015 Or be explicitly found inapplicable. See JH Merryman, 'Toward a Theory of Citations: an Empirical Study of the Citation Practice of the California Supreme Court in 1950, 1960 and 1970' (1978) 50 Southern California Law Review, 420–1.

1016 HP Glenn, 'Persuasive Authority' (1987) 32 McGill Law Journal, 263.

1017 C Flanders, 'Towards a Theory of Persuasive Authority' (2009) 62 Oklamhoma Law Review, 58–64.

1018 M Bobek, *Comparative Reasoning in European Supreme Courts* (Oxford University Press 2013), 25–7.

1019 CH Mendes, *Constitutional Courts and Deliberative Democracy* (Oxford University Press 2013), 181–2.

1020 Y Lupu and E Voeten, 'Precedent in International Courts: A Network Analysis of Case Citations by the European Court of Human Right' (2012) British Journal of Political Science 1, 1.

1021 D Fausten et al., 'A Century of Citation Practice on the Supreme Court of Victoria' (2007) 31 Melbourne University Law Review, 733, 738; and Y Lupu and E Voeten, 'Precedent in

is also a way to show that judicial decisions are constrained by the law, and that there is only one correct legal answer which is independent of the use of judicial discretion.[1022] In contrast, a court that simply disregards its past decisions may disturb legitimately formed expectations and might create the impression that its rulings are arbitrary and *ad hoc*.[1023] This does not mean, however, that courts cannot overturn precedents when this is justified with solid arguments.

A second type of citable authority is the jurisdiction of other courts, whether they are on an equal footing or higher in the judicial hierarchy. References to other courts are considered one of the most important forms of judicial conversation because they display consideration for each other's arguments.[1024] Also, references to each other's case law maintain the coherence of the judicial system.[1025] Prior studies have shown that court opinions are often among the most cited authorities. It is likely that this preference is rooted in the idea that courts speak the same legal language.[1026]

Citing judgments of the *domestic judiciary* mostly serves to clarify how the challenged legislation is currently interpreted. In the Belgian legal order, the Court of Cassation and the Council of State are the highest courts in civil and administrative matters. Within their area of expertise, their case law has considerable authority.

Depending on the status of the *international* or *supranational judiciary* in a legal order, their case law may also carry considerable weight. Within the European context, the case law of the ECJ and the ECtHR is considered most decisive. By referring to these authorities, domestic (constitutional) courts may strengthen their own position.[1027] In countries outside the European Union, the focus is more on international treaties. For instance, in the case law of the SACC, international law has played a vital role in shaping the laws in South Africa and in protecting the rights enshrined in the Constitution of South Africa.[1028]

International Courts: A Network Analysis of Case Citations by the European Court of Human Rights' (2012) British Journal of Political Science 1, 7.

1022 S Dothan, *Reputation and Judicial Tactics* (Cambridge University Press 2015), 37.

1023 C Flanders, 'Towards a Theory of Persuasive Authority' (2009) 62 Oklamhoma Law Review, 55, 83.

1024 See P Popelier, 'Judicial Conversations in Mulitlevel Constitutionalism. The Belgian Case' in M Claes et al. (eds.), *Constitutional Conversations in Europe – Actors, Topics and Procedures* (Intersentia 2012), 76.

1025 CH Mendes, *Constitutional Courts and Deliberative Democracy* (Oxford University Press 2013), 183–4 and 189–94.

1026 C Flanders, 'Towards a Theory of Persuasive Authority' (2009) 62 Oklamhoma Law Review, 55, 69–72.

1027 P Popelier, 'Judicial Conversations in Mulitlevel Constitutionalism. The Belgian Case' in M Claes et al. (eds.), *Constitutional Conversations in Europe – Actors, Topics and Procedures* (Intersentia 2012), 99.

1028 CD Zungu, 'The Role, Relevance and Application of International Law in South Africa' (2015) 8 International Journal of Sustainable Development, 85, 88.

The USSC has equally used international law to help resolve major legal controversies.[1029]

Further, courts may cite the case law of *foreign courts*. There is particular and growing interest in this phenomenon,[1030] for a series of reasons. Constitutional courts increasingly face common issues.[1031] By treating similar cases alike, courts create a sort of uniformity across jurisdictional systems.[1032] This increases legal stability and predictability and enhances the perception of fairness.[1033] However, some have expressed concerns regarding the citation of foreign decisions. Before considering or applying a decision from a foreign court, they argue, the basis and reasoning of the foreign decision must be considered in the context of the originating country.[1034] Also, while supranational sources have obtained authority through their implementation, foreign (case) law remains non-binding. Hence, applying such non-binding sources to resolve domestic cases may endanger the legitimacy of the resulting judicial decision.[1035] Nonetheless, comparative constitutional analysis offers unique opportunities to learn about new methods of analysis and new approaches to issues that domestic courts have yet to address. In sum, engaging in judicial conversation may lead to better-reasoned outcomes and increases the Court's legitimacy.[1036]

Third, legislative history documents may shed light on the underlying policy objective *(ratio legis)* and the *ex ante* evaluation of the challenged provisions. Parliamentary preparatory documents, such as the preamble, explanatory memoranda or arguments exchanged during parliamentary debates, may prove particularly helpful when there is discussion on how the challenged legislation should be understood. References to these documents reflect that the Court

1029 For more information on the use of international law by the US Supreme Court, see DL Sloss et al. (eds.), *International Law in the U.S. Supreme Court* (Cambridge University Press 2012).

1030 This interest in 'judicial internationalisation' had spread more broadly than citation patterns. For example see: U Bentele, 'Mining for Gold: the Constitutional Court of South Africa's Experience with Comparative Constitutional Law' 37 (2009) Georgia Journal of International and Comparative Law, 219; M Bobek, *Comparative Reasoning in European Supreme Courts* (Oxford University Press 2013); T Groppi, 'Le Recours aux Précédents Étrangers par les Juges Constitutionnels' in F Hourquebie and MC Pontoreau (eds.), *La Motivation des Décisions des Cours Suprêmes et Cours Constitutionelles* (Bruylant 2012); and E Mak, *Judicial Decision-making in a Globalised World: a Comparative Analysis of the Changing Practices of Western Highest Courts* (Hart Publishing 2013).

1031 C Moon, 'Comparative Constitutional Analysis: Should the United States Supreme Court Join the Dialogue?' (2003) 12 Washington University Journal of Law & Policy, 229, 245.

1032 A 'transnational judicial community'. See C Flanders, 'Towards a Theory of Persuasive Authority' (2009) 62 Oklamhoma Law Review, 55, 86.

1033 Ibid., 75.

1034 C Moon, 'Comparative Constitutional Analysis: Should the United States Supreme Court Join the Dialogue?' (2003) 12 Washington University Journal of Law & Policy, 229, 245.

1035 E Mak, *Judicial Decision-making in a Globalised World: a Comparative Analysis of the Changing Practices of Western Highest Courts* (Hart Publishing 2013), 29.

1036 P Popelier, 'Judicial Conversations in Mulitlevel Constitutionalism. The Belgian Case' in M Claes et al. (eds.), *Constitutional Conversations in Europe – Actors, Topics and Procedures* (Intersentia 2012), 99.

does not only wish to persuade, but can also be persuaded in return. The legislature is considered to have considerable expertise and resources to pursue its policy objectives. Hence, courts may refer to these documents to show deference to the legislator. Yet legislative history documents may also be cited to argue that legislation is (un)justifiable. For example, an *ex ante* legislative evaluation or the input of other consulted actors may demonstrate that the policy objective is (il)legitimate or that the consequences of the law are (not) disproportionally harmful in comparison with the policy objective. Citing legislative history documents guarantees, to a certain extent, the objectivity and controllability of the judicial investigation. Moreover, previous research has shown that when courts use this method to uncover the policy goal, the legislator may be stimulated to express their aims more clearly.[1037]

The fourth type of authority, such as academic articles, scientific studies and news sources, are considered to have a principal utility as research aids.[1038] Some constitutional questions require expert knowledge, in particular when the legislation under review may be based on normative assumptions that need empirical clarification (see *supra*, section 1.3.2.4.).[1039] The argumentative space implied in the proportionality test compels courts to look for evidence to substantiate their assessments.[1040] Scientific evidence can be brought forward by any participant in the review procedure, either to support or challenge the legislation under review.[1041] In the US, for example, it is said that many of these citations indirectly stem from evidence brought forward by *amici curiae*.[1042] For instance, social science studies might show that the measures taken are not suitable to achieve the policy goal or that the costs outweigh the benefits of the provision through which the policy rationale is implemented.[1043]

1037 JH Gerards, *Judicial Review in Equal Treatment Cases* (Martinus Nijhoff Publishers 2005), 37.

1038 JH Merryman, 'Toward a Theory of Citations: an Empirical Study of the Citation Practice of the California Supreme Court in 1950, 1960 and 1970' (1978) 50 Southern California Law Review, 381, 423.

1039 N Petersen, 'Avoiding the Common-wisdom Fallacy: the Role of Social Sciences in Constitutional Adjudication' (2013) 11 International Journal of Constitutional Law, 294. For examples, see G Cumming, *Expert Evidence Deficiencies in the Judgments of the Court of the European Union and the European Court of Human Rights* (Kluwer 2014), 113 and further.

1040 A Alemanno, 'The Emergence of the Evidence-based Judicial Reflex: A Response to Bar-Siman-Tov's Semiprocedural Review' (2013) 1 Theory and Practice of Legislation, 1, 3.

1041 When these documents are brought forward by the legislator, serving to demonstrate that the policy options have been properly investigated, they can also been understood as 'legislative history documents'.

1042 Another reason is the propensity of the USSC to cite social science evidence in capital punishment cases and cases relating to the Bill of Rights: R Smyth, 'What do Intermediate Appellate Courts Cite? A Quantitative Study of the Citation Practice of Australian State Supreme Courts' (1999) 21 Adelaide Law Review, 51, 67.

1043 CH Mendes, *Constitutional Courts and Deliberative Democracy* (Oxford University Press 2013), 45; L Alexander, 'The Banality of Legal Reasoning' (1998) 73 Notre Dame Law Review, 517; and D Fausten, I Nielsen and R Smyth, 'A Century of Citation Practice on the Supreme Court of Victoria' (2007) 31 Melbourne University Law Review, 733, 742.

In that sense, an important reason to cite scientific evidence is to criticise the development of the law or to make recommendations to the legislator for future reforms.[1044] Scientific studies may also qualify as legislative history documents, in particular when the study has been executed during the parliamentary process. In that case, they are usually brought forward in the review procedure by the legislator to demonstrate that the policy options have been properly investigated.[1045]

When credible scientific evidence is presented, this may strengthen the justificatory ground for the judicial outcome. Yet, by mentioning them explicitly, these sources become verifiable. This may be a benefit, but also a pitfall. Citing scientific evidence may prompt others to raise concerns regarding the authenticity and credibility of these authorities. This is especially delicate for empirical studies, since judges are usually not familiar with the statistical language used in these studies. Also, some argue that, by citing academic literature, courts indicate that they seek out the sources that suit their own preferences instead of following legal constraints.[1046]

Finally, the cited authorities should be relevant to the case. Which of these persuasive authorities are selected depends on the topic of the dispute and the pleas that were raised by the parties.[1047] For example, when the case before the court concerns administrative law, it would be appropriate to take into account the administrative jurisdiction. Also, when a court is required to review legislation against international law, it seems relevant to explore the case law of the international court competent to interpret that law. Such citation patterns would show that the BeCC relies on relevant authorities to reach a conclusion.

6.3. CITING AUTHORITIES: CODING THE COURT'S CASE LAW

In line with other constitutional courts, the BeCC cites authorities that can be categorised into one of the four types discussed above: precedents, (inter)national

1044 I Nielsen and R Smyth, 'One Hundred Years of Citation of Authority on the Supreme Court of New South Wales' (2008) 31 University of New South Wales Law Journal, 193.

1045 Some scholars have noticed a global trend towards the use of more procedural arguments (referring to the legislative procedure) as a part of substantive judicial review. This would translate into more citations of scientific evidence (brought forward in the legislative procedure) and consultation input: A Alemanno, 'The Emergence of the Evidence-based Judicial Reflex: A Response to Bar-Siman-Tov's Semiprocedural Review' (2013) Theory and Practice of Legislation, 1.

1046 S Dothan, *Reputation and Judicial Tactics* (Cambridge 2015), 38.

1047 M Shapiro and A Stone Sweet, *On Law, Politics and Judicialization* (Oxford University Press 2002), 238; and C Flanders, 'Towards a Theory of Persuasive Authority' (2009) 62 Oklamhoma Law Review, 55, 69.

case law,[1048] legislative history documents and secondary authorities. The nine most common references in the BeCC's case law were coded as dichotomous variables (0=no citation, 1=citation to this authority). An overview of these variables can be found in table 6.1. The numbers in the last column indicate the number of cases (n) in which each dichotomous variable was coded, and their proportion (%) of the total number of cases (n=3145).

Additionally, for each case, the values for each of these variables (0/1) were added up to a count variable (min. 0–max. 9). This variable represents the citation density within a particular case (*CIT_DENSITY*) and can serve as a reasonable proxy for the judicial effort put into producing a qualitative ruling. Previous studies have confirmed that cases with more citations carry more weight.[1049] Section 6.5. will be explore whether citing more authorities can be understood as a strategy to legitimise the judicial decision.

Table 6.1. Overview of the results for the different citation variables

Type of authority	Variables	
Precedents	Precedents	791 (25%)
(Inter)national case law	Case law of the Court of Cassation	313 (10%)
	Case law of the Council of State	89 (3%)
	Case law of the European Court of Justice	146 (5%)
	Case law of the European Court of Human Rights	327 (10%)
Legislative history documents	Parliamentary preparatory documents	2689 (86%)
	Political agreements	85 (3%)
	Legislative advisory opinion of the Council of State	247 (8%)
Secondary authorities	Scientific studies	71 (2%)
Citation density	*CIT_DENSITY*	Mean = 1.5

In the previous section, it has been argued that the Court should cite authorities that are relevant with regard to the subject of the legislation under review and the pleas raised by the parties. To determine the extent to which the legal substance of a case is related to referencing, correlations are calculated between the different authorities and (1) the references norms against which the legislation is reviewed and (2) the legal domain in which the case is situated.[1050]

1048 The BeCC is not known to cite any foreign (case) law, making it redundant to include a variable for this type of authority.

1049 FB Cross et al., 'Citations in the U.S. Supreme Court: an Empirical Study of their Use and Significance' (2010) 2 University of Illinois Law Review, 489, 519; DJ Walsh, 'On the Meaning and Pattern of Legal Citations: Evidence from State Wrongful Discharge Precedent Cases' (1997) 31 Law & Society Review, 337.

1050 Only correlations above 0.1 that are significant to the 0,001 level (***) are discussed in the results section.

The numbers in the last column of the tables below indicate the proportion of the total number of cases (n=3145) that the Court reviewed against these reference norms (table 6.2) or which proportion of these cases related to these different legal domains (table 6.3).

Table 6.2. Overview of the results for the different reference norms that can be invoked in a review procedure before the Belgian Constitutional Court

Dichotomous variables: reference norms	
The competence allocating rules	15%
The equality clause	88%
Other fundamental rights in the Belgian Constitution	23%
European legislation	6%
European Convention on Human Rights	23%
Other International law treaties	9%
General principles of law	9%

Table 6.3. Overview of the results for the different legal domains into which a case before the Belgian Constitutional Court can be categorised

Dichotomous variables: legal domains	
Law of persons and family law	4%
Tax law	14%
Judicial organisation and civil procedure	10%
Constitutional law	2%
Spatial planning	3%
Environmental and energy law	3%
Other administrative law (e.g. discipline matters)	3%
Labour and social security law	14%
Educational law	5%
Migration law	4%
Commercial and financial law	6%
Substantive and procedural criminal law	10%
Property law and special contracts	1%
Cultural issues	3%
Social services	3%
Combination	5%
Other	10%

6.4. CITING AUTHORITIES: DESCRIPTIVE TRENDS AND EVOLUTION IN TIME

6.4.1. EVOLUTION IN CITATION DENSITY

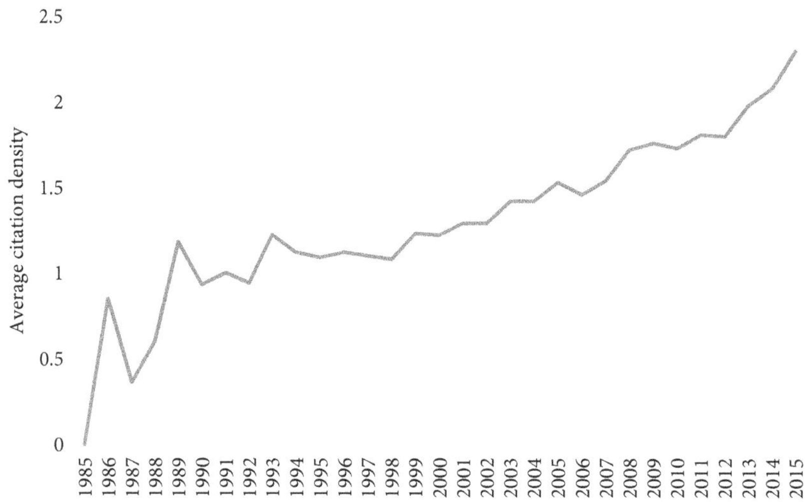

Figure 6.1. Evolution in citation density

Figure 6.1 demonstrates that the average number of different citations per case has steadily increased over the years. This suggests that the Court increasingly incorporates a more diverse range of sources and knowledge into its decision-making process. Several reasons can explain this upward trend. To begin with, the pool of available authorities has increased. For instance, as more time passes since the establishment of the BeCC, the more likely it becomes that the judges may find precedents or other (inter)national case law relevant to the case before them.[1051] Next, the growing volume of legal information is also more and more accessible due to changes in information technology.[1052] The existence of proper searching tools reduces the citation costs for the preparation of judgments

[1051] FB Cross et al., 'Citations in the U.S. Supreme Court: an Empirical Study of their Use and Significance' (2010) 2 University of Illinois Law Review, 489, 531–3; and Y Lupu and E Voeten, 'Precedent in International Courts: A Network Analysis of Case Citations by the European Court of Human Right' (2012) British Journal of Political Science 1, 19.

[1052] I Nielsen and R Smyth, 'One Hundred Years of Citation of Authority on the Supreme Court of New South Wales' (2008) 31 University of New South Wales Law Journal, 189, 212.

considerably.[1053] In addition, the number of law clerks who may supply those citations for the court has increased over the years.[1054] Having additional drafting assistance has been said to produce lengthier and better-supported rulings.[1055] Finally, some have argued that the acceleration in socio-economic changes has intensified the struggle between competing interests and has increased the demands on courts to be seen to be administering due process. This may result in an increase in citations, since judges have to seek legitimacy in the eyes of these competing interests.[1056]

Yet, with an average of almost 2.5 different citations per ruling in 2015, the BeCC cites less authorities than its counterparts in common law systems. Also, the Court still proclaims rulings that do not contain any citations of authorities, although this proportion of cases has decreased over the years.[1057] As mentioned before, reasoning style may partially explain this difference in citations patterns. Like many European courts, the BeCC does not have the tradition of making public all the sources used in its decision-making procedure. In addition, when judges have more control over their dockets – which is usually the case in common law courts – they will presumably choose to hear a higher proportion of salient cases.[1058] As will be discussed below, the more salient a case is, the more strongly the Court will ground its ruling in citations of a variety of authorities. Hence, a higher proportion of salient cases may push the average citation levels upward. Nonetheless, some have argued that lower citation levels may raise certain concerns. If judges are, by virtue of this tradition, not inclined or allowed to openly cite their source of inspiration, will they not be, over time, less likely to keep looking for it?[1059]

1053 JH Merryman, 'Toward a Theory of Citations: an Empirical Study of the Citation Practice of the California Supreme Court in 1950, 1960 and 1970' (1978) 50 Southern California Law Review, 381, 426–7.

1054 Initially, a maximum of ten legal secretaries could assist the judges (article 23 of the Special Law from 1983). In 1989, this amount was increased to a maximum of 14 (article 35 of the Special Law from 1989). Nowadays, a maximum of 24 legal secretaries work for the Court (although only 18 are currently employed).

1055 R Smyth, 'What do Intermediate Appellate Courts Cite? A Quantitative Study of the Citation Practice of Australian State Supreme Courts' (1999) 21 Adelaide Law Review, 51, 60; FB Cross et al., 'Citations in the U.S. Supreme Court: an Empirical Study of their Use and Significance' (2010) 2 University of Illinois Law Review, 489, 531–3.

1056 R Smyth, 'Trends in the Citation Practice of the Supreme Court of Queensland over the Course of the Twenthieth Century' (2009) 28 The University of Queensland Review, 39, 54.

1057 In total, 9.4% do not contain any citation of authority. In 2015, however, this percentage dropped to 2.5%.

1058 LM Friedman et al., 'State Supreme Courts: A Century of Citation' (1981) 33 Stanford Law Review 773, 778, 783, 800.

1059 M Bobek, *Comparative Reasoning in European Supreme Courts* (Oxford University Press 2013), 223. Bobek formulated this concern about citations of foreign jurisdictions, but this might be valid for the citation practice in general.

6.4.2. PRECEDENTS

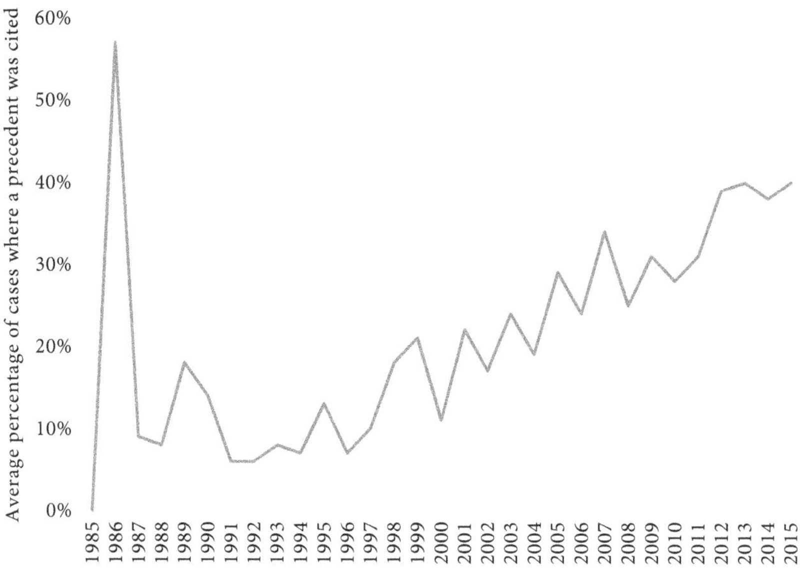

Figure 6.2. Precedents

In approximately one fourth of the rulings, the Court cites its own case law. Figure 6.2 demonstrates that, on average, there is an upward trend towards more citations of precedents. The average percentages have to be interpreted in light of the number of rulings proclaimed in each year. For example, the peak in 1986 (57%) only represents nine cases, while 40% of the cases in 2015 represent a number of 64 cases. As mentioned before, the increased tendency of the Court to cite precedents may be explained by the fact that, over time, the volume of citable cases has grown considerably.[1060]

The Court uses citations of precedents for several reasons. First, these citations may serve to legitimate an outcome with far-reaching consequences.[1061] More specifically, when previous case law has pointed out that a legislative initiative is required, and the legislator has not acted upon this request, this gives the Court a strong mandate to invalidate or modulate the challenged legislation.[1062] For instance, the BeCC has repeatedly criticised the unequal treatment

1060 R Smyth, 'Trends in the Citation Practice of the Supreme Court of Queensland over the Course of the Twenthieth Century' (2009) 28 The University of Queensland Review, 39, 54.

1061 Precedents may empower the Court to react more intensely. See CH Mendes, *Constitutional Courts and Deliberative Democracy* (Oxford University Press 2013), 219, referring to a quote of from justice of the South African Constitutional Court.

1062 For example, BeCC case no 10/2016, 21 January 2016, building on the precedents of BeCC case no 56/93, 8 July 1993, and BeCC case no 125/2011, 7 July 2011.

between so-called 'workmen', on the one hand, and 'service employees' on the other. Already in 1993, the criterion selected to differentiate between these categories, in particular the mainly 'manual' or 'intellectual' nature of their work, was dismissed by the Court for not being objective. Yet the Court initially allowed the legislator some time to gradually equate the status of workmen and employees.[1063] The legislator acted upon this request but inadequately. Hence, a series of new procedures were initiated before the Court. In these more recent cases, the Court stated that – so many years after its initial ruling – a gradual evaluation can no longer be considered a reasonable approach. The Court argued that, by allowing a manifest discrimination to persist, the legislator had violated the Constitution.[1064] In short, the Court built on its precedents as a way to justify the establishment of a constitutional infringement.

On the other hand, the BeCC uses its precedents to avoid an overload of work. In particular, the judge-rapporteur may ask for a summary procedure when the preliminary question evidently calls for a negative reply or when the case is manifestly unfounded or relatively straightforward.[1065] The data demonstrates that the BeCC refers to precedents in 61.9% of these cases.[1066] This suggests that this summary procedure is mostly used for cases relating to issues on which the BeCC has already taken a stance. For example, in case no 82/2015,[1067] relating to a certain tax provision, the BeCC stated that a similar *and* the same challenged legal provision had already been declared unconstitutional in previous case law.[1068] The BeCC simply took over the reasoning from the earlier cases, thus avoiding losing time or energy.

The results suggest that the BeCC takes into account its precedents more prominently when the challenged legislation concerns a migration issue.[1069] When studying these cases in more detail, one can infer a certain pattern. Instead of referring to one 'landmark' case, the BeCC prefers to cite recent cases which, in turn, build on older cases. This results in a certain through-line that connects the most recent cases to, ultimately, the oldest cases relating to migration law.[1070] This practice of building continuously on more recent precedents also

1063 BeCC case no 56/93, 1 July 1993, B.6.2.

1064 BeCC case no 125/2011, 7 July 2011, B.4.3; BeCC case no 187/2014, 18 December, B.6; and BeCC case no 10/2016, 21 January 2016, B.7.

1065 Article 72 of the Special Law on the Constitutional Court.

1066 In contrast, precedents only occur in 17% of cases decided in a 'normal' restricted session, and in 31% of cases decided in plenary session. Also, the summary procedure does not significantly correlate with any of the other citation categories.

1067 BeCC case no 82/2015, 28 May 2015.

1068 BeCC case no 35/2005, 16 February 2005; and BeCC case no 7/2015, 22 January 2015.

1069 The Court refers to precedents in 48% of the cases related to migration law (vs an average of 25%).

1070 An example of a such a line of case law is: BeCC case no 133/2015, 1 October 2015; BeCC case no 95/2014, 30 June 2014; BeCC case no 135/2011, 27 July 2011; BeCC case no 21/2001, 1 March 2001; BeCC case no 80/99, 30 June 1999; and BeCC case no 51/94, 29 June 1994.

appears in other subject matters, such as the law of persons/family law[1071] and criminal law.[1072] Studies on other courts have led to similar observations.[1073] In these studies, several potential explanations were put forward. First, judges might prefer to cite judgments that they wrote. Also, the stock of older decisions will decline over time because cases may be overruled. Lastly, recent cases may be more relevant if the social context has changed over time.[1074] Building on precedents also gives the Court the opportunity to differentiate between similar, but not equal, situations, and therefore refine the boundaries of the Constitution imposed upon the legislator.

6.4.3. CASE LAW OF (INTER)NATIONAL COURTS

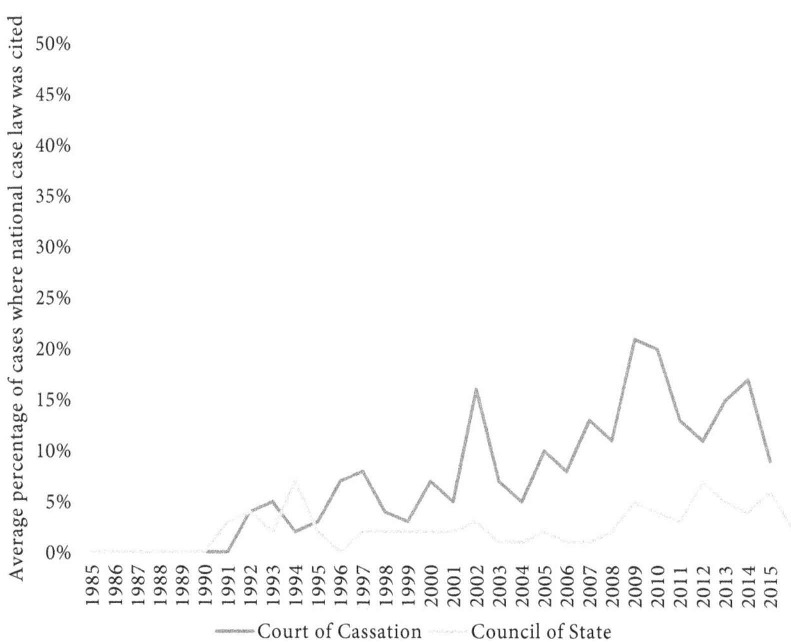

Figure 6.3. National case law

1071 For example: BeCC case no 118/2014, 17 July 2014; BeCC case no 165/2013, 5 December 2013; BeCC case no 54/2011, 6 April 2011; BeCC case no 144/2010, 16 December 2010; BeCC case no 112/2003, 17 September 2003; and BeCC case no 36/96, 6 June 1996.

1072 For example: BeCC case no 123/2014, 19 September 2014; BeCC case no 178/2013, 19 December 2013; BeCC case no 5/2007, 11 January 2007; BeCC case no 24/2005, 26 January 2005; and BeCC case no104/2003, 22 July 2003.

1073 For example: S Dothan, *Reputation and Judicial Tactics* (Cambridge 2015), 23; and Y Schachar, R Harris and M Gross, 'Citation Practices of the Supreme Court, Quantitative Analysis' (1996) 27 Hebrew University Law Review, 119.

1074 R Smyth, 'What do Intermediate Appellate Courts Cite? A Quantitative Study of the Citation Practice of Australian State Supreme Courts' (1999) 21 Adelaide Law Review, 51, 62–3; and

The results indicate that the Court is less keen to cite case law of other courts than its own precedents. First, although citations of the Court of Cassation's case law have fluctuated strongly over the years, figure 6.3 suggests a slight upward trend (average: 10%). A large majority of the cases in which the BeCC cites the case law of the Court of Cassation (87%) are preliminary questions.[1075] This makes sense considering that these questions often deal with the interpretation of an existing legal provision. In principle, it belongs to the Court of Cassation, the final appellate court in criminal and civil proceedings, to determine how legal provisions should be applied in practice. Hence, it is no surprise that the BeCC especially takes into account case law of the Court of Cassation in cases that relate to criminal law.[1076] Often, the referring judge in the preliminary proceedings founds his interpretation on the case law of the Court of Cassation. If so, the BeCC does not limit its citations to recent case law but, on the contrary, regularly refers to cases that are at least a few years old.[1077] Sometimes the BeCC even deviates from the interpretation given by the Court of Cassation.[1078]

In annulment procedures, the BeCC very rarely cites the case law of the Court of Cassation. However, these citations did occur more frequently in the years 2002, 2009 and 2014, which explains the peaks in figure 6.3. In annulment procedures, there may not be as much case law of the Court of Cassation to cite, since the challenged legislation has not yet been applied in practice. Also, these citations generally serve other functions, for example to explain the situation prior to the new legislation or to specify that the legislator wanted to legally consolidate a certain judicial interpretation.[1079]

A similar upward trend cannot be noted for the case law of the administrative judiciary.[1080] Moreover, the number of cases where the Court refers to this

I Nielsen and R Smyth, 'One Hundred Years of Citation of Authority on the Supreme Court of New South Wales' (2008) 31 University of New South Wales Law Journal, 189, 206.

1075 The Court cites case law of the Court of Cassation in 13% of the preliminary rulings, and in 4% of the annulment procedures (independent samples t-test; equal variance not assumed; p=0.000).

1076 The Court cites case law of the Court of Cassation in 21% of the cases related to criminal law. For example, BeCC case no 112/2015, 17 September 2015, B.12.4.2, cites Cass, 27 September 2011, case no 501.

1077 For example, in BeCC case no 2014/163, 6 November 2014, the BeCC refers to case law that dates back to 1973.

1078 These cases usually result in a 'double interpretation' outcome in which the BeCC states that two interpretations are possible but only one is constitutional. For example, see BeCC case no 127/2015, 24 September 2015, B.12.

1079 For example: BeCC case no 2002/086, 8 May 2002; BeCC case no 2009/196, 3 December 2009; BeCC case no 2014/120, 17 September 2014, B.4.4.

1080 Most citations concern case law of the Council of State but, occasionally, the BeCC also refers to the Council of Migration Law Litigation (e.g. BeCC case no 2014/001, 16 January 2014, B.8.2) or to the Council for Permit Disputes (BeCC case no 2015/158, 4 November 2015, B.5.1). No citations are known of the case law of the council for disputes about decisions on study progress.

authority is very limited (3%). A possible explanation is that the administrative jurisdiction may simply not be relevant as often as the case law of the Court of Cassation. In particular, the results demonstrate that these citations occur more frequently in preliminary procedures[1081] that relate to spatial planning and 'other' administrative law issues (e.g. disciplinary matters).[1082] Together, these subject matters only represent 7% of the cases, whereas criminal law for example represents 10% of the cases. Nonetheless, this shows that the BeCC does refer to these authorities when they are relevant to the case.

Similarly, in preliminary procedures, the administrative case law tends to be used to interpret the legislation under review.[1083] In annulment procedures, these citations generally occur when the legislation under review concerns a validation of a previous executive decision which was invalidated by the administrative judiciary. For example, in case no 119/2015, the Court stated that the challenged spatial planning legislation served to validate a previous executive decision that

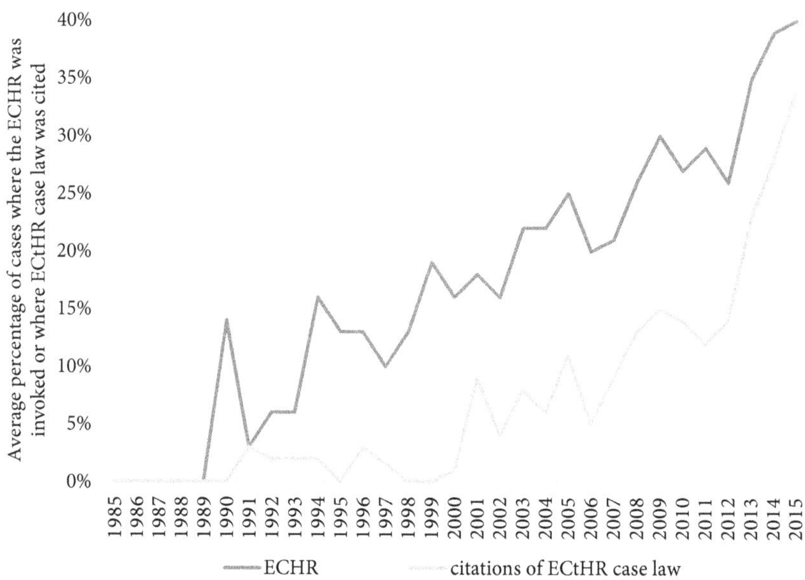

Figure 6.4. Case law of the European Court of Human Rights and the relation with the European Convention on Human Rights as invoked reference norm

1081 The Court cites case law of the Court of Cassation in 4% of the preliminary rulings, and in 2% of the annulment procedures (independent samples t-test; equal variance not assumed; p=0.021).

1082 The Court cites case law of the administrative judiciary in, respectively, 14% and 12% of these cases.

1083 For example, BeCC case no 158/2015, 4 November 2015. In this case, the Court follows the interpretation of the Council for Permit Disputes (in particular case no A/2013/0753, 17 December 2013, and case no A/2014/0012, 14 January 2014).

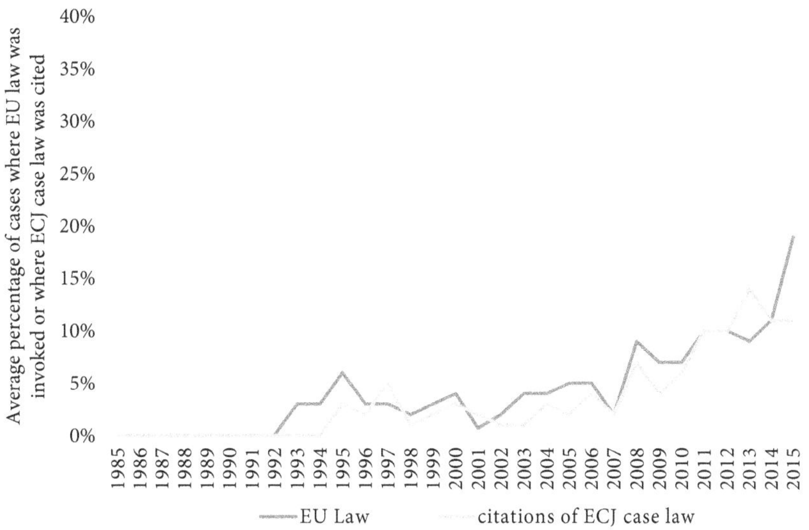

Figure 6.5. Case law of the European Court of Justice and the relation with European law as invoked reference norm

had been declared inapplicable by the Council of State because it entailed an unconstitutional discrimination.[1084] In these cases, the administrative case law can shed light on the grounds for the previous invalidation, assisting the Court in evaluating whether the legislator has succeeded in remedying this error.

As shown in figures 6.4 and 6.5, the BeCC increasingly accepts the intrusion of ECJ and especially ECtHR case law into its jurisdiction.[1085] Although the Court cited these authorities in 5% and 10% of the cases respectively, the results indicate that the BeCC has become more oriented towards international than national case law. Initially, the BeCC only had jurisdiction to review legislation against competence allocating rules. During this period (1985–1989), there was evidently little room for European case law. Yet, in 1989, the BeCC was additionally given the competence to review against certain *constitutional* fundamental rights. At the time, the European legal order was already in place and institutions such as the ECJ and ECtHR had risen to considerable importance. Through the equality principle, the BeCC incorporated international norms, including European law, into its set of reference norms (see *supra*, section 2.2.1.).

1084 For example, BeCC case no 119/2015, 17 September 2015, B.2.1-2, referring to the Council of State, case no 214.791, 12 August 2011, and case no 220/536, 12 September 2012.

1085 Previous, more limited, studies on the BeCC have already suggested the existence of these tendencies: see P Popelier, 'Judicial Conversations in Mulitlevel Constitutionalism. The Belgian Case' in M Claes et al. (eds.), *Constitutional Conversations in Europe – Actors, Topics and Procedures* (Intersentia 2012), 86; and S Lambrecht, 'The Attitude of Four Supreme Courts Towards the European Court of Human Rights: Strasbourg has Spoken ...' in S Besson and AR Ziegler (eds.), *Le Juge en Droit International et Européen – The Judge in International and European Law* (Schulthess 2013), 312–15.

Moreover, the BeCC stated that an 'extricable' bond exists between analogous human rights in the Constitution and human rights treaties, such as the ECHR. Considering the timing, there was already a considerable amount of ECJ and ECtHR judgments to cite.[1086] Nonetheless, although the data shows that the BeCC has been reviewing legislation against these international norms since 1990, figures 6.4 and 6.5 show that the share of cases in which the BeCC cites ECtHR and ECJ case law have long been limited, with a noticeable 'turn' in 2000 towards ECtHR case law and again after 2006–2007 towards both judicial institutions.

Considering the bond between human rights provisions in the Constitution and in the ECHR, the case law of the ECtHR is considered a major source for the interpretation of constitutional rights.[1087] However, before 2000, the BeCC did not frequently cite ECtHR case law in cases in which it had to apply the ECHR.[1088] Nonetheless, the relation between the invocation of the ECHR and ECtHR case law has grown stronger ever since.[1089] These results suggest that something other than an increased tendency to invoke the ECHR is additionally pushing these citation levels upwards. An alternative explanation may be that the Court, and more specifically the law clerks who prepare the judgments, are nowadays more oriented towards European jurisdictions. Also, the ECtHR itself encourages domestic supreme courts to take into account (to a greater extent) its case law. More specifically, the ECtHR states that a broader margin of appreciation is given when its case law was comprehensively analysed.[1090] Even so, in 2015, the BeCC still neglected to mention relevant ECtHR case law in 27% of the cases in which it was requested to apply the ECHR.[1091] Although in some of these cases the ECtHR may simply not have produced any relevant case law on the particular issue at hand, some scholars have argued that

---

1086 P Popelier, ibid., 89: "In contrast with, for example the German Bundesverfassungsgericht, the BeCC is therefore not hampered by a long tradition of constitutional review giving rise to a comprehensive national doctrine of fundamental rights."

1087 P Popelier, 'Judicial Conversations in Mulitlevel Constitutionalism. The Belgian Case' in M Claes et al. (eds.), *Constitutional Conversations in Europe – Actors, Topics and Procedures* (Intersentia 2012), 89.

1088 More precisely, in only 6% of these cases.

1089 In the period 2000–2015, the Court referred to ECtHR case law in 41% of the cases where it had to apply the ECHR. In 2015, this percentage peaked (63%) and the correlation ECtHR-ECHR has become very strong (0.672, p=0.000).

1090 See for example: ECtHR Axel Springer AG v. Germany, n°39954/08, 7 February 2012, §88; and ECtHR, von Hannover v. Germany, n°40660/08, 60641/08, 7 February 2012, §107. See: S Lambrecht, 'The Attitude of Four Supreme Courts Towards the European Court of Human Rights: Strasbourg has Spoken …' in S Besson and AR Ziegler (eds.), *Le Juge en Droit International et Européen – The Judge in International and European Law* (Schulthess 2013), 304; and P Popelier and C Van De Heyning, 'Procedural Rationality: Giving Teeth to the Proportionality Analysis' (2013) European Constitutional Law Review, 259.

1091 For example, BeCC case no 16/2015, 12 February 2015.

disregarding ECtHR case law *when it is available* may not only cause issues for the margin of appreciation given by the ECtHR, but might also go against basic principles of transparency and the adequacy of reasoning.[1092]

The ECtHR especially seems to shape the BeCC's decisions relating to the law of persons and family law, criminal law and migration issues.[1093] The BeCC is less willing to accept this kind of intrusion of ECtHR case law in other subject matters. This can only be partially explained by the prominence of articles 6 (right to a fair trial) and 8 (right to respect for one's private and family life) of the ECHR as reference norms in the BeCC's case law.[1094] The results suggest that interest groups are particularly drawn to migration and criminal legislation and that they attempt to build stronger claims by relating their pleas to the ECHR and other international human rights treaties.[1095] In addition, as recent cases no 101/2015[1096] and no 155/2015[1097] confirm, ECtHR case law also serves as an inspiration in cases related to persons and family law or criminal law, even when these articles were not invoked.

Figure 6.5 demonstrates that the ECJ plays a less prominent role in the BeCC's case law. Yet, the results indicate the Court does rely on the ECJ case law when appropriate. First, there is a strong relation between these citations and the invocation of EU law, already in the early years after the Court's establishment. In contrast to what was said above on the ECHR-ECtHR combination, the BeCC always relied strongly on the ECJ for guidance when interpreting EU law. The correlation between the invocation of EU law and ECJ case law has remained relatively stable and did not intensify in a similar way to the ECtHR case law.[1098] Second, the Court is inclined to cite ECJ law as an authority when the legislation under review has been adopted to fulfil an international obligation, such as the implementation of a European directive.[1099] Third, these citations evidently also appear in rulings that follow a preliminary procedure before the ECJ, initiated by the BeCC.[1100] Nonetheless, the BeCC still regularly fails to demonstrate that it took into account relevant ECJ case law when appropriate, as in one of the three situations

---

1092 S Lambrecht, 'The Attitude of Four Supreme Courts Towards the European Court of Human Rights: Strasbourg has Spoken ...' in S Besson and AR Ziegler (eds.), *Le Juge en Droit International et Européen – The Judge in International and European Law* (Schulthess 2013), 315.

1093 Citations of ECtHR case law appeared in, respectively, 27%, 21% and 22% of these cases (vs an average of 10%).

1094 S Lambrecht, 'The Attitude of Four Supreme Courts Towards the European Court of Human Rights: Strasbourg has Spoken ...' in S Besson and AR Ziegler (eds.), *Le Juge en Droit International et Européen – The Judge in International and European Law* (Schulthess 2013), 315.

1095 See *supra*, sections 4.2.2.1. and 4.2.2.2.

1096 BeCC case no 101/2015, 2 July 2015.

1097 BeCC case no 155/2015, 29 October 2015.

1098 Correlation 0.460, p=0,000.

1099 The Court cited ECJ case law in 28% of these cases.

1100 The Court cited ECJ case law in 58% of these cases.

mentioned above. For instance, in 2015, the BeCC did not cite any ECJ case law in more than half (55%) of the cases where such a citation would have been relevant.[1101] Although this does not mean that ECJ case law was not consulted, exhibiting such consultations more strongly would enhance the transparency and quality of the BeCC's reasoning.

ECJ case law is particularly referred to in cases related to environmental or energy law.[1102] Previously, it has been noted that the involvement of business companies is more pronounced in these cases, and that they – more than any other type of litigants – tend to link their claim to European law.[1103] For instance, in case no 106/2014,[1104] several energy companies challenged legislation aiming to initiate the demolition of nuclear power plants. In their request for annulment, the companies invoked European directives and the Treaty on the functioning of the European Union. Yet, with reference to several cases of the ECJ, the Court rejected their request.

In conclusion, although there is room for improvement, these results confirm the BeCC's reputation for taking a Europe-friendly stance.[1105] While the case law of the Court of Cassation and the combined administrative courts explicitly contributed to shaping constitutional decisions in 17% of BeCC's rulings in 2014–2015, the ECJ and ECtHR together were cited in 38% of these rulings. This is in line with a more general trend in continental Europe. Studies have confirmed that both the ECHR and EU law also play a considerable role in the decision-making process of other European constitutional courts.[1106]

6.4.4. LEGISLATIVE HISTORY DOCUMENTS

Regarding the legislative history documents, figure 6.6 shows that the BeCC consistently looks into the preparatory parliamentary documents. Since 1993, these percentages have remained relatively stable and – in comparison to any other authority – very high (average: 86%). References to other preparatory documents, in particular political agreements (average: 3%) and *ex ante* advisory opinions of the Council of State (average: 8%), appear less frequently.

1101 For example, BeCC case no 9/2015, 28 January 2015. In this case, the BeCC was requested to review legislation relating to the fight against terrorism, implementing a European framework decision.

1102 The Court referred to ECJ case law in 12% of these cases (vs an average of 5%).

1103 See *supra*, sections 4.2.2.1. and 4.2.2.2.

1104 BeCC case no 106/2014, 17 July 2014.

1105 P Popelier, 'Judicial Conversations in Mulitlevel Constitutionalism. The Belgian Case' in M Claes et al. (eds.), *Constitutional Conversations in Europe – Actors, Topics and Procedures* (Intersentia 2012), 81.

1106 E Mak, *Judicial Decision-making in a Globalised World: A Comparative Analysis of the Changing Practices of Western Highest Courts* (Hart Publishing 2013).

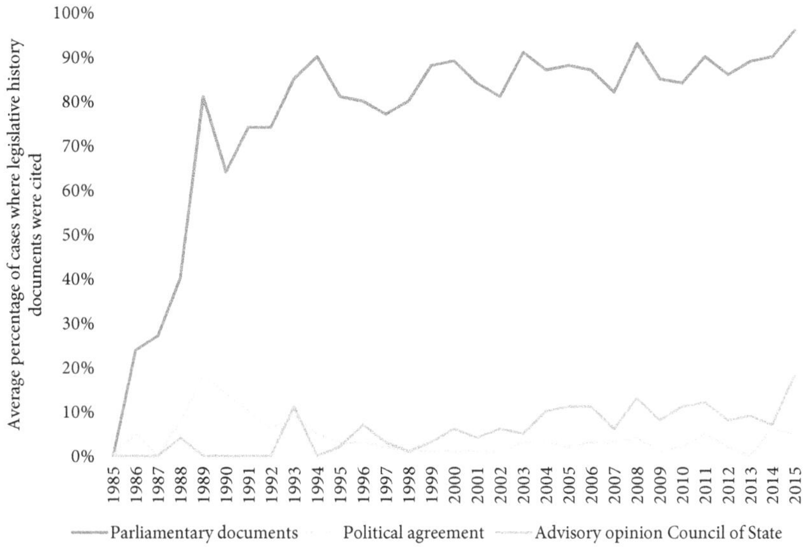

Figure 6.6. Legislative history documents

First, the parliamentary preparatory documents (such as the legislative initiative, the report of parliamentary commissions, reports on the plenary sessions) primarily serve to shed light on the underlying policy objective. These citations occur most when the BeCC is requested to review against the equality clause (88%). In this type of rights adjudication, the BeCC developed a step-by-step proportionality analysis, inspired by the case law of the ECtHR.[1107] The last step, the 'justification test', requires an evaluation of the legitimacy of the legislative objective, its necessity and the causality and proportionality between this objective and the challenged legal provision. Logically, the parliamentary documents are an important guideline for making this evaluation. Nonetheless, the BeCC also regularly cites parliamentary documents in cases relating to a conflict of competences (79%). In these cases, the consultation of parliamentary documents serves another purpose. In order to judge whether the legislation under review violates the competence allocating rules, the BeCC does not only look into the parliamentary documents preceding the challenged legislation itself, but also those relating to the allocating rules.[1108] In particular, references to these latter documents can enlighten how the boundaries between particular federal or regional competences should be interpreted.

This tradition of relying heavily on parliamentary preparatory documents is not necessarily shared by other constitutional courts. In the United States

[1107] For more information, see chapter 7.

[1108] For example, BeCC case no 80/2015, 28 May 2015, B.3.2, B.4.1 (relating to the competence allocating rules) and B.12 (relating to the challenged legislation).

for instance, the use of legislative history for the purpose of ascertaining the intention of the legislature has been much more contested.[1109] Initially, evidence of intent was limited to the plain meaning of the legislative text because this was considered to be more objective. Gradually, more authority was given to legislative history, particularly to ensure that the USSC was not reading its own values into the text. Yet, in contrast with the BeCC, the USSC still seems reluctant to be strongly influenced by these documents in judicial proceedings.[1110]

Another type of legislative history document that the Court can cite are political agreements. In Belgium, laws related to the organisation of the state, such as electoral legislation or legislation that implements a state reform, often follow difficult political negotiations that culminated in such an agreement. Hence, it is not surprising that citations of these agreements mostly appear in cases related to the organisation of state.[1111] For instance, in case no 57/2014, the Court stated that one of the challenged provisions, introducing a new procedure for the appointment of mayors in communities with special language facilities, resulted from the political agreement of 2011 on the sixth state reform. The Court went on to state that the challenged provision aimed to end the continuing disagreement on these appointments between the Dutch-speaking and French-speaking communities.[1112] This reflects the Court's reluctance to meddle in cases related to the organisation of the state if this could upset the agreement and revive the political conflict. However, citations of political agreements also appear in cases relating to other subject matters, reflecting the Belgian political practice of searching for a broad consensus amongst linguistic, political and/or social partners (see *supra*, section 2.2.2.). For example, the BeCC acknowledged the importance of cooperation in social matters.[1113] Also, with regard to the law enforcement reform, the BeCC repeatedly argued that a partial annulment would upset the balanced character of the overall 1988 'octopus agreement'.[1114]

1109 For example, WN Eskridge, *Dynamic Statutory Interpretation* (Harvard University Press 1994), 205 and further. Eskridge describes, in detail, the value of legislative history documents in adjudication between 1892–1994. See also McNollgast, 'Legislative Intent: The Use of Positive Political Theory in Statutory Interpretation' (1994) 57 Law and Contemporary Problems, 3; and A Barak, *The Judge in a Democracy* (Princeton University Press 2006), 125.

1110 Ibid., 220–7. Also, there has been a strong debate between Justices Breyer and Scalia on the use of the purposive approach. See S Breyer, 'Making Our Democracy Work: The Yale Lectures' (2011) 120 Yale Law Journal, 1999, 2017.

1111 The Court cited political agreements in 22% of these cases.

1112 BeCC case no 57/2014, 3 April 2014, B.6.5.

1113 For example, BeCC case no 116/2015, 17 September 2015. The BeCC confirms (B.12) that the challenged legislation constitutes a compromise that has been adopted after long and difficult negotiations with the social partners.

1114 For example: BeCC case no 64/1999, 9 June 1999, B.4.3; BeCC case no 149/2006, 11 November 2006, B.6; BeCC case no 11/2007, 17 January 2007, B.4; and BeCC case no 22/2015, 19 February, B.9.

Finally, the Court can rely on the advisory opinion of the Council of State. This institution is responsible for the *ex ante* screening of legislation, which comprises an evaluation of its conformity with the Constitution, European law, human rights treaties and the competence allocating rules.[1115] These opinions are, however, not binding and therefore regularly discarded by the legislative branch.[1116] Although they are equally accessible, both to the parties involved in the procedure and to the judges, as the parliamentary documents,[1117] the number of citations of these opinions is limited (8%). Figure 6.6 shows a slow increase, with a recent peak in 2015 (18%). Yet, this seems rather a one-off outlier than the beginning of an actual trend.[1118]

Besides the fact that the advisory opinions are not always relevant to solving the case, there are several additional plausible reasons for this low citation rate. First, there may not be an opinion available on the piece of legislation that is brought before the Court, either because no opinion was requested,[1119] or because the Council of State did not have enough time to execute an in-depth investigation.[1120] Although the BeCC does not consider the absence of an advisory opinion as a reason *in se* to declare legislation unconstitutional,[1121] it equally does not prevent the Court from establishing a violation.

In addition, even when the Council has considerable time to produce its opinion, some problems of constitutionality may be missed. Because of the *in abstracto* nature of its examination, the Council cannot anticipate the consequences for each individual affected by the legislative proposal.[1122] Some problems may only arise when the legislation is applied in practice, resulting in a constitutional review procedure. The data confirms that citations of advisory opinions are especially lacking in preliminary procedures, meaning

---

1115 Therefore, these opinions are considered a 'constitutional goldmine': see J Velaers, *De Grondwet en de Raad van State, Afdeling wetgeving: Vijftig jaar adviezen aan wetgevende vergaderingen, in het licht van de rechtspraak van het Arbitragehof* (Maklu 1999), 13.

1116 OECD, *Better regulation in Europe: Belgium* (OECD 2010), 98; and J Velaers, ibid., 13, 919.

1117 In contrast with many advisory opinions on proposals concerning executive decisions, they are made accessible online, together with the other parliamentary documents. See articles 2–3 of the law on the Council of State.

1118 Preliminary results from 2016 (citation of advisory opinions of the Council of State in 11% of the cases) suggest that it may not be a significant trend.

1119 The legislator is not obliged to request an advisory opinion when the proposal is introduced by one the parliamentary representatives (instead of the executive), nor when the legislative provision is introduced in the later phase of the legislative process, in particular through an amendment.

1120 OECD, *Better Regulation in Europe: Belgium* (OECD 2010), 11: "A large number of draft regulations are submitted to the Council of State under the 'urgency procedure' (95%) which severely limits its capacity to carry out effective checks."

1121 For example: BeCC case no 103/2000, 11 October 2000, B.4.-5; and BeCC case no 5/2010, 27 May 2010, B.9.

1122 J Velaers, *De Grondwet en de Raad van State, Afdeling wetgeving: Vijftig jaar adviezen aan wetgevende vergaderingen, in het licht van de rechtspraak van het Arbitragehof* (Maklu 1999), 66.

that the Court is less likely to find remarks on the issue in the advisory opinion when it evaluates legislation that has already been applied in practice (for a considerable time).[1123]

Finally, there are reasons to believe that the Court sometimes strategically omits an explicit citation of an advisory opinion. In particular, when the Court cites the opinion only to deviate from it, this would accentuate the disagreement between both institutions. This can decrease the authority of both the advisory and the judicial opinion. The data confirm that citations of the advisory opinions, only to deviate from them, are exceptional.[1124] Although these results may be interpreted as a sign of quasi-permanent alignment between the advisory opinions and the opinions of the Court, this is not necessarily the case. For example, with regard to the competence conflict cases, it has been noted that the Court is more inclined to interpret regional competences broadly, while the Council shows more reluctance on that matter.[1125] Yet the data shows that the Court is actually somewhat more inclined to cite the advisory opinion in competence conflict cases,[1126] and in particular when the legislation under review deals with education or state organisation.[1127] This suggests that strategic citation behaviour, omitting the citation of the advisory opinion, may either occur more often in fundamental rights cases or that there are indeed very few divergences in opinion between the Council of State and the Court.

The results confirm that the Court almost exclusively cites an advisory opinion when its decision is in line with the arguments of the Council. On the one hand, it seems more difficult for the legislator to justify legislation that has been previously disapproved by the Council of State.[1128] On the other hand, when the Council approved the proposal,[1129] or offered criticism that was

---

1123 In particular, these citations appear in 14% of the annulment procedures and 5% of the preliminary procedures (independent samples t-test; unequal variance, p=0.000).

1124 For example, BeCC case no 133/2015, 1 October 2015, in contrast with the advisory opinion on the legislative proposal of 3 June 2013 with regard to the rights of refugees, *Parl Doc* no 53-2853/001, 66.

1125 J Velaers, *De Grondwet en de Raad van State, Afdeling wetgeving: Vijftig jaar adviezen aan wetgevende vergaderingen, in het licht van de rechtspraak van het Arbitragehof* (Maklu 1999), 908.

1126 In particular, the Court cites advisory opinions in 10% of the competence conflict cases, and even in 15% of the mixed cases (vs an average of 8%).

1127 In particular, the Court cited an advisory opinion in 14% and 13%, respectively, of the cases related to education or state organisation.

1128 For example, BeCC case no 2/2016, 14 January 2016, B.2.2, in line with the advisory opinion on the legislative proposal of 25 November 2013 introducing the double surname for children and adoptees (name of the father and mother), *Parl Doc* 2013–14, no 53-3145/001, 36–7. Other examples include: BeCC case no 20/2014, 29 January 2014, B.10; and BeCC case no 1/2015, 22 January 2015, B.6.3.

1129 For example, BeCC case no 63/2015, 21 May 2015, B.7-8, in line with the advisory opinion on the legislative proposal of 11 April 2013 with regard to the rights of detainees, *Parl Doc* 2012/13, no 53-2744/001, 14.

subsequently adequately refuted,[1130] or implemented,[1131] by the legislator, the Court cites these opinions to support the rejection of the constitutional challenge.

In conclusion, legislative history documents play an important role in Belgian constitutional adjudication. The Court consistently cites parliamentary documents to establish the legislative purpose underlying the challenged provisions. Yet, while these documents may be cited rather *pro forma*, the advisory opinions seem to contribute more substantively to the BeCC's decision. Remarks of the Council of State on the constitutionality of the proposed provision are usually supported by the Court. This is promising, because notwithstanding the non-binding character of the advisory opinions, the *ex ante* evaluation may indirectly and substantially affect the quality of legislation.

6.4.5. SECONDARY AUTHORITIES

While the judges on the BeCC may be *looking into* secondary authorities at the present time during the judicial decision-making process, any such research is hardly reflected in their citation patterns. In particular, no references were made to academic scholarship, and scientific studies appeared in a mere 2% of the cases.[1132] Also, there is no sustained increase in these citations over the years (making it redundant to present the results in a graph).

Notwithstanding the limited number of references to scientific evidence, some relevant patterns appear in the Court's case law. Generally, the BeCC uses scientific evidence as part of the substantive evaluation of the challenged legislation or to judge the quality of the law-making process.[1133]

First, as part of the substantive reasoning, such evidence can either demonstrate or contradict the reasonableness of legislation. More specifically, evidence is mostly cited to underpin the Court's evaluation when applying

---

1130 For example, BeCC case no 92/2015, 18 June 2015, B.37.3-7, in line with the advisory opinion on the legislative proposal of 12 December 2002 with regard to taxes imposed on medication fabricators, in line with *Parl Doc* 2012–13, no 53-2561/001, 143–4.

1131 For example, BeCC case no 179/2014, 10 December 2014, in line with the advisory opinion on the legislative proposal of 27 December 2012 with regard to the procedure before the Belgian institution responsible for competition law, *Parl Doc* no 53-2591/001, 158–62.

1132 Only 71 cases contained a reference to a scientific study. Even this number is somewhat overstated, as several of these judgments are linked, in particular because they dealt with the same issue since one ruling followed a previous ruling in which the Court referred a preliminary question to the ECJ.

1133 On the dual meaning of evidence-based judicial review, see I Barr-Siman-Tov, 'The Dual Meaning of Evidence-Based Judicial Review of Legislation' (2016) 4 Theory and Practice of Legislation, 107–33. In addition, there are also cases in which the evidence did not play a role in the final assessment but merely served to situate or interpret the challenged provision. For example: BeCC case no 176/2009, 12 November 2009; and BeCC case no 69/2010, 10 June 2010.

the justification test, and in particular when analysing the suitability[1134] or necessity[1135] step (see *infra*, chapter 7). The defending party may bring forward studies that have been used during the law-making procedure,[1136] or studies may be submitted to the Court by one of the initiating or intervening parties. Only exceptionally will the Court request the parties to submit evidence to support their arguments.[1137]

Second, although the Court does occasionally reproach the legislator for not taking into account certain scientific data,[1138] the claim that no scientific studies were conducted is not a reason *as such* to declare legislation unconstitutional.[1139] Hence, like other courts,[1140] the BeCC rejects a purely procedural approach. Nonetheless, the Court does sometimes consider the presence of studies, as such, as proof that Parliament made a reasonable decision.[1141]

A more detailed analysis of these citations shows that the Court mostly cites scientific studies as evidence that the law is reasonable.[1142] Even though the Court sometimes questions the value of evidence brought forward by the legislator, it usually follows the legislator's lead when no other contradicting evidence can be found.[1143] Moreover, even when litigants introduce additional expertise to prove the opposite, the BeCC is reluctant to enter into a scientific debate.[1144] It does not feel called upon to question the quality of the studies,

---

1134 For example: BeCC case no 50/2015, 30 April 2015; and BeCC case no 89/2011, 31 May 2011 (the measure was found not suitable).

1135 For example, BeCC case no 142/2015, 15 October 2015 (the measure was found necessary).

1136 In that sense, these references could have also qualified as 'legislative history documents'.

1137 BeCC case no 29/1996, 15 May 1996; BeCC case no 89/2011, 31 May 2011.

1138 For example, BeCC case no 9/2007, 11 January 2007.

1139 The Court declared itself not competent to judge whether legislation should have been preceded by consultations, studies or expert investigations in BeCC case no 193/2006, 5 December 2006, B.15. Also, the Court has stated that no constitutional provision obliges the legislator the base their decisions on scientific or statistical evidence. The legislator has a large discretionary power to take the measures that, according to their views, respond to the expectations of the citizens: BeCC case no 110/2008, 31 July 2008, B.8.4.

1140 I Bar-Siman-Tov, 'The Dual Meaning of Evidence-Based Judicial Review of Legislation' (2016) Theory and Practice of Legislation, 107, 113. As discussed in this article, the Israeli Supreme Court also held "that it will not invalidate a law solely on the grounds that it was not enacted through a deliberative evidence-based legislative process". Similarly, the USSC has held that there is no general formal requirement upon Congress to make findings of facts or to follow an evidence-based legislative process in order to legislate.

1141 For example, BeCC case no 4/2011, 13 January 2011.

1142 For a more extensive overview see P Popelier and J De Jaegere, 'Evidence-based Judicial Review of Legislation in Divided States: the Belgian Case' (2016) 4 Theory and Practice of Legislation, 187–208.

1143 For example, BeCC case no 180/2015, 17 December 2015. Similarly, the government is given more leeway when no concluding evidence is available: BeCC case no 182/2008, 18 December 2008.

1144 For example: BeCC case no 50/2015, 30 April 2015 (stating that the government can reasonably rely on its own studies); and BeCC case no 50/2011, 6 April 2011 (stating that the evidence brought forward by the litigants was not convincing).

let alone to go as far as to formulate standards to ascertain the reliability of scientific evidence.[1145] Nonetheless, exceptionally, evidence-based judicial review has led to the establishment of a constitutional infringement.[1146]

An interesting example is case no 186/2005,[1147] in which the BeCC dealt with a tax law stimulating the manufacturing of environmentally friendly products. Several companies had asked for an annulment because the law promoted reusable products with a tax relief, but excluded products made from recycled materials. The BeCC made references to several scientific studies, proving that the environmental impact of the production of recycled products, under specific conditions, can be equally low as for reusable products. Therefore, the exclusion of recycled products was said to be disproportionate to the legislative goal. The BeCC agreed and specified that it was the legislator's task to enumerate the conditions under which recycled products could also profit from the tax relief. Moreover, the BeCC explicitly stated that the legislator should take into account the results of the scientific studies.[1148] Not only did the BeCC thus use external sources to justify its own decision, it equally stimulated the legislator to consider the strength of this scientific argument and, if appropriate, to rewrite the legislation.

This example shows that some constitutional questions require expert knowledge, in particular when the Court has to weigh the costs and benefits of the rules through which the policy decision rationale is implemented (proportionality analysis, see chapter 7). Therefore, it is striking that, compared to all the other authorities discussed above, scientific sources continue to play only a marginal role in the BeCC's case law. The question remains as to why the Court does not exhibit such an 'evidence-based reflex'.[1149]

First, these low citation rates may be due to the unavailability of scientific evidence. The various Belgian governments (some more than others) are not celebrated for the quality of the *ex ante* evaluation of their legislative proposals.[1150] Evidently, the lack of documents demonstrating the evidence-based character of

---

1145 With regard to expert testimony, see the standards established by the US Supreme Court in *Daubert v. Merell Dow Pharmaceuticals*, 509 U.S. 579 (1993).

1146 In particular, when the legislator does not convincingly explain why it has departed from expert advice (e.g. BeCC case no 196/2011, 22 December 2011 and BeCC case no 8/2014, 23 January 2014), or when the litigants bring forward persuasive evidence (e.g. BeCC case no 1/93, 7 January 1993 and BeCC case no 37/2011, 15 March 2011).

1147 BeCC case no 186/2005, 14 December 2005.

1148 Ibid., B.15.5.

1149 Also see P Popelier and J De Jaegere, 'Evidence-based Judicial Review of Legislation in Divided States: the Belgian Case' (2016) 4 Theory and Practice of Legislation, 187–208. The authors discuss additional theories that may explain the restricted use of evidence (constitutional mandate and the political context). Yet, they found that the first has little explanatory power. The latter will be discussed in the section on the Court's strategic citation patterns.

1150 For an overview, see P Popelier and J De Jaegere, 'Evidence-based Judicial Review of Legislation in Divided States: the Belgian Case' (2016) 4 Theory and Practice of Legislation, 187–208.

the challenged legislation prevents the Court from citing them. In addition, the litigants involved may not have the knowledge or resources to produce or gather scientific studies that can undermine the legislator's assumptions.[1151] In contrast with other countries, the Belgian system does not allow *amici curiae* without a personal interest in the case, such as academics, to bring forward evidence.[1152] Finally, although the Court is allowed to take investigative measures, it rarely does so.[1153] Also, the Court estimates that it can only take such measures when they are useful for the collection of factual information.[1154] Some have argued that this excludes the collection of information from experts and academics.[1155]

Next, notwithstanding the specific knowledge and experience of the judges, they cannot have expertise on each issue that is raised. As mentioned before, lawyers in continental Europe, are usually not trained to interpret or evaluate the accuracy or reliability of empirical evidence. The lack of sufficient background in interferential statistics makes it difficult to evaluate the assumed causalities underlying legislative decisions. Again, *amici* would be able to fill in the gaps by assessing the strength of evidence and putting it in perspective.

This contrasts immensely with the citation practices of Anglo-American countries, where these secondary sources play an important role.

First, scientific studies, especially from social science, have found their way into common law rulings.[1156] In particular, the US Supreme Court is known to cite this type of authority.[1157] A famous case in which the US Supreme Court cited (in a footnote) a number of social science studies was *Brown v. Board of Education* (1954). In this case, the USSC used psychological evidence to establish that the racial segregation of schools caused psychological harm to black students, and thus violated the equal protection of the Fourteenth Amendment.[1158]

1151 D Shelton, 'The Participation of Non-governmental Organizations in International Judicial Proceedings' (1994) 88 The American Journal of International Law, 611, 615; and A Maamouri, 'L'Amicus Curiae et la Motivation des Décisions des Cours Suprêmes Américaine et Canadienne' in F Hourquebie and M-C Pontoreau (eds.), *La Motivation des Décisions des Cours Suprêmes et Cours Constitutionelles* (Bruylant 2012), 129.

1152 For a discussion on *amici curiae*, see *supra*, chapter 2, section 2.4.

1153 See *supra*, section 2.5.1.

1154 BeCC case no 29/2010, 18 March 2010, B.4.

1155 E Maes, *De Rol van een Grondwettelijk Hof in Rechtsstatelijk Perspectief* (KULeuven, Institute for Constitutional Law 2016), 513.

1156 For example, during the period 1985–1990, the Supreme Court of Canada cited academic scholarship in an average of 40% in its decisions: V Black and N Richter (1993), 'Did she Mention My Name?: Citation of Academic Authority by the Supreme Court of Canada' (1993) Dalhousie Law Journal, 377, 382.

1157 *Lochner v. New York*, 198 US 45, 59 (1905), was the first major constitutional case in which the decision to strike down a law was based on the proportionality enquiry and on scrutiny of general empirical evidence: P Yowell, 'Proportionality in United States Constitutional Law' in L Lazarus, C McCrudden and N Bowled (eds.), *Reasoning Rights: Comparative Judicial Engagement* (Hart Publishing 2014), 110.

1158 N Petersen, 'Avoiding the Common-wisdom Fallacy: the Role of Social Sciences in Constitutional Adjudication' (2013) 11 International Journal of Constitutional Law, 294–5.

In the decades since *Brown*, social science research has been frequently invoked to demonstrate the (in)validity of empirical assumptions made in the process of creating legislation.[1159] This is said to be partially due to the large amount of public interest litigation and *amicus curiae* involvement in US cases.[1160] This kind of litigation would involve either parties or issues (or both) that are much more likely to place such authorities before the courts.[1161] Empirical research on the USSC has repeatedly shown that this external input has a significant influence on the Court's case law.[1162] In addition, the South African Constitutional Court is also known to employ scientific evidence when evaluating the rationale of challenged legislation. An example is the *Makwanyane* case.[1163] In this case, the SACC found that there is no evidence that the death penalty is a greater deterrent of crime than imprisonment, and therefore that the death sentence was ineffective and thus unconstitutional.

Second, supreme courts in common law countries regularly cite academic work.[1164] Although there were some critical voices at first,[1165] in general, this practice is now widely accepted. These citations are usually included in footnotes, like in academic scholarship. Although the internal drafts of the BeCC's rulings probably include references to such literature, they are not as

---

1159 J Monahan and L Walker, 'Judicial Use of Social Science Research' in E Mertz (ed.), *The Role of Social Science in Law*' (Ashgate 2008), 25.

1160 Another reason is the propensity of the US Supreme Court to cite social science evidence in capital punishment cases and cases relating to the Bill of Rights: R Smyth, 'What do Intermediate Appellate Courts Cite? a Quantitative Study of the Citation Practice of Australian State Supreme Courts' (1999) 21 Adelaide Law Review, 51, 67.

1161 D Fausten, I Nielsen and R Smyth, 'A Century of Citation Practice on the Supreme Court of Victoria' (2007) 31 Melbourne University Law Review, 733, 761.

1162 For example: GA Caldeira and JR Wright, 'Amici Curiae before the Supreme Court: Who participates, When and How Much?' (1990) 52 The Journal of Politics, 782; JF Spriggs and PJ Wahlbeck 'Amici Curiae and the Role of Information at the Supreme Court' (1997) 50 Political Research Quartely, 365; and PM Collins, 'Lobbyist before the U.S. Supreme Court: Investigating the influence of Amicus Curiae Briefs' (2007) 60 Political Research Quarterly, 55.

1163 Constitutional Court of South Africa, *S v. Makwanyane and Another* (CCT3/94), 6 June 1995.

1164 For example: LM Friedman et al., 'State Supreme Courts: A Century of citation' (1981) 33 Stanford Law Review, 773, 814; V Black and N Richter, 'Did she Mention My Name?: Citation of academic Authority by the Supreme Court of Canada' (1993) Dalhousie Law Journal, 377; R Smyth, 'What do Intermediate Appellate Courts Cite? A Quantitative Study of the Citation Practice of Australian State Supreme Courts' (1999) 21 Adelaide Law Review, 51; D Fausten, I Nielsen and R Smyth, 'A Century of Citation Practice on the Supreme Court of Victoria' (2007) 31 Melbourne University Law Review, 733; JJ Hasko, 'Persuasion in the Court: Nonlegal Materials in U.S. Supreme Court Opinions' (2002) 94 Law Library Journal, 427.

1165 For example, some judges have argued that the Canadian Supreme Court is not sufficiently selective in weighing up academic authorities to decide which are worth citing and that academic citations might reduce the authority of the judge: D Fausten, I Nielsen and R Smyth, 'A Century of Citation Practice on the Supreme Court of Victoria' (2007) 31 Melbourne University Law Review, 733, 743. See also R Smyth, 'What do Intermediate Appellate Courts Cite? A Quantitative Study of the Citation Practice of Australian State Supreme Courts' (1999) 21 Adelaide Law Review, 51, 56–7.

such published on the website. Including these references would reveal how and by whom judgments are prepared. For example, some studies in the US have suggested that the tendency of the US Supreme Court to cite some sources more than others might be attributable to the fact that law clerks prefer to cite scholars or periodicals that are connected to the university from which they graduated.[1166] Another reason that may explain the Court's reluctance to cite academic work is to avoid the criticism that judges would pick the sources that suit their preferences instead of following legal constraints.[1167]

In conclusion, to stimulate more evidence-based judicial review, the scientific competence of judicial decision-makers should be increased and the technical input into the judicial process should be improved.[1168] Until then, the Belgian Constitutional Court, and constitutional courts in continental Europe more generally, may remain reluctant to use and cite scientific studies.

6.5. STRATEGIC CONSIDERATIONS UNDERLYING CITATION PRACTICES

6.5.1. INTRODUCTION: CITATIONS OF EXTERNAL AUTHORITIES AS A LEGITIMATISATION STRATEGY

While this section has so far concentrated on *which* authorities have been cited over the years, in what follows an explanation for the variation in citation density will be sought. In general, figure 6.7. shows that there is considerable variance in the use of citations by the BeCC. On average, the Court cites between one and two authorities to support its decision. When the BeCC cites one type of authority, this is usually the parliamentary documents.[1169] In 10% of the cases, the BeCC even chose not to cite any authority. At the other end of the spectrum, only 1% of cases were documented more extensively with 5 or more cited authorities.

The question remains as to which case features push citation density upward. Citations are believed to serve the primary function of legitimation for the audience the Court addresses.[1170] Without other legal incentives to

---

1166 For example, W Daniels, 'Far Beyond the Law Reports: Secondary Source Citations in United States Supreme Court Opinions October Terms 1900, 1940 and 1978' (1983) 76 Law Library Journal, 1.

1167 S Dothan, *Reputation and Judicial Tactics* (Cambridge 2015), 38.

1168 S Jasanoff and D Nelkin, 'Science, Technology and the Limits of Judicial Competence' in WA Thomas (ed.), *Science and Law: An Essential Alliance* (Westview Press 1983), 16–17.

1169 In 91.7% of the cases where the BeCC referred to one authority, these were parliamentary documents; and in 5.6% of cases these were precedents.

1170 FB Cross et al., 'Citations in the U.S. Supreme Court: an Empirical Study of their Use and Significance' (2010) 2 University of Illinois Law Review, 489, 509, 525 and further.

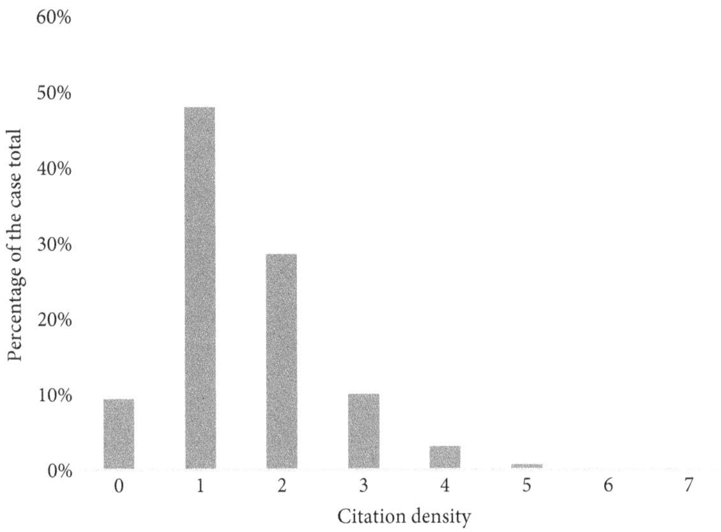

Figure 6.7. Citation density

stimulate compliance, courts must partially rely on a qualitative reason-giving to convince their audience to comply with their rulings.[1171] Systematic studies on the implementation of US Supreme Court opinions have suggested that greater precision in the wording of an opinion does indeed promote implementation.[1172]

If a case relates to a relatively easy and uncontroversial question, a concise reason-giving can suffice. In those cases, it seems reasonable to expect a rather limited number of citations. Some cases require more legitimation, and thus more effort.[1173] In particular, when judging a salient issue, courts may estimate that a more detailed account of all considered arguments is needed.[1174]

1171 P McCormick 'The Supreme Court Cites the Supreme Court: Follow-up Citation on the Supreme Court of Canada, 1989–1993' (1995) 33 Osgoode Hall Law Journal, 453–4; D Fausten, I Nielsen and R Smyth, 'A Century of Citation Practice on the Supreme Court of Victoria' (2007) 31 Melbourne University Law Review, 733–4; M Claes et al., 'Introduction: on Constitutional Conversations' in M Claes et al. (eds.), *Constitutional Conversations in Europe – Actors, Topics and Procedures* (Intersentia 2012), 1. But it is important to note that compliance also depends on other factors, such as ideological congruence with the decision, resources and other case characteristics.

1172 L Baum, 'Implementation of Judicial Decisions' (1976) 4 American Politics Research, 86; and RC Black et al., *US Supreme Court Opinions and Their Audiences* (Cambridge University Press 2016).

1173 LM Friedman et al., 'State Supreme Courts: A Century of Citation' (1981) 33 Stanford Law Review, 773, 777.

1174 An "elaborate display of reasoning from authority": P Harris, 'Difficult Cases and the Display of Authority' (1985) 1 Journal of Law, Economics and Organization, 209–10.

In general, these cases have higher visibility and raise major policy questions. Hence, more time and energy will be expended on shaping the content of the majority opinion than in relatively trivial disputes.[1175] Studies have shown that cases with more citations carry more weight.[1176] Therefore, it is hypothesised that citation density is pushed upwards by the presence of one of the salience indicators, in particular when: (1) the case has been covered in the media; (2) a large or diverse group of litigants participated in the procedure; and (3) the Court has deliberated in plenary session. In addition, it is hypothesised that the BeCC will ground its rulings more strongly in citations when the challenged legislation has been invalidated or modulated.

6.5.2. HYPOTHESES

Firstly, the prominent media coverage of a case may prompt the Court to ground its opinion more strongly in external authorities. When there has been attention for the case during the judicial decision-making procedure, the Court probably anticipates that the ruling will also be under public scrutiny. Hence, underpinning the ruling more carefully would allow the news media to portray the Court's decision closer to how the Court would like it portrayed.[1177] Another reason to expect more citations in media-covered cases is that many of these cases relate to politically controversial issues. One can expect that the Court would have a special concern for legitimating such rulings.[1178] To increase the chances of compliance, an important tactic may be to support the judgment with a reasoning that hides its judicial discretion.[1179] Courts may try to avoid taking a stand on a sensitive issue by taking refuge in external authority sources, for example by referencing international (case) law or scientific studies.[1180] For these reasons, the first hypothesis is that more media coverage pushes citation levels upwards.

1175 L Epstein and JA Segal, 'Measuring Issue Salience' (2000) 44 Amercian Journal of Political Science, 66; and TS Clark et al., 'Measuring the Political Salience of Supreme Court Cases' (2015) 3 Journal of Law and Courts, 37, 59.

1176 FB Cross et al., 'Citations in the U.S. Supreme Court: an Empirical Study of their Use and Significance' (2010) 2 University of Illinois Law Review, 489, 519; and DJ Walsh, 'On the Meaning and Pattern of Legal Citations: Evidence from State Wrongful Discharge Precedent Cases' (1997) 31 Law & Society Review, 337.

1177 RC Black et al., *US Supreme Court Opinions and Their Audiences* (Cambridge University Press 2016), 38.

1178 FB Cross et al., 'Citations in the U.S. Supreme Court: an Empirical Study of their Use and Significance' (2010) 2 University of Illinois Law Review, 489, 543.

1179 S Dothan, *Reputation and Judicial Tactics* (Cambridge 2015), 25–6.

1180 P Popelier, 'The Belgian Constitutional Court: Guardian of Consensus Democracy or Venue for Deliberation?' in A Alen et al., *Liber Amicorum Marc Bossuyt* (Intersentia 2013), 496.

Hypothesis 1: The BeCC will cite more authorities when a case has been covered by the news media prior to the decision.

Next, the involvement of a large and diverse group of litigants may equally result in a higher citation density. First, more participation indicates that the case is more difficult or troublesome than others, hence requiring a more extensive search for, and thus display of, authorities.[1181] Also, the amount and variety of information for consideration and analysis tend to increase when more litigants participate in the procedure. This would expose the judges to a broader range of rationales for each possible outcome, requiring a more fully elaborate discussion. The Court is expected to address all arguments brought forward in the review procedure. Hence, it is hypothesised that more participation results in judgments that are underpinned with more citations of external authorities.

Hypothesis 2: The BeCC will cite more authorities when a large and/or diverse group of litigants participates in the review procedure.

Further, the handling of the case in plenary session can push citation levels upward. As mentioned before, judges display higher levels of engagement with a topic that is important to them than when it is not. In particular, research has shown that more intra-court bargaining occurs in salient cases.[1182] Moreover, when the BeCC deliberates in plenary session, the double parity rule is strictly applied. Hence, a compromise needs to be found between all sub-groups within the Court (Dutch-speaking and French-speaking judges, former politicians and legal experts). In order to reach a majority opinion, the judges must win the support of their colleagues. To do so, they can employ different tactics including persuasion by information and arguments.[1183] While arguing with each other, judges set out alternatives, elaborate on their potential consequences and discuss their criteria of validity.[1184] The judges can rely on external authorities to convince each other to follow their lead. If so, these internal discussions may push citation density upwards. Research on the US Supreme Court has shown that the more heterogeneous the group of judges, the more citations are used.[1185] Therefore, it is hypothesised that rulings

1181 P Harris, 'Difficult Cases and the Display of Authority' (1985) 1 Journal of Law, Economics and Organization, 209, 213.

1182 L Epstein and JA Segal, 'Measuring Issue Salience' (2000) 44 Amercian Journal of Political Science, 66; TS Clark et al., 'Measuring the Political Salience of Supreme Court Cases' (2015) 3 Journal of Law and Courts, 37, 66.

1183 JB Grossman and RS Wells, 'Constitutional Law and Judicial Policy Making' (John Wiley & Sons 1972), 235.

1184 LA Kornhauser and LG Sager, 'Unpacking the Court' (1986) 96 Yale Law Journal, 82, 101.

1185 FB Cross et al., 'Citations in the U.S. Supreme Court: an Empirical Study of their Use and Significance' (2010) 2 University of Illinois Law Review, 489, 551.

that were produced by the Court in plenary session will be documented with more citations.

Hypothesis 3: The BeCC will cite more authorities when it deliberates on the case in plenary session.

Finally, stronger justification may be needed in cases where the Court denounces the legislator's choices. In particular, more citations can be expected when the Court proclaims a simple or modulated declaration of unconstitutionality (from now on: invalidation or modulation, see chapter 5). These rulings can be defined as 'legally salient' because they influence the development of the law, regardless of whether or not they are known to the public.[1186] Because they are more likely to be subject to criticism, this would make the Court more concerned to legitimatise them.[1187] In particular, when anticipating pushback from political actors, courts are more inclined to signal that the decision was compelled by external authorities rather than ideological reasons.[1188] If not, judges may risk being perceived as agents of a political minority trying to impose its policy preferences on democratically elected legislators. In addition, explaining why legislation is found (un)constitutional allows the Court's audience to comprehend the outcome and respond accordingly.[1189] Also, the more clearly the Court enunciates its opinion and the implications that should follow, the easier it is to monitor whether the legislator has complied with the ruling.[1190] Hence, more transparency makes it more difficult for the legislator to evade a decision.[1191] For these reasons, judgments in

1186 TA Collins and CA Cooper, 'Case Salience and Media Coverage of Supreme Court Decisions: Toward a New Measure' (2012) 65 Political Research Quartely, 396; and TS Clark et al., 'Measuring the Political Salience of Supreme Court Cases' (2015) 3 Journal of Law and Courts, 37.

1187 DJ Walsh, 'On the Meaning and Pattern of Legal Citations: Evidence from State Wrongful Discharge Precedent Cases' (1997) 31 Law & Society Review, 362; FB Cross et al., 'Citations in the U.S. Supreme Court: an Empirical Study of their Use and Significance' (2010) 2 University of Illinois Law Review, 489, 541–3; and Y Lupu and E Voeten, 'Precedent in International Courts: A Network Analysis of Case Citations by the European Court of Human Rights' (2012) British Journal of Political Science 1, 11.

1188 See FB Cross et al., ibid., 489, 528. These authors argue that citations should therefore be interpreted as a 'mask' behind which the court hides the true basis of the decision.

1189 I Nielsen and R Smyth, 'One Hundred Years of Citation of Authority on the Supreme Court of New South Wales' (2008) 31 University of New South Wales Law Journal, 189: "a fourth reason for citing authority, and in particular secondary authority, is to critise the development of the law or make recommendations to parliament for a law reform."

1190 RC Black et al., *US Supreme Court Opinions and their Audiences* (Cambridge University Press 2016), 11.

1191 G Vanberg, *The Politics of Constitutional Review in Germany* (Cambridge University Press 2005), 48–9.

which the Court (partially) invalidates or modulates legislation are considered candidates for more citations.

Hypothesis 4: The BeCC will cite more authorities when it (partially) invalidates or modulates the challenged legislation.

6.5.3. OPERATIONALISATION

To test these hypotheses, a Poisson model is estimated with citation density as the dependent variable. Poisson regression is an accurate model when the dependent variable is a count variable which does not have an overly dispersed distribution (see figure 6.7).[1192] As explanatory variables, the model includes each of the salience indicators (see chapter 4), a variable tracking the case outcome as well as two control variables. The case outcome variable has four categories, in particular for when no violation is found (0) or when the ruling includes a modulation (1), invalidation (2) or both (3). The control variables are the number of pleas - meaning a point of criticism - that were raised by the litigants and the type of procedure. The number of pleas may affect the Court's citation practice because the BeCC is, in principle, inclined to respond to each of these points raised by the litigants. In this sense, the number of pleas dealt with by the Court is a reasonable proxy for the length of the ruling.[1193] The type of procedure was also added as a control variable because the establishment of violation has more far-reaching consequences in an annulment than in a preliminary procedure. In particular, annulled legislation is retroactively removed from the legal order, while preliminary outcomes do not have the same *erga omnes* effect. Hence, the BeCC may feel inclined to justify annulment outcomes more thoroughly.

Since citation density has evolved over time (see figure 6.1), a multilevel Poisson model was also estimated to control for the year in which the case could be situated (1985–2015, n=31). However, since the intra-class correlation (ICC) was very low (0.0637) and the direction and size of the effects were very similar, the simpler model can be reported.[1194]

1192 The mean of citation density is 1.52, and variance is 0.942. Hence, there is no over-dispersion (in that case, a negative binomial regression would have been more appropriate).

1193 These pleas are discussed in the 'B-part' of the ruling (the reason-giving of the Court itself). The judgments also include an A-part with an overview of the litigants' arguments, but the section may vary in length in a way that is unrelated to the Court's reason-giving. Moreover, only authorities cited in the B-part were coded.

1194 The variation of the year level (VAR1) was 0.064 and the variation of the individual level (VAR2) 0.942. ICC was calculated as follows: VAR1 / (VAR1 + VAR2).

6.5.4. RESULTS

Table 6.4. Citation density – model effects (* = p<0.001; ** = p<0.01; * = p<0.05)**

	MODEL 1		MODEL 2		MODEL 3		MODEL 4		MODEL 5		FULL MODEL 6	
	B (standard error)	Exp (B)	B (standard error)	Exp (B)	B (standard error)	Exp (B)	B (standard error)	Exp (B)	B (standard error)	Exp (B)	B (standard error)	Exp (B)
Intercept	0.394*** (0.0152)	1.483	0.274*** (0.0196)	1.315	0.363*** (0.0286)	1.438	0.371*** (0.0191)	1.448	0.206*** (0.0336)	1.229	0.164*** (0.0366)	1.179
Explanatory Variables												
* **Media attention**												
– No articles (REF)	/	/	/	/	/	/	/	/	/	/	/	/
– 1–5 articles	0.211*** (0.0574)	1.235							0.076 (0.0590)	1.078	0.032 (0.0604)	1.033
– >5 articles	0.509*** (0.0836)	1.663							0.232 ** (0.0873)	1.261	0.182* (0.0881)	1.200
***Plenary session** (REF=0)			0.351*** (0.0290)	1.420					0.295 *** (0.0305)	1.343	0.280 *** (0.0307)	1.323
* **Participation diversity**												
– One type of litigant involved (REF)	/	/	/	/	/	/	/	/	/	/	/	/
– Only referring judge (preliminary procedures)					0.062 (0.0536)	1.064			0.085 (0.0542)	1.088	0.109 (0.0562)	1.115
– 2 types of litigants involved					0.081* (0.0338)	1.094			0.053 (0.0340)	1.054	0.036 (0.0343)	1.037
– >2 types of litigants involved					0.192*** (0.05)	1.212			0.136** (0.0507)	1.146	0.086 (0.0517)	1.090

***Involvement of individuals**												
– No individual involved (REF)	/	/	/	/	/	/	/	/	/	/	/	/
– 1–5 individuals involved					−0.029 (0.0333)	0.972			0.001 (0.0336)	1.001	0.021 (0.0349)	1.021
– >5 individuals involved					0.273*** (0.0549)	1.314			0.226*** (0.0555)	1.253	0.145* (0.0579)	1.155
***Violation found**												
– No violation found (REF)	/	/	/	/	/	/	/	/	/	/	/	/
– (partial) modulation							0.153*** (0.0356)	1.165	0.103** (0.0363)	1.109	0.086* (0.0367)	1.090
– (partial) invalidation							0.010 (0.0408)	1.011	−0.036 (0.0411)	0.965	−0.037 (0.0415)	0.964
– (partial) modulation *and* invalidation							0.525*** (0.0816)	1.689	0.289*** (0.0843)	1.335	0.078 (0.0901)	1.082
Control Variables												
***Type of procedure** (REF= preliminary procedure)											0.019 (0.0377)	1.019
***Number of pleas**											0.025*** (0.0035)	1.026
Goodness of fit												
Deviance	2059.714 (0.656)		1958.831 (0.623)		2045.884 (0.652)		2052.478 (0.653)		1888.694 (0.603)		1843.020 (0.589)	
Pearson Chi Square	1886.068 (0.600)		1749.114 (0.557)		1872.968 (0.597)		1874.262 (0.597)		1672.488 (0.534)		1621.664 (0.518)	
Likelihood ratio-square	43.005***		143.888***		56.835***		50.241***		214.024***		259.699***	

The 'goodness of fit' demonstrates that all models accurately estimate the effects of the explanatory and control variables, but that the full model (including all variables) fits the data best. In principle, the intercept equals the citation density when all other variables in the model are evaluated at zero. However, in both models, there are no cases that meet that condition and, therefore, the intercept loses it practical meaning. The other parameter estimates show the effect size of the independent variables on citation density, when all other variables are held constant. For each model, the first column shows the logs of the expected increase. However, to facilitate the interpretation of the estimates, a second column with exponential estimates was added. These numbers indicate the multiplication of citation density when a certain independent variable is present rather than absent. Overall, the hypotheses on the relation between case salience and citation practices are strongly supported by the data, while the findings concerning the case outcome are somewhat inconsistent.

6.5.4.1. *Case Salience*

Table 6.5. The average percentage of citations of the different types of authorities, in relation to the categories of salience indicators

CITATIONS OF:	Overall mean	Media attention			Plenary session		Participation diversity				Group of individuals		
		0	*1-5*	*>5*	*no*	*yes*	*1*	*0*	*2*	*3*	*0*	*1-5*	*>5*
Precedents	25	25	25	35	22	31	22	34	27	27	26	23	34
Court of Cassation	10	10	8	7	8	13	9	14	10	10	9	11	6
Administrative Judiciary	5	3	2	2	2	4	2	0	5	8	2	3	5
ECJ case law	5	4	9	18	2	9	4	4	5	9	6	3	10
ECtHR case law	10	10	17	35	5	20	11	11	10	10	9	10	20
Parliamentary preparatory documents	85	85	93	97	83	89	85	84	87	87	85	85	94
Political agreements	3	2	6	12	2	4	2	0	4	7	3	2	12
Advisory opinions Council of State	8	7	15	27	5	12	7	5	8	15	8	7	16
Scientific evidence	2	2	5	13	1	4	2	1	2	6	3	2	7

First, the results demonstrate that citation density increases in line with the extent of news coverage a case has received prior to the ruling. In particular, when no attention has been given, the average citation density is 1.5. This increases slightly to 1.8 when the case received some attention (1–5 journal articles), and more strongly to an average of 2.5 when the case has been intensively covered by the news media (>5). Although the effect of a little news media attention becomes insignificant once other factors are taken into account, extensive coverage continues to push citation density upwards in the full model. Hence, even within groups of cases in which the same number of pleas were raised, those that received extensive media attention are referenced with 20% more citations. In chapter 4, an in-depth analysis of media coverage demonstrated that newspaper journalists are drawn to controversial or politically salient cases with a potential far-reaching impact. Hence, this result confirms the hypothesis that the Court uses citations of authorities as a means to legitimate these decisions for its audience.

When looking into the relation between media coverage and the different types of citations, the findings show that the Court increasingly relies on *all* authorities, except for national case law. This may be explained by the fact that the latter citations occur more frequently in preliminary judgments, while the news media are drawn to annulment procedures.[1195]

Further, the news media's propensity to cover politically controversial cases is reflected in the Court's case law. In particular, in intensively covered cases, the Court refers four times more to political agreements. An example is case no 57/2014,[1196] related to a special appointment procedure for mayors in six 'suburb communities' around Brussels. Although these communities are part of the Flemish territory, many of their citizens (and political candidates) are French-speaking. The special procedure was introduced to end continuing conflicts related to the appointment of French-speaking mayors in these suburbs. In the parliamentary preparatory documents, the legislator emphasised that the challenged provision stemmed from the search for a balance between the interests of the different linguistic communities in Belgium, and was necessary to ensure the political peace.[1197] Yet several politicians from a Flemish political party disagreed and initiated an annulment procedure against the provision. The news media reported that the Court was now called upon to judge in this politically delicate matter.[1198] In the ruling, the Court took over the legislator's arguments, with reference to the political agreement on

---

1195 See *supra*, chapter 4, section 4.3.1.

1196 BeCC case no 57/2014, 3 April 2014.

1197 See the legislative proposition introducing the challenged provision: *Parl Doc* Senate 2011–2012, no 5-1565/1.

1198 For example: De Standaard, 4 May 2013, "*Raad van State danst rond randburgemeesters. Grondwettelijk Hof moet advies uitbrengen*"; and La Libre Belgique, 6 May 2013, "*Les bourgmestres réfractaires devant la Cour constitutionnelle?*".

the 2011 state reform which had resulted in the adoption of the challenged provision.[1199] The Court additionally argued that the introduction of the new procedure should be understood as an integral part of the choices made by the *constitutional* legislator, making the Court incompetent to review the provision against the Constitution. As a result, all pleas were rejected.

In addition, the data suggests that more media attention stimulates the Court to refer to scientific evidence if it is relevant to the case. An example is case no 7/2012,[1200] in which the Court reviewed a Flemish decree regulating the schooling system for Dutch-speaking students in Brussels. Because these students generally have more difficulties finding a school in Brussels, where the majority of citizens are French-speaking, the Flemish legislator introduced a system to preserve a percentage (55%) of the school capacity for the Dutch-speaking students.[1201] However, this meant that less capacity remained for other foreign students who would have to apply at a French-speaking school. Hence, the provision could result in an over-population of the latter schools and create a political conflict between the different linguistic communities. The French-speaking community initiated an annulment procedure, to which the news media paid considerable attention.[1202] One of its arguments was that the preserved capacity of 55% was in excess of demand and therefore discriminatory. Yet the Court found that numerical evidence could demonstrate the real need for the provision.[1203] Importantly, this evidence was brought forward by the Flemish legislator at the explicit request of the Court itself. This search for external authority may be understood as a judicial strategy to legitimatise the decision without upsetting sensitive political interests.

Second, the results show that citation density is strongly related to the extent to which the case is perceived as salient by the judges themselves. In particular, it pushes the average citation density to 1.9 (vs 1.3). Moreover, panel size is related to citation density independently of the other considerations, such as the extent of news media attention or the number of pleas raised by the litigants. In particular, the full model shows that a plenary session is most strongly related (an increase of 33%) to citation density. These findings suggest that the judicial

1199 In addition to the political agreement (B.6.5) and parliamentary preparatory documents, the Court also referred to the advisory opinion of the Council of State (B.6.3) and precedents (B.6.6): citation density=4.

1200 BeCC case no 7/2012, 18 January 2002.

1201 See the justification underlying the amendment that introduced the challenged provision: *Parl Doc* Flemish Parliament, 2009–2010, no 526/2, 33.

1202 For example: De Standaard, 7 March 2011, "*Schoolstrijd in Brussel. Franstalige politici willen migranten verschuiven naar Vlaamse scholen*"; and Le Soir, 8 March 2011, "*Enseignement. Pas tous égaux devant l'école? Décret flamand: recours en annulation*".

1203 BeCC case no 7/2012, 18 January 2002, B.21.3-4. In the ruling, the Court also referred to parliamentary preparatory documents (citation density 2).

perception of case salience, whether this is induced by political or legal reasons, affects how much effort the judges put into producing a qualitative decision. In addition, this result may be a reflection of a more elaborate internal deliberation process in which the judges rely on external authorities to persuade each other.

More specifically, a deliberation in plenary session results in more citations of *all* types of authorities, but especially of ECtHR case law. Above, it has been noted that more plenary sessions were registered when the Court reviewed migration law, and also when the litigants invoked EU law and the ECHR.[1204] Hence, the findings demonstrate that this is equally reflected in the Court's citation patterns. An example of a case where the Court, in plenary session, extensively referenced its decision without the case being covered in the news media or the involvement of a large, diverse group of litigants is case no 1/2014.[1205] In this case, the Court looked into the (lack of) appeal possibilities for refugees from 'secure countries' against the decision not to offer them asylum. In principle, a full appeal suspends the previous decision and allows the appeal judge to look into new elements. Yet, in order to accelerate the procedure, the legislator introduced a more limited appeal procedure for these specific refugees.[1206] Building on both ECtHR and ECJ case law, the Court stated that the criterion for differentiation (nationality) was not relevant and that the provision was disproportionate to the legislative purpose.[1207] The challenged provision was partly invalidated. In sum, although the case was not particularly controversial, its legal complexity did prompt some of the judges to request a plenary session and resulted in a more densely referenced ruling.

Finally, the findings with regard to participation variables are twofold. On the one hand, while the involvement of individuals *as such* does not increase citation density, it does when a large group of individuals (>5) participated. In particular, this results in an increase from 1.5 to 2 cited authorities. Again, the result remains positive and significant, even when all other variables are included in the model. The full model shows that 16% more authorities are cited when a large group of individuals is involved.

With regard to the type of cited authorities, the results are almost parallel to the relation with media coverage. In particular, citations of national case law are limited and the numbers of all other types of authorities increase. For instance, in case no 189/2005,[1208] the Court reviewed a Walloon decree related to noise

---

1204 See *supra*, chapter 4, section 4.5.2.

1205 BeCC case no 1/2014, 16 January 2014.

1206 *Parl Doc* Senate 2011–2012, 5-1364/3, 2.

1207 BeCC case no 1/2014, 16 January 2014, B.11-12. In this ruling, the Court also cited parliamentary preparatory documents, a precedent, and case law of the administrative judiciary (citation density 5).

1208 BeCC case no 189/2005, 14 December 2005.

pollution caused by night flights, challenged by a group of citizens living in the vicinity of the airport (together with an association defending their interests). The litigants argued that the new regulations would decrease their quality of life and, secondly, that this was not adequately compensated by other measures. In order to strengthen their claim, they built their memoranda on scientific studies, ECtHR case law and precedents. Although their claim was rejected, the Court provided an answer for each of the points raised by the litigants, with reference to the same external authorities.[1209] In sum, although the news media did not show any interest in the case, the fact that the decree could have far-reaching consequences for a large group of citizens indirectly resulted in an elaborately documented ruling.

On the other hand, the relation between more diversity within the groups of participants – when other categories of participants (such as interest groups, companies) are added – and citation density seems to be more limited. For each additional type of litigant involved in the procedure, citation density increases slightly.[1210] But, while in the models without control variables a significant result for the participation of a more diverse group (>2) of litigants is shown, the significance of the result disappears in the full model. The results reveal, however, that the effect of litigant diversity may be intertwined with the effect of the number of pleas. More specifically, a more diverse group of litigants will try to challenge legislation on more grounds (increasing the number of pleas) which, in turn, increases citation density.[1211] With each additional plea that is raised, citation density increases by 3%. This is consistent with findings on Anglo-American courts, where citation density was found to be linked to the length of the ruling.[1212] With regard to the type of authority cited, the findings indicate that the Court uses more citations of precedents and the case law of the Court of Cassation when addressing the referring judge in a preliminary ruling (reference category). Considering that preliminary questions often deal with the interpretation of an existing legal provision, it makes sense that the BeCC relies on the Court of Cassation's case law to explain how that provision should be applied in practice. Cases that attract a diverse group of litigants (>2) are underpinned with more citations to all types of authorities except, surprisingly, ECtHR case law.

1209 In particular, the Court cited parliamentary preparatory documents, a precedent, case law of the ECtHR and scientific evidence (citation density 4).

1210 In particular, 1=1.43; 2=1.59; 3=1.8; 4=1.83; 5=2. Only when participation diversity was at its maximum (one case, seven types of litigants involved, in particular BeCC case no 110/1999, 14 October 1999) does citation density decrease again (=1).

1211 There is a positive correlation between participation rate and the number of pleas (Phi 0.214***).

1212 I Nielsen and R Smyth, 'One Hundred Years of Citation of Authority on the Supreme Court of New South Wales' (2008) 31 University of New South Wales Law Journal, 189, 199.

Figure 6.8. Citation density in relation to case salience

In addition to understanding the results concerning the separate salience indicators, it is enlightening to visualise the relation between aggregated case salience and citation density. In particular, as demonstrated by figure 6.8, there is a sustained increase in the average number of different cited authorities from non-salient to highly salient cases. In comparison with an average ruling, highly salient cases are documented with more citations of advisory opinions of the Council of State (x2), ECJ and ECtHR case law (x3), political agreements (x5) and scientific evidence (x8).

First, the BeCC seems more likely to back its decision with a reference to the advisory opinion of the Council of State when the case's importance increases. The results show that several (highly) salient cases were actually built on the existence of a sceptical opinion of the Council of State. Hence, the origin of this reference is not the Court's own investigation, but rather the attention given to the opinion by the news media and/or litigants. One example is the school inspection case,[1213] where the initiating parties built on several advisory opinions on previous state reforms to argue that the challenged legislation conflicted with the competence allocating rules.[1214] The Court, taking over this reasoning, partly annulled the challenged provisions.[1215] Another example of a moderately salient case is the fiscal amnesty case,[1216] where the news media reported on the sceptical

1213 BeCC case no 124/2010, 28 October 2010.

1214 *Parl Doc* Chamber 1977–1978, no 461/25 and *Parl Doc* Senate 1979–1980, no 434/40. The Court also cited the advisory opinion on the challenged legislation (*Parl Doc* Flemish Parliament 2006–2007, no 1163/2).

1215 BeCC case no 124/2010, 28 October 2010, B.18.5, B.26.5. The Court equally referred to parliamentary preparatory documents and a political agreement (citation density 3).

1216 BeCC case no 72/2005, 20 April 2005.

advisory opinion of the Council of State.[1217] In their memoranda, the litigants argued that the legislation did not respond effectively to the points of criticism raised. Yet the Court disagreed and declared the legislation constitutional.[1218] Finally, the citation may also originate from arguments brought forward by the defending party. For example, in the weapon regulation case,[1219] the federal legislator stated that the Council of State had acknowledged its competence to regulate the matter, which was confirmed by the BeCC.[1220]

Next, more citations to international and supranational case law were registered in highly salient cases. The findings indicate that these references to ECtHR or ECJ case law always resulted from the invocation of the ECHR or EU law by one of the litigants.[1221] For instance, in case no 90/94,[1222] a forerunner of the famous *BHV* case, the litigants objected that French-speaking citizens living in the BHV constituency who were elected as representatives in the Flemish Parliament were obliged to their take their oath in Dutch. In addition to arguing that this situation was discriminatory, they invoked article 3 of the first protocol of the ECHR relating to the right to democratic representation. Yet, as stated first by the defending party,[1223] and confirmed by the BeCC,[1224] the ECtHR does not consider this obligation contrary to the invoked article 3. The challenged provision was declared constitutional. Another example is the tobacco advertising case, where the litigants argued that the ban on such advertising was contrary to the 'free movement of goods' within the European Union. The Court answered that, as confirmed by ECJ case law,[1225] the prohibition on tobacco advertising does not conflict with European law because the measure aimed to protect public health.[1226]

1217 Financieel Ekonomische Tijd, 11 October 2003, *"Raad van State ziet graten in fiscale amnestie. Wetsontwerp loopt voor Arbitragehof risico op vernietiging"*; De Standaard, 19 December 2003, *"Regering verwerpt kritiek Raad van State op fiscale amnestie"*.

1218 BeCC case no 72/2005, 20 April 2005, B.9.2-3. The Court equally referred to parliamentary preparatory documents (citation density 2).

1219 BeCC case no 154/2007, 19 December 2007. See section 4.5.

1220 Ibid., B.18.2. The Court equally referred to parliamentary preparatory documents, the case law of the ECtHR and the Court of Cassation, and precedents (citation density 5).

1221 One exception is BeCC case no 141/2013. Yet, although the litigants did not request to review against EU law, they did refer to ECJ case law to underpin their challenge.

1222 BeCC case no 90/94, 22 December 1994.

1223 Ibid., A.11.2.

1224 Ibid., B.4.20, referring to ECtHR case no 9267/81, *Mathieu-Mohin and Clerfayt v Belgium*, 2 March 1987, point 57. In addition, the Court also referred to a political agreement (citation density 2).

1225 The Court did not refer to a specific case, but almost literally took over the reasoning of the defending party, who cited in their memorandum ECJ C-267/91 and C-268/91, 24 November 1993, (Keck and Mithouard). The Court also referred to preparatory parliamentary documents (citation density 2).

1226 BeCC case no 102/1999, 30 September 1999.

As discussed in the descriptive analysis, the Court cited ECtHR case law and ECJ case law in only 37% and 42%, respectively, of the cases where it reviewed against the ECHR and EU law. Although this relation has grown stronger over the years, it is remarkable that, in (some very old) highly salient cases, the Court *always* explicitly backs it decision with the case law of the ECtHR or ECJ. This suggests that the Court is more inclined to demonstrate that its decision is authorised by higher sources of law when it anticipates that the case outcome may have far-reaching (political) consequences. Importantly, courts generally do not want to be perceived as political actors but as institutions bound by the law. Hence, referencing the ruling with these authorities can be understood as a strategy to depoliticise the judicial decision.

Further, the Court's propensity to cite political agreements in highly salient cases reflects the politically controversial nature of these cases. It shows that the Court is willing to explicitly stress either the balanced character of the challenged legislation or the threat posed to a previously found political balance. The latter situation can be illustrated by the above-mentioned school inspection case, where the Court found that the challenged provisions conflicted with previously established agreements between politicians from the Dutch-speaking and French-speaking communities.[1227] An example of the first situation can be found in the aforementioned case no 96/2014, related to the division of the BHV judicial district.[1228] The challenged provisions were part of a larger political compromise on the sixth state reform. The Court confirmed that the challenged provisions contributed to the legitimate objective of maintaining political peace.[1229] Although it was acknowledged that this purpose cannot justify any unequal treatment, in particular when it is not an essential element of the reform, the Court declared the majority of the challenged provisions constitutional.[1230] Hence, this ruling reflects a judicial decision-making process centred on protecting the agreement established at the political level.

Finally, there is a very sharp increase of citations of scientific evidence in highly salient cases. These citations may serve to prove that the legislator has made a reasonable decision, but can also be used to establish a violation. An example of the first situation is the case related to the French-speaking Community's school

---

1227 BeCC case no 124/2010, 28 October 2010, for example B.16.1.

1228 BeCC case no 96/2014, 30 June 2014. See *supra*, section 5.5.4.2.

1229 Ibid., B.49. In addition to a political agreement, the Court also cited parliamentary preparatory documents, case law of the ECJ and the advisory opinion of the Council of State (citation density 4).

1230 Many of the challenged provisions were considered 'essential elements' of the state reform, approved by the *constitutional* legislator, making the Court incompetent to review them against the Constitution (e.g. B.63.1-2, B.109.2). Also, non-essential elements were considered justified: see B.80.3-4 (even though the challenged provision could result in certain practical problems).

enrolment policy.[1231] The challenged provision introduced an enrolment system based on an 'index number', determined by factors such as the distance between the student's residence and the school and his or her socio-economic situation. The French-speaking Community argued that the measurement for this last factor was based on an academic study. Nonetheless, the litigants questioned legislator's competence to estimate the socio-economic situation of students who lived in the Flemish Region but who wanted to enrol in a school in the French-speaking Community. The Court, however, simply stated that the study allowed the legislator to calculate the socio-economic situation for students living anywhere in Belgium, and the plea was rejected.[1232] The second situation can be illustrated by the smoking ban case,[1233] in which the litigants challenged the unequal treatment of bars where food was served and those where it wasn't. To protect the second category of bars against a profit loss, the legislator had provided an exemption to the immediate application of the ban. Yet the litigants presented to the Court scientific evidence that undermined the legislator's assumption that the smoking ban could inflict economic harm. Rather, because of the ban, these bars would attract other costumers. The Court relied on these studies to establish a violation.[1234] In cases such as these, it seems improbable that the invocation of scientific evidence alone triggered more media attention and more participation. Rather, the results indicate that, notwithstanding the case outcome, the Court is more likely to cite scientific studies when the case's importance increases. As with the references to ECJ and ECtHR case law, this behaviour can be understood as a strategy to depoliticise and at the same time legitimise the judicial outcome.

6.5.4.2. *Case Outcome*

In contrast to the above, the case outcome hypothesis is only partly confirmed by the data. When no violation is found, the Court refers to an average of 1.4 authorities. While the proclamation of a modulation is documented with slightly more citations (1.7), the citation density remains at the same level when the case results in an invalidation (1.5). When the ruling results in both a modulation and invalidation, citation density increases more sharply to 2.5 authorities.

1231 For example, BeCC case no 4/2011, 13 January 2011.

1232 Ibid., B.17.3.

1233 BeCC case no 37/2011, 15 March 2011. For example: De Standaard, 8 December 2009, "*Liga tegen Kanker wil nieuwe rookwet vernietigen*"; La Libre Belgique, 26 January 2010, "*Société. Horeca. Tabac: requête en annulation*"; De Morgen, 26 January 2010, "*Snackproducenten vechten rookverbod aan bij Grondwettelijk Hof*"; and Le Soir, 12 May 2010, "*Horeca sans tabac: risque d'annulation. La Cour constitutionnelle a débouté des entreprises du secteur, qui gardent espoir*".

1234 BeCC case no 37/2011, 15 March 2011, B.8.2.

Table 6.6. The average percentages of citations of the different types of authorities in relation to the case outcome

	Overall mean	Case outcome			
		Acceptation	Modulation	Invalidation	Modulation and invalidation
Precedents	25	23	29	24	43
Court of Cassation	10	9	15	7	14
Administrative Judiciary	5	3	3	2	5
ECJ	5	4	5	5	14
ECtHR	10	9	15	7	14
Parliamentary preparatory documents	85	84	88	88	89
Political agreements	3	3	1	4	5
Advisory opinions Council of State	8	6	9	9	34
Scientific evidence	2	2	2	3	3

In the full model, only the proclamation of a modulation is positively and significantly related to the number of cited authorities. In particular, citation density increases by 9% once the ruling includes a modulated outcome. Yet, it should be noted that this increase is more modest than any of the effects of the salience indicators. As shown in table 6.6, modulated outcomes are documented with more citations of the case law of the Court of Cassation and the ECtHR. The first increase may simply be explained by the fact that preliminary questions more regularly result in a modulation, and that they also include more citations of Court of Cassation case law (see 3.1.4.3.). Hence, in these rulings, the BeCC addresses the referring judge – or any judge who wishes to apply the challenged provision.[1235] Further, as demonstrated in the previous chapter, the Court is more likely to proclaim a modulated outcome in salient cases, rather than bluntly disapprove of the challenged legislation. Combining this result with the finding that salient cases include more citations of ECtHR case law offers an explanation for the second increase.[1236] Hence, both the case outcome and how this is referenced may be a reflection of the Court's strategic behaviour in salient cases.

1235 Some recent examples are: BeCC case no 19/2015, 12 February 2015; and BeCC case no 127/2015, 24 September 2015.

1236 Some recent examples are: BeCC case no 34/2015, 12 March 2015; and BeCC case no 44/2015, 23 April 2015.

Conversely, none of the models indicate that the invalidation of legislation is related to citation density.[1237] At first sight, this is a surprising result. In comparison with a modulated outcome, an invalidation confronts the legislator in a more direct way. In an annulment procedure, such an outcome leads to the retroactive removal of the invalidated provision from the legal order. When the outcome was proclaimed in a preliminary ruling, the judiciary and the administration should declare the invalidated provision inapplicable. Therefore, one would expect that the Court has a stronger incentive to legitimise an invalidation with more citations of authorities. Yet this hypothesis is not supported by the data. Other scholars have also found inconsistent results with regard to the effect of finding a violation. While a study on the US Supreme Court suggested a significant effect,[1238] a similar study on citations by the ECtHR only suggested a very modest and insignificant effect.[1239]

The results for the last outcome category, the proclamation of both an invalidation and modulation, are inconsistent. While both models without the control variables indicate that such a 'double' outcome does push citation density upwards, the result becomes insignificant in the full model. Yet this result should be interpreted in relation to the number of pleas. As mentioned above, citation density increases by 3% for each additional plea raised by the litigants. The results show that 'double' outcomes were registered in cases where far more pleas were invoked.[1240] For this reason, these rulings are generally referenced with more citations of authorities.[1241] However, when comparing rulings in which the same number of pleas were raised, a double outcome is not significantly related to citation density.[1242]

In sum, the results demonstrate the Court's propensity to use more citations when it proclaims a modulated outcome. There are two (parallel) explanations for this result. First, as mentioned above, increased citation density can be understood as an integral part of the Court's strategic behaviour in salient cases. Second, although modulated outcomes do not confront the legislature in the same way as in invalidation, they are also not necessarily more deferential.

1237 An example of a case that resulted in an invalidation, but which was very concisely reasoned, is BeCC case no 44/2014, 13 March 2014. Without referring to one authority, the Court concluded that there was no reasonable justification for the unequal treatment between sexes introduced by the challenged legislation.

1238 FB Cross et al., 'Citations in the U.S. Supreme Court: an Empirical Study of their Use and Significance' (2010) 2 University of Illinois Law Review, 489, 544.

1239 The effect was found to be significant only at the 0.072 level. See Y Lupu and E Voeten, 'Precedent in International Courts: A Network Analysis of Case Citations by the European Court of Human Right' (2012) British Journal of Political Science 1, 25.

1240 In these 65 rulings, an average of 10 pleas were invoked by the litigants, while the overall average number of pleas is 2 (which is also the average for the other case outcome categories).

1241 Some recent examples are: BeCC case no 103/2015, 16 July 2015 (13 pleas, citation density 5); and BeCC case no 152/2015, 29 October 2015 (17 pleas, citation density 4).

1242 For example, BeCC case no 119/2015, 17 September 2015 (14 pleas, citation density 4).

In principle, a modulated outcome does not alter the text of the challenged provision(s) but rather a normative aspect of it.[1243] In some modulations, the Court intervenes in the democratic process by stating that Parliament should repair an infringement, for instance by filling a legislative gap. In other modulations, the Court even states that – without a textual modification – the judiciary and administration should apply the legislation in its modulated sense. Yet it is not evident that they should apply this legislation in a manner that conflicts with its explicit text. Therefore, modulated outcomes are associated with judicial activism,[1244] or even with the violation of the separation of powers principle.[1245] From this perspective, it is less surprising that the Court is more inclined to signal that the decision was compelled by external authorities. If not, the outcome may risk being perceived as a political decision taken by non-democratically elected judges.

6.6. CONCLUSION

While many scholars in civil law countries generally focus on the normative value of the judicial reason-giving requirement, little is known about how courts in these countries actually shape their opinion. Although the set of explicitly cited authorities may only partially reflect the reasoning process that the Court has gone through,[1246] a large 'n-analysis' of citation practices can provide more insight into how judges justify their decisions. In particular, it shows which authorities are considered legitimate, how this has evolved over time, and can explain why some cases are referenced more elaborately than others. As stated at the end of the previous chapter, by studying the case outcome alone, important

---

1243 G Rosoux and F Tulkens, 'Considérations Théoriques et Pratiques sur la Portée des Arrêts de la Cour d'Arbitrage' in V Thiry, B Renauld and JT Debry (eds.), *La Cour d'Arbitrage: un Juge Comme les Autres?* (Éditions du jeune barreau de Liège 2004), 111.

1244 M De Visser, *Constitutional Review in Europe: A Comparative Analysis* (Hart Publishing 2014), 303–4.

1245 AR Brewer-Carias, *Constitutional Courts as Positive Legislators: A Comparative Law Study*, (Cambridge University Press 2011), 38–40.

1246 There is a difference between the process of discovery (where judges are looking for a solution) and of representation (where judges are seeking to convince others that their solution is correct). Not all sources that were consulted will be explicitly cited and some citations might just serve as *ex post* justification without having genuinely contributed to reaching the decision. See M Bobek, *Comparative Reasoning in European Supreme Courts* (Oxford University Press 2013), 222, 225. See also MC Ponthoreau, 'L'Énigme de la Motivation Encore et Toujours l'Éclairage Comparatif' in F Hourquebie and MC Pontoreau (eds.), *La Motivation des Décisions des Cours Suprêmes et Cours Constitutionelles* (Bruylant 2012), 6. Further, a bare citation count does not consider the manner in which the authority was cited: see FB Cross et al., 'Citations in the U.S. Supreme Court: an Empirical Study of their Use and Significance' (2010) 2 University of Illinois Law Review, 489, 521.

aspects of judicial (strategic) behaviour may be missed. By exploring the reason-giving practice of the Belgian Constitutional Court, this chapter aimed to improve our understanding of judicial functioning. Although this study relates to a single court, one can argue that the implications of this analysis extend beyond Belgium. Constitutional courts of other European countries share many of the same institutional characteristics as the BeCC, as well as the requirement to give reasons and the non-unified style of reason-giving. Hence, these results may be of interest to scholars from other European countries.

First, the results show that a large majority of the cases (91%) were documented with a reference to at least one authority. Further, over the years there has been a trend towards citing more authorities. Yet, in terms of which authorities get cited, the BeCC takes a prudent approach. Often, rulings are documented with only one *routine* citation to parliamentary documents. On average, less than half (46.5%) of the Court's rulings contain references to external authorities other than parliamentary documents. However, citation patterns have broadened considerably. In 2015, the proportion of cases that were documented with either no citations or with merely one *routine* citation dropped to 27.5%. Further, the BeCC has an (increasingly) strong preference for citations of judicial decisions, whether they are their own or from other (inter)national courts. This is consistent with studies on Anglo-American courts, which show that they prefer to cite decisions from other judges who speak the same judicial language. This study also confirms the (increasingly) Europe-friendly reputation of the BeCC. In 2015, the proportion of cases with citations of either the ECJ or ECtHR climbed to 38%. However, the BeCC does not follow the global trend of citing decisions of foreign national courts. It has been noticed that this is not uncommon among European courts that already give European (case) law an important role.[1247] Another point of contrast with common law courts is that the BeCC rarely resorts to sources other than traditional legal authorities (such as case law). Citations of information from other sources, such as scientific studies, academic work or advice from expert organisations, are very scarce. The proportion of cases citing these authorities also hardly grew over the years. Old citation habits persist, no doubt, because judges still feel that only legal authorities are legitimate or because they want to avoid criticism.

With regard to variety in citation density, it is apparent that salient cases are documented with more authorities than non-controversial cases. To begin with, a larger panel size, extensive media coverage and the involvement of a large group of individuals increases citation density, independently of case

[1247] M Bobek, *Comparative Reasoning in European Supreme Courts* (Oxford University Press 2013), 195. Bobek states that there is an inverse correlation between the amount of mandatory foreign sources (such as the ECJ and ECtHR) and non-mandatory foreign inspiration.

outcome, the number of pleas and the type of procedure. These findings imply that courts respond to external incentives and that citations serve the purpose of legitimating decisions to a public audience. On the one hand, more citations of political agreements in salient cases reflect their politically controversial nature. On the other hand, the increase in citations of external authorities indicates that the Court looks for ways to show its decision is compelled by these sources, rather than by political motives. In contrast, the results are inconsistent with regard to the relation between citation density and the case outcome. An increase of citation density when the Court invalidates or modulates would serve the purpose of convincing the legislator to repair the established unconstitutionality. Yet, the results indicate that there is only an increase of citations when the Court proclaims a modulation, and the effect size is also more modest than for each of the salience indicators. Hence, a tentative conclusion is that the BeCC references its rulings more strongly when a case is salient, irrespective of the outcome of the case.

Finally, although this chapter contained some profound findings, it also provides a base from which a great deal of further research may proceed. An extended empirical study might include an actual citation count for each separate category of authority or an identification of the citation (e.g. *which* precedent was cited). In particular, identifying the citations would allow researchers to execute a network analysis between them.[1248] Another advance would be to add a qualitative approach that is capable of probing more deeply, such as interviews with court personnel.[1249] Finally, it would be enlightening to test whether the thoroughness of the BeCC's justification effectively stimulates compliance with its decisions.

1248 For example J Staben, 'Colourful Case Law: Citation Analysis of the German Constitutional Court's Jurisprudence', https://verfassungsblog.de/farbenfrohe-rechtsprechung-verweisungsanalyse-von-entscheidungen-des-bundesverfassungsgerichts (26 January 2015). This method focuses on the connection of entities and looks for conclusions regarding the nature of certain networks and potential relations within them. The pictured overall network is created by the decisions depicted as dots and the references as lines connecting the dots.

1249 DS Law and WC Chang, 'The Limits of Global Judicial Dialogue' (2011) 86 Washington Law Review 523, 527.

CHAPTER 7
PROPORTIONALITY ANALYSIS

7.1. INTRODUCTION

In the previous section, the manner in which a constitutional court can strengthen a ruling's justificatory ground by referring to relevant, persuasive authorities was explored. However, a proper use of citations is not the only way to build a clear, convincing reason-giving. In this chapter, the focus is on the structure of the justificatory ground, and in particular on the application of the proportionality analysis as an argumentative framework in fundamental rights adjudication. In short, this framework sets out the conditions for a limitation of a constitutionally protected right to be permissible.[1250] Essentially, the interference with this right should be reasonably justified.[1251] This justification test consists of four stages, exploring whether: (1) the legislation pursues a legitimate goal; (2) there is a causal relation between the provision and the policy goal (suitability stage); (3) the measure infringes fundamental rights no more than necessary to accomplish this goal (necessity stage); and (4) the measure does not have a disproportionately severe effect on the persons to whom it applies (proportionality stage *sensu stricto*).[1252] In principle, each step is assessed cumulatively, and failure of a measure to comply with one of the steps will render the measure unjustified. This four-stage test has become the most prominent method for adjudicating in fundamental rights cases around the world.[1253]

1250 A Barak, *Proportionality: Constitutional Rights and Their Limitations* (Cambridge University Press 2012), 131.

1251 This is the core of the analysis. For a comparative analysis between European continental countries, Canada, the UK, the US and South Africa, see P Yowell, 'Proportionality in United States Constitutional Law' in L Lazarus, C McCrudden and N Bowled (eds.), *Reasoning Rights: Comparative Judicial Engagement* (Hart Publishing 2014).

1252 B Pirker, *Proportionality Analysis and Models of Judicial Review: A Theoretical and Comparative Study* (Europa Law Publishing 2014), 15; and A Barak, *Proportionality: Constitutional Rights and Their Limitations* (Cambridge University Press 2012), 243 and further.

1253 For more information on the emergence of proportionality analysis as a global constitutional standard and judge-made doctrine, see: A Stone Sweet and J Mathews 'Proportionality Balancing and Global Constitutionalism' (2008) 47 Colombia Journal of Transnational Law, 73; and K Möller, 'Constructing the Proportionality Test: An Emerging Global Conversation' in L Lazarus, C McCrudden and N Bowles (eds.), *Reasoning Rights: Comparative Judicial Engagement* (Hart Publishing 2014), 31 and further.

It gives courts the possibility of evaluating the reasonableness of legislation.[1254] Although the review method is not without its critics,[1255] it is usually praised as a way to ensure that legal measures are not excessive in relation to the social problems they are intended to solve.

Importantly, the proportionality analysis leaves considerable room for judicial discretion.[1256] Instead of adhering to strict manifestations of the law, a court can move within the – not so strictly defined – boundaries of the justification test.[1257] Therefore, it is important to understand which factors and processes may influence its application in practice.[1258] Notwithstanding the prominence of the proportionality analysis in constitutional adjudication, there is very little empirical knowledge on its application in practice.[1259] This is partly due to the fact that judicial behaviour studies are usually limited to case outcomes (circumventing the justificatory ground), and partly because many empirical analyses concentrate on the US Supreme Court, a court that does not explicitly integrate the proportionality analysis in its case law. Considering that the test is executed by the BeCC on a regular basis, an empirical analysis can reveal which factors explain the variation in its application between different types of cases.

The plan of this chapter is as follows. First, how courts can use the proportionality analysis as a way to build a clear, convincing justificatory

---

1254 P Popelier and AA Patiño Álvarez, 'Deliberative Practices of Constitutional Courts in Consolidated and Non-Consolidated Democracies' in P Popelier, A Mazmanyan and W Vandenbruwaene (eds.), *The Role of Constitutional Courts in Multilevel Governance* (Intersentia 2013), 215.

1255 The perceived danger is that it may lead to courts assessing which objectives are opportune, putting their own policy preferences in the place of those of the legislative branch. See A Barak, *Proportionality: Constitutional Rights and Their Limitations* (Cambridge University Press 2012), 481 and further. For an extensive overview of critical literature, see N Petersen, *Proportionality and Judicial Activism* (Cambridge University Press 2017), 4–6.

1256 For instance, Belgian scholars have argued that the execution of the proportionality analysis "does not exclude that [...] extra-judicial considerations determine the decisions made." They have added that "anyone who believes that it can be mastered in its entirety and can lead to predictable results when subjected to review is mistaken": M Adams and D Vanheule, 'The Theory and Practice of Constitutional Review in the Civil Law: The Case of Belgium' in LJ Wintgens (ed.), *The Theory and Practice of Legislation* (Ashgate 2005), 213.

1257 S Dothan, *Reputation and Judicial Tactics* (Cambridge 2015), 36.

1258 Therefore, this chapter contributes to a particular line of scholarship which focuses on the way the proportionality test operates (or ought to operate) in practice, in the actual resolution of cases. On this and other lines of research with regard to the proportionality analysis, see K Möller, *The Global Model of Constitutional Rights* (Oxford University Press 2012), 33.

1259 The first sample of empirical evidence in this regard was provided in R Sulitzeany-Kenan, M Kremnitzer and S Alon, 'Facts, Preferences and Doctrine: An Empirical Analysis of the Proportionality Judgment' (2015) 50 Law & Society Review, 348. Yet this study was executed in an abstract, experimental setting and does not analyse the actual application by a particular court. Another recent publication contains a descriptive analysis of the case law of the German, South African and Canadian Constitutional Courts: N Petersen, *Proportionality and Judicial Activism* (Cambridge University Press 2017).

ground for the ruling (7.2.) will be explored. In short, following its sequential structure enhances the transparency and rationality of the decision and can, therefore, stimulate compliance with the outcome. Section 7.3. explains which data were collected to analyse the Court's application of the proportionality analysis. In particular, in each case where the test failed, the manner in which the Court labelled its arguments in order to reach this conclusion has been coded. Following this, two analyses are carried out on the collected data - one with a descriptive and one with an explanatory focus. First, in section 7.4., the registrations for each separate variable are discussed, providing an in-depth qualitative analysis. The focus is on the signals that reach the legislative branch by formulating the proportionality analysis in a particular way. Second, the application of the proportionality analysis is studied from a strategic perspective (7.5.). The main idea is that the Court can employ vaguer language, thus not applying the proportionality to its full extent, as a strategy to protect itself against institutional challenges while striking down a policy to which it objects. Building on other empirical research relating to opinion clarity, a set of five hypotheses is developed. These hypotheses concern the relation between case salience, international human rights law and legislative deficiencies, and the application of the proportionality analysis to establish a violation. A logit model is tested to explore which factors may affect the Court's case law.

7.2. A DELIBERATIVE PERSPECTIVE: A STRUCTURED APPROACH TO THE PROPORTIONALITY ANALYSIS

One of the ideas expressed in the normative framework is that a main source of legitimacy is a justification grounded in arguments that are reasonably acceptable to others, rather than authority. When legislation is challenged before a constitutional court, the proportionality analysis provides a framework to evaluate the justification given by the legislator. At the same time, it can also be used as a method to structure the justificatory ground of the judicial decision.[1260]

Although the test has been accepted globally as a method of constitutional adjudication, there are differences between courts with regard to how they construct the test and the emphasis that they place on the different stages. Some courts apply the test to its full extent, as a structured framework that should be followed in a sequential order, while others approach the four stages as factors

1260 As Matthias Kumm put it, "proportionality based judicial review institutionalizes a right to justification that is connected to a particular conception of legitimate legal authority": M Kumm, 'The Idea of Socratic Contestation and the Right to Justification: The Point of Rights-Based Proportionality Review' (2010) Law and Ethics Human Rights, 142.

to be taken into account in one global test. The latter approach usually ends with the conclusion that 'all things considered' the challenged measures are either constitutional or not.[1261]

While applying the justification test to its full extent should be encouraged from a deliberative perspective, a looser approach provides courts more leeway to strategically formulate an opinion when pushback is expected from the legislative branch. As will be further explored in the descriptive analysis, the BeCC has a more mixed approach, opting to be specific in some cases and vaguer in others. Explaining this variation in the case law of the BeCC will be the main focus of the regression analysis. Yet, before embarking upon the empirical analysis, this section provides an overview of the advantages of the structured approach. This provides the necessary background to evaluate the Court's case law from a deliberative perspective.

First, the proportionality analysis provides a structure which guides judges through their reasoning process. It breaks down the complex question of whether a policy decision is constitutionally legitimate into a series of smaller questions that can be analysed one by one. If properly applied, this ensures that the judicial analysis addresses comprehensively all relevant issues, instead of blending questions that should be addressed separately.[1262] By not skipping ahead to the last stage (proportionality *sensu stricto*) or engaging in a mere broad-brush balancing, fundamental rights receive protection that cannot be "balanced away".[1263] Experimental research has shown that applying the full proportionality analysis reduces the probability that legislation passes the test.[1264] Although the aim of the proportionality analysis should not be to establish more violations, such findings suggest that a structured approach provides more protection for citizens than broad-brush balancing.

Next, the framework functions as a filter reducing the number and quality of reasons to be taken into account.[1265] The structured approach clarifies which information will be relevant at each stage of the enquiry, making the

---

1261 Brems and Lavrysen nominate these approaches 'vertical' and 'horizontal': E Brems and L Lavrysen, 'Don't Use a Sledgehammer to Crack a Nut: Less Restrictive Means in the Case Law of the European Court of Human Rights' (2015) 15 Human Rights Law Review, 139, 141.

1262 K Möller, *The Global Model of Constitutional Rights* (Oxford University Press 2012), 179; and A Barak, *Proportionality: Constitutional Rights and Their Limitations* (Cambridge University Press 2012), 461.

1263 A Baker, 'Proportionality' in H Fenwick (ed.), *Judicial Review* (LexisNexis 2014), 274.

1264 In contrast to an unstructured approach or an approach that only involves the strict balancing test, see R Sulitzeany-Kenan, M Kremnitzer and S Alon, 'Facts, Preferences and Doctrine: An Empirical Analysis of the Proportionality Judgment' (2015) 50 Law & Society Review, 348, 373.

1265 CH Mendes, *Constitutional Courts and Deliberative Democracy* (Oxford University Press 2013), 59.

decision-making procedure more efficient.[1266] In particular, while the 'legitimate purpose' and 'balancing' stages invoke a normative judgment, the 'suitability' and 'necessity' tests mainly entail factual assessment of the means-end relation. Although the framework does not dictate one correct answer,[1267] it obliges the court to operate within reasonable boundaries. Arguments based on personal bias, coercion or other irrational motives cannot be acceptable.[1268] Research has shown that the effect of such legally irrelevant elements is less pronounced under a full application of the proportionality analysis.[1269] Drawing on case-relevant information, rather than being driven by political pressure and personal opinion, is important for ensuring public support for the decision.[1270] When the reason-giving is perceived as a 'cover-up' for the fact that the Court is actually making its decision according to its own beliefs, this would undermine the legitimacy-securing potential of the proportionality analysis.[1271]

Further, the fixed character of the framework enhances transparency on how the decision came about.[1272] In particular, by following the structured approach, it is articulated more precisely why a particular decision is unconstitutional. This assists litigants, the legislator and broader communities to better understand how the Court has reached a conclusion.[1273] By explaining which of the standards has not been met, the Court makes clear whether and how much space is left for legislative response.[1274] Systematic studies on the

1266 B Challenor, 'The Balancing Act: A Case for Structured Proportionality Under the Second Limb of the Lange Test' (2015) 40 The University of Western Australia Law Review, 294; and T-I Harbo, 'The Function of the Proportionality Principle in EU Law' (2010) 16 European Law Journal, 158, 160–1.

1267 A Stone Sweet and J Mathews, 'Proportionality Balancing and Global Constitutionalism' (2008) 47 Colombia Journal of Transnational Law, 73, 77–8.

1268 M Cohen-Eliya and I Porat, 'Proportionality and the Culture of Justification' (2011) 59 American Journal of Comparative Law, 463, 480; and JH Gerards, *Judicial Review in Equal Treatment Cases* (Martinus Nijhoff Publishers 2005), 659.

1269 R Sulitzeany-Kenan, M Kremnitzer and S Alon, 'Facts, Preferences and Doctrine: An Empirical Analysis of the Proportionality Judgment' (2015) 50 Law & Society Review, 348, 377.

1270 See A Stone Sweet and J Mathews, 'Proportionality Balancing and Global Constitutionalism' (2008) 47 Colombia Journal of Transnational Law, 73, 9; and E Brems and L Lavrysen, 'Procedural Justice in Human Rights Adjudication: the European Court of Human Rights' (2013) 35 Human Rights Quarterly, 176, 180.

1271 T-I Harbo, 'The Function of the Proportionality Principle in EU Law' (2010) 16 European Law Journal, 158, 182.

1272 JL Gibson, 'From Simplicity to Complexity: The Development of Theory in the Study of Judicial Behavior' (1983) 5 Political Behavior, 7, 15; JH Gerards, *Judicial Review in Equal Treatment Cases* (Martinus Nijhoff Publishers 2005), 69–70; and A Barak, *Proportionality: Constitutional Rights and Their Limitations* (Cambridge University Press 2012), 462.

1273 C Henckels, *Proportionality and Deference in Investor-State Arbitration* (Cambridge University Press 2015), 27.

1274 The proportionality analysis enables a 'bridge' or 'dialogue' between legislature and judiciary. See A Barak, *Proportionality: Constitutional Rights and Their Limitations* (Cambridge University Press 2012), 466 and further.

implementation of US Supreme Court opinions have suggested that greater precision in the wording of an opinion does indeed promote implementation.[1275] Although the legislature can come up with alternative solutions to advance its own views, following the Court's advice makes it more likely that future challenges are rejected.[1276] Yet this potential for opinion clarity can only be realised when the Court is clear on which elements the test comprises and on the role played by each.[1277] In the long run, a better understanding of the Court's case law increases confidence in the Court as an institution.[1278]

A final reason for courts to apply the full proportionality analysis is that this may prompt the legislator to adopt the same standard of approach and act reasonably.[1279] The proportionality analysis is not specifically designed for implementation by courts, but may serve as a general test for the limitation of rights.[1280] Scholars have argued that the rise of the proportionality analysis can be explained as part of the global spread of a 'culture of justification', a constitutional culture which puts justification at its centre. Moreover, the proportionality analysis is considered the central device for ensuring the flourishing of a culture of justification. The judiciary in particular is identified as an institution that has the tools to impose rationality and reasonableness on other authorities.[1281]

1275 L Baum, 'Implementation of Judicial Decisions' (1976) 4 American Politics Research, 86; and RC Black et al., *US Supreme Court Opinions and Their Audiences* (Cambridge University Press 2016).

1276 C Bateup, 'Expanding the Conversation: American and Canadian Experiences of Constitutional Dialogue in Comparative Perspective' (2006) 44 New York University Public Law and Legal Theory Working Papers, 6, 8–9.

1277 M Elliott, 'Proportionality and Deference: The Importance of a Structured Approach' in C Forsyth et al. (eds.), *Effective Judicial Review: A Cornerstone of Good Governance* (Oxford University Press 2010), 266; and E Brems and L Lavrysen, 'Don't Use a Sledgehammer to Crack a Nut: Less Restrictive Means in the Case Law of the European Court of Human Rights' (2015) 15 Human Rights Law Review, 145.

1278 B Challenor, 'The Balancing Act: A Case for Structured Proportionality Under the Second Limb of the Lange Test' (2015) 40 The University of Western Australia Law Review, 267, 293; and A Barak, *Proportionality: Constitutional Rights and their limitations* (Cambridge University Press 2012), 463.

1279 P Popelier and AA Patiño Álvarez, 'Deliberative Practices of Constitutional Courts in Consolidated and Non-Consolidated Democracies' in P Popelier, A Mazmanyan and W Vandenbruwaene (eds.), *The Role of Constitutional Courts in Multilevel Governance* (Intersentia 2013), 215.

1280 J Rivers, 'Proportionality and Variable Intensity of Review' (2006) 65 Cambridge Law Journal, 174, 182; and A Barak, *Proportionality: Constitutional Rights and Their Limitations* (Cambridge University Press 2012), 462.

1281 M Cohen-Eliya and I Porat, 'Proportionality and the Culture of Justification' (2011) 59 American Journal of Comparative Law, 463.

7.3. ESTABLISHING A VIOLATION ON THE BASIS OF THE PROPORTIONALITY ANALYSIS: CODING THE COURT'S CASE LAW

The vast majority of the cases brought before the BeCC deal with a challenge based on a violation of a constitutionally protected fundamental right.[1282] Moreover, inspired by the case law of the ECtHR,[1283] the Court has adopted the proportionality analysis as a framework to investigate these challenges.[1284] In particular, shortly after the Court received the competence to review legislation against articles 10 and 11 of the Constitution (equality clause), it ruled that "an unequal treatment may be allowed insofar as there is an objective and reasonable justification for the criterion for differentiation."[1285] From 1994 onwards, the BeCC changed the standard formulation to "insofar as the differentiation is rooted in an objective criterion and is reasonable justified."[1286] Hence, the Court's approach consists of two steps.[1287] First, the Court examines whether the differential treatment is based upon an objective criterion and second, whether the measure is justified. As mentioned above, the justification test entails four steps: (1) an examination of the legitimacy of the legislative objective, and (2) the suitability, (3) necessity, and (4) proportionality of the challenged measure in relation to that objective.

To analyse how the Court applies this test in practice, a specific subset of cases is examined: those fundamental rights cases where the proportionality analysis led to the establishment of a violation (n=631).[1288] A descriptive

---

1282 In 86% of the annulment procedures, the BeCC is requested to review against fundamental rights (of which 15% are in conjunction with competence allocating rules). In preliminary procedures, this rises to 92% (of which 0.2% are joined with a competence conflict). Litigants usually invoke articles 10 and 11 of the Constitution (principle of equality), possibly with other constitutionally or internationally protected rights or freedoms.

1283 ECtHR, *the Belgian Linguistic case*, No 6, 23 July 1968. Yet the ECtHR was in turn inspired by the German Constitutional Court. From Germany, the principle of proportionality spread to most other European countries, the ECJ, the ECtHR and a number of jurisdictions outside Europe. See D Grimm, 'Proportionality in Canadian and German Constitutional Jurisprudence' (2007) 57 University of Toronto Law Review, 383, 384.

1284 The proportionality principle can also play a role in the context of a Belgian competence conflict case: see W Van Gerven, 'The Effect of Proportionality on the Actions of Member States of the European Community: National Viewpoints from Continental Europe' in E Ellis (ed.), *The Principle of Proportionality in the Laws of Europe* (Hart Publishing 1999), 53.

1285 BeCC case no 21/89, 13 July 1989.

1286 BeCC case no 1/94, 13 January 1994, B.2.3.

1287 In some cases, the Court adds another preliminary step, investigating whether the categories of persons who are deemed to be treated unequally, are actually comparable (comparability test). Violations found during this step are very rare. See P Popelier, *Procederen voor het Grondwettelijk Hof* (Intersentia 2008), 103–4.

1288 In particular, when one of the pleas resulted in an invalidation, modulated declaration of (un)constitutionality or an extrinsic gap. For similar reasons, as explained in footnote 919, double interpretation outcomes were not included in this list.

and explanatory analysis of this subset can provide particularly interesting perspectives. First, in the descriptive section, the focus is on how the Court communicates with the legislative branch. In the chapter on case outcomes, it has been argued that a legislative response is usually only expected when the Court proclaims an invalidation or modulation – in other words, when a violation has been established. In those cases, the Court can provide assistance on which direction to take by indicating more precisely – with reference to the separate stages – why the proportionality analysis failed. Conversely, when rejecting the challenge, the Court should in principle clear all stages of the sequential proportionality analysis. Second, when establishing a violation, there is a more pronounced conflict between the Court and the parliamentary majority.[1289] When anticipating pushback from the legislative branch, the Court may attenuate the ruling by adapting how it applies the proportionality analysis. This would be in line with the previous findings in chapter 5, which showed that strategic considerations do not necessarily determine *whether* a violation is found, but may affect how the ruling is formulated *if* one is established. In particular, in the majority of the (highly) salient cases, a substantive or temporal modulation is proclaimed. This does not mean that no variation in the application of the proportionality analysis is expected in cases where no violation is established,[1290] but that this is likely to be affected by other dynamics.[1291] In particular, considering that, overall, less resistance is anticipated in these cases,[1292] there is no similar need to use strategies to stimulate the legislator to comply.[1293]

1289 N Petersen, *Proportionality and Judicial Activism* (Cambridge University Press 2017), 10.

1290 Prior research has shown that, in these cases, the BeCC is equally reluctant to ground its decision on a reference to all four stages of the proportionality analysis. See M Adams and D Vanheule, 'The Theory and Practice of Constitutional Review in the Civil Law: The Case of Belgium' in LJ Wintgens (ed.), *The Theory and Practice of Legislation* (Ashgate 2005), 212.

1291 Belgian scholars have already noted that in a number of decisions involving social, fiscal or environmental policy, where no violation was found, the Court has engaged in hardly any proportional assessment. They argue that this applies particularly when the legislation is the expression of a political project on which there is a broad social consensus or which has been difficult to achieve, or where a balance between the linguistic communities is sought. For example: BeCC case no 26/1990, 14 July 1990; M Adams and D Vanheule, 'The Theory and Practice of Constitutional Review in the Civil Law: The Case of Belgium' in LJ Wintgens (ed.), *The Theory and Practice of Legislation* (Ashgate 2005), 212.

1292 Petersen argues that confirming legislation does not pose a 'legitimacy issue' because the legislator is spared: N Petersen, *Proportionality and Judicial Activism* (Cambridge University Press 2017), 95. It should be noted, however, that this argument does not hold when the Court deals with a competence conflict, where governments of different state levels are opposing each other. Yet, the focus in this chapter is on fundamental rights cases.

1293 For instance, Petersen noted that the SACC uses balancing frequently in cases where it did not overturn legislation, while it is extremely reluctant to do so when establishing a violation. As Peterson explains, the court only needs to act prudently in the latter cases, in order to secure its institutional position (which is already weak): N Petersen, *Proportionality and Judicial Activism* (Cambridge University Press 2017), 148, 154.

For each case in this subset of data, one of seven dichotomous variables was coded. An overview can be found in table 7.1. The last column of this table presents the number of cases (n) where each variable was coded and the proportion (%) of the total number of cases in which the proportionality analysis led to the finding of a violation (n=631).[1294]

The first five variables (a–e) refer to situations where the Court explicitly mentioned the stage at which the proportionality analysis found the constitutional violation. In other words, in these cases, the Court was specific on the grounds for establishing the violation. The other two variables (f–g) were coded in cases where the Court only concluded that the legislation was 'not (reasonably) justified' (f) or where it simply stated there was 'discrimination' or a 'violation of articles 10 and 11 of the Constitution' (g). Hence, in contrast to the first five situations, the Court remains vaguer on why a violation was established. Importantly, the collected data reflect the classification that the Court *itself* gave its arguments. Using this classification has the advantage of giving insight into what the Court finds a proper way to formulate its decision. Whether or not the Court has correctly labelled its arguments may be subject to debate.[1295] Yet the focus here is on how the Court uses the proportionality analysis as a method to draft the justificatory ground for its decisions. A more in-depth discussion on these sequential stages follows in the descriptive analysis (7.4.).

Table 7.1. Overview of the variables related to the application of the proportionality analysis

	Dichotomous variables	
Specific	(a) The challenged measure is not objective	4 (1%)
	(b) The legislative objective underlying the challenged measure is not legitimate	0 (0%)
	(c) The challenged measure is not suitable to advance the legislative objective	117 (19%)
	(d) There are less restrictive means to advance the legislative objective	22 (4%)
	(e) The challenged measure is disproportionately harmful	233 (37%)
Vague	(f) Only conclusion: the challenged measure is 'unreasonable'	285 (45%)
	(g) There is 'discrimination' or a 'violation of articles 10 and 11 the Constitution'	48 (8%)

1294 Yet the latter number is lower than the total sum of the registrations for each variable (n=713). On the one hand, the BeCC often treats multiple pleas in one case, making it possible that, for example, it finds some measures to be unsuitable and others unnecessary. On the other hand, the BeCC occasionally finds a measure to be, for example, unnecessary and disproportionate at the same time.

1295 N Petersen, *Proportionality and Judicial Activism* (Cambridge University Press 2017), 101.

7.4. THE COURT'S APPLICATION OF THE STEP-BY-STEP FRAMEWORK: DESCRIPTIVE AND QUALITATIVE ANALYSIS

In what follows, the selected subset of the data is analysed qualitatively. In particular, for each variable mentioned in table 7.1. above, explanations are explored for the (in)frequent occurrence of that particular situation. Although the number of registrations for each variable is somewhat limited for an extensive statistical analysis in this descriptive section, the qualitative approach allows for the development of a more in-depth analysis of the registered cases and to contextualise the results. The findings are illustrated by several examples from the BeCC's case law.

7.4.1. THE OBJECTIVITY OF THE CRITERION FOR DIFFERENTIATION (N=4)

Before engaging in the justification test, the Court evaluates whether the criterion for differentiation is determined by objective facts or by personal or subjective appreciation.[1296] However, in the vast majority of cases, this 'objectivity stage' ends in an approving conclusion saying that 'the criterion for unequal treatment is objective'.[1297] Hence, most constitutional infringements are established in a later phase of the proportionality analysis.

Only on rare occasions has the BeCC explicitly called into question the objectivity of the criterion for unequal treatment (n=4). Of those cases, two relate to the same topic – the harmonisation of labour regulations for 'workmen' and 'service employees'.[1298] The criterion selected by the legislature, the mainly 'manual' or 'intellectual' nature of their work, was dismissed by the Court because it was not considered objective (nor reasonably justifiable).[1299]

1296 J Theunis, 'Het Gelijkheidsbeginsel' in A Alen et al., *Doorwerking publiekrecht in het privaatrecht* (Mys&Breesch 1997), 138. This step is usually not mentioned in literature on the proportionality analysis: see P Yowell, 'Proportionality in United States Constitutional Law' in L Lazarus, C McCrudden and N Bowles (eds.), *Reasoning Rights: Comparative Judicial Engagement* (Hart Publishing 2014), 90: "Many formal statements of the European proportionality inquiry follow the four-step template described above: (1) legitimacy, (2) suitability, (3) necessity, and (4) balancing".

1297 Recent examples of cases where the measure was found objective, but nonetheless irrelevant and therefore declared unconstitutional include: BeCC case no 112/2016, 14 July 2016, B.7-8; and BeCC case no 148/2016, 24 November 2016, B.7.

1298 "*Arbeiders en bedienden*".

1299 See: BeCC case no 2011/125, 7 July 2011, B.3.1; and BeCC case no 2014/187, 18 December 2014, B.5. The first case where the Court formulated this criticism was BeCC case no 56/93, 1 July 1993, B.6.2.1, but no violation was established in this case.

In addition, two other cases were coded in this category: one relating to company law[1300] and another one relating to social security law.[1301] In both cases, the Court questioned not only the objectivity of the challenged measure, but also its suitability.[1302] Hence, in none of the above cases did the BeCC find legislation unconstitutional for the *single* reason that the criterion for unequal treatment was not objective.

There are two possible explanations for the limited number of cases in this category and the constant blending with other stages of the proportionality analysis. First, the Court may be reluctant to invalidate legislation during this preliminary stage because this would intrude upon the legislator's policy freedom. However, a more probable explanation is that very few legislative actions are rooted in a subjective criterion for unequal treatment. One can expect that such initiatives are filtered out during the legislative procedure and, therefore, do not reach the Court.

7.4.2. ILLEGITIMATE POLICY OBJECTIVE (N=0)

Once it is established that the measure is based on an objective criterion, the following step is the four-stage justification test. Since this test mainly entails a means-ends comparison, the BeCC's starting point is to ascertain the legislator's intentions. To do so, it can resort to preparatory parliamentary documents. As discussed in section 6.4.4., the BeCC refers almost automatically to these documents, especially in fundamental rights cases. In addition, the defending party may also introduce new *post hoc* arguments during the review procedure. In particular, some policy decisions may have been implemented for reasons deemed unacceptable at the moment the case is lodged before the Court, but can still be justified by reference to other legitimate purposes. However, the Court should be careful when the terms of the law are influenced by an earlier purpose which now may be incapable or unnecessary to achieve the new aim.[1303]

Essentially, by adopting the measure, the legislator should aim to further a legitimate purpose. This aim cannot go against the democratic values of the state, such as the equal status of all human beings or the equal respect that must be shown to (ethical) beliefs.[1304] For example, an illegitimate purpose would

1300 BeCC case no 102/2010, B.8.4.

1301 BeCC case no 32/2009, B.13.3.

1302 In particular, the Court stated there was "no relevant objective criterion" (BeCC case no 2009/032) and "no objective and pertinent criterion" (BeCC case no 2010/102).

1303 For examples from the ECtHR case law, see J Rivers, 'Proportionality and Variable Intensity of Review' (2006) 65 Cambridge Law Journal, 174.

1304 K Möller, *The Global Model of Constitutional Rights* (Oxford University Press 2012), 188.

be to discriminate on the ground of racial differences or sexual preferences.[1305] Some scholars argue that the legislator should show he is constitutionally-authorised to take the challenged measure.[1306] Pursuing an illegitimate purpose makes the statute unconstitutional *in se*, which is different from a purpose that may be legitimate but cannot justify the measure (for instance, because it is not important enough).[1307] An evaluation of this importance occurs at a later stage of the analysis, in particular during the proportionality test *sensu stricto*, which involves weighing up the harms caused against the benefits of the infringing measure. Hence, the 'legitimate purpose' requirement leaves considerable room to the legislative branch to shape policy according to its views on which social or economic goals to pursue.[1308] Hence, the threshold for rejecting legislation during this step is very high. Nonetheless, including it in the review process can have a disciplining effect on the legislator. By forcing them to identify permissible arguments whose actual strength can then be examined in the later stages of the test, the Court keeps the legislative branch on the right track.[1309]

The data confirm that the Court – similarly to other constitutional and international courts[1310] – is extremely reluctant to label the legislative

[1305] An example from the South African Constitutional Court is SACC case no CCT 49/03, *Bhe and Others v. Khayelitsha Magistrate and Others*, 15 October 2004. In this ruling, the SACC stated that the challenged provision "was enacted as part of a racist programme intent on entrenching division and subordination". Another example is SACC case no CCT 11/98, *National Coalition for Gay and Lesbian Equality and Another v. Minister of Justice and Others*, 9 October 1988, relating to a provision that made sexual intercourse between consenting males a criminal offence. The Court stated that "the enforcement of the private moral views of a section of the community, which are based to a large extent on nothing more than prejudice, cannot qualify as such a legitimate purpose." See also N Petersen, 'Proportionality and the Incommensurability Challenge – Some Lessons from the South African Constitutional Court' (2013) New York University Public Law and Legal Theory Working Papers, 1, 10, footnote 68.

[1306] A Stone Sweet and J Mathews 'Proportionality Balancing and Global Constitutionalism' (2008) 47 Colombia Journal of Transnational Law, 73, 76.

[1307] In some other jurisdictions, this stage is characterised in another way. The Canadian Constitutional Court, for example, states that the objective must be of "sufficient importance to warrant overriding a constitutionally protected right or freedom". See D Grimm, 'Proportionality in Canadian and German Constitutional Jurisprudence' (2007) 57 University of Toronto Law Review, 383, 388.

[1308] J Rivers, 'Proportionality and Variable Intensity of Review' (2006) 65 Cambridge Law Journal, 174, 196.

[1309] K Möller, *The Global Model of Constitutional Rights* (Oxford University Press 2012), 190–1.

[1310] See for example: D Grimm, 'Proportionality in Canadian and German Constitutional Jurisprudence' (2007) 57 University of Toronto Law Review, 383, 388–93; and A Barak, 'Proportional Effect: The Israeli Experience' (2008) 57 University of Toronto Law Review, 369, 371. The ECJ, ECtHR and WTO are entirely focused on the relationship between means and ends: J Rivers, 'Proportionality and Variable Intensity of Review' (2006) 65 Cambridge Law Journal, 174, 196; Y Arai-Takahashi, *The Margin of Appreciation Doctrine and the Principle of Proportionality in the Jurisprudence of the ECtHR* (Intersentia 2002), 11; and JH Gerards, *Judicial Review in Equal Treatment Cases* (Martinus Nijhoff Publishers 2005), 32–3.

objective 'illegitimate'.[1311] Conversely, the Court does regularly mention that the legislative purpose is legitimate.[1312] There are several explanations for this finding. First, legislative initiatives prompted by an illegitimate purpose are likely to be filtered out by Parliament – and therefore do not reach the Court. Next, explicitly claiming the legislator has pursued an illegitimate aim is delicate in light of the need to respect the separation of powers. In principle, it is a prerogative of the legislative branch to determine which policy goals to pursue. Hence, not making an explicit claim about the illegitimacy of the stated objective may be a sign that the Court wants to avoid criticism that it is making decisions that are principally reserved for the legislative branch.

Rather than declaring a legislative purpose 'illegitimate', the Court prefers to express scepticism and to state that the measure cannot be justified by that purpose (see *infra*, section 7.4.6.). In particular, in some cases a negative attitude of the Court towards the legislative purpose could be ascertained.[1313] For instance, in case no 198/2005,[1314] the BeCC objected that the challenged fiscal regulation was driven by merely financial considerations. Without explicitly labelling the legislative objective 'illegitimate', the Court did argue that such an objective was insufficient to justify the challenged measure.[1315] Another example where the Court questioned the desirability of the stated purpose is case no 33/93.[1316] The preparatory parliamentary documents showed that the legislative measure was merely a validation of an executive decision. By taking the measure, the legislator had wanted to 'secure' their decision. Yet the Court argued that this justification was insufficient, in particular because the validation was driven by the willingness to avoid a review by the Council of State (which alone is competent to review executive decisions).[1317] Notwithstanding the negative attitude towards the legislative objective, the Court again did not explicitly label it illegitimate. Stating that the purpose is 'insufficient' to justify

---

1311 Competence conflict cases are not included in this subset of data, which means that this conclusion cannot be generalised for all cases. For instance, in BeCC case no 41/2010, 29 April 2010, the Court found that the pursued objective was not lawful, in particular because it conflicted with the principle of economic and monetary union within the Belgian territory.

1312 BeCC case no 47/2016, 24 March 2016, B.4.2 ("improving the efficacy of fiscal controls is an objective of general importance, and pursuing it is legitimate."); BeCC case no 79/2016, 25 May 2016, B.6.5 ("the legitimate choice of the legislator to responsabilize the principals, in the fight against social fraud"); BeCC case no 84/2016, 2 June 2016, B.8 ("familial peace and legal certainty are legitimate purposes"); and BeCC case no 2016/123, 22 September 2016, B.10 ("the legitimate purpose of avoiding misuse when picking up non-menial garbage").

1313 In particular, this attitude was registered in 27 cases, a large majority of which led to the finding of a constitutional violation. In particular, only in two of these cases were all pleas rejected.

1314 BeCC case no 198/2005, 21 December 2005.

1315 Ibid., B.6.

1316 BeCC case no 33/93, 11 April 1993.

1317 Ibid., B.2.

the measure does not confront the legislator in the same way as a verdict of illegitimacy would. Hence, this may be understood as a strategy of the Court to avoid a conflict with the legislator and to protect itself against reprisals.

7.4.3. SUITABILITY (N=117)

Further, the suitability test[1318] sets out a factual and normative plausibility threshold.[1319] More specifically, a measure is not suitable when it cannot advance the stated purpose. Such unsuitability can be due to alternative motives or to a lack of diligence when drafting the measure. First, the measure may be adopted to pursue another objective than the one reported by the legislature. Hence, the review procedure can reveal that the means are ineffective to advance that objective. Secondly, the effectiveness of a measure may not have been appropriately investigated.[1320] Such *ex ante* legislative evaluation may be circumvented due to time pressure, or because it was not considered necessary in order to ensure its acceptance. In particular, the political success of the measure often depends on whether the general public *believes* that the measures are effective.[1321] When the Court criticises the relevance of the measures taken, this sends a particular signal to the legislative branch. More specifically, the legislator may be allowed to pursue the same policy goal, but through other, more suitable means.

In principle, the evaluation of the causality between the intended goal and the means chosen should be ascertained on the basis of standards which derive from scientific perceptions of cause and effect. Yet this may prove particularly difficult when the court is confronted with complex issues or a policy area where a large number of factors determine the effects of a particular measure. When the measure has already been in place for a while, it is easier to determine whether the intended effects have been achieved. However, when this is not the case, the court should make a probability estimation of the measure's effectiveness. In a previous part of this book (see *infra*, section 2.3.2.4.), it has been discussed how courts may deal with such empirical questions. In general, a court cannot require absolute certainty of a proven result, nor should the mere statement that a result ought to be achieved be found sufficient.[1322]

1318 Also known as the rationality or rational connection test.

1319 J Rivers, 'Proportionality and Variable Intensity of Review' (2006) 65 Cambridge Law Journal, 174, 189; A Barak, *Proportionality: Constitutional Rights and their Limitations* (Cambridge University Press 2012), 131; and B Pirker, *Proportionality Analysis and Models of Judicial Review: A Theoretical and Comparative Study* (Europa Law Publishing 2014), 26.

1320 N Petersen, *Proportionality and Judicial Activism* (Cambridge University Press 2017), 47.

1321 Ibid., 47.

1322 B Pirker, *Proportionality Analysis and Models of Judicial Review: A Theoretical and Comparative Study* (Europa Law Publishing 2014).

In order to know how effective a policy might be, a court is often reliant on others to provide evidence. In particular, it can attach weight to the decision-maker's (or another party's) expertise in the course of arriving at its decision.[1323]

Often in cases before the BeCC there is uncertainty on whether any particular measure chosen by the legislator will achieve its end. Sometimes, the BeCC shows deference to the legislative branch by approving legislation notwithstanding the uncertainty on the challenged measure's adequacy. For instance, in case no 41/93,[1324] there were doubts about the dissuasive effect of a tax on specific waste materials. Yet the Court confirmed that it belongs to the democratically elected branch to evaluate which measures are appropriate. The Court declared the legislation constitutional, although the measure was said not to be completely adequate to advance the stated purpose.[1325]

Nonetheless, the data shows that the BeCC does occasionally establish a constitutional violation due to a lack of causal relation between the challenged measure and the stated purpose.[1326] In particular, the results show that this situation occurred in approximately one fifth of the studied subset of cases (n=117, 19%). The BeCC employs a variety of wordings (not pertinent,[1327] relevant,[1328] adequate[1329] or effective[1330]) to indicate that the measure could not advance the stated purpose.

The Court's evaluation of the measure's effectiveness is usually based on an analytical – and not empirical – understanding of cause and effect. An example can be found in case no 39/90,[1331] relating to the formal recognition of a child by its biological father. To avoid recognitions by men who are not the biological father but claim that they are as a gesture to the mother, the legislator made the recognition conditional on the permission of the mother. However, this condition is ineffective because the mother can give this permission even though she is well aware that the man in question is not the biological father.[1332]

1323 M Elliott, 'Proportionality and Deference: The Importance of a Structured Approach' in C Forsyth et al. (eds.), *Effective Judicial Review: A Cornerstone of Good Governance* (Oxford University Press 2010), 272; and J Rivers, 'Proportionality and Variable Intensity of Review' (2006) 65 Cambridge Law Journal, 174, 200.

1324 BeCC case no 41/93, 3 June 1993.

1325 Ibid., B.3.7–8.

1326 This contrasts, for example, to the case law of the Israeli Constitutional Court. See A Barak, 'Proportional Effect: The Israeli experience' (2008) 57 University of Toronto Law Review, 369, 372–3.

1327 For example, BeCC case no 3/2015, 22 January 2015, B.9.3.

1328 For example, BeCC case no 8/2014, 23 January 2014, B.19.

1329 For example, BeCC case no 60/2012, 3 May 2012, B.6.

1330 For example, BeCC case no 152/2015, 29 October 2015, B.71.3.

1331 BeCC case no 39/90, 21 December 1990.

1332 Moreover, in response to other arguments brought forward by the legislator to justify the condition of the permission, the Court also found the measure unnecessary and disproportional: ibid, B.4.3.1-3.

Another example is case no 152/2015,[1333] related to certain appointment rules for judges. The BeCC noted that the legislator had installed these rules in order to consistently guarantee the capability of these judges. However, considering that some judges were exempt from these rules, the measures taken were not effective to guarantee this legislative purpose.[1334]

Hence, the Court is reluctant to rely on (scientific) expertise when evaluating a measure's adequacy.[1335] Only in five cases was a reference to scientific evidence registered *and* the measure found unsuitable. Moreover, solely in case no 89/2011[1336] did the evidence discussed actually help to reach that conclusion. Remarkably, in that case the Court had been instructed by the ECJ to check for evidence. Therefore, the Court requested the government of the French-speaking Community to bring forward documents that could substantiate their arguments. On the basis thereof, the Court invalidated some of the challenged measures because they were not relevant to ensure the protection of public health. In the other cases, the evidence was either discussed in another part of the judgment or the expertise did not deal with the effectiveness of the challenged measure. The Court's reluctance to deal with empirical evidence has already been discussed in the chapter on its citation practices. Yet, without engaging in a more empirical understanding of cause and effect, the BeCC's application of the suitability test retains a rather *ad hoc* character. It can be recommended that the Court develop a set of rules determining the distribution of burden of proof among the parties involved in the review procedure.

7.4.4. NECESSITY (N=23)

Next, the necessity stage[1337] involves an evaluation of whether the policy objective could have been effectively pursued by other measures that are less burdensome or disadvantageous. Such 'excess breadth' often presents a risk for minority groups, in particular when their rights are limited for the sake of the public interest.[1338] The protection of these minorities against the abuses

1333 BeCC case no 152/2015, 29 October 2015.

1334 Ibid., B.71.2-3.

1335 In contrast to the USSC, which is more inclined to look into empirical evidence to evaluate a measure's effectiveness: see P Yowell, 'Proportionality in United States Constitutional Law' in L Lazarus, C McCrudden and N Bowled (eds.), *Reasoning Rights: Comparative Judicial Engagement* (Hart Publishing 2014), 95, 110.

1336 BeCC case no 89/2011, 31 May 2011, B.4.8, B.6-7, B.9.2.1-B.11.3.

1337 Also known as the least restrictive means or subsidiarity test.

1338 E Brems and L Lavrysen, 'Don't Use a Sledgehammer to Crack a Nut: Less Restrictive Means in the Case Law of the European Court of Human Rights' (2015) 15 Human Rights Law Review, 139, 146. These authors give the example of security measures in the post 9/11 context, which may be particularly harmful for Muslims.

of majority rule is an essential aspect of the Court's role as a deliberative institution. The signal that reaches the legislator when the measure is found unnecessary is that he may be able to pursue the same objective but by less invasive means. More generally, the necessity test should prompt the legislator to engage closely with the effects of the measures he wants to impose. He should consider all alternatives in relation to the stated objective and the fundamental rights in question. Sometimes, courts explicitly put forward alternatives that would have been acceptable. Nonetheless, this cannot prevent the legislator from investigating and opting for other alternatives.

In principle, the necessity test implies a judicial assessment of the availability and quality of hypothetical alternatives. In order to render the legislation truly unnecessary, the alternative measures should realise the purpose 'at the same level of intensity and efficiency'.[1339] Just like in the previous stage, this search for optimisation requires a factual evaluation of the effects of the challenged measure *and* of the alternative measures.[1340] This often involves a degree of speculation and raises the same issues, relating to the availability of factual and technical knowledge, which emerge at the suitability stage.[1341] Evaluating alternatives is not only a difficult and time-consuming exercise, but also one that is usually reserved for the political branch. In principle, the legislator has more expertise or can rely on more expertise (though consultations) in order to find the least restrictive means. Yet if the Court simply accepts the legislator's assessment, it would fail to provide protection against majoritarian abuses.[1342] Evidence on alternative means, their restrictiveness and effectiveness, can also be provided by the parties challenging the legislation on that ground.[1343] Most courts (such as the BeCC) are unwilling to impose a high burden of proof by requiring 'cogent and persuasive' evidence in connection to the necessity test.[1344] The reality of policy-making is that there

---

1339 A Barak, *Proportionality: Constitutional Rights and their limitations* (Cambridge University Press 2012), 323.

1340 M Elliott, 'Proportionality and Deference: The Importance of a Structured Approach' in C Forsyth et al. (eds.), *Effective Judicial Review: A Cornerstone of Good Governance* (Oxford University Press 2010), 270.

1341 E Brems and L Lavrysen, 'Don't Use a Sledgehammer to Crack a Nut: Less Restrictive Means in the Case Law of the European Court of Human Rights' (2015) 15 Human Rights Law Review, 139, 147.

1342 Ibid., 147.

1343 In Canada, this information is usually brought forward by the parties: D Grimm, 'Proportionality in Canadian and German Constitutional Jurisprudence' (2007) 57 University of Toronto Law Review, 383, 388–93.

1344 For a discussion of the case law of the Canadian and German Supreme Courts, see D Grimm, ibid., 390. Cases before the USSC are usually centred on the minimal impairment test. Consistent with its approach to the efficacy of challenged means, the USSC often relies on empirical evidence when evaluating the alternatives. See: P Yowell, 'Proportionality in United States Constitutional Law' in L Lazarus, C McCrudden and N Bowled (eds.), *Reasoning Rights: Comparative Judicial Engagement* (Hart Publishing 2014), 110; and C Bateup, 'Expanding

is often uncertainty as to the precise effects of the various alternatives. Because of the practical difficulties arising during this stage, some even argue that courts should limit their evaluation to whether the measure is a reasonably adequate attempt to solve the problem (the suitability stage).[1345]

Generally, the BeCC is reluctant to look into alternative measures. In several rulings, the Court has explicitly declared itself incompetent to evaluate whether the pursued purpose could have been reached with other, less burdensome measures. An example is one of the first cases dealing with alleged unequal treatment, case no 23/89,[1346] where the Court stated that the review against the equality principle only entails an evaluation of the objective and adequate nature of the challenged measure, and the proportionality between the measure and the stated purpose.[1347] Such a statement, based on the idea that it is up to legislator to compare and select appropriate measures, has been repeated in several other, more recent rulings.[1348]

Nonetheless, the Court does rarely invalidate legislation with reference to the unnecessary character of the challenged measure (n=22). If so, the Court usually adds that the policy purpose could be advanced by other, less intrusive measures. More specifically, the Court either points at an existing measure that can serve as alternative,[1349] or formulates suggestions for new measures to adopt.[1350,1351] An example of the first situation can be found in case no 101/2015. In order to ensure the 'liveability' of neighbourhoods with social housing projects, the legislator allowed housing services to dissolve a tenure agreement without prior judicial oversight. Yet the BeCC argued there were already possibilities for taking action against tenants who acted in breach of the housing agreement, making it unnecessary to take away this judicial guarantee.[1352] An example of a case where the Court suggested adopting an alternative was case no 88/2012.[1353] The challenged measure was part of a reform

the Conversation: American and Canadian Experiences of Constitutional Dialogue in Comparative Perspective' (2006) 44 New York University Public Law and Legal Theory Working Papers, 6, 8–9.

1345 B Challenor, 'The Balancing Act: A Case for Structured Proportionality Under the Second Limb of the Lange Test' (2015) 40 The University of Western Australia Law Review, 267, 276 and further.

1346 BeCC case no 23/89, 13 October 1989.

1347 Ibid., B.2.7.

1348 BeCC case no 37/98, 1 April 1998, B.5.2; BeCC case no 35/2003, 25 March 2003, B.13.8; and BeCC case no 110/2008, 31 July 2008, B.8.3, B.8.5.

1349 For example: BeCC case no 101/2008, 10 July 2008, B.25.1; and BeCC case no 169/2013, 19 December 2013, B.21.2.

1350 For example: BeCC case no 25/2007, 30 January 2007, B.12; BeCC case no 88/2012, 12 July 2012, B.37.

1351 In some cases, the Court mentions that there exist alternative measures, without specifying which exactly. For example: BeCC case no 39/90, 21 December 1990, B.4.3; and BeCC case no 16/2005, 19 January 2005, B.6.2.

1352 BeCC case no 101/2008, 10 July 2008, B.24.2-B.26.

1353 BeCC case no 88/2012, 12 July 2012.

of the administrative procedure in migration issues. In order to accelerate the procedure, the legislator had abolished the possibility (which was previously an obligation) for the initiating party to introduce an additional memorandum. The Court argued that this absolute abolition infringed the rights of the defence. The Court suggested, instead, making the additional memorandum optional and introducing a strict deadline.[1354] Exceptionally, the Court merely states that the measures are unnecessary, without even considering the possibility of existing or hypothetical alternatives. An example is the above-mentioned case no 23/89. In particular, the BeCC denounced the provision because the challenged measures disproportionally infringed the constitutionally protected freedom of expression, "without this being necessary to advance the stated purpose".[1355] The Court's reluctance in this case can be explained by the fact that it had, in the same ruling, declared itself incompetent to judge alternative measures.

Not only is a failure at the necessity stage rare, it is usually not the single decisive element in establishing a violation. More specifically, like many other courts,[1356] the BeCC usually combines this conclusion with either a failure at the proportionality or suitability stage. The ambiguity in the Court's approach is reflected, again, in case no 23/89. In this early ruling, the Court drew an explicit equivalence between the necessity and balancing stages. In several other cases, the Court has continued this approach.[1357] Another interesting example is case no 172/2015, where the Court reviewed legislation relating to the retirement rights of citizens who were victimised during the Second World War. Because the granting of this pension was made conditional on a continuing residence in Belgium, there was a potential conflict with the freedom of movement and residence within the European Union. Therefore, the Court referred to ECJ case law to underpin its decision. In particular, the BeCC cited an ECJ ruling in which it was concluded that a similar measure (in Poland) violated European law.[1358] In particular, the ECJ argued that:

> while the restriction [...] is capable of being justified by objective considerations of public interest [...], that restriction must also not be disproportionate in the light

1354 Ibid., B.37.

1355 BeCC case no 23/89, 13 October 1989, B.2.13. Another example is BeCC case no 29/95, 4 April 1995, B.17.

1356 This single test can be expressed as follows: 'does a governmental measure excessively impair or burden an individual right in comparison to the value of the aim to be achieved?'. See P Yowell, 'Proportionality in United States Constitutional Law' in L Lazarus, C McCrudden and N Bowles (eds.), *Reasoning Rights: Comparative Judicial Engagement* (Hart Publishing 2014), 91.

1357 In 17 out of the 22 cases which failed the necessity stage, this conclusion was combined with a failure of the proportionality test *sensu stricto*.

1358 ECJ C-499/06, *Halina Nerkowska v. Zakład Ubezpieczeń Społecznych Oddział w Koszalinie*, 22 May 2008.

> of the objective pursued. […] The requirement of residence […] must be held to be disproportionate, since it goes beyond what is necessary […][1359]

The BeCC simply concluded that the measure violated articles 10 and 11 of the Constitution "for the same reasons". In other rulings, the Court fuses the necessity and suitability stages. For instance, in case no 39/2007,[1360] it needed to evaluate certain mathematical formulae to calculate an insurance contribution. The litigants, several insurance companies, argued that the chosen formulae could harm their interests without a proper justification. The Court found that the pertinence of the formulae could not be established and that, at the same time, other, less invasive means were available to secure the legislator's purpose.[1361]

Only occasionally is the existence of less intrusive means alone sufficient to mean that the challenged measure violates the Constitution. This was the case in case no 105/2007,[1362] where the Court dealt with criminal procedure legislation. In some specific procedures (e.g. relating to terrorism), the legislator had authorised a single court to evaluate the regularity of the criminal investigation, without the possibility of appeal against their decision. The legislator argued that this served the purpose of protecting the confidentiality of sensitive information. Yet the Court stated that this measure was unnecessary to secure this purpose, in particular because any Belgian judge is bound by professional confidentiality. Hence, the legislative goal could be secured without taking any measures, while at the same time guaranteeing the right of appeal.[1363]

The practice of fusing several stages into one has been criticised as judicially insincere because it obscures the internal logic and structure of the proportionality analysis.[1364] Clarity on what elements the proportionality analysis comprises and the role played by each is essential to the interests of opinion clarity and transparency. Also, as discussed below, the impact of the judicial decision on the breadth of legislative discretion is different when the narrow proportionality test is failed than when it is established that less restrictive means are available.[1365]

1359 Ibid., 40 and 43.

1360 BeCC case no 39/2007.

1361 Ibid., B.14.

1362 BeCC case no 105/2007, 19 July 2007.

1363 Ibid., B.16.4-B.16-6.

1364 M Cohen-Eliya and I Porat, 'Proportionality and the Culture of Justification' (2011) 59 American Journal of Comparative Law, 463; and M Elliott, 'Proportionality and Deference: The Importance of a Structured Approach' in C Forsyth et al. (eds.), *Effective Judicial Review: A Cornerstone of Good Governance* (Oxford University Press 2010), 268.

1365 M Elliott, 'Proportionality and Deference: The Importance of a Structured Approach' in C Forsyth et al. (eds.), *Effective Judicial Review: A Cornerstone of Good Governance* (Oxford University Press 2010), 268. See *infra*, on the discussion on the proportionality test *sensu stricto*.

In conclusion, although the necessity stage can be conceived as logically distinct from the other stages, the BeCC mostly takes into account the existence of alternative, less burdensome measures as an element in the overall evaluation of the measure's justifiability.[1366] This reluctance to engage more strongly in a factual evaluation of various alternatives reflects that the Court does not want to enter into the policy debate. By doing so, the Court can avoid the criticism that it is making decisions that actually should be made by the legislative branch.

7.4.5. PROPORTIONALITY *SENSU STRICTO* (N=233)

Finally, the proportionality test *sensu stricto* relates to the actual balance between the potential harm caused by the measure and the benefits to be gained. Even if the challenged measure is suitable and necessary, it may still violate the Constitution if it produces an impact that outweighs the benefits achieved by the measure.[1367] The more deleterious the effect of the measure, the more important the policy goal will have to be. Although this balancing exercise comes at the end, it is often considered the core of the justification test.[1368]

The costs and benefits to be weighed are generally not quantifiable, and thus not commensurable with mathematical analysis.[1369] Therefore, in contrast to the factual thresholds built into the suitability and necessity tests, there are no common yardsticks against which to measure different values. As a mainly normative evaluation, the proportionality test gives the Court more discretion to weigh the values and interests at stake.[1370] If the Court establishes a violation with reference to the balancing stage, it has to justify why the valuation of the competing interests at stake is superior to the valuation of the legislative objective. The balancing stage is often looked on with distrust because it can

1366 This ambiguity is equally reflected in the literature on the BeCC. For example, Theunis does not integrate necessity as a separate stage, but merges it with the proportionality stage *sensu stricto*. Yet, to describe the latter stage he uses a metaphor similar to 'don't use a sledgehammer to crack a nut', which is usually mentioned in relation to the necessity stage: J Theunis, 'Het Gelijkheidsbeginsel' in A Alen et al., *Doorwerking Publiekrecht in het Privaatrecht* (Mys & Breesch 1997); and E Brems and L Lavrysen, 'Don't Use a Sledgehammer to Crack a Nut: Less Restrictive Means in the Case Law of the European Court of Human Rights' (2015) 15 Human Rights Law Review, 139.

1367 A Baker, 'Proportionality' in H Fenwick (ed.), *Judicial Review* (LexisNexis 2014), 283.

1368 M Cohen-Eliya and I Porat, 'Proportionality and the Culture of Justification' (2011) 59 American Journal of Comparative Law, 463.

1369 J Rivers, 'Proportionality and Variable Intensity of Review' (2006) 65 Cambridge Law Journal, 174, 201; and M Elliott, 'Proportionality and Deference: The Importance of a Structured Approach' in C Forsyth et al. (eds.), *Effective Judicial Review: A Cornerstone of Good Governance* (Oxford University Press 2010), 281.

1370 E Brems and L Lavrysen, 'Don't Use a Sledgehammer to Crack a Nut: Less Restrictive Means in the Case Law of the European Court of Human Rights' (2015) 15 Human Rights Law Review, 139, 145.

enable courts to pass judgment on the appropriateness of legislation, while they are actually only competent to assess its legality. Moreover, the Court should evaluate the measure's proportional nature after all previous stages have been cleared. If so, the finding of a violation during this stage would mean that even the least restrictive means are unacceptable. In other words, while the suitability and necessity tests are concerned with whether the stated objective can be pursued *in a particular way*, the proportionality test *sensu stricto* would determine whether it can be pursued *at all*.[1371] Because of the impact of such a decision upon the breadth of legislative discretion, it is considered a bolder judicial endeavour than invalidating legislation during one of the previous stages.

Notwithstanding these reservations, the data show that the BeCC is not reluctant to declare legislation disproportionate. Moreover, there are as many contemporary cases as cases from the early stages of the Court's existence where an infringement is established by reference to the balancing stage. At the time the BeCC was established, the proportionality analysis was already widely accepted and used by other European courts. As Petersen argued, the probability that a court uses the balancing stage is in line with the strength of their institutional position and the degree to which the proportionality test is accepted in legal scholarship.[1372] Hence, it is not surprising that the balancing stage is prominent in the BeCC's case law. Another explanation could be the Court's reluctance to engage with a factual evaluation of the suitability and necessity stages. When there is no concluding evidence available, the Court may want to circumvent the suitability and necessity stages and leap over to the conclusion.[1373]

Usually, the Court does not clear all previous stages before engaging in the proportionality analysis *sensu stricto*. Hence, in contrast to the above, these rulings do not necessarily indicate that the objective cannot be pursued *at all*. A good example illustrating the Court's approach is case no 105/2013,[1374] where the BeCC evaluated the existing conditions for initiating a challenge against the presumption of paternity. In particular, the provision excluded the possibility for a potential biological father to take this initiative when there is an affective relation (*'bezit van staat'*) between the child and its mother's husband. The BeCC argued that the legislative purpose underlying this condition, in particular protecting 'familial peace' and the child's interests, is legitimate.

1371 M Elliott, 'Proportionality and Deference: The Importance of a Structured Approach' in C Forsyth et al. (eds.), *Effective Judicial Review: A Cornerstone of Good Governance* (Oxford University Press 2010), 267.

1372 N Petersen, *Proportionality and Judicial Activism* (Cambridge University Press 2017), 14.

1373 C Henckels, *Proportionality and Deference in Investor-State Arbitration* (Cambridge University Press 2015), 43: "Deference is relevant where courts and tribunals make decisions in situations of normative or empirical uncertainty."

1374 BeCC case no 105/2013, 9 July 2013.

In addition, the measure was considered pertinent to pursue this goal, in particular by preventing biological reality from always prevailing over a socio-affective situation. Yet, by introducing the existence of such an affective relation as an *absolute* ground for inadmissibility, the regular judiciary (applying the measure in practice) cannot take into account the interests of all parties involved. Hence, the potential harm caused to the biological father was found to be disproportional to the benefits to be gained. The measure was thus declared invalid.[1375] The Court did not explicitly investigate whether less restrictive means were available. Hence, the ruling remains unclear on whether other measures that are not as *absolute* may have been considered acceptable. Rulings such as these are very common because the BeCC usually circumvents the necessity stage, or fuses both stages into one (see *supra*, section 7.4.4.). Moreover, in some rulings, the BeCC only focuses on the proportionality test *sensu stricto*, without addressing any of the prior stages explicitly.[1376]

Case no 105/2013 is additionally interesting from another perspective. The conclusion on the proportionate nature of the challenged measures conflicts with previous case law of the BeCC. In particular, in earlier cases, the Court judged that a measure allowing only the mother, child and husband (excluding outsiders claiming to be the biological father) to challenge the established paternity, was proportionate. Moreover, it was considered in the interest of the child to avoid the disruption of "familial peace".[1377] This confirms that the balancing test is not a mathematical exercise and that the weight of particular values and interests may evolve over time.

7.4.6. THE COURT CONCLUDES THAT THE MEASURE IS 'NOT (REASONABLY) JUSTIFIED' (N=285)

The BeCC does not always make explicit why the proportionality analysis was failed. In many cases (n=285), the Court circumvents the individual stages and goes right to the conclusion of the justification test, in particular by stating the measure is 'not (reasonably) justified'. Hence, the Court refers to the justification test but merely qualifies the given reasons as 'insufficient', without applying the proportionality framework. Therefore, the following questions remain unanswered: are the reasons insufficient in the sense that they cannot

1375 Ibid., B.5-11. The condition as an absolute ground for admissibility is also considered disproportionate for the other persons allowed to challenge the assumption of paternity, in particular the husband (BeCC case no 20/2011, 3 February 2011, B.10) and the child (BeCC case no 2013/147, 7 November 2013, B.18).

1376 For example: BeCC case no 89/2004, 19 May 2004, B.5; BeCC case no 181/2008, B.25.1-B.25.4; and BeCC case no 94/2015, 25 June 2015, B.7.2-B.10-1.

1377 BeCC case no 41/1997, B.11; BeCC case no 12/1998, B.6.2; and BeCC case no 56/2001, B.5-B.9.

justify *any* legislative action (illegitimate)? Can they not justify that particular measure because it is ineffective or unnecessary (suitability or necessity test)? Or, are the reasons insufficient because they are not important or strong *enough* in comparison to the severity of the limitation on the fundamental right (proportionality test *sensu stricto*)?

An example is case no 63/2011,[1378] relating to a tax reduction measure. In order to lighten the 'financial burden' of having children, a reduction was introduced for those citizens who have at least two children living with them. The referring judge interpreted this rule as such that the reduction could only be granted to the parent who lives in the house where the children have their *official* residence. The BeCC concluded that the measure, interpreted as such, was not justified. In particular, the Court argued that the reduction should be (partially) granted to each parent if the children in practice reside at both their houses. The measure was invalidated, without the Court suggesting an alternative interpretation.[1379] In cases such as these, the Court does not apply the structural reasoning scheme despite giving the impression that it has. In particular, the Court's own reference to the 'justification test' creates the expectation that it will deal with the issues raised in a certain manner. This is not only confusing, but can also be perceived as a 'cover up' for the fact that the Court is actually making its decision according to its own views.

7.4.7. THE COURT STATES THAT THE 'LEGISLATION IS DISCRIMINATORY/UNCONSTITUTIONAL' (N=48)

The last variable represents the residual category of cases. In most of these cases, a violation was established but no justification test was applied. The BeCC simply finds that the challenged provisions are 'discriminatory' or 'violate articles 10 and 11 of the Constitution'.

In case no 104/2006,[1380] for example, the BeCC reviewed criminal procedural legislation relating to violations of international humanitarian law. The legislation allows that, under certain circumstances, a pending procedure can be withdrawn from the Belgian criminal courts, except where one of the litigants is of Belgian nationality. A similar exception was not provided for refugees. The BeCC concluded that this differential treatment of Belgian citizens and refugees violated articles 10, 11 and 191 of the Constitution.[1381]

Another example is case no 36/2011,[1382] relating to the competences of the Council of State. In principle, the Council of State may review decisions of any

1378 BeCC case no 63/2011, 5 May 2011.
1379 Ibid., B.4.2.
1380 BeCC case no 104/2006, 21 June 2006.
1381 Ibid., B.5-B.11.
1382 BeCC case no 36/2011, 10 March 2011.

Belgian administration. For instance, a decision that changes the employment conditions of their individual staff members can be brought before the Council because they may be disguised disciplining sanctions. Yet, because the Council of State is not considered an administration itself, its own staff members are not allowed to lodge such an appeal. The BeCC stated that the lack of any possibility for appeal violates articles 10 and 11 of the Constitution. It was argued that the challenged measures were not unconstitutional *in se*, only the absence of a legislative provision installing such a possibility for staff members of the Council of State.[1383]

7.5. STRATEGIC CONSIDERATIONS UNDERLYING THE APPLICATION OF THE PROPORTIONALITY ANALYSIS

7.5.1. INTRODUCTION: OPINION CLARITY AS A DOUBLE-EDGED SWORD

Each case presents a unique set of facts and principles which may prompt the Court to be creative when applying the proportionality analysis. The conceptual abstractness of the proportionality principle and the flexibility of the framework may result in inconsistency across cases.[1384] The descriptive results demonstrated that the BeCC generally takes a prudent approach when executing the proportionality analysis. Although all elements of the structured framework are – to some extent – present in the case law, the Court usually does not follow them in a strictly separated, sequential order. In particular, neither the failure of the objectivity or the necessity stage is sufficient to establish a constitutional violation. In addition, when the Court states that a certain stage has been failed, this does not mean the Court has explicitly cleared all previous stages. This situation occurs most often in rulings where the challenged legislation fails the last step (proportionality test *sensu stricto*), without an explicit evaluation of the legitimacy of the stated objective and the suitability and necessity of the measures taken. Most importantly, however, in more than half of the studied cases, the BeCC found a violation without addressing any of the stages of the proportionality analysis. Although the failure of the previous stages may be implied, such an unstructured approach can render the

1383 Ibid., B.3-B.6.

1384 R Sulitzeany-Kenan, M Kremnitzer and S Alon, 'Facts, Preferences and Doctrine: An Empirical Analysis of the Proportionality Judgment' (2015) 50 Law & Society Review, 348, 353.

result less transparent and may be (perceived as) arbitrary.[1385] The legislative branch is left in the dark on *whether* or *how* it is entitled to realise its objectives.[1386]

This varying degree of opinion clarity presents us with a puzzle. Without other legal incentives to ensure implementation, courts are aware that they must formulate their rulings in such a way as to stimulate compliance.[1387] At first sight, one might expect that courts are inclined to be as clear as possible on why legislation is found unconstitutional. In short, by framing its decisions in doctrinal terms, the Court can stimulate public support and compliance by the legislator.[1388] Yet, as discussed in the descriptive section, all stages of the proportionality analysis may entail difficult empirical or normative evaluations.[1389] Also, greater precision can be counterproductive. In some cases, the Court may anticipate that establishing a violation with explicit reference to one of the separate stages will be met with resistance. When the legislative branch is determined not to comply with the judicial decision, more precision can highlight the court's ineffectiveness. This may undermine the perception that the Court's rulings should be respected. An alternative strategy can be to establish a violation but be vaguer on the grounds, when this better serves the purpose of ensuring implementation while at the same time securing the Court's institutional legitimacy.[1390] This would dispel the suspicion that the Court is interfering with the legislator's prerogatives.[1391] If the Court is perceived as a political actor with its own agenda, this would undermine its legitimacy and thus weaken its institutional position.[1392] Also, a vague opinion leaves more room for the legislative branch to respond to the ruling in a way that best suits

---

1385 D Grimm, 'Proportionality in Canadian and German Constitutional Jurisprudence' (2007) 57 University of Toronto Law Review, 383, 397.

1386 M Elliott, 'Proportionality and Deference: The Importance of a Structured Approach' in C Forsyth et al. (eds.), *Effective Judicial Review: A Cornerstone of Good Governance* (Oxford University Press 2010), 267.

1387 Yet compliance also depends on other factors such as ideological congruence, resources, etc. See JK Staton and G Vanberg, 'The Value of Vagueness: Delegation, Defiance and Judicial Opinions' (2008) 52 American Journal of Political Science, 504, 515.

1388 N Petersen, *Proportionality and Judicial Activism* (Cambridge University Press 2017), 10.

1389 Ibid., 10.

1390 Staton and Vanberg relate vagueness to uncertainty on the policy implications of the ruling. The more clearly the Court articulates what the ruling demands from the legislative branch, the stronger the ruling scores on the measure of opinion clarity. See JK Staton and G Vanberg, 'The Value of Vagueness: Delegation, Defiance and Judicial Opinions' (2008) 52 American Journal of Political Science, 504.

1391 N Petersen, *Proportionality and Judicial Activism* (Cambridge University Press 2017), 96. Although Petersen's research starts from the same idea that courts strategically adapt their application of the proportionality analysis in order to ensure compliance, his research question and collected data differ considerably. In particular, Petersen argues that the Court is prompted to refrain from balancing (*sensu stricto*) and, instead, relies on the other stages of the analysis or other arguments as an alternative strategy. Cases where the Court did not specify why the proportionality analysis failed were merged with the balancing stage.

1392 Ibid., 93.

its policy choices, even if the Court ultimately opposes the elected branches in the substance of its decision. In other words, the Court fulfils its duty to uphold the Constitution while maintaining a certain degree of deference.[1393]

In conclusion, opinion clarity (or its flip side, vagueness) is a double-edged sword.[1394] Assuming that the BeCC cares about compliance with its rulings, both strategies can be considered as reasonable alternative tools to deal with potential resistance to its decisions. The question arises as to *why* the Court is specific in some cases, but resorts to vaguer language in other cases. This may be dictated by the area of law in which the case is situated, or the substance of the conflicting interests at stake.[1395] In addition, without a fixed standard approach, the person who writes the first opinion draft (presumably one of the law clerks) has a large influence on how the ruling is formulated. Nonetheless, there are reasons to believe that external considerations also influence how the Court applies the proportionality analysis. In what follows, I explore which case-specific factors may push the Court in one of two opposite directions. In other words, the analysis aims to explain why the BeCC may be more inclined to write a vague opinion in one case, but prefers to be more precise in another.

7.5.2. HYPOTHESES

Media attention may be related to opinion clarity in two contrasting ways. First, when a case has been covered (extensively) in the newspapers prior to the decision, this points at its politically controversial character. In these cases, the decision to establish a violation will be likely to meet opposition from the legislative branch. In particular, when the political stakes are higher, the legislator will be more likely to risk the costs of non-compliance.[1396] To soften anticipated resistance and avoid public backlash, while at the same time establishing a constitutional violation, the Court may feel more inclined to conceal its decision behind an evasively drafted justification. This result would be in line with the findings in chapter 5, where the regression models indicated that the Court strategically attenuates the outcome (by opting for a modulation) when pushback is expected from the political branch. In short, it is hypothesised that the Court is more

---

1393 A Kavanagh, *Constitutional Review under the UK Human Rights Act* (Cambridge University Press 2009), 186, 200.

1394 As Staton and Vanberg stated, "Under some conditions, increasing sensitivity to non-compliance always results in more ambiguous opinions [...]. Under other circumstances, such sensitivity may result in more specific or in more ambiguous opinions." See JK Staton and G Vanberg, 'The Value of Vagueness: Delegation, Defiance and Judicial Opinions' (2008) 52 American Journal of Political Science, 504, 513.

1395 T-I Harbo, 'The Function of the Proportionality Principle in EU Law' (2010) 16 European Law Journal, 158, 180.

1396 JK Staton and G Vanberg, ibid., 513.

likely to produce a vague opinion when the case has received considerable media attention prior to the decision.

Yet, as mentioned before, when a case receives media attention during the decision-making procedure, the media is also more likely to cover the final decision. Media coverage allows others, such as actors involved in the procedure and the general public, to monitor legislative implementation of judicial decisions. Being clear on the grounds for establishing the violation makes it easier for the Court's audience to detect evasive manoeuvres by the legislator.[1397] This increases the threat to the legislator of losing public support when it attempts to evade the judicial outcome. Hence, opinion clarity may be a more rewarding strategy to ensure compliance than producing a vaguer opinion.[1398] Systematic studies on the implementation of US Supreme Court opinions have suggested that greater precision in the wording of an opinion does indeed promote implementation.[1399] In addition, the news media equally provides the link between the Court's reasoning style and its public legitimacy. As Petersen argues, if the public disapprove of the methodological approach of the Court, the image of the Court will be severely damaged.[1400] Hence, when the Court anticipates it will be under public scrutiny, it might be inclined to apply the doctrinally supported proportionality analysis more rigorously. Therefore, an alternative hypothesis is that more media attention will increase the likelihood that the Court is more specific on the grounds for establishing a violation.

Hypothesis 1a: The more media attention a case receives before the decision is taken, the more likely it is that the Court will produce a vague opinion.

Hypothesis 1b: The more media attention a case receives before the decision is taken, the less likely it is that the Court will produce a vague opinion.

Next, there may be a significant relation between who participated in the procedure and how the Court formulates the justificatory ground. The involvement of large or diverse group of participants indicates that the case is perceived as more salient than others. Also, as discussed in chapter 4, the news media are interested in cases that potentially affect a larger number of people. As mentioned above, opinion clarity can help the public monitor the legislative reaction after an invalidation. Hence, more intense participation may increase the threat to the legislator of losing public support after evasion, protecting the

1397 JK Staton and G Vanberg, ibid., 507.

1398 RC Black et al., *US Supreme Court Opinions and their Audiences* (Cambridge University Press 2016), 11.

1399 L Baum, 'Implementation of judicial decisions' (1976) 4 American Politics Research 86; and RC Black et al., *US Supreme Court Opinions and their Audiences* (Cambridge University Press 2016).

1400 N Petersen, *Proportionality and Judicial Activism* (Cambridge University Press 2017), 94.

outcome from political reprisals.[1401] In those cases, opinion clarity may be a more rewarding strategy to ensure compliance than producing a vaguer opinion. In addition, the more litigants are involved in the case, the more arguments are brought forward. When the memoranda introduced by the participants focus on the measure's relevance, necessity or proportionality, the Court can integrate these arguments into its opinion. For these reasons, it is hypothesised that the Court will produce clearer opinions when more participants are involved in the case.

Hypothesis 2: The probability that the Court produces a vague opinion will decrease, when a large group of individuals or a more diverse group of participants is involved.

Opinion clarity may also be related to panel size. Research on the USSC has shown that each additional justice added to the majority coalition increases the number of demands to be taken into account, resulting in a more diluted opinion.[1402] The same study showed that judges write clearer dissenting than majority opinions. Although Belgian judges are not allowed to publish separate opinions, it is possible that the same mechanism is operating when they deliberate in plenary session. In these cases, the double parity rule is strictly applied: as many French-speaking as Dutch-speaking judges, and as many ex-politicians as 'professional' judges participate in the deliberation process. To reach one single opinion, some give and take is inevitable. This can result in a ruling to which all judges can assent, but that has lost some of its clarity.

Hypothesis 3: When the Court deliberates in plenary session, it is more likely to produce a vague opinion.

In addition, the BeCC's rulings may be affected by international case law. By linking it to analogous provisions in the Constitution, the BeCC has incorporated international human rights treaties into its case law. Hence, in fundamental right adjudication, the Court can rely for guidance on the case law of the international courts competent to interpret and apply these treaties. As demonstrated by the citation analysis in a previous chapter, the BeCC increasingly accepts the intrusion of ECJ and ECtHR case law into its jurisdiction. Considering the bond between human rights provisions in the Constitution and the ECHR, it can be expected that the case law of the ECtHR is a major reference point in

---

1401 G Vanberg, *The Politics of Constitutional Review in Germany* (Cambridge University Press 2005), 96.

1402 RJ Owens and J Wedekins, 'Justices and Legal Clarity: Analyzing the Complexity of Supreme Court Opinions' (2011) 45 Law & Society Review, 1032–3. The results for the effect of 'Majority Coalition Size' on the complexity of the USSC decision showed that unanimous opinions are the most complex, followed by majorities with eight or seven justices. Majorities with five or six justices write the clearest opinions.

fundamental rights adjudication.[1403] The case law of the ECtHR served as an inspiration to adopt the proportionality analysis as an argumentative framework in the review procedure.[1404] Research has shown that, although the ECtHR does not follow the proportionality analysis structure rigorously, it engages in similar testing in the context of almost every Convention right.[1405] Elements can be found of all the separate stages, although the focus is on the final balancing stage.[1406] When the BeCC turns to the ECtHR for guidance, it is likely that it will reproduce the ECtHR's conclusion. In particular, in line with the ECtHR's ruling, it will clarify which stage of the proportionality analysis was failed. Hence, it is hypothesised that the BeCC will be less likely to produce a vague opinion when it refers to ECtHR case law. In addition, although ECJ case law seems less relevant in fundamental rights adjudication, it should be noted that the ECJ has also gradually developed a catalogue of human rights.[1407] The citation analysis showed that the ECJ has an impact in cases where the legislation under review has been adopted to implement a European directive or in rulings following a preliminary reference to the ECJ. The ECJ usually structures the proportionality analysis more carefully, in particular with three consecutive stages (suitability-necessity-narrow proportionality).[1408] Therefore, it is hypothesised that in rulings where ECJ case law is involved, the BeCC will be less likely to produce a vague opinion.

Hypothesis 4a: The Court will be less likely to produce a vague opinion when it can rely on ECtHR case law.

Hypothesis 4b: The Court will be less likely to produce a vague opinion when it can rely on ECJ case law.

The final hypothesis concerns the relation between previous legislative deficiencies and the Court's application of the proportionality analysis. Considering this

[1403] P Popelier, 'Judicial Conversations in Mulitlevel Constitutionalism. The Belgian Case' in M Claes et al. (eds.), *Constitutional Conversations in Europe – Actors, Topics and Procedures* (Intersentia 2012), 89.

[1404] ECtHR, *the Belgian Linguistic case*, No 6, 23 July 1968. Yet this ECtHR case law was in turn inspired by the German Constitutional Court. From Germany, the principle of proportionality spread to most other European countries, the ECJ, ECtHR and a number of jurisdictions outside Europe. See D Grimm, 'Proportionality in Canadian and German Constitutional Jurisprudence' (2007) 57 University of Toronto Law Review, 383–4.

[1405] J Rivers, 'Proportionality and Variable Intensity of Review' (2006) 65 Cambridge Law Journal, 174, 182, 187; and T-I Harbo, *The Function of Proportionality Analysis in European Law* (Brill Nijhoff 2015), 12.

[1406] Y Arai-Takahashi, *The Margin of Appreciation Doctrine and the Principle of Proportionality in the Jurisprudence of the ECHR* (Intersentia 2002), 15.

[1407] M De Visser, *Constitutional Review in Europe: A Comparative Analysis* (Hart Publishing 2014), 269 and further.

[1408] T-I Harbo, *The Function of Proportionality Analysis in European Law* (Brill Nijhoff 2015), 12.

analysis mainly entails a means-ends comparison, the BeCC's starting point is to ascertain the legislator's intentions. Without clearing this first hurdle, it becomes difficult to evaluate whether the challenged measures are suitable and necessary to pursue this goal, and whether this is proportional to the potential harm inflicted by the measure. Hence, a structured approach may be hindered when there is a lack of information on the legislator's objective. To ascertain this purpose, the Court usually resorts to preparatory parliamentary documents. Yet, in some cases, the Court makes no reference to these documents.[1409] The absence of such a reference may be due to a deficiency in the legislative process, in particular when the legislator has not properly justified the unequal treatment. Another option is that the constitutional violation is due to a legislative lacuna, and not the result of a purposeful exclusion – which would explain that no preparatory documents are available. Finally, the Court may deliberately abstain from referring to the parliamentary documents, for instance when balancing this purpose against other values is particularly delicate. In other cases, the Court explicitly states that, based on the parliamentary preparatory documents, it could not ascertain which goals the legislator wanted to pursue.[1410] In this situation, it is clear that the legislator's shortcomings during the parliamentary procedure prevent the Court from engaging in a full proportionality analysis. In short, the hypothesis is made that the Court will be more likely to produce a vague opinion when the legislator's objective cannot be or has not been ascertained.

Hypothesis 5a: The Court will be more likely to produce a vague opinion when it has not referred to preparatory parliamentary documents.

Hypothesis 5b: The Court will be more likely to produce a vague opinion when the legislative objective could not be ascertained from the preparatory parliamentary documents.

7.5.3. OPERATIONALISATION

The dependent variable tracks whether the Court, when it established a violation in a fundamental rights case, produced a precise or vague opinion. For the purpose of this research, 'opinion clarity' is identified with the account given by the Court on the proportionality analysis.[1411] In particular, the Court is 'precise'

1409 For example, BeCC case no 36/2011, 10 March 2011.

1410 For example, BeCC case no 54/2015, 7 May 2015.

1411 Other scholars have measured opinion clarity in another way, such as Staton and Vanberg (see *supra*, footnote 1383). Owens and Wedekins used psychology software that targets and measures cognitive complexity by identifying certain words known to be associated with

when it establishes a violation with reference to one of the separate stages of the proportionality analysis (a-e). Conversely, a ruling is identified as 'vague' when the Court does not refer to these stages, but simply concludes that the challenged legislation is unjustified, discriminatory or unconstitutional (f–g). In other words, the set of seven variables is recoded in one dichotomous variable (0=clarity, 1=vague).[1412,1413]

Given the binary nature of the dependent variable(s), a logit model is estimated to analyse its relation to the different explanatory variables. Seven models are estimated to explore the odds on producing a vague opinion: one for each salience indicator (see chapter 4), one with all salience indicators combined, one with the two variables tracking whether a reference was made to ECtHR or ECJ case law, and one with the variables related to whether the legislative purpose could not be or has not been ascertained. An in-depth analysis of these models can demonstrate whether the clarity of the ruling is significantly related to case salience, international case law, legislative deficiencies or a combination of these factors.

Table 7.2. Overview of the descriptive results of the explanatory variables in the subset of cases and in the total number of cases

Explanatory variables	**N (%) within the subset of cases**	**N (%) within the total**
Media attention		
– No articles (REF)	576 (91%)	2907 (92%)
– 1–5 articles	39 (6%)	178 (6%)
– >5 articles	16 (3%)	60 (2%)
Panel size		
– Plenary session	280 (44%)	1173 (37%)
Participation diversity		
– One type of litigant involved	337 (53%)	1640 (52%)

(continued)

cognitive processes. The dependent variable was the cognitive complexity score of each opinion: see RJ Owens and J Wedekins, 'Justices and Legal Clarity: Analyzing the Complexity of Supreme Court Opinions' (2011) 45 Law & Society Review, 1032–3.

1412 Precise (n=329); vague (n=302). In 27 cases, a combination of both precise and vague language was registered. These cases were integrated into the dummy-variable as value zero, in order to keep the other category (vagueness) as 'pure' as possible. It is this judicial practice which is explained and studied from a strategic perspective.

1413 This dichotomisation is robust, considering that the result of the explanatory variables is very similar for all variables in groups 'zero' and 'one'. One exception is panel size, but in none of the models was this variable significant, which indicates that it simply does not affect opinion clarity. Therefore, each case can be categorised into one of these two options, with very little information loss. The robustness check consisted of testing two multinomial models, one with categories 0=vague, 1=relevant and 2=proportional (considering that the objective and

Table 7.2 *continued*

Explanatory variables	N (%) within the subset of cases	N (%) within the total
– Only referring judge (in preliminary procedures)	83 (13%)	319 (10%)
– 2 types of litigants involved	183 (29%)	910 (29%)
– >2 types of litigants involved	28 (4%)	276 (9%)
Involvement of individuals		
– No individuals involved	231 (37%)	1299 (41%)
– 1–5 individuals involved	340 (54%)	1625 (52%)
– > 5 individuals involved	60 (10%)	221 (7%)
Ascertaining the legislative objective		
– No reference to preparatory parliamentary documents	44 (7%)	327 (10%)
– Reference to the lack of justification given by the legislator	50 (8%)	84 (3%)
Influence of human rights case law		
– Reference to ECtHR case law	89 (14%)	327 (10%)
– Reference to ECJ case law	33 (5%)	146 (5%)

7.5.4. RESULTS

The goodness of fit tests indicate that most models accurately estimate the effects of the independent variables. In particular, the Omnibus Test of Model Coefficients shows that the Chi Square is significant except for models 2 and 3, meaning that all other models are better at predicting opinion vagueness than a null-model. The Hosmer and Lemeshow test indicates that all models fit the data. In comparison to the more limited models (1–6), the log-likelihood shows that the least unexplained observations remain in the full model. The findings indicate that, in this model, although most variables go in the expected direction,[1414] a few of them yield a significant effect. In particular, only references to the ECtHR case law, the two variables relating to the legislative objective, and the participation of a diverse group of litigants are significantly related to opinion clarity. In other words, while hypotheses 4 and 5 are largely supported by the data, the results with regard to salience indicators (hypotheses 1 to 3) are mixed.

necessity stage almost always overlap with category 1 or 2) and one with categories 0=precise, 1=not reasonably justified and 2=no justification test executed.

1414 The exception is the participation of a large group of individuals. While it was argued that their involvement may push to court to be more specific, the results suggest it may have an opposite effect (although not a significant one).

Table 7.3. Application of the proportionality analysis – model effects (* = p<0.001; ** = p<0.01; * = p<0.05)**

	MODEL 1		MODEL 2		MODEL 3		MODEL 4		MODEL 5		MODEL 6		FULL MODEL 7	
	B (standard error)	Exp (B)	B (standard error)	Exp (B)	B (standard error)	Exp (B)	B (standard error)	Exp (B)	B (standard error)	Exp (B)	B (standard error)	Exp (B)	B (standard error)	Exp (B)
Intercept	−0.069 (0.083)	0.933	−0.040 (0.107)	0.961	−0.181 (0.175)	0.835	−0.146 (0.188)	0.864	−0.228** (0.087)	0.796	0.043 (0.087)	1.044	−0.255 (0.194)	0.775
Explanatory Variables														
***Media attention**														
– No articles (REF)	/	/	/	/	/	/	/	/	/	/	/	/	/	/
– 1–5 articles	0.327 (0.334)	1.387					0.391 (0.351)	1.478					0.459 (0.358)	1.583
– >5 articles	−1.876* (0.761)	0.153					−1.751* (0.773)	0.174					−1.459 (0.796)	0.232
***Plenary session** (REF=0)			−0.089 (0.160)	0.915			−0.032 (0.170)	0.969					0.146 (0.182)	1.158
***Participation diversity**														
– One type of litigant involved (REF)	/	/	/	/	/	/	/	/	/	/	/	/	/	/
– Only referring judge (preliminary procedures)					0.546 (0.284)	1.727	0.523 (0.286)	1.687					0.473 (0.293)	1.605

– 2 types of litigants involved					0.116 (0.189)	1.123	0.095 (0.193)	1.100					0.058 (0.197)	1.060
– >2 types of litigants involved					−0.831 (0.443)	0.435	−0.775 (0.452)	0.461					−0.983* (0.468)	0.374
***Involvement of individuals**														
– No individual involved (REF)	/	/	/	/	/	/	/	/	/	/	/	/	/	/
– 1–5 individuals involved					−0.008 (0.198)	0.992	−0.019 (0.200)	0.981					−0.013 (0.205)	0.988
– >5 individuals involved					0.299 (0.322)	1.349	0.309 (0.327)	1.362					0.422 (0.338)	1.525
***Ascertaining the legislative objective**														
– Reference to preparatory parliamentary documents (REF=1)									0.887** (0.330)	2.429			0.778* (0.337)	2.177

(continued)

Table 7.3 *continued*

	MODEL 1		MODEL 2		MODEL 3		MODEL 4		MODEL 5		MODEL 6		FULL MODEL 7	
	B (standard error)	Exp (B)	B (standard error)	Exp (B)	B (standard error)	Exp (B)	B (standard error)	Exp (B)	B (standard error)	Exp (B)	B (standard error)	Exp (B)	B (standard error)	Exp (B)
– Reference to the lack of justification given by the legislator (REF=0)									1.173*** (0.327)	3.230			1.191*** (0.336)	3.289
***Influence of human rights case law**														
– Reference to ECtHR case law (REF=0)											−0.861*** (0.247)	0.423	−0.808** (0.267)	0.446
– Reference to ECJ case law (REF=0)											−0.129 (0.369)	0.879	−0.069 (0.407)	0.933

Goodness of fit														
−2 Log-likelihood	863.290		873.454		863.088		853.748		853.255		860.302		823.925	
Chi Square	10.306 (0.006)		0.307 (0.580)		10.508 (0.062)		19.848 (0.011)		20.506 (0.000)		13.459 (0.001)		49.671 (0.000)	
Hosmer & Lemeshow	0.000 (1)		0.000		1.143 (0.950)		7.588 (0.475)		0.000 (1)		0.401 (0.527)		6.502 (0.591)	
Nagelkerke R^2	0.022		0.001		0.022		0.041		0.043		0.028		0.101	

First, in line with hypothesis 1b, the Court is usually more precise on the grounds for establishing a violation in intensively covered cases. In particular, the average opinion vagueness increases from 48% (no media attention) to 56% (little attention), but decreases to 13% when the case is covered in more than five newspaper articles. Models 1 (with only media attention) and 4 (with the salience indicators combined) reveal a significant result for extensive coverage, decreasing the odds on a vague opinion considerably (85% and 83%, respectively).[1415] This suggests that when political resistance is anticipated, but external actors will be able to monitor evasion manoeuvers due to media attention, the Court is more inclined to be specific on the grounds for establishing a violation. Being precise may not only stimulate the implementation of its ruling, but can also protect the Court against criticism when it is under public scrutiny. In particular, by binding itself to the proportionality analysis in intensively covered cases, the Court may aim to ensure that the decision is perceived as determined by legal principles, instead of political considerations.[1416] In other words, in intensively covered cases, the benefit of using specific language to prompt a legislative response outweighs the Court's concern for the institutional implications. Conversely, when there is little attention on the case, the potential costs that the legislature must bear in case of non-compliance are lower. The results imply that, in those cases, the Court's concerns for the consequences of a lack of legislative response more often get the upper hand.[1417]

In the full model, the p-value for the 'extensive coverage' is just above the significance threshold of 0.05.[1418] A probable explanation is that this variable is correlated to the factors added in the full model. More specifically, within this subset of data, more references to ECtHR and ECJ case law were registered in cases that were covered in the news media.[1419] This is in line with the findings discussed in chapter 6 on citation practices. In particular, the Court strategically grounds its rulings more strongly in controversial cases in order to legitimise the decision to an external audience. As discussed below, references to ECtHR

1415 In model 1, the p-value=0.031.

1416 T-I Harbo, 'The Function of the Proportionality Principle in EU Law' (2010) 16 European Law Journal 158, 164.

1417 Staton and Vanberg argue that the balance between these concerns does not only depend on the contours of the case, but also on the general institutional standing of and public support for the Court, which determines its leverage to ensure compliance. The authors compare Germany and the US (strong) with Russia and Bulgaria (weak). See JK Staton and G Vanberg, 'The Value of Vagueness: Delegation, Defiance and Judicial Opinions' (2008) 52 American Journal of Political Science, 504, 515.

1418 P-value=0.067 (>5 newspaper articles).

1419 In particular, within the subset of data, references to ECtHR case law were made in 13% of the cases that received no attention, 18% of cases covered in 1–5 articles and 50% of extensively covered cases (Phi 0.126, p-value=0.000). For references to ECJ case law, this distribution is 4%, 10% and 38% (Phi 0.105, p-value=0.000).

case law significantly prompt the Court to produce a precise opinion. Hence the results indicate that, when comparing cases with and without a reference to the ECHR, more media attention does not additionally push the Court in that direction.[1420] In addition, there may also be correlation between media coverage and the variables related to the legislative objective. In particular, in the group of cases that received extensive media attention, there are fewer cases where no reference was made to parliamentary documents.[1421] As discussed below, the absence of such a reference significantly increases the probability that the Court produces a vague opinion. And vice versa: when the legislative objective can be ascertained, the odds on a vague opinion decrease considerably. Thus, the results again indicate that more media attention does not additionally push the Court in that direction.[1422]

Next, no support is found for the hypothesis related to panel size. None of the models that include this variable (2, 4 and 7) reveal a significant effect. The average opinion vagueness is almost equal for the rulings decided in plenary and restricted session.[1423] This may be explained by the institutional setting in which the Court has to function. In particular, the individual judges are not allowed to publish separate opinions and each ruling is the result of a compromise between the different (sub-groups of) judges. Hence, independently from the panel size, the judges are permanently obliged to find common ground. This is in contrast with the institutional framework of the USSC, where judges can decide to concede to the majority opinion or publish a separate opinion. In that setting, larger majority coalitions are known to produce more diluted opinions.[1424]

The results for the final two salience indicators, related to who participated in the procedure, are again mixed. First, the findings indicate that the size of the group of individuals involved in the procedure is not related to how the Court formulates its opinion. In particular, in none of the models where it

1420 Nonetheless, the data does show that – within the group of cases where a reference was made to ECtHR case law – less vague opinions were proclaimed in the cases that received extensive attention. Hence, it remains plausible that there is a significant result that may become apparent when adding new cases to the subset of data.

1421 In particular, within the subset of data, references to parliamentary documents were made in 85% of the cases that received no attention, 93% of cases covered in 1–5 articles and 97% of extensively covered cases (Phi 0.071, p-value=0.000).

1422 Nonetheless, the data does demonstrate that – within the group of cases where the legislative objective could be ascertained – less vague opinions were proclaimed in the cases that received extensive media attention. Hence, it remains plausible that there is a significant result that will become apparent when adding new cases to the subset of data.

1423 In particular, 47% (plenary session) vs 49% (restricted session).

1424 The results showed that, for each additional judge in the majority coalition, the complexity score of the ruling increases by 0.107 units: RJ Owens and J Wedekins, 'Justices and Legal Clarity: Analyzing the Complexity of Supreme Court Opinions' (2011) 45 Law & Society Review, 1032–3.

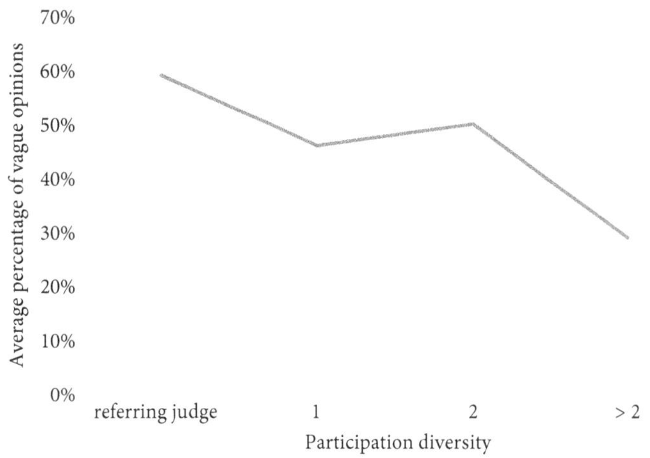

Figure 7.1. Average opinion vagueness in relation to participation diversity

was integrated (3, 4 nor 7) did this factor have a significant result.[1425] Next, more diversity within the group of participants equally does seem to related to opinion clarity. As demonstrated by figure 7.1, a large majority of the preliminary questions where only the referring judge was involved resulted in vague opinions (59%). When one or two types of litigants participated in the procedure, this percentage drops slightly (46% and 50%). Finally, it decreases considerably in cases where more than three litigants were involved (29%). Although no significant result was found for such increased participation diversity in models 3 and 4, the full model – which fits the data best – does reveal a significant result.[1426] Hence, the results indicate that – controlling for all other factors – more intense participation is a trigger for the Court to be more specific on the grounds for establishing a violation. The more litigants participate in the procedure, the more information the Court has to rely on when formulating its opinion. Moreover, preliminary questions that are drawn up by the referring judge, without any involvement at a later stage by other litigants, often relate to an uncontroversial issue.[1427] Conversely, the participation of more than two types of litigants points to the delicate nature of that case.[1428] Hence, this result

1425 In 51% of the cases where no individual was involved, the Court produced a vague opinion. This decreases to 46% when 1–5 individuals participated and increases slightly to 52% when more than 5 were involved.

1426 P-value=0.036. In model 3, this p-value was 0.060 and in model 4 it was 0.086.

1427 These cases receive the least media coverage (an average of 0.02 articles) and are least decided in plenary session (30%), in comparison to cases where one or more litigants are involved.

1428 In particular, these cases receive more media attention (an average of 1.7 articles) and are more regularly treated in plenary session (47%). See chapter 4, sections 4.3. and 4.4.

confirms that the Court is actually more inclined to be precise in controversial cases, in particular when it anticipates that a broader audience will monitor legislative implementation.

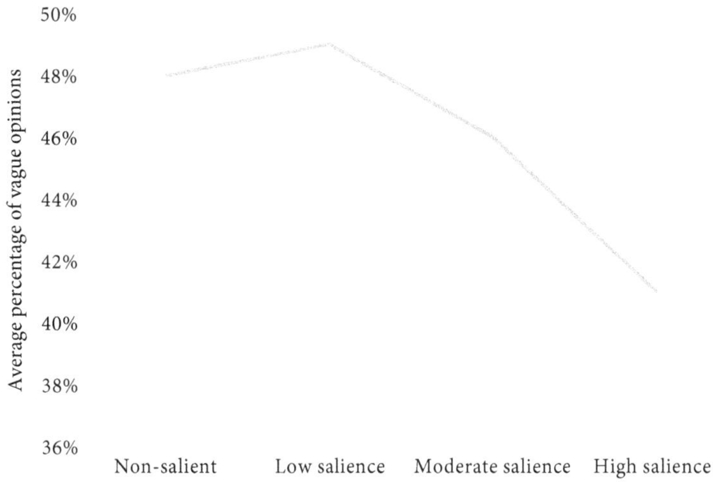

Figure 7.2. Average opinion vagueness in relation to case salience

In line with the presentation of the results in the previous chapters, figure 7.2 gives an overview of the relation between 'aggregated salience' (such as defined in chapter 4) and the Court's application of the proportionality analysis. Yet, in contrast to the results for the outcomes and citation practices, this figure does not indicate that highly salient cases are treated considerably differently than other cases. In particular, there is only a slight decrease in average opinion vagueness. This should be understood in relation to the above-mentioned diverging effects of the separate salience indicators. In particular, while more media attention and participation diversity may decrease the odds on a vague opinion, no similar relation was found for panel size and the size of the group of individuals. Therefore, it is not surprising that highly salient cases – where all these indicators are combined – are treated similarly to low or medium salient cases.

Nonetheless, the results demonstrate that the combination of extensive media attention and a diverse group of litigants creates a setting in which producing a precise opinion is considered the most rewarding strategy. A first example is the already discussed weapon regulations case.[1429] The challenged provisions were intended to protect citizens against crimes with firearms and initially met with broad political and public support. Due to a shooting incident, the decision-making process had been accelerated and resulted in regulations that were

[1429] BeCC case no 154/2007, 19 December 2007. See section 4.5.

considered amongst the strictest in the world.[1430] Yet, as argued by the litigants, some citizens may own a firearm for recreational, sporting or historical reasons without any intention to commit a crime with it.[1431] The Court found that, in light of the general interest in protection, it is neither adequate nor proportional to tighten the existing rules for owners of firearms without good reason – considering the limited danger of these weapons.[1432] A second example is the smoking ban case,[1433] discussed earlier, where the Court dealt with an exemption to the immediate application of the ban for bars where no food was served. The Court noted that the main purpose of the ban was to protect non-smoking employees and customers. The exemption was motivated by the argument that the immediate application could inflict economic harm on these particular bars. Yet, the litigants presented to the Court scientific evidence that undermined that assumption. The Court concluded that the criterion of differentiation (serving food) was not pertinent in the light of the general purpose of the law. In sum, in intensively covered cases where a diverse group of litigants is involved, the Court considers opinion clarity a better alternative than vagueness.

Yet, the variables that are most strongly linked to opinion vagueness are related to the lack of information on the legislative objective. More precisely, the odds on a vague opinion increases significantly, by 117%, when no reference was made to preparatory parliamentary documents, and by 229% when the Court specifies that, based on those documents, the legislative objective could not be ascertained. More specifically, in 66% and 72% of these cases respectively, a vaguer opinion was published. Hence, the results confirm that in these two situations, the Court is prevented from applying a full proportionality analysis. Importantly, proportionality-based judicial review institutionalises the right to demand a public, reasons-based justification.[1434] The absence of a reference to parliamentary documents can be due to a deficiency in the legislative process, for example when the discrimination resulted from forgetfulness such as the aforementioned case no 36/2011. In addition, a statement that the preparatory documents lack a justification for the constitutional infringement can certainly be interpreted as criticism of the legislative procedure. For instance, in case no 54/2015,[1435] the Court reviewed a fiscal measure with

---

1430 V Verlinden, *De Hoeders van de Wet* (die Keure 2010), 223.

1431 A petition was lodged before the Court by three types of litigants: several individual firearm owners; a business buying and selling firearms; and associations acting in the interest of one or both. Their judicial action was covered by the news media. See for example: De Morgen, 25 July 2006, "*Wapenliefhebbers naar Arbitragehof tegen wapenwet*"; and Le Soir, 26 July 2006, "*Armes. La Cour d'arbitrage saisie d'une requête en annulation. Les armuriers flinguent la loi*".

1432 BeCC case no 154/2007, 19 December 2007, B.51.2.

1433 BeCC case no 37/2011, 15 March 2011. See *supra*, section 6.5.4.1.

1434 M Kumm, 'The Idea of Socratic Contestation and the Right to Justification: The Point of Rights-Based Proportionality Review' (2010) Law and Ethics Human Rights, 142.

1435 BeCC case no 54/2015, 7 May 2015.

retroactive consequences. The Court stated that it could not be deduced from parliamentary documents or from the defending party's memorandum why this retroactive effect was introduced. This statement was immediately followed by the conclusion stating that the retroactive nature of the challenged measure was 'unjustified' and therefore unconstitutional.[1436] A remark like this should prompt the legislator to adopt the proportionality framework.[1437]

Further, in cases where a reference was made to ECtHR case law, opinion vagueness decreases significantly, by 55%. In particular, while the average opinion vagueness in cases where no such reference was made is 51%, this drops to 30% when ECtHR case law is cited in the opinion. This result confirms that, when the Court's opinion is guided by ECtHR case law, it is more likely to clarify why the proportionality analysis was failed. Moreover, the prominence of the proportionality stage *sensu stricto* in the ECtHR judgments[1438] is reflected in the Court's case law.[1439] This is not unsurprising, considering that the BeCC's initial adoption of the proportionality analysis was inspired by ECtHR case law. In addition, considering the authority of the ECtHR as a supranational institution, its judgments carry considerable weight. By referring to this case law as a source of authority, the Court can address the legislator more directly but at the same time avoid the criticism that it is interfering with legislative discretion. Although opinion clarity also increases when a similar reference is made to ECJ case law, this result is not significant. This result cannot be a reflection of opinion vagueness in ECJ case law, because this court actually applies the proportionality framework more rigorously than the ECtHR. Rather, it suggests that the impact of the ECJ in fundamental rights adjudication is more limited.[1440]

An example of a case where the impact of international human rights case law is reflected in the Court's application of the proportionality analysis is the data retention case, discussed above.[1441] In order to combat serious crime and

---

1436 Ibid., B.13.

1437 P Popelier and AA Patiño Álvarez, 'Deliberative Practices of Constitutional Courts in Consolidated and Non-Consolidated Democracies' in P Popelier, A Mazmanyan and W Vandenbruwaene (eds.), *The Role of Constitutional Courts in Multilevel Governance* (Intersentia 2013), 215.

1438 J Rivers, 'Proportionality and Variable Intensity of Review' (2006) 65 Cambridge Law Journal, 174, 182, 187: "In practice, the ECtHR engages in balancing in the context of almost every Convention Right [...] balancing rights and public interest is endemic under the Convention"; and Y Arai-Takahashi, *The Margin of Appreciation Doctrine and the Principle of Proportionality in the Jurisprudence of the ECHR* (Intersentia 2002), 193.

1439 In particular, of the 233 cases where the Court explicitly stated that the measure fails the proportionality test, 54 (23%) also contained a reference to ECtHR case law. This is a significant increase in comparison to the number of references to ECtHR case law in the total number of cases (10%).

1440 In particular, when such a reference is made, opinion vagueness drops to 42%, while it increases to 48% when the Court does not refer to ECJ case law. An independent samples t-test confirms that this difference is not significant (equal variances not assumed; $p=0.526$).

1441 BeCC case no 84/2015, 11 June 2015.

terrorism, the federal legislator installed a mechanism to store private data. But no restrictions were built into the law, such as limiting its scope of application to persons suspected of criminal activities. To underpin its ruling, the Court cited both ECtHR and ECJ case law indicating that such almost unlimited ability to store private data is disproportional to the purpose of combatting serious crime and terrorism.[1442] The Court stated that 'for the same reasons', the data retention law violates the Constitution. Hence, this ruling shows how a previous and similar proportionality analysis executed by the ECtHR (or ECJ) can affect how the BeCC formulates its opinion.

7.6. CONCLUSION

Given the global prominence of the proportionality analysis in constitutional adjudication, it is important to study which factors may affect its application in concrete cases. By analysing the BeCC's case law, this chapter provides some new and valuable insights. First, the descriptive analysis revealed that the Court rarely declares legislation unconstitutional on the grounds of an illegitimate purpose or the subjective nature of the criterion for unequal treatment. On the one hand, this may indicate that such legislative proposals are filtered out during the legislative process. On the other hand, the Court may be reluctant to label its arguments as such because this could provoke the criticism that it is interfering with the legislator's prerogatives. In addition, the results showed that the suitability and especially the necessity stage are less prominent in the Court's case law compared to the balancing stage *sensu stricto*. Moreover, when the Court establishes a violation with reference to the balancing stage, often it has not cleared the previous stages. A possible explanation is that the Court circumvents the suitability and necessity stages because they often require a factual evaluation of cause and effect. Executing this evaluation is particularly difficult when there is no evidence available, or when there is empirical uncertainty on the matter. Although the balancing stage also entails a difficult normative evaluation, the judges – especially those with a legal background – may feel more comfortable with this approach. Yet, engaging in a full proportionality analysis, which would include mechanisms to distribute the burden of proof, would enhance the transparency on how the decision came about and increase its persuasiveness. Also, by pointing out more precisely why the violation was established, the Court can increase its influence on policy outcomes. Yet, in more than half of the subset of cases, the Court refrains from referring to any of the stages of

1442 Ibid., B.9, referring to, for example: ECJ C-293/12, *Digital Rights Ireland Ltd*, 8 April 2014; ECJ C-594/12 *Kärtner Landesregiering a.o.*; ECtHR case no 9248/81, *Leander/Sweden*, 26 March 1987; ECtHR case no 28341/95, *Rotaru/Romania*, 4 May 2000; and ECtHR case no 54934/00, *Weber and Saravia/Germany*, 29 June 2006.

the proportionality analysis to establish a violation. By simply mentioning that the provision is 'unjustified', 'discriminatory' or 'unconstitutional', the Court provides even less assistance to the legislator for when it designs a new initiative in conformity with the Constitution. Hence, the question that arose was why the Court, in these cases, produces a vague opinion.

For that purpose, several hypotheses were developed with regard to the determinants of opinion clarity. In particular, it was argued that constitutional courts develop strategies to avoid the criticism that they are interfering with the legislator's prerogatives. Additional hypotheses were developed with regard to the availability of information on the legislative objective and the influence of human rights case law. The regression models revealed several interesting findings. When the Court is vague on the grounds for establishing a violation, this is primarily due to a lack of sufficient information on the legislative objective underlying the challenged measure. In that sense, legislative shortcomings prevent the Court from applying the proportionality test to its full extent. Next, the results showed that the Court's reasoning patterns are influenced by the ECtHR. In some cases, there is ECtHR case law available related to the same or a similar measure as that challenged before the BeCC. In those cases, the BeCC is likely to adopt the conclusion – with reference to a certain stage of the proportionality analysis – of the ECtHR. Finally, the results of the salience indicators on opinion clarity are mixed. Neither panel size nor the size of the group of involved individuals is significantly related to how the Court formulates its opinion. Yet, the significant result in relation to participation diversity revealed by the model suggested that when more litigants bring forward arguments on which the Court can rely, the more likely the Court can or will ascertain why the proportionality analysis failed. Moreover, producing a clearer opinion may also be interpreted as a specific judicial strategy to stimulate compliance. When a diverse group of litigants is involved, and especially when the case has been intensively covered by the news media, the legislative reaction to the ruling is likely to be under public scrutiny. Such monitoring can stimulate implementation, which decreases the risk for the Court that open legislative defiance will threaten its institutional standing. Hence, producing a clearer opinion can protect the Court against reprisals while striking down a policy to which it objects.

CONCLUSION

By systematically analysing the case law of the Belgian Constitutional Court, this book contributes to the scholarly debate on the role of constitutional courts in democratic systems. The main research question relates to how the BeCC balances its role as a deliberative institution against its functioning in a political system defined by consociational features by behaving strategically in salient cases. The interdisciplinary methodology used to answer this question is particularly innovative. While normative and empirical projects usually travel on largely separate tracks, this book sought to integrate both approaches. In particular, the case law of the Court was evaluated empirically from two angles: (a) to what extent does the Court employ the discussed deliberative 'judicial good practices'; and (b) to what extent is the Court's performance affected by strategic considerations? A final relevant sub-question, that addresses the normative implications of the empirical findings, is: (c) whether such strategic behaviour corresponds with the deliberative expectations weighing on the Court?

In what follows, it is first discussed why an in-depth scrutiny of the three selected judicial practices – case outcomes, citation practices and the application of the proportionality analysis – generates new insights into the judicial behaviour of constitutional courts. Next, an overview is given of the main results. Overall, the findings show that the Belgian Constitutional Court has developed into a venue for deliberation but that, simultaneously, it exhibits strategic behaviour in order to ensure compliance with its rulings and to protect itself against institutional reprisals. Following that, it is argued that the Court's strategic behaviour can be understood as part of the deliberative performance, and that the third sub-question should therefore be answered positively. Finally, there is a consideration of some recommendations for both the Court and the legislator.

Three main aspects of the Court's case law were explored: case outcomes, citation practices and the application of the proportionality analysis. First, scholars traditionally concentrate on whether the individual ideological preferences of judges predict their decision to invalidate legislation or not. The analysis on case outcomes in this book offers a new perspective because it takes into account the effect of collegial dynamics and because it integrates a variety of 'in-between' modulated outcomes. The analysis of the citation practices provides a window into the reason-giving culture and performance of the BeCC. In contrast to common law countries, the BeCC – like many other courts in continental Europe – tends to be more selective when grounding its rulings in external authorities such as (inter)national case law and scientific evidence. Finally, the examination of the proportionality analysis adds a new and unique layer to the current knowledge on strategic judicial behaviour. Notwithstanding the global prominence of the proportional analysis in constitutional studies, very little is known about the factors and processes that influence its application in practice. More generally, by linking the strategical model to other aspects of the ruling than the case outcome, this analysis gives new insights into how judges adapt their rulings in order to stimulate compliance.

In the normative framework, a multi-dimensional definition was given for 'deliberative performance'. In particular, a deliberative institution should: (1) provide an inclusive forum; (2) deliberate internally; (3) produce a transparent written decision; (4) justify that decision by rational arguments; and (5) enhance constitutional dialogue. It was argued that performing in line with these five sub-components enhances the quality and legitimacy of an institution's decision. Because the legislative decision-making process is often criticised for a lack of inclusiveness, transparency and rationality – precisely the key concepts in the given definition – a constitutional court can offer an alternative route. The analysis of the BeCC's case law shows that the Court engages in such a deliberative enterprise.

First, although to the letter of the law there is no middle way between invalidating legislation or rejecting the challenge, the Court has developed a variety of 'substantive modulations'. Such creative outcomes indicate how the legislation should be interpreted or altered in order for it to be applied in a constitutional way. In addition, the Court can also temper the retroactive effect of an invalidation (only recently in preliminary rulings). Substantive and temporal modulations leave room for and initiate an interactive engagement with other actors involved in the review procedure – the legislator, the litigants and the judiciary. They instruct these actors on how to interpret and apply, but also, more generally, how to amend and draft legislation. The results indicate that the Court, over the years and especially in fundamental rights cases, has become more and more willing to provide such assistance. Although there is room for improvement, as is explained below, this highlights the Court's potential to catalyse deliberation outside the scope of the review procedure.

Second, the quality of the Court's reasoning – understood as the extent to which it relies on external authorities – has improved considerably. Most rulings are documented with reference to at least one authority. Although there is usually a routine citation of parliamentary documents, results show that the average citation density has increased over the years. In particular, the Court increasingly makes use of precedents and of ECtHR and ECJ case law. The first increase can logically be explained by the increase in the volume of the BeCC's own case law. Moreover, the results indicate that the Court cites precedents to avoid an overload of work, but also to legitimise an act of judicial activism, in particular when the legislator repeatedly makes the same mistake. The latter increase points at the BeCC's pro-European inclination. Although the Court is overall less keen to cite national case law, the results show that the Court does so when relevant to the case. For instance, the Court cites the case law of the administrative jurisdiction in cases relating to spatial planning. Finally, scientific evidence only plays a marginal role in the BeCC's case law. Usually, the cited evidence is brought forward by the legislator and serves to prove the reasonableness of the legislative decision. Yet, as will be discussed below, executing the proportionality analysis – and in particular the suitability and necessity test – often requires empirical clarifications. The law allows the Court to invite the parties to present additional evidence, or ask expert advice, but these options are rarely used. It was said that this reluctance of the Court may be explained by the limited availability of such evidence. Another explanation may be that the Court wants to prevent its active engagement, as opposed to the passive collection of all arguments brought forward, from being perceived as some form of bias. Also, considering their limited background in empirical methodology, the judges may not feel comfortable interpreting such evidence or estimating its reliability. As will be discussed below, two possible solutions are to allow *amici curiae* with expert knowledge to introduce a memorandum and to improve the acquaintance of the judges with contemporary scientific methods (including statistics).

Third, the examination of the Court's application of the proportionality analysis shows that, when establishing a violation, it very rarely follows the sequential structure of the proportionality analysis. Further, the results reveal the prominence of the balancing stage *sensu stricto*. It was argued that this can primarily be explained by a reluctance to declare a legislative purpose illegitimate, or the chosen means unsuitable or unnecessary. First, the Court may want to avoid the criticism that, by labelling the objective illegitimate, it infringes upon the prerogative of the elected politicians to define which goals to pursue. Second, in line with the previous argument on the use of scientific evidence, the judges may not feel called upon to estimate the effectiveness of the chosen measure or possible alternatives. Although the balancing stage also entails a difficult normative evaluation, they may prefer to avoid making empirical evaluations. Finally, in more than half of the subset of cases, the Court refrains from referring to any of the stages of the proportionality analysis and simply mentions that the provision is 'unjustified', 'discriminatory' or 'unconstitutional'. These rulings provide the least assistance to the legislator on how to amend the current of new draft legislation and were identified as 'vague opinions'. Overall, in order to enhance the transparency on how the decision came about and increase its persuasiveness, this author recommends that the Court engages more strongly in a full proportionality analysis. Yet this poses similar difficulties with regard to the availability of evidence and the distribution of the burden of proof. As will be discussed below, opening up the review procedure to *amici curiae* and broadening the quantitative (including statistical) skills of the judges may provide a solution.

Building on judicial behaviour theories, this book argues that 'the strategic model' may offer an explanation for variation in the Court's case law. The strategic model assumes that the Court adapts its behaviour in line with the anticipated reactions of others, which are expected to be more pronounced in salient cases. In chapter 4, a new and unique view on contemporaneous case salience was developed, based on three objective, independent measures: increased media attention, the participation of a large and/or diverse group of litigants and a deliberation in plenary session. These measures were included as independent variables in the regression models in chapters 5, 6 and 7. These results indicate that the Court acts differently in salient cases in order to strategically stimulate short- and long-term compliance with its decision.

First, the Court has considerable discretion to select the outcome it finds appropriate. The results in chapter 5 on the case outcomes were presented in two steps. First, a positive relation was found between case salience and the finding of a violation. In particular, more violations are established in cases that were decided in plenary session and that were extensively covered by the news media during the judicial procedure. The same can be said for the cases where a larger group of individuals was involved, but not where more diversity within the group of litigants was registered. This does not necessarily reflect strategic behaviour, but rather that the anticipation of the finding of a violation attracts more attention from the news media, litigants and the Court itself. In the second step, the model only included those cases where a violation was established. This analysis suggests that increased case salience – and particularly extensive news media attention before the Court ruling – prompts the Court to act more prudently by proclaiming a substantive and temporal modulation. Often, increased media attention points at the politically sensitive nature of the case. The same can be said for a plenary session, which was the factor with the second largest effect size in this model. Proclaiming a simple invalidation in politically controversial cases may be met with resistance, which can eventually threaten the Court's institutional standing or result in loss of public support. The findings imply that the Court, when anticipating this risk, strategically resorts to an outcome that is phrased in less outspoken terms.

Next, chapter 6 looked into the variation in citation density, which was understood here as a proxy for the judicial effort put into the ruling. The results demonstrate that more effort is expended on the grounding of salient cases than in simple, non-controversial cases. Again, the factors that were shown to be most strongly related to citation density were the plenary session and extensive media coverage. In addition, more authorities are cited in cases where a large group of individuals is involved. These findings imply that courts respond to external incentives and that citations serve the purpose of legitimating decisions to a public audience. In particular, when resistance against the judicial decision is anticipated, a strategy to stimulate compliance is to show that the decision was compelled by external authorities. This is confirmed by the Court's particularly strong reliance, in these cases, on international case law and scientific studies. Further, the results also indicate that more input (collected internally, provided by the litigants or in the public forum) generates a more strongly grounded judicial reason-giving. This can, in turn, provide a stronger basis for future policy decisions. Remarkably, the results do not reveal a similar incentive to use more citations when the Court wants to (partially) invalidate or modulate the challenged legislation. When the case results in a modulation, the ruling is usually underpinned with somewhat more authorities than when the challenge is rejected. Yet, this result can be explained by the fact that more modulations are proclaimed in salient cases (see chapter 5). Hence, the conclusion is that the BeCC grounds its rulings more strongly when a case is salient, irrespective of the outcome of this case.

Finally, variation in the application of the proportionality analysis was explored for a specific subset of cases. In particular, the analysis concentrated on when the Court – if a violation is established in a fundamental rights case – refers to a specific stage of the proportionality analysis or writes a vaguer opinion where the legislation is simply declared 'unjustified' or 'unconstitutional'. Although precise language is generally believed to stimulate compliance, some scholars have identified the producing of vaguer opinions as a strategy for a court to protect itself against institutional reprisals while striking down a policy to which it objects. Yet, the results show that the use of vagueness by the BeCC is primarily prompted by the lack of sufficient information on the legislative objective underlying the challenged measure. This indicates that legislative deficiencies, such as not giving a justification for the measures the legislator wants to impose, are reflected in the Court's case law. Next, the results show that ECtHR case law is also strongly linked to how the BeCC applies the proportionality analysis. In particular, the BeCC tends to be more precise on the grounds for establishing a violation when the ECtHR has ruled on a similar issue, in which case that court probably phrased its decision with reference to a specific stage of the proportionality analysis. In contrast to the previous two chapters, the relation between case salience and opinion vagueness was found to be limited. In particular, the models show that opinion clarity is not related to panel size nor to the size of the group of individuals. Nonetheless, extensive media attention and more diversity within the group of litigants correspond with the Court being more specific on the grounds for establishing a violation. This suggests that, although this is not the main determinant of opinion vagueness, the Court considers it a better strategy to be precise rather than vague in order to stimulate compliance with the ruling. Moreover, by using the proportionality analysis – which is a globally accepted doctrine for solving constitutional questions – the Court may aim to depoliticise its rulings. This is consistent with the Court's propensity to cite more external authorities in controversial cases. Finally, the result may reflect that the input provided by litigants assists the Court in building the justificatory ground for its decision. The more litigants participate in the procedure, the more information the Court may have at its disposal. Similarly, to the proper use of citations, justifying its decision with reference to the proportionality analysis can, in turn, assist the legislator when amending or drafting legislation.

In sum, these empirical results have important implications for the study of judicial behaviour. The empirical analyses show that looking into case outcomes alone underestimates the extent to which courts respond to external incentives and can act strategically in order to maximise their effectiveness. Thus, agreement is found with other scholars who argue that empirical analyses of judicial opinions should concentrate on more nuanced measures that represent the richer content of those opinions which legal scholars regard as fundamental.[1443]

Further, a relevant question is whether such strategic behaviour can be aligned with the deliberative expectations weighing on the Court. As explained in the normative framework, a deliberative court should treat cases equally, be responsive to rational arguments and to all points of view, and be independent of political pressure. Some argue that strategic behaviour conflicts with that deliberative ideal. It would show that judges are not primarily motivated to decide cases based upon an independent assessment of the law and facts.[1444] Instead, the decision is based on prudential calculations about possible (political) consequences. If reasons are expressed not to convince or support an argument, but to please the audience, the implied attitude would be one of anticipation and appeasement, rather than one of good arguments.[1445] In that sense, it is said, judges are guided by similar mechanisms as the elected branch.[1446] Indeed, by letting strategic considerations prevail, the Court would be undermining its unique institutional role of protecting basic constitutional values and

---

1443 For example: F Maltzman, FJ Spriggs and PJ Wahlbeck, 'Strategy and Judicial Choice: New Institutionalist Approaches to Supreme Court Decision Making' in CW Clayton and H Gillman (eds.), *Supreme Court Decision-Making: New Institutional Approaches* (University of Chicago Press 1999), 61; KE Whittington, 'Once More Unto the Breach: Postbehavioralist Approaches to Judicial Politics' (2000) Law and Social Enquiry, 601; B Friedman, 'Taking Law seriously' (2006) 4 Perspectives on Politics, 261, 265; and JK Staton and G Vanberg, 'The Value of Vagueness: Delegation, Defiance and Judicial Opinions' (2008) 52 American Journal of Political Science, 504, 506.

1444 B Friedman 'The Politics of Judicial Review' (2005) 84 Texas Law Review, 257, 270.

1445 I Venzke, 'Judicial Authority and Styles of Reasoning: The Self-presentation between Legalism and Deliberation' (2016) 4 Amsterdam Law School Legal Studies Research Paper, 1, 3,17.

1446 WF Murphy, *Elements of Judicial Strategy* (University of Chicago Press 1964), 209; and FB Cross and BJ Nelson, 'Strategic Institutional Effects on Supreme Court Decision-making' (2001) 95 Northwestern University Law Review, 1437, 1442.

minority rights.[1447] Therefore, strategic behaviour is believed to cast doubt on the critical and potentially legitimating role that courts can play.[1448]

Yet, in this author's view and based on the research conducted, exhibiting strategic behaviour does not necessarily mean that the judges do not decide cases in good faith based on their best understanding of the law. While the above-mentioned sceptics assume that political constraints determine the case outcome in an arbitrary way, strategic behaviour can also be reflected in other circumstantial aspects of the ruling. Although constitutional scrutiny does not allow the Court to react to anticipated reactions in a manner that is not justifiable, it does leave room for the Court to address its audience with prudence, anticipating the future response. The justification given by the Court should be sincere, meaning that judges would stand by these same arguments in diverse cases. Courts should be committed to do nothing that they are not prepared to justify through rational arguments. In that sense, a court can be principled, yet pragmatic. From the three main empirical analyses on the BeCC, it could be deduced that strategic considerations in salient cases usually result in more substantive and temporal modulations, more citations to external authorities and more precise references to the different stages of the proportionality analysis. Although this does not mean that all rulings enjoy transparent, clear and rational underpinnings, overall such behaviour does not conflict with the deliberative ideal.

Rather, these findings reflect the Court's willingness to engage in dialogue with its audience. More and more private petitioners find their way to the BeCC, suggesting an institutional openness to listen to various viewpoints. In turn, the Court's rulings generate information that can be taken into account in new rounds of deliberation, in particular by the legislative branch. Through modulated rulings, references to external authority and to the proportionality analysis, the Court can signal which type of legislative response is suitable and appropriate. It should be emphasised that it is precisely this circulation of arguments that defines the deliberative component. Importantly, constitutional litigation cannot function as a sole forum for deliberation. The legislative branch remains well equipped to decide in which direction public policy should go. The Court, then, can offer *ex post* protection against arbitrary decision-making

---

1447 Friedman argues that this threatens the "hope of constitutional review": B Friedman, 'Taking Law Seriously' (2006) 4 Perspectives on Politics, 261, 264: "If political constraints are too strong, then normative theories that support judicial review as protecting minority rights against a wilful majority at least require nuance". Also see WN Eskridge and PP Frickey, 'Foreword: Law as Equilibrium' (1994) Harvard Law Review, 26, 76; and G Vanberg, *The Politics of Constitutional Review in Germany* (Cambridge University Press 2005), 176.

1448 I Venzke, 'Judicial Authority and Styles of Reasoning: The Self-presentation between Legalism and Deliberation' (2016) 4 Amsterdam Law School Legal Studies Research Paper, 1, 3; and FB Cross and BJ Nelson, 'Strategic Institutional Effects on Supreme Court Decision-making' (2001) 95 Northwestern University Law Review, 1437, 1447 and further.

and function as an agenda-setter and shaper for future policy-making. In that sense, the Court and the legislator act as partners. Also, it remains vital that civil society is engaged with other fora such as Parliament, and that these fora are held accountable through mechanisms other than constitutional review.[1449] Finally, the role of the news media cannot be underestimated. Its role is to draw attention to the case outcomes that require a legislative response. Based on an exploration of the extent of media attention for different types of outcomes, it was concluded that a ruling's newsworthiness mainly depends on the visible impact it has on public policy-making. The removal of provisions from the legal order particularly draws the attention of journalists, and even more so when the retroactive effect of this removal is tempered. Overall, substantive modulations receive far less public attention. Considering that many modulations have a large impact on the content of legislation and require legislative action to provide the necessary legal certainty, a lack of public attention for these outcomes is potentially problematic. Without public oversight, the legislator may be more likely to take the risk of ignoring the judicial decision. Agenda-setters have more influence when it is difficult or costly for decision-makers to ignore their proposals.[1450] When the legislative response to the judicial opinion is under public scrutiny, it becomes more costly for the legislator to take that risk.

Also, strategic behaviour can secure, instead of inhibit, the Court's capacity to live up to deliberative expectations. First, by adjusting its rulings in order to make them more acceptable, the Court actually enhances the consequential character of its case law. Non-compliance with its rulings would diminish the court's effectiveness, not only in the short term but also from a long-term perspective. Although the Court's institutional security is relatively strong,[1451] there is always a risk of losing institutional mechanisms that shape its deliberative potential. Hence, by continuingly taking into account the anticipated behaviour of others, the Court protects its institutional security and legitimacy for future cases.[1452]

Finally, these practices reflect that a consensus must be found amid a pluralist group of judges. In the second chapter, it was argued that diversity

---

1449 E Cameron, 'A South African Perspective on the Judicial Development of Socio-Economic Rights' in L Lazarus, C McCrudden and N Bowles (eds.), *Reasoning Rights: Comparative Judicial Engagement* (Hart Publishing 2014), 338.

1450 G Tsebelis, 'The Power of the European Parliament as a Conditional Agenda Setter' (1995) 88 American Political Science Review, 129.

1451 Altering the institutional framework of the BeCC would require altering the Constitution and/or the Special Act on the Constitutional Court. This requires a special majority in Parliament.

1452 T Roux, *The Politics of Principle: the First South African Constitutional Court, 1995–2005* (Cambridge University Press 2013), 67, 371; A Kavanagh, *Constitutional Review under the UK Human Rights Act* (Cambridge University Press 2009), 199; and CH Mendes, *Constitutional Courts and Deliberative Democracy* (Oxford University Press 2013), 199.

within a constitutional court can improve its deliberative performance. Often, controversial cases are decided in plenary session – which means that the ruling needs to be acceptable to both the Dutch-speaking and French-speaking judges, and to both the legal specialists and former politicians. The results indicate that this collegial internal deliberation process amplifies the available arguments and information and results in rulings that are more elaborately and precisely reasoned.

Nonetheless, there is always room for improvement. First, an evaluation of the Court's case law revealed many inconsistencies, which can obscure the messages the Court sends. First, the Court has developed a broad scale of modulated case dicta, without always being clear on what these dicta practically entail for the regular judiciary, administration or even the legislator. There is no sharp line between interpretative modulations and dicta that constructively alter the legislation, neither between modulations that broaden or limit the scope of the legislation. Also, not all rulings that include a constructive modulation give proper instructions on how to apply the altered legislation. When no legislative response follows those rulings, these outcomes undermine the principle of legal certainty. Therefore, based on these findings, this author would recommend the Court to pay more attention to how it phrases modulated case dicta. More consistency and clearer instructions in *all* modulated rulings would increase the overall transparency of the Court's case law. Next, the Court should engage in a full proportionality analysis. Following the structured approach makes sure that legislation that passes constitutional scrutiny is actually suitable, necessary and proportional to a legitimate policy objective. Also, it enhances transparency on how the decision came about. By articulating more precisely why a particular decision is unconstitutional, the Court provides assistance to the legislator, the litigants and the general public in news round of debate. Finally, it may prompt the legislator to adopt the same standard of approach and act reasonably. In that sense, the Court can contribute to the globally spreading 'culture of justification'.

Also, as explained above, the BeCC is reluctant to engage in the globally emerging phenomenon of evidence-based judicial review of legislation. This judicial good practice relates to the rational component of deliberative performance, and more specifically to the substantive quality of the given arguments. When the Court applies the proportionality analysis to evaluate whether a limitation on a constitutionally protected right is permissible, it often has to estimate the efficacy of means and the nature and acceptability of side-effects. This is a factual enquiry, and might require specific expert knowledge. Yet, notwithstanding the Court's broad investigative possibilities, it is rather reluctant to actively seek evidence to substantiate its decision, for instance by inviting experts to give advice.

An alternative system, which would avoid the Court having to select the experts it wants to hear, is to provide access to *amici curiae*. These do not necessarily have a personal interest in the outcome of the case, but can bring forward specific expert knowledge to aid the Court in making its decision. Moreover, the Court can use this additional information to underpin its judgment. This can contribute to the evidence-based quality of the Court's reasoning and, in turn, that of the potential policy response following the ruling. Therefore, a system with *amici* would allow the Court to enhance its deliberative performance. As explained in section 2.4.2., other judicial institutions already offer this opportunity, be it under the condition of acceptance by the involved parties and/or the Court itself. Empirical research on the influence of *amicus* briefs has repeatedly shown that this external input has a significant effect on the opinions of these courts.[1453]

There are various ways to organise an *amicus curiae* system in practice. An open system would provide the largest access possibilities, but might threaten the economics of judicial efficiency. Therefore, many courts try to limit the amount of *amicus* briefs.[1454] For example, some courts require that an *amicus* requests permission to write a memorandum. Another possibility is that the Court uses a sort of docket control, to select only those memoranda that are useful for the case. Whether the Court accepts the request or the memorandum can depend on various criteria, such as originality, novelty and the quality of the submitted expertise. Transparency on these criteria and, in each specific case, the reason(s) why the request is accepted or rejected, is essential.[1455] Notwithstanding how the system would be organised in practice, this author believes that an extended accessibility would enhance the BeCC's deliberative potential. It increases the probability that valuable, evidence-based information can be incorporated into the Court's proceedings.

Yet case-by-case mechanisms for the incorporation of expertise, such as *amicus* briefs, do not necessarily guarantee that rulings will be evidence-based. Moreover, more external input also brings into the Court questions relating to the quality and interpretation of evidence. Earlier, it was argued that judges may not feel comfortable interpreting empirical evidence or estimating its reliability, considering their limited background in advanced quantitative methods. Hence, a second recommendation is to better facilitate the Court on this point. A possibility is to appoint one or more judges or law clerks with some background in statistics.[1456] Having this judge(s) or law clerk(s) participating

1453 See *supra*, footnotes 456–461.

1454 For an overview, see D Shelton, 'The Participation of Nongovernmental Organizations in International Judicial Proceedings' (1994) 88 The American Journal of International Law, 617–19.

1455 N Bürli, 'Amicus Curiae as a Means to Reinforce the Legitimacy of the European Court of Human Rights' in S Flogaitis, T Zwart and J Fraser (eds.), *The European Court of Human Rights and its Discontents* (Edward Elgar 2013), 144.

1456 A Vermeule, *Law and the Limits of Reason* (Oxford University Press 2009), 138, 153.

in the decision-making process can help the Court to recognise the force of the 'better argument'.[1457] When uncertainty prevails, it must be decided whom to grant the benefit of the doubt. Giving deference to the legislator can be reasonable, but not if this decision is taken on an *ad hoc* basis. Therefore, a final recommendation for the Court is to develop a set of rules determining the distribution of the burden of proof amongst the parties involved in the review procedure. This would enhance the transparency of the Court's reason-giving, and may prompt others to fill in the gaps to allow the Court, and the legislator, to produce evidence-based outcomes.

1457 Ibid., 152 and further.

CODEBOOK

1. IDENTIFICATION OF THE PROCEDURE AND LEGISLATION UNDER REVIEW

Variable name	*Label + additional explanation (if needed)*	*Codes*
VAR1a	Identification case 1 *(Own identification – to sort the cases chronologically)*	Year/number (e.g. 1998/002; 2014/064)
VAR1b	Identification case 2 *(Official identification used by the BeCC – to link this database to the media database of the Court)*	Number/year (e.g. 1/98; 65/2004)
VAR2	Type of Procedure	1 = preliminary ruling 2 = annulment procedure 3 = combination
VAR3	Preliminary question to the ECJ *(Did the BeCC refer a preliminary question to the ECJ with regard to this case, before the ruling?)*	0 = no 1 = yes
VAR4	Legislation under review implements supranational law *(Is the legislation under review an implementation of international/ supranational law?)*	0 = no 1 = yes
VAR5	Legal domain	1 = The Law of persons and family law 2 = Tax law 3 = Judicial organisation and civil procedure 4 = Commercial and finance law 5 = Intellectual property 6 = Environmental and energy law 7 = Spatial planning 8 = (Other) administrative law 9 = Cultural law 10 = Labour and social security law 11 = Substantive and procedural criminal law

Variable name	*Label + additional explanation (if needed)*	*Codes*
		12 = Fundamental rights and freedoms 13 = Educational law 14 = Organisation of the state 15 = Migration law 16 = Social services 17 = Other 18 = Combination 19 = The law of property and special contracts
VAR6	Date of initial request *(Date of the first petition (annulment procedure) or the referring case (preliminary procedure))*	DD/MM/YYYY
VAR7	Date of ruling *(When was the ruling published?)*	DD/MM/YYYY

2. PARTIES INVOLVED IN THE PROCEDURE

VAR8	Defending party	1) Federal state 2) Flemish community/region 3) French-speaking community 4) Walloon region 5) German-speaking community 6) Brussel-capital region 7) Joint community commission 8) French-speaking community commission 9) Combination of a federal and regional entity
VAR9a	Number of initiating individuals *(How many individuals initiated the procedure?)*	0 = none 1 = between 1–5 individuals 2 = between 5–20 individuals 3 = more than 20 individuals
VAR9b	Number of 'new' intervening individuals *(How many individuals were involved as a 'new' intervening party – in the case of a preliminary procedure, not involved in the procedure a quo)*	idem

VAR9c	Individuals involved as intervening party who were also involved in the procedure *a quo.* *(Only in preliminary procedure: the individuals involved as an intervening party were also involved in the procedure a quo)*	0 = no / 1 = yes
VAR10	Interest group	0 = none 1 = initiating party 2 = intervening party 3 = initiating and intervening party 4-7 *(only for preliminary procedure)* 4 = the litigant involved in the procedure before the referring judge raised the preliminary question and intervenes in the procedure before the BeCC 5 = the litigant involved in the procedure before the referring judge raised the preliminary question and, together with another litigant from that category, intervenes in the procedure before the BeCC 6 = the litigant involved in the procedure before the referring judge did not raise the preliminary question but intervenes in the procedure before the BeCC 7 = the litigant involved in the procedure before the referring judge did not raise the preliminary question but, together with another litigant from that category, intervenes in the procedure before the BeCC
VAR11	Companies	idem
VAR12	Local government	idem
VAR13	Public institution or private institution with task of general interest	idem
VAR14	Federal goverment	idem
VAR15	Regional government	idem
VAR16	President parliamentary assembly	idem
VAR17	Political actor	idem
VAR18	Composition of the Court *(The number of judges involved in the deliberation process)*	1 = seven judges (procedure article 71) 2 = seven judges (limited procedure article 72) 3 = plenary session (10/12 judges)

3. ARGUMENTATION ANALYSES

3.1. REFERENCE NORMS

VAR19	**Number of pleas**	**Number**
VAR20a	Reference norm – equality clause (articles 10 & 11, 171 C°)	0 = no 1 = yes, invoked by one of the parties 2 = yes, invoked by the court
VAR20b	Reference norm – other fundamental rights included in the Belgian Constitution	idem
VAR20c	Reference norm – competence allocating rules	idem
VAR20d	Reference norm – federal loyalty related to the competence allocating rules	idem
VAR20e	Reference norm – proportionality related to the competence allocating rules	idem
VAR20f	Reference norm EU law	idem
VAR20g	Reference norm ECHR	idem
VAR20h	Reference norm other international law	idem
VAR20i	Reference norm general principles of law	idem

3.2. CITATIONS

3.2.1. Parliamentary Documents

VAR21a	No citation parliamentary documents *(The BeCC doesn't refer to the legislative goal (as mentioned in preparatory documents) of the legislation under review)*	0 = no / 1 = yes
VAR21b	Citation parliamentary documents neutral *(The BeCC has a neutral attitude towards the legislative goal)*	0 = no / 1 = yes
VAR21c	Citation parliamentary documents positive *(The BeCC has a positive attitude towards the legislative goal)*	0 = no / 1 = yes
VAR21d	Citation parliamentary documents negative *(The BeCC has a negative attitude towards the legislative goal)*	0 = no / 1 = yes
VAR21e	Citation parliamentary documents discrepancy *(The BeCC notes a discrepancy between the legislative goal and the legislative text)*	0 = no / 1 = yes
VAR21f	Citation parliamentary documents goal not specified *(The BeCC notes that the legislative goal was not specified / is not clear)*	0 = no / 1 = yes
VAR21g	Citation parliamentary documents unclear *(The reference to the legislative goal is unclear)*	0 = no / 1 = yes
VAR21h	Citation of parliamentary documents relating to the reference norm	0 = no / 1 = yes

3.2.2. *Other Authorities*

VAR22a	Citation political agreement	0 = no 1 = reference to a specific political agreement 2 = reference to general political principles 3 = combination
VAR22b	Citation case law ECJ = the European Court of Justice	0 = no / 1 = yes
VAR22c	Citation case law ECtHR = the European Court of Human Rights	0 = no / 1 = yes
VAR22d	Citation case law Cassation = the Court of Cassation	0 = no / 1 = yes
VAR22e	Citation case law administrative courts = the Council of State, educational decisions and migration issues	0 = no / 1 = yes
VAR22f	Citation precedents	0 = no / 1 = yes
VAR22g	Citation advisory opinion Council of State	0 = no / 1 = yes
VAR22h	Citation scientific studies	0 = no / 1 = yes
VAR22i	Citation other	0 = no / 1 = yes

4. THE COURT'S RULING

VAR23a	Declaration of unconstitutionality *(The challenged provision is found unconstitutional)*	Number of pleas
VAR23b	Modulated declaration of unconstitutionality *(The challenged provision is found unconstitutional 'to the extent that')*	Number of pleas
VAR23c	Declaration of constitutionality *(The challenged provision is found constitutional)*	Number of pleas
VAR23d	Modulated declaration of constitutionality *(The challenged provision is found constitutional 'under the condition that')*	Number of pleas
VAR23e	Extrinsic lacuna *(The challenged provision is found constitutional, but there is an extrinsic gap in the legal system)*	Number of pleas
VAR23f	Double interpretation *(Unconstitutional if interpreted in one way, but constitutional if interpreted in another way)*	Number of pleas
VAR24	Temporal modulation	0 = no / 1 = yes

BIBLIOGRAPHY

Abraham HJ, *Justices and Presidents: a Political History of Appointments to the Supreme Court* (Oxford University Press 1974) 310p

Abrahamson SS and Lessard G, 'Interbranch Communications: The Next Generation' in F Magnum (ed.), *Conference on Assessing the Effects of Legislation on the Workload of the Courts: Papers and Proceedings* (Diane Publishing 1995) 173p

Adams M and Vanheule D, 'The Theory and Practice of Constitutional Review in the Civil Law: the Case of Belgium' in LJ Wintgens (ed.), *The Theory and Practice of Legislation* (Ashgate 2005) 368p

Agnoloni T and Pagallo U, 'The Power Laws of the ICC, and their Relevance for Legal Scholars' in A Rotolo (ed.), *Legal Knowledge and Information Systems* (IOS Press 2015) 212p

Alemanno A, 'The Emergence of the Evidence-based Judicial Reflex: A Response to Bar-Siman-Tov's Semiprocedural Review' (2013) 1 The Theory and Practice of Legislation 1

Alexander L, 'The Banality of Legal Reasoning' (1998) 73 Notre Dame Law Review 517

Allen MD and Haider-Markel DP, 'Connecting Supreme Court Decisions, Media Coverage and Public Opinion: The Case of Lawrence v. Texas' (2006) 27 The American Review of Politics 209

Arai-Takahashi Y, *The Margin of Appreciation Doctrine and the Principle of Proportionality in the Jurisprudence of the ECHR* (Intersentia 2002) 300p

Armingeon K, 'The Effects of Negotiation Democracy: A Comparative Analysis' (2002) 41 European Journal of Political Research 81

——, 'Democracy, Consociational' in B Badie (ed.), International Encyclopedia of Political Science (Sage publications 2011) 1190p

Bailey MA and Maltzman F, *The Constrained Court* (Princeton University Press 2011) 216p

Baird V, 'The Effect of Politically Salient Decisions on the U.S. Supreme Court's Agenda' (2004) 66 The Journal of Politics 755

Baker A, 'Proportionality', 255–308, in H Fenwick (ed.), *Judicial Review* (LexisNexis 2014) 881p

Barak A, *The Judge in a Democracy* (Princeton University Press 2006) 368p

——, 'Proportional Effect: The Israeli Experience' (2008) 57 University of Toronto Law Review 369

——, *Proportionality: Constitutional Rights and Their Limitations* (Cambridge University Press 2012) 638p

Barbier de la Serre E and Sibony AL, 'Expert Evidence before the EC Courts' (2008) 45 Common Market Law Review 941

Bar-Siman-Tov I, 'The Dual Meaning of Evidence-Based Judicial Review of Legislation' (2016) 4 Theory and Practice of Legislation 107

Bartels B, *Heterogeneity in Supreme Court Decision Making: How Situational Factors Shape Preference-Based Behavior* (PhD Dissertation Ohio State University 2006) 295p

Bateup C, 'The Dialogic Promise: Assessing the Normative Potential of Theories of Constitutional Dialogue' (2006) 71 Brooklyn Law Review 1109

——, 'Expanding the Conversation: American and Canadian Experiences of Constitutional Dialogue in Comparative Perspective' (2006) 44 New York University Public Law and Legal Theory Working Papers 1

Baum L, 'Implementation of Judicial Decisions' (1976) 4 American Politics Research 86

——, *Judges and Their Audiences: a Perspective on Judicial Behaviour* (Princeton University Press 2006) 231p

——, 'Motivation and Judicial Behavior' (2007) Paper prepared for the Workshop on Exploring the Judicial Mind, University of Virginia, 1

Behrendt C, *Le Juge Constitutionnel, un Législateur-cadre Positif: Les Normes Juridictionnelles Relatives à la Production et au Contenu de Norms Législatives Futures – une Analyse Comparative en Droit Français, Belge et Allemand* (Doctoral thesis at the University Paris I Panthéon-Sorbonne 2005) 540p

Bentele U, 'Mining for Gold: The Constitutional Court of South Africa's Experience with Comparative Constitutional Law' 37 (2009) Georgia Journal of International and Comparative Law 219

Beyers J, 'Policy Issues, Organisational Format and the Political Strategies of Interest Organisations' (2008) 31 West European Politics 1188

Bickel AM, 'Foreword: The Passive Virtues' (1961) Faculty Scholarship Series 40

Bielen S, Marneffe W and Vereeck L, 'An Empirical Analysis of Case Disposition Time in Belgium' (2015) 11 Review of Law and Economics 293

Black RC, Sorenson MW and Johnson TR, 'Toward an Actor-Based Measure of Supreme Court Case Salience: Information-Seeking and Engagement during Oral Arguments' (2012) 66 Political Research Quartely 804

Black RC et al., *US Supreme Court Opinions and Their Audiences* (Cambridge University Press 2016) 196p

Black V and Richter N, 'Did she Mention My Name?: Citation of Academic Authority by the Supreme Court of Canada' (1993) Dalhousie Law Journal 377

Bobek M, *Comparative Reasoning in European Supreme Courts* (Oxford University Press 2013) 307p

Bogaards M, 'The Uneasy Relationship between Empirical and Normative Types in Consociational Theory' (2000) 12 Journal of Theoretical Politics 395

——, 'Democracy and Power-sharing in Multinational States: Thematic Introduction' (2006) 8 International Journal on Multicultural Societies 119

Bohne E, 'The Politics of the *Ex Ante* Evaluation of Legislation' in J Verschuuren (ed.), *The Impact of Legislation* (Martinus Nijhoff 2009) 280p

Boucké T and Vandaele K, *Het sociaal overleg in België* (Academia Press 2003) 89p

Boularbah H, 'Interpretation ou qualification de la norme controlee et dessaisissement de juge a quo' in *Liber Amicorum Paul Martens* (Larcier 2007) 1008p

Brems E and Lavrysen L, 'Procedural Justice in Human Rights Adjudication: The European Court of Human Rights' (2013) 35 Human Rights Quarterly 176

——, 'Don't Use a Sledgehammer to Crack a Nut: Less Restrictive Means in the Case Law of the European Court of Human Rights' (2015) 15 Human Rights Law Review 139

Brewer-Carias AR, *Constitutional Courts as Positive Legislators: A Comparative Law Study* (Cambridge University Press 2011) 962p

Breyer S, 'Making Our Democracy Work: The Yale Lectures' (2011) 120 Yale Law Journal 1999

Bustamate T, 'The Ongoing Search for Legitimacy: Can a "Pragmatic yet Principled" Deliberative Model Justify the Authority of Constitutional Courts?' (2015) 78 The Modern Law Review 372

Bustos A and Jacobi T, 'Strategic Judicial Preference Revelation' (2014) 57 The Journal of Law and Economics 113

Bürli N, 'Amicus Curiae as a Means to Reinforce the Legitimacy of the European Court of Human Rights' in S Flogaitis, T Zwart and J Fraser (eds.), *The European Court of Human Rights and its Discontents* (Edward Elgar 2013) 217p

Caldeira GA and Wright JR, 'Amici Curiae before the Supreme Court: Who Participates, When and How Much?' (1990) 52 The Journal of Politics 782

Caluwaerts D, (2012), *Confrontation and Communication: Deliberative Democracy in Divided Belgium* (Peter Lang 2012) 227p

Cameron E, 'A South African Perspective on the Judicial Development of Socio-Economic Rights' in L Lazarus, C McCrudden and N Bowles (eds.), *Reasoning Rights: Comparative Judicial Engagement* (Hart Publishing 2014) 392p

Challenor B, 'The Balancing Act: A Case for Structured Proportionality Under the Second Limb of the Lange Test' (2015) 40 The University of Western Australia Law Review 267

Chandrachud C, 'Measuring Constitutional Case Salience in the Indian Supreme Court' (2014) 42 Journal Indian Law and Society 42

Cichowski RA, 'Civil Society and the European Convention of Human Rights' in J Christoffersen and MR Madsen, *The European Court of Human Rights between Law en Politics* (Oxford University Press 2011) 256p

Claes M et al., 'Introduction: on Constitutional Conversations' in M Claes et al. (eds.), *Constitutional Conversations in Europe – Actors, Topics and Procedures* (Intersentia 2012) 399p

Clark TS et al., 'Measuring the Political Salience of Supreme Court Cases' (2015) 3 Journal of Law and Courts 37

Cohen-Eliya M and Porat I 'Proportionality and the Culture of Justification' (2011) 59 American Journal of Comparative Law 463

Collins PM, 'Lobbyist before the U.S. Supreme Court: Investigating the Influence of Amicus Curiae Briefs' (2007) 60 Political Research Quarterly 55

——, *Friends of the Supreme Court: Interest Groups and Judicial Decision Making*, (Oxford University Press 2008) 248p

Collins TA and Cooper CA, 'Case Salience and Media Coverage of Supreme Court Decisions: Toward a New Measure' (2012) 65 Political Research Quartely 396

Comella VF, *Constitutional Courts and Democratic Values*, (Yale University Press 2009) 238p

Courtis C, 'Rationality, Reasonableness and Proportionality: Testing the Use of Standards of Scrutiny in the Constitutional Review of Legislation' (2011) 4 Constitutional Court Review 31

Cross FB et al., 'Citations in the U.S. Supreme Court: an Empirical Study of Their Use and Significance.' (2010) 2 University of Illinois Law Review 489

Cross FB and Nelson BJ, 'Strategic Institutional Effects on Supreme Court Decision-making' (2001) 95 Northwestern University Law Review 1437

Cumming G, *Expert Evidence Definiciencies in the Judgments of the Court of the European Union and the European Court of Human Rights* (Kluwer 2014) 251p

Czapanskiy KS and Manjoo R, 'The Right of Public Participation in the Law-making Process and the Role of Legislature in the Promotion of this Right' 19 (2008) Duke Journal of Comparative and International Law 1

Dahl R, *On Democracy* (Yale University Press 1998) 224p

Daniels W, 'Far Beyond the Law Reports: Secondary Source Citations in United States Supreme Court Opinions October Terms 1900, 1940 and 1978' (1983) 76 Law Library Journal 1

De Fine Licht J et al., 'When Does Transparency Generate Legitimacy? Experimenting on a Context-Bound Relationship' (2014) 27 Governance: An International Journal of Policy, Administration and Institutions 111

De Jaegere J, 'Actieve Rechtsvorming door het Grondwettelijk Hof: Waar Ligt De Grens?' (2014) 1 Tijdschrift voor Bestuurswetenschappen en Publiek Recht 22

De Visser M, *Constitutional Review in Europe: A Comparative Analysis* (Hart Publishing 2014) 528p

Decroo H, 'De Invloed van de Arresten van het Arbitragehof op het Parlementaire Werk' (2001) Rechtskundig Weekblad 259

Deschouwer K, 'From Consociation to Federation: How the Belgian Parties Won' in KR Luther and K Deschouwer (eds.), *Party Elites in Divided Societies: Political Parties in Consociational Democracy* (Routledge 1999) 312p

——, 'And the Peace Goes On? Consociational Democracy and Belgian Politics in the Twenty-first Century' (2006) 29 West European Politics, 895

Dewachter W, *Besluitvorming in Politiek België* (Acco 1992) 371p

Dothan S, *Reputation and Judicial Tactics* (Cambridge 2015) 336p

Dryzek JS, *Deliberative Democracy and Beyond* (Oxford University Press 2000) 195p

——, 'Legitimacy and Economy in Deliberative Democracy' (2001) 29 Political Theory 651

——, 'Deliberative Democracy in Divided Societies: Alternatives to Agonism and Analgesia' (2005) 33 Political Theory 218

——, 'Democratization as Deliberative Capacity Building' (2008) 42 Comparative Political Studies 1379

Du Plessis L, 'The Status and Role of Legislation in South Africa as a Constitutional Democracy: some Exploratory Observations' (2011) 14 Potchefstroom Electronic Law Journal 92

Dworkin R, *A Matter of Principle* (Harvard University Press 1985) 425p

——, *Freedom's Law: the Moral Reading of the American Constitution* (Oxford University Press 1996) 427p

Dyevre A, 'Unifying the Field of Comparative Judicial Politics: Towards a General Theory on Judicial Behaviour' (2010) 2 European Political Science Review 297

Elliott M, 'Proportionality and Deference: The Importance of a Structured Approach' in C Forsyth et al. (eds.), *Effective Judicial Review: A Cornerstone of Good Governance* (Oxford University Press 2010) 800p

Elster J, 'The Market and the Forum' in J Bohman and W Regh (eds.), *Essays on Reason and Politics: Deliberative Democracy*, (Massachusetts Institute of Technology 1997) 451p

Elster J et al., *Deliberative Democracy* (Cambridge University 1998) 282p

Ely JH, 'Toward a Representation-reinforcing Mode of Judicial Review' (1978) 37 Maryland law review, 451

Epstein L and Knight J, 'Toward a Strategic Revolution in Judicial Politics: a Look Back, a Look Ahead' (2000) 53 Political Research Quarterly 625

——, *The Choices Justices Make* (CQ Press 1998) 224p

Epstein L, Knight J and Murphy WF, 'The Interactive Nature of Judicial Decision Making' in N Maveety (ed.), *The Pioneers of Judicial Behaviour* (University of Michigan Press 2003) 433p

Epstein L and Segal JA, 'Measuring Issue Salience' (2000) 44 Amercian Journal of Political Science 66

Eskridge WN, *Dynamic Statutory Interpretation* (Harvard University Press 1994) 205p

Eskridge WN and Frickey PP, 'Foreword: Law as Equilibrium' (1994) Harvard Law Review 26

Esman MJ, (2004), *An Introduction to Ethnic Conflict* (Polity Press 2004) 232p

Fausten D et al., 'A Century of Citation Practice on the Supreme Court of Victoria' (2007) 31 Melbourne University Law Review 733

Fearon JD, 'Deliberation as Discussion' in J Elster, *Deliberative Democracy* (Cambridge University Press 1998) 282p

Ferejohn J and Pasquino P, 'The Countermajoritarian Opportunity' (2010) 13 Journal of Constitutional Law 353

——, 'Constitutional Courts as Deliberative Institutions' in W Sadurski (ed.), *Constitutional Justice, East and West: Democratic Legitimacy and Constitutional Courts in a Comparative Perspective* (Kluwer 2002) 457p

Ferejohn J, Rosenbluth F and Shipan CR, 'Comparative Judicial Politics' in C Boix and SC Stokes (eds.), *Oxford Handbook of Comparative Politics* (Oxford University Press 2009) 1021p

Feyen S, 'Afwijkende Meningsuitingen in het Belgische Grondwettelijk Hof: Mensenrechtelijk Beschermd, Wenselijk of Gevaarlijk?' in A Alen and J Theunis, *Leuvense Staatsrechtelijke Standpunten*, (Die Keure 2012) 479p

Fish ES, 'Choosing Constitutional Remedies' (2016) 63 UCLA Law Review 322

Fishkin JS, *When the People Speak: Deliberative Democracy and Public Consultation* (Oxford University Press 2009) 256p

Fiss O, *The Law as it could Be* (New York University Press 2003) 291p

Flanders C, 'Towards a Theory of Persuasive Authority' (2009) 62 Oklamhoma Law Review 55

Fontana D, 'Docket Control and the Success of Constitutional Courts' in T Ginsburg and R Dixon (eds.), *Comparative Constitutional Law* (Edward Elgar 2011) 680p

Friedman B 'The Politics of Judicial Review' (2005) 84 Texas Law Review 257

——, 'Taking Law Seriously' (2006) 4 Perspectives on Politics 261

Friedman LM et al., 'State Supreme Courts: A Century of Citation' (1981) 33 Stanford Law Review 773

Gardbaum S, 'The Structure and Scope of Constitutional Rights' in T Ginsburg and R Dixon (eds.), *Comparative Constitutional Law* (Edward Elgar 2011), 680p

Gargarella R, 'Full Representation, Deliberation and Impartiality', 260–280, in J Elster (ed.), *Deliberative Democracy* (Cambridge University Press 1998) 282p

Garoupa N et al., 'Judging under Political Pressure: an Empirical Analysis of Constitutional Review Voting in the Spanish Constitutional Court' (2013) 29 Journal of Law, Economics and Organization 1

Gerards JH, *Judicial Review in Equal Treatment Cases* (Martinus Nijhoff Publishers 2005) 774p

Gibson JL, 'From Simplicity to Complexity: The Development of Theory in the Study of Judicial Behavior' (1983) 5 Political Behavior 7

Gibson JL and Caldeira GA, 'Defenders of Democracy? Legitimacy, Popular Acceptance, and the South African Constitutional Court' (2003) 65 The Journal of Politics 1

Ginsburg T, 'The Global Spread of Constitutional Review' in KE Whittington, RD Kelemen and GA Caldeira (eds.), *The Oxford Handbook of Law and Politics* (Oxford University Press 2010) 815p

Glenn HP, 'Persuasive Authority' (1987) 32 McGill Law Journal 261

Goris A, Muylle K and Van Der Hulst M, 'Twintig jaar Arbitragehof v. Wetgever: van Vertrouwen naar Dialoog' in A Alen (ed.), *Twintig Jaar Arbitragehof* (Kluwer 2005) 168p

Grajzl P and Zajc K, 'Litigation and the Timing of Settlement: Evidence from Commercial Disputes' (2016) 44 European Journal of Law and Economics 1

Grembi V and Garoupa N, 'Delays in Medical Malpractice Litigation in Civil Law Jurisdictions: Some Evidence from the Italian Court of Cassation' (2013) 8 Health Economics, Policy and Law 423

——, 'Judicial Review and Political Partisanship: Moving from Consensual to Majoritarian Democracy' (2015) 43 International Review of Law and Economics 32

Grimm D, 'Proportionality in Canadian and German Constitutional Jurisprudence' (2007) 57 University of Toronto Law Review 383

Grimmelikhuijsen SG and Meijer AJ, 'The Effects of Transparency on the Perceived Trustworthiness of a Government Organization: Evidence from an Online Experiment' (2012) Journal of Public Administration Research and Theory Advance Access 1

Groppi T, 'Le Recours aux Précédents Étrangers par les Juges Constitutionnels', 47–86, in F Hourquebie and MC Pontoreau (eds.), *La Motivation des Décisions des Cours Suprêmes et Cours Constitutionelles* (Bruylant 2012) 310p

Grossman JB and Wells RS, 'Constitutional Law and Judicial Policy Making' (John Wiley & Sons 1972) 1379p

Guarniere C and Pederzoli P, *The Power of Judges: a Comparative Study of Courts and Democracy* (Oxford University Press 2003) 235p

Guttman A and Thompson D, 'Deliberative Democracy Beyond Process' (2002) 10 The Journal of Political Philosophy 153

——, 'Democracy and Disagreement' in RA Dahl, I Shapiro and JA Cheibub (eds.), *The Democracy Sourcebook* (MIT Press 2003) 556p

Habermas J, *Between Facts and Norms: Contributions to a Discourse Theory of Law and Democracy* (Polity 1996), 631p

Haider-Markel DP, Allen MD and Johansen M, 'Understanding Variations in Media Coverage of U.S. Supreme Court decisions' (2006) 11 The International Journal of Press/Politics 64

Hamilton A. 'A View of the Constitituion of the Judicial Department in Relation to the Tenure of Good Behaviour' in J Madison, A Hamilton and J Jay, *The Federalist Papers*, (Penguin Books 1788) 517p

Hammond TH, Bonneau CW and Sheehan RS, *Strategic Behavior and Policy Choice on the U.S. Supreme Court* (Stanford University Press 2005) 328p

Harbo T-I, 'The Function of the Proportionality Principle in EU Law' (2010) 16 European Law Journal 158

Harris P, 'Difficult Cases and the Display of Authority' (1985) 1 Journal of Law, Economics and Organization 209

Hasko J, 'Persuasion in the Court: Nonlegal Materials in U.S. Supreme Court Opinions' (2002) 94 Law Library Journal 427

Hausman D, 'Government Noncompliance with Constitutional Court Orders in South Africa' in L Bartels and CW Bonneau (eds.), *Making Law and Courts Research Relevant* (Routledge 2014) 260p

Heise M, 'The Past, Present and Future of Empirical Legal Scholarship: Judicial Decision Making and the New Empiricism' (2002) 4 University of Illinois Law Review 819

Henckels C, *Proportionality and Deference in Investor-State Arbitration* (Cambridge University Press 2015) 266p

Hönnige C, 'Beyond Judicialization: Why We Need More Comparative Research about Constitutional Courts' (2011) European Political Science 346

Hopper R, 'Post-Apartheid South Africa: Evaluating South Africa's Institutional Design' (2008) 5 Opticon1826 1

Inoue T, 'Two Models of Democracy: How to Make Demos and Hercules Collaborate in Public Deliberation' in LJ Wintgens (ed.), *The Theory and Practice of Legislation: Essays in Legisprudence* (Ashgate 2005) 368p

Kantorowicz J and Garoupa N, 'An Empirical Analysis of Constitutional Review Voting in the Polish Constitutional Tribunal' (2015) 27 Constitutional Political Economy 66

Kavanagh A, *Constitutional Review under the UK Human Rights Act* (Cambridge University Press 2009) 470p

Kelemen K, 'Dissenting Opinions in Constitutional Courts' (2013) 14 German Law Journal 1345

Klein D and Mitchell G, *The Psychology of Judicial Decision Making* (Oxford University Press 2010) 360p

Klug H, *The Constitution of South Africa: a Contextual Analysis* (Hart Publishing 2010) 319p

Knight J and Johnson J, 'Aggregation and Deliberation: on the Possibility of Democatic Legitimacy' (1994) 22 Political Theory 277

Kornhauser LA and Sager LG, 'Unpacking the Court' (1986) 96 Yale Law Journal 82

Krislov S, 'The Amicus Curiae Brief: From Friendschip to Advocacy' (1963) 72 Yale Law Journal, 694

Kumm M, 'The Idea of Socratic Contestation and the Right to Justification: The Point of Rights-Based Review' (2010) Law and Ethics Human Rights 142

Lambrecht S, 'The Attitude of Four Supreme Courts Towards the European Court of Human Rights: Strasbourg has Spoken …', in S Besson and AR Ziegler (eds.), *Le Juge en Droit International et Européen – The Judge in International and European Law* (Schulthess 2013) 343p

Larsson O and Naurin D, 'Judicial Independence and Political Uncertainty: How the Risk of Override Affects the Court of Justice of the EU' (2016) 70 International Organization 377

Lasser M, *Judicial Deliberations: a Comparative Analysis of Judical Transparancy and Legitimacy* (Oxford University Press 2004) 381p

Law DS and Chang WC, 'The Limits of Global Judicial Dialogue' (2011) 86 Washington Law Review 523

Lax JR and Cameron CM, 'Bargaining and Opinion Assignment on the US Supreme Court' (2007) 23 The Journal of Law, Economics & Organization, 292

Lewis A, *Politics in West Africa* (Oxford University Press 1965) 90p

Lijphart A, *Democracies: Patterns of Majoritarian and Consensus Government in Twenty-one Countries* (Yale University Press 1984) 229p

—— 'Consociational Democracy' (1969) 21 World Politics 207

——, *Democracy in Plural Societies: a Comparative Exploration* (Yale University Press 1977) 248p

——, 'Consociational Theory: Problems and Prospects. A Reply' (1981) 13 Comparative Politics 355

——, *Conflict and Coexistence in Belgium. The Dynamics of a Culturally Divided Society* (University of California, Institute of International Studies 1981) 171p

——, *Power-sharing in South Africa* (Institute of International Studies, University of Berkely 1985) 178p

——, *Patterns of Democracy*, (Yale University Press 1999) 351p

——, 'The Wave of Power Sharing Democracy', 37–54, in A Reynolds (ed.), *The Architecture of Democracy. Constitutional Design, Conflict Management and Democracy* (Oxford University Press 2002) 507p

——, '*Thinking about Democracy: Power Sharing and Majority Rule in Theory and Practice*' (Routledge 2008) 306p

——, *Patterns of Democracy: Government Forms and Performance in Thirty-six Countries* (Yale University Press 2012) 348p

Lombart B, 'Les Techniques d'Arrêts de la Cour d'Arbitrage' (1996) RBDC 352

Lucy W, 'Adjudication' in J Coleman and S Shapiro (eds.), *The Oxford Handbook of Jurisprudence and Philosophy of Law* (Oxford University Press 2002) 1064p

Luna E, 'Constitutional Road Maps' (2000) 90 Journal of Criminal Law and Criminology 1125

Lupu Y and Voeten E, 'Precedent in International Courts: a Network Analysis of Case Citations by the European Court of Human Rights' (2012) British Journal of Political Science 1

Maamouri A, 'L'Amicus Curiae et la Motivation des Décisions des Cours Suprêmes Américaine et Canadienne', 117–140, in F Hourquebie and MC Pontoreau (eds.), *La Motivation des Décisions des Cours Suprêmes et Cours Constitutionelles* (Bruylant 2012) 310p

Maes E, *De Rol van een Grondwettelijk Hof in Rechtsstatelijk Perspectief* (KULeuven, Institute for Constitutional Law 2016) 598p

Mak E, *Judicial Decision-making in a Globalised World: A Comparative Analysis of the Changing Practices of Western Highest Courts* (Hart Publishing 2013) 272p

Makau JM and Marty DL, *Dialogue and Deliberation* (Waveland Press 2013) 283p

Maltzman F, Spriggs FJ and Wahlbeck PJ, 'Strategy and Judicial Choice: New Institutionalist Approaches to Supreme Court Decision Making' in CW Clayton and H Gillman (eds.), *Supreme Court Decision-Making: New Institutional Approaches* (University of Chicago Press 1999) 358p

Maltzman F, Spriggs JE and Wahlbeck PJ, *Crafting Law on the Supreme Court: The Collegial Game* (Cambridge University Press, 2000) 224p

Manfredi CP and Kelly JB, 'Six Degrees of Dialogue: a Response to Hogg and Bushell' (1999) 37 Osgoode Hall Law Journal 513

Marneffe W and Poel K, 'De Federale Regelgevingsimpactanalyse: een Stand van Zaken na Zes Maanden' (2014) Tijdschrift voor Wetgeving 193

Maruste R, 'The Role of the Constitutional Court in Democratic Society' (2007) Juridica International 8

Mastor W, 'L'Effet Performative des Opinions Séparées sur la Motivation des Décisions Constitutionnelles Majoritaires', in F Hourquebie and MC Pontoreau (eds.), *La Motivation des Décisions des Cours Suprêmes et Cours Constitutionelles* (Bruylant 2012) 310p

Maveety N (ed.), *The Pioneers of Judicial Behaviour* (University of Michigan Press 2003) 433p

Mazmanyan A, 'Majoritarianism, Deliberation and Accountability as Institutional Instincts of Constitutional Court', in A Mazmanyan, P Popelier and W Vandenbruwaene (eds.), *The Role of Constitutional Courts in Mulitlevel Governance* (Intersentia 2013) 310p

McCormick P, 'Judical Authority and the Provincial Courts of Appeal: A Statistical Investigation of Citation Practices' (1993) Manitoba Law Journal 286

——, 'The Supreme Court Cites the Supreme Court: Follow-up Citation on the Supreme Court of Canada, 1989–1993' (1995) 33 Osgoode Hall Law Journal 453

McNollgast, 'Legislative Intent: The Use of Positive Political Theory in Statutory Interpretation' (1994) 57 Law and Contemporary Problems 3

Mendes CH, *Constitutional Courts and Deliberative Democracy* (Oxford University Press 2013) 249p

Merryman JH, 'Toward a Theory of Citations: an Empirical Study of the Citation Practice of the California Supreme Court in 1950, 1960 and 1970' (1978) 50 Southern California Law Review 381

Meuwese A and Snel M, 'Constitutional Dialogue: An Overview', (2013) 9 Utrecht Law Review 129

Möller K, *The Global Model of Constitutional Rights* (Oxford University Press 2012) 240p

——, 'Constructing the Proportionality Test: An Emerging Global Conversation' in L Lazarus, C McCrudden and N Bowles (eds.), *Reasoning Rights: Comparative Judicial Engagement* (Hart Publishing 2014) 392p

Monahan J and Walker L, 'Judicial Use of Social Science Research' in E Mertz (ed.), *The Role of Social Science in Law* (Ashgate 2008) 648p

Moon C, 'Comparative Constitutional Analysis: Should the United States Supreme Court Join the Dialogue?' (2003) 12 Washington University Journal of Law & Policy 229

Murphy WF, *Elements of Judicial Strategy* (University of Chicago Press 1964) 256p
Nelissen B, 'Judicial Loyalty Through Dissent or Why The Timing is Perfect for Belgium to Embrace Separate Opinions' (2011) 15 EJCL 1
Nielsen I and Smyth R 'One Hundred Years of Citation of Authority on the Supreme Court of New South Wales' (2008) 31 University of New South Wales Law Journal 189
Nyati L, 'Public Participation: What Has the Constitutional Court Given the Public?' (2008) 15 Law, Democracy & Development Law Journal 102
OECD, *Better Regulation in Europe* (OECD 2010)
O'Flynn I, 'Deliberative Democracy, the Public Interest and the Consociational Model' (2010) 58 Political Studies 572
O'Leary B, 'Debating Consociational Politics: Normative and Explanatory Arguments' in S Noel (ed.), *From Power Sharing to Democracy: Post-Conflict Institutions in Ethnically Divided Societies* (McGill-Queen's Press 2005) 312p
Owens RJ and Wedekins J, 'Justices and Legal Clarity: Analyzing the Complexity of Supreme Court Opinions' (2011) 45 Law & Society Review 1027
Parkinson J, *Deliberating in the Real World: Problems of Legitimacy in Deliberative Democracy* (Oxford University Press 2006) 209p
Perry HW, *Deciding to Decide: Agenda Setting in the United States Supreme Court* (Harvard University Press 1991) 316p
Peters G, 'Consociationalism, Corruption and Chocolate: Belgian Exceptionalism' (2006) 29 West European Politics 1079
Petersen N, 'Proportionality and the Incommensurability Challenge – Some Lessons from the South African Constitutional Court' (2013) New York University Public Law and Legal Theory Working Papers 405
——, 'Avoiding the Common-wisdom Fallacy: the Role of Social Sciences in Constitutional Adjudication' (2013) 11 International Journal of Constitutional Law 294
——, *Proportionality and Judicial Activism* (Cambridge University Press 2017) 258p
Pinard D, 'A Plea for Conceptual Consistency in Constitutional Remedies' 18 National Journal of Constitutional Law 105
Pirker B, *Proportionality Analysis and Models of Judicial Review: A Theoretical and Comparative Study* (Europa Law Publishing 2014) 452p
Ponthoreau MC, 'L'Énigme de la Motivation Encore et Toujours l'Éclairage Comparatif', 6–24, in F Hourquebie and MC Pontoreau (eds.), *La Motivation des Décisions des Cours Suprêmes et Cours Constitutionelles* (Bruylant 2012) 310p
Popelier P, 'Mosaic Laws and Arrangement Laws: A Common Practice Respectively Not So Common Practice' (2005) European Journal of Law Reform 47
——, *Procederen voor het Grondwettelijk Hof* (Intersentia 2008) 426p
——, 'De doorwerking van Prejudiciële Arresten van het Grondwettelijk Hof in de Rechtspraak' (2010) CDPK 393
——, 'Judicial Conversations in Multilevel Constitutionalism: the Belgian Case' in M Claes et al. (eds.), *Constitutional Conversations in Europe* (Intersentia 2012) 400p
——, 'The Court as Regulatory Watchdog: the Procedural Approach in the Case Law of the European Court of Human Rights', 249–267, in P Popelier A Mazmanyan and W Vandenbruwaene (eds.), *The Role of Constitutional Courts in Multilevel Governance* (Intersentia 2013) 310p

——, 'The Belgian Constitutional Court: Guardian of Consensus Democracy or Venue for Deliberation?' in A Alen et al., *Liber Amicorum Marc Bossuyt* (Intersentia 2013) 974p

Popelier P and De Jaegere J, 'Evidence-based Judicial Review of Legislation in Divided States: the Belgian Case' (2016) 4 Theory and Practice of Legislation 187

Popelier P and Lemmens K, *The Constitution of Belgium: A Contextual Analysis* (Bloomsbury 2015) 312p

Popelier P and Patiño Álvarez AA, 'Deliberative Practices of Constitutional Courts in Consolidated and Non-Consolidated Democracies' in P Popelier, A Mazmanyan and W Vandenbruwaene (eds.), *The Role of Constitutional Courts in Multilevel Governance* (Intersentia 2013) 310p

Popelier P and Van De Heyning C, 'Procedural Rationality: Giving Teeth to the Proportionality Analysis' (2013) 9 European Constitutional Law Review 260

Popelier P. and Voermans W, 'Europeanization, Constitutional Review and Consensus Politics in the Low Countries' in J Beyers, H Vollaard and P Dumont (eds.), *European Integration and Consensus Politics in the Low Countries*, (London 2015) 250p

Popelier P and Voermans W, 'Europeanization, Constitutional Review and Consensus Politics in the Low Countries' in H Vollaard, J Beyers and P Dumont (eds.), *European Integration and Consensus Politics in the Low Countries* (Routledge 2015) 250p

Popelier P, Verstraelen S, Vanheule D and Vanlerberghe B, 'The Effect of Judicial Decisions in Time: Comparative Notes' in P Popelier et al. (eds.), *The Effects of Judicial Decisions in Time* (Intersentia 2014) 285p

Popelier P et al., *Consultaties in de Wetgevingspraktijk* (Politeia 2008) 170p

——, 'Transparant Consulteren in Vlaanderen: de Spanning Tussen Rationeel Wetgevingsmodel en Besluitvormingspraktijk' (2012) Tijdschrift voor Wetgeving 6

Posner RA, 'Statutory Interpretation in the Classroom and in the Courtroom' (1983) 50 University of Chicago Law Review 800

——, *How Judges Think* (Harvard University Press 2008) 387p

Rawls J, *Political Liberalism* (Columbia University Press 1993) 401p

Rivers J, 'Proportionality, Discretion and the Second Law of Balancing' in G Pavlakos (ed.), *Law, Rights and Discourse: The Legal Philosophy of Robert Alexy* (Hart Publishing 2007) 377p

——, 'Proportionality and Variable Intensity of Review' (2006) 65 Cambridge Law Journal 174

Rigaux MF and Renauld B, *La Cour Constitutionelle* (Bruylant 2009) 330p

Roux T, *The Politics of Principle: the First South African Constitutional Court, 1995–2005* (Cambridge University Press 2013) 167

Rosanvallon P, *Le Bon Gouvernement* (Seuil 2015) 416p

Rosenfeld M, 'The United States of America' in J Bell and M-L Paris (eds.), *Right-Based Constitutional Review: Constitutional Courts in a Changing Landscape* (Edward Elgar 2016) 464p

Rosoux G, 'Les Réserves d'Interprétation dans la Jurisprudence de la Cour d'Arbitrage: une Alternative à l'Annulation' (2001) 3 RBDC 403

Rosoux G and Tulkens F, 'Considérations Théoriques et Pratiques sur la Portée des Arrêts de la Cour d'Arbitrage' in V Thiry, B Renauld and JT Debry (eds.), *La Cour d'Arbitrage: un Juge Comme les Autres?* (Éditions du jeune barreau de Liège 2004) 303p

Sadurski W, *Rights Before Courts: a Study of Constitutional Courts in Postcommunist States of Central and Eastern Europe* (Springer 2008) 376p

Sager LG, *Justice in Plainclothes: a Theory of American Constitutional Practice* (Yale University Press 2006) 260p

Sartori G, *Comparative Constitutional Engineering: an Inquiry into Structures, Incentives and Outcomes* (New York University Press 1994) 231p

Schachar Y, Harris R and Gross M, 'Citation Practices of the Supreme Court, Quantitative Analysis' (1996) 27 Hebrew University Law Review 119

Schudson M, *The Power of News* (Harvard University Press 1995) 288p

Seidman AW, Seidman RB and Matsiborchuk V, 'Legislative Deliberation and the Drafting Process: The Drafter's Role' (2015) Theory and Practice of Legislation 341

Segal JA and Spaeth HJ, *The Supreme Court and the Attitudinal Model Revisited* (Cambridge University 2002) 459p

Sinardet D, 'From Consociational Consciousness to Majoritarian Myth: Consociational Democracy, Multi-level Politics and the Belgian Case of Brussels-Halle-Vilvoorde' (2010) 45 Acta Politica 347

Shapiro M, 'The Giving Reasons Requirement' (1992) 179 The University of Chicago Legal Forum 179

Shapiro M and Stone Sweet A, *On Law, Politics and Judicialization* (Oxford University Press 2002) 417p

Shelton D, 'The Participation of Nongovernmental Organizations in International Judicial Proceedings' (1994) 88 The American Journal of International Law 611–642

Sill K et al., 'Media Coverage of the U.S. Supreme Court: How Do Journalists Assess the Importance of Court Decisions?' (2013) 20 Political Communication 1

Sloss DL et al. (eds.), *International Law in the U.S. Supreme Court* (Cambridge University Press 2012) 632p

Smyth R, 'What do Intermediate Appellate Courts Cite? A Quantitative Study of the Citation Practice of Australian State Supreme Courts' (1999) 21 Adelaide Law Review 51

——, 'Trends in the Citation Practice of the Supreme Court of Queensland over the Course of the Twenthieth Century' (2009) 28 The University of Queensland Review 39

——, 'Judicial Citations – an Empirical Study of Citation Practice in the New Zealand Court of Appeal' (2000) 31 Victoria University of Wellington Law Review 847

Songer DR, Johnson SW, Ostberg CL and Wetstein MA, *Law, Ideology and Collegiality: Judicial Behaviour in the Supreme Court of Canada* (McGill Queen's University Press, 2012) 222p

Spiller PT and Gely R, 'Strategic Judicial Decision Making' in GA Caldeira, RD Keleman and KE Whittington (eds.), *The Oxford Handbook of Law and Politics* (Oxford University Press 2008) 832p

Spreutels J, Alen A and Meerschaut F, Rapport Belge sur les cours constitutionelles et les medias, publié après le 7ème conference des chefs d'institution de l'associations des cours constitutionelles ayant en partage l'usage du français, 28–30 April 2014, 1–42.

Spriggs JF and Wahlbeck PJ, 'Amici Curiae and the Role of Information at the Supreme Court' (1997) 50 Political Research Quartely 365

Staben J, 'Colourful Case Law: Citation Analysis of the German Constitutional Court's Jurisprudence', https://verfassungsblog.de/farbenfrohe-rechtsprechung-verweisungsanalyse-von-entscheidungen-des-bundesverfassungsgerichts (26 January 2015)

Staton JK, 'Constitutional Review and the Selective Promotion of Case Results' (2006) 50 American Journal of Political Salience 98

Staton JK and Vanberg G, 'The Value of Vagueness: Delegation, Defiance and Judicial Opinions' (2008) 52 American Journal of Political Science 504

Steiner HJ, 'Ideals and Counter-Ideals in the Struggle Over Autonomy Regimes for Minorities' (1991) Notre Dame Law Review 1539

Stone Sweet A and Mathews J, 'Proportionality Balancing and Global Constitutionalism' (2008) 47 Colombia Journal of Transnational Law 73

Sulitzeany-Kenan R, Kremnitzer M and Alon S, 'Facts, Preferences and Doctrine: An Empirical Analysis of the Proportionality Judgment' (2015) 50 Law & Society Review 348

Sunstein C, 'Health-Health Trade-offs', 232–259, in J Elster (ed.), *Deliberative Democracy* (Cambridge University Press 1998) 282p

——, *One Case at a Time: Judicial Minimalism on the Supreme Court* (Harvard University Press 1999) 290p

——, *Designing Democracy* (Oxford University Press 2001) 292p

Swart M, 'Left out in the Cold? Crafting Constitutional Remedies for the Poorest of the Poor' (2005) 21 South African Journal on Human Rights 215

Théry L, 'Markante Arresten uit Twintig Jaar Rechtspraak van het Arbitragehof: een Vergelijking tussen de Vommentaren in de Rechtsleer en de Weerklank in de Geschreven Pers' (2006) 7 TBP 387

Théry L and Dupont N, 'Het Grondwettelijk Hof en "de Doos van Pandora": Leerzaam Professioneel Ramptoerisme of Rechtsleer Nijgend Naar Sensatieberichtgeving' (2012) CDPK 594

Theunis J, 'Het Gelijkheidsbeginsel' in A Alen et al., *Doorwerking Publiekrecht in het Privaatrecht* (Mys&Breesch 1997) 577p

T'Kindt P and Van Nieuwenhove J, 'De Federale Voorafgaande Regelgevingsimpactanalyse (RIA) – een Wassen Neus of een Stapje Vooruit?' (2014) Tijdschrift voor Wetgeving 168

Treanor WM, 'Judicial Review before Marbury' (2005) Stanford Law Review 58, 455

Tremblay LB, 'The Legitimacy of Judicial Review: The Limits of Dialogue between Courts and Legislatures' ¾ 2005 ICON 617

T Tridimas, *The General Principles of EU Law* (Oxford University Press 2006) 591p

Tsebelis G, 'The Power of the European Parliament as a Conditional Agenda Setter' (1995) 88 American Political Science Review 129

Unah I and Hancock AM, 'U.S. Supreme Court Decision Making, Case Salience and the Attitudinal Model' (2006) 28 Law & Policy 295

Vanberg G, 'Legislative-Judicial Relations: a Game-Theoretic Approach to Constitutional Review' (2001) 45 Amercian Journal of Political Science 346

——, *The Politics of Constitutional Review in Germany* (Cambridge University Press 2005) 195p

Valadez JM, *Deliberative Democracy, Political Legitimacy and Self-determination in Multicultural Societies* (Westview Press 2001) 320p

Vandenberghe H, 'De Beleidsmatige Reactie op Arresten van het Grondwettelijk Hof' (2010) CDPK 366

Van der hulst M, 'Het Parlement als Wetgever. Medeverantwoordelijk voor wat Misgaat? Ja. Kop van Jut? Nee bedankt!' in P Popelier and Van Nieuwenhove J (eds.), *Wie maakt de wet?* (die Keure 2006) 303p

Van Gerven W, 'The Effect of Proportionality on the Actions of Member States of the European Community: National Viewpoints from Continental Europe' in E Ellis (ed.), *The Principle of Proportionality in the Laws of Europe* (Hart Publishing 1999) 224p

Van Gestel R and De Poorter J, 'Putting Evidence-Based Law Making to the Test: Judicial Review of Legislative Rationality' (2016) 4 Theory and Practice of Legislation 155

Van Hoecke M, 'Constitutional Courts and Deliberative Democracy' in A Mazmanyan, P Popelier and W Vandenbruwaene (eds.), *The Role of Constitutional Courts in Mulitlevel Governance* (Intersentia 2013) 310p

Van Humbeeck P, 'Wetgevingsbeleid in Vlaanderen op Niveau van de Uitvoerende Macht: een Update van de Uitdagingen voor Betere Regelgeving', 93–138, in P Popelier and J Van Nieuwenhove (eds.), *Wie maakt de wet?* (die Keure 2006) 303p

Van Nieuwenhove J, 'Programmawetten: voor Verbetering Vatbaar?' in P Popelier and Van Nieuwenhove J (eds.), *Wie maakt de wet?* (die Keure 2006) 303p

Velaers J, *Van Arbitragehof tot Grondwettelijk Hof* (Maklu 1990) 478p

——, *De Grondwet en de Raad van State, Afdeling wetgeving: Vijftig jaar Adviezen aan Wetgevende Vergaderingen, in het Licht van de Rechtspraak van het Arbitragehof* (Maklu 1999) 1034p

Venzke I, 'Judicial Authority and Styles of Reasoning: The Self-presentation between Legalism and Deliberation' (2016) 4 Amsterdam Law School Legal Studies Research Paper 1

Verdussen M, 'La Responsabilité Civile du Fait de Légiférer en Violation de la Constitution' in D Renders (ed.), *La responsabilité des pouvoirs publics* (Bruylant 2016) 694p

Verlinden V, *De Hoeders van de Wet* (die Keure 2010) 748p

Vermeule A, 'Should We Have Lay Justices?' (2006) 134 Harvard Public Law Working Paper 1

——, *Law and the Limits of Reason* (Oxford University Press 2009) 220p

Verrijdt W, 'De Plicht tot Uitvoering van Arresten van het Grondwettelijk Hof' in A Alen, S Sottiaux, *Leuvense Staatsrechtelijke Standpunten 2* (die Keure 2010) 369p

Verstraelen S, 'Constitutionele Dialoog als een Lens: Onderzoek naar het Wetgevend Optreden na de Vaststelling van een Ongrondwettige Lacune door het Grondwettelijk Hof' (2016) Tijdschrift voor Wetgeving 19

——, 'The Temporal Limitation of Judicial Decisions: The Need for Flexibility Versus the Quest for Uniformity' (2013) 14 German Law Journal 1687

——, *Rechterlijk Overgangsrecht in het Publiek en Privaat Procesrecht: Nieuwe Ontwikkelingen Aangaande de Werking in de Tijd van Vonnissen en Arresten* (Intersentia 2015) 456p

Vining Jr RL and Wilhelm T, 'Measuring Case Salience in State Courts of Last Resort' (2011) 64 Political Research Quartely 559

Vuye H, 'Het Parlement als Wetgevende macht, Historisch en Prospectief', 3–35, in P Popelier and J Van Nieuwenhove (eds.), *Wie maakt de wet?* (Die Keure 2006) 303p

Waldron J, *Law and Disagreement* (Oxford University Press 1999) 332p

——, 'The Core of the Case against Judicial Review' (2006) 115 Yale Law Journal 134

——, 'Judges as Moral Reasoners' (2009) International Journal of Constitutional Law 2

Walsh DJ, 'On the Meaning and Pattern of Legal Citations: Evidence from State Wrongful Discharge Precedent Cases' (1997) 31 Law & Society Review 337

Weingast BR, 'Rational-choice Institutionalism' in I Katznelson and HV Milners (eds.), *Political Science: The State of the Discipline* (WW Norton & Company 2002) 1040p

Westéus M, 'Settlement Probability Asymmetries in the Swedish Labour Court' (2014) 38 European Journal of Law and Economics 485

White CA and Boussiakou I, 'Separate Opinions in the European Court of Human Rights' (2009) 9 Human Rights Law Review 37

Whittington KE, 'Once More Unto the Breach: Postbehavioralist Approaches to Judicial Politics' (2000) Law and Social Enquiry 601

Witte E, Craeybeckx J and Meynen A, *Politieke Geschiedenis van België: van 1830 tot Heden* (Standaard uitgeverij 2007) 584p

Wrightsman LS, 'Persuasion in the Decision Making of US Supreme Court Judges' in D Klein and G Mitchell (eds.), *The Psychology of Judicial Decision Making* (Oxford University Press 2010) 360p

Yee AS, 'Cross-National Concepts in Supranational Governance: State-Society Relations and EU Policy' (2004) 17 Governance 487

Young EA, 'The Continuity of Statutory and Constitutional Interpretation: an Essay for Phil Frickey' (2010) 98 California Law Review 1371

Yowell P, 'Proportionality in United States Constitutional Law' in L Lazarus, C McCrudden and N Bowled (eds.), *Reasoning Rights: Comparative Judicial Engagement* (Hart Publishing 2014) 432p

Yung CR, 'A Typology of Judging Styles' (2015) 107 Northwestern University Law Review 1757

Zungu CD, 'The Role, Relevance and Application of International Law in South Africa' (2015) 8 International Journal of Sustainable Development 85

Zurn CF, *Deliberative Democracy and the Institutions of Judicial Review* (Cambridge University Press 2007) 530p

OTHER SOURCES

Speech by president Jean Spreutels during the formal hearing on the occasion of his inauguration, 26 June 2013.

Speech by president André Alen during the formal hearing on the occasion of his inauguration, 5 February 2013.

Speech by president André Alen during the formal hearing on the occasion of the inauguration of judge Riet Leysen, 19 March 2014

INDEX

ABOUT THE AUTHOR

Josephine De Jaegere is an associated researcher at the University of Antwerp, Belgium. She is affiliated with both the Faculty of Law and the Faculty of Social Sciences. She is also a member of the standing group on Law & Politics of the European Consortium on Political Research. She is currently working as a legal advisor specialising in matters of constitutional law at the Belgian Ministry of Justice.

www.ingramcontent.com/pod-product-compliance
Ingram Content Group UK Ltd.
Pitfield, Milton Keynes, MK11 3LW, UK
UKHW051846100926
8556IPUK00005B/483

9 781780 686943